A Primer on
Integrating Psychotherapies for
Children and Adolescents

A Primer on Integrating Psychotherapies for Children and Adolescents

Sebastiano Santostefano

JASON ARONSON INC.
Northvale, New Jersey
London

Production Editor: Robert D. Hack

This book was set in 10 pt. Adobe Caslon by Alpha Graphics of Pittsfield, NH and printed and bound by Book-mart Press, Inc. of North Bergen, NJ.

Library of Congress Cataloging-in-Publication Data

Santostefano, Sebastiano, 1929–
    A primer on integrating psychotherapies for children and
adolescents / Sebastiano Santostefano.
        p.   cm.
    Includes bibliographical references and index.
    ISBN 0-7657-0109-X (alk. paper)
    1. Child psychotherapy—Philosophy.   2. Eclectic psychotherapy.
3. Adolescent psychotherapy—Philosophy.   4. Child psychotherapy.
5. Adolescent psychotherapy.
    RJ504.S253   1998
    618.92'8914—dc21   97-29509

Printed in the United States of America on acid-free paper. For information and catalog write to Jason Aronson Inc., 230 Livingston Street, Northvale, New Jersey 07647-1726. Or visit our website: http://www.aronson.com

To Susan, our cave, and its treasures
that continue to grow within
in spite of storms without:
Damon, Natalie, Stephanie, Jessica, and Cristiano.
And to our Sebbie whose brilliant flight
continues in another world.

Contents

Preface

According to Schneider (1990), psychology is at a critical crossroads. One of the forces the discipline faces, which I believe applies equally to child psychotherapy, is a centrifugal trend that results in disunity, divisiveness, and self-limiting specialization. Paraphrasing a quote from his illuminating discussion, child therapists read only what they must to help them in their own specialty. The specialties in child therapy are well known, each segregated from the other: psychodynamic therapy, cognitive therapy, behavioral therapy, and cognitive-behavioral therapy. And most therapists have been trained to conceptualize their work in one of these frameworks (Schact 1984). Three clinical reports that appeared nearly a century ago could be viewed as forecasting this segregation.

In 1905 Shephard Ivory Franz (Santostefano 1976a) described his efforts to train a patient who had had a paralytic stroke to speak. His goal was to teach the patient the name of familiar colors, numerical digits, four lines from a written text, and the German word for *pen*, a piece of information the patient did not have as part of his past. In his attempt to achieve this goal, Franz designed techniques that reflect present-day principles of cognitive therapy. First he selected a finite amount of information for the patient to master—six colors, nine numerical digits, one line of a text—presenting it in a stepwise fashion starting with simple patterns of information and gradually shifting to more complex ones. A given piece of information was presented repeatedly, a few minutes each day over many days. In carefully prescribing the complexity of information, and in repeatedly asking the patient to manage it, Franz suggested that a cognitive "habit" or function was being structured.

In 1909 Freud reported the treatment of a 5-year-old boy, conducted by his father and supervised by Freud. This case set the stage for the emphasis given in psychodynamic child psychotherapy to the use of interpretation as the main tool that brings unconscious motives to conscious awareness, thereby resolving conflict and relieving the problem behavior. The boy was afraid that horses would bite him, a fear that generalized to other large animals. Freud stated his broad treatment plan clearly: "I arranged with Hans's father that he should tell the boy that all this business about horses was a piece of nonsense and nothing more. The truth was, his father was to say, that he was fond of his mother and wanted to be taken into her bed. The reason he was afraid of horses now was that he had taken so much interest in their widdlers" (p. 28) as well as his own. And so father, over many months, delivered interpretations to his son that would gradually "enlighten him" of the notion that his oedipal longings for mother resulted in the fear that he would lose his widdler at the bite of horses: Hans said, "Don't put your finger to the white horse, it'll bite you." Father responded, "I say, it strikes me that it isn't the horse you mean, but a widdler, that one mustn't put one's hand to" (p. 29).

In 1924 Mary Cover Jones described her attempts to help Peter overcome his fear of rabbits and furry objects using a technique that forecast the emergence of behavioral therapies. She extinguished the fear by pairing the noxious stimulus (a caged rabbit) with pleasurable stimuli and responses (eating food). Initially, while the child ate at a table, the caged rabbit was placed at some distance. Over a number of meals, as the child showed no signs of fear, the cage was moved closer, step by step. In the last phase the rabbit was released at the table while the child ate happily.

After these first clinical reports representing the beginnings of different approaches, segregation in psychotherapy was, and is, tenaciously maintained. During the past several years, however, interest in psychotherapy integration has been growing (Garfield 1994). This interest is reflected by the formation of the Society for the Exploration of Psychotherapy Integration (SEPI), the journal of this society launched in 1991, and by the appearance of two handbooks (Norcross and Goldfried 1992, Stricker and Gold 1993). The fact that interest in psychotherapy integration is growing and receiving recognition is also reflected by the fact that Arkowitz (1992) was invited to write a chapter on "Integrative Theories of Therapy" for the volume published to honor the centennial of the American Psychological Association (Freedkeim 1992). Interest in integration is also reflected by paradigm shifts that have been occurring in each camp of psychotherapy. Cognitive and behavioral therapists are becoming interested in learning about clients from the inside (their meanings and fantasies) as well as from overt behaviors and conscious thoughts, while psychodynamic therapists are becoming interested in learning about clients from the outside (aspects of relationships that are corrective) as well as from inferred unconscious motives and meanings (Messer and Winokur 1984). Stimulated by these developments, debates among segregated camps of adult psychotherapy are ongoing (e.g., Mahoney 1993, Wachtel 1994).

It is my impression, however, that mainstream child psychotherapy remains severely segregated, and that, relative to the field of adult psychotherapy, little or no attention is being paid to integration. This impression derives from my teaching courses and presenting at programs attended over the years by graduate students in clinical, school, counseling, and social work programs; psychiatric residents; and trainees in child psychoanalysis. This volume is intended to contribute to the desegregation of child psychotherapy, provide one model of integration, and stimulate interest in integration. Therefore, the reader will not find cookbook recipes that define how one should conduct psychotherapy with children and adolescents who have been assigned to one or another diagnostic category. Such volumes are available (e.g., Reinecke and Dattilio 1996). Instead, the reader will find a therapeutic model and technical guidelines, framed within a developmental-dialectical perspective, that result from integrating child psychotherapies and that can be applied to all or most children, whatever their diagnoses. The model and methods I present to stimulate interest in integrating child psychotherapies evolved over the past three decades, influenced by the continuous interpenetration of my research activities and clinical experiences.

My interest in integration has roots in childhood experiences I have discussed elsewhere (Santostefano 1997, in press). But beginning with the adolescence of my professional development, after military service as a medic, I enrolled in the University of Connecticut and decided to switch from a pre-med major to psychology, discovering that I was fascinated by philosophy and the mind. At that time, in that program, behaviorism and animal research were emphasized, leaving me with the nagging feeling that the dilemmas of life were not being addressed. Yet I was fascinated by the animal experiments of Gestalt psychology, which were not part of the ethos of behaviorism. Familiar to some, one classic experiment went something like this: a monkey was placed in a cage, along with a stick and chair. A banana hung out of reach on a string from the ceiling. Leaping, the monkey reached for the banana but to no avail. Then the monkey took the stick and swung at the banana, or stood on the chair reaching upwards, repeatedly trying each solution and still failing to retrieve the banana. After many efforts, the "sacred moment" of insight came. The monkey stood on the chair, stick in hand, reached up, and easily obtained the banana. Experiments such as these aroused in me what were then vague notions about the relation between action and insight, and the importance of integrating actions and their meanings with cognitive activity, notions that would surface in graduate school and eventually find their way into my views concerning psychotherapy with children.

While attending graduate school courses in psychotherapy, we were assigned undergraduates who had applied for treatment. One of my cases, a member of the varsity wrestling team, from time to time asked to walk around outside or sit on the steps. I noticed that thoughts and feelings he experienced when walking about were different from those he experienced when sitting in the office. And I noticed that particular memories about his mother occurred to him when he repeatedly rubbed the palm of his hand against the cement steps. My supervisor, William Snyder, representing one prevailing view (still maintained in some quarters) that therapy should take place in an office, advised me to explore within myself why I went outside. But he did listen to my wondering whether there was more to what happens in therapy than reflections and interpretations by the therapist. Influenced by such questions, I conducted research for my doctoral dissertation on the topic of actions as measures of personality (Santostefano 1960a, 1962), which later continued as a program of studies on the relations among action, fantasy, and language as modes of expression (e.g., Santostefano 1965a,b, 1968a,b, 1977).

After receiving my doctorate, I enrolled in a two-year postdoctoral program in clinical child psychology at the University of Colorado Medical Center where I was supervised by psychoanalytically oriented psychologists and psychoanalysts to whom I am indebted (John Conger, John Benjamin, Gaston Blom, and others). After completing my postdoctoral, I continued on the staff of the medical center and, with the benefit of an NIMH Career Teacher Award, spent time with George Klein and David Rapaport, two psychologists-psychoanalysts. These tutorials sparked my interest in understanding cognitive functioning within personality and development, an interest that also led to a series of initial studies (e.g., Santostefano 1964a,b). In addition, while continuing clinical work, I participated in several research projects that provided me with the opportunity to continue my interest in studying the meanings of actions and gestures. As one example, in a study of monozygotic twin children, I asked each twin (with the other absent) to stand on one of two wooden boxes, identical save that one was half the height of the other. The actions the twins took predicted which child was dominant and which deferent in their relationship, as determined later by treatment sessions.

Throughout this time I was receiving intensive supervision in child psychotherapy; however, my studies of the relationship among action, cognition, meaning, and development continually impacted what I did in treatment sessions. As one example, I began twice-weekly sessions with "Albert" in the best way I knew at the time and within the psychoanalytic tradition to which I had made a commitment. I entered each session sustained by the conviction that if I could help this boy successfully resolve his unconscious conflicts, he would loosen his constriction and inhibition and perform better at home and school. As treatment progressed, I noticed behaviors that suggested to me that whatever else troubled the boy, he simply was not experiencing stimulation around him, stimulation *I* took for granted *he* was taking for granted. For example, when touching surfaces of different textures, he did not spontaneously show signs that he was aware of differences. And when we entered the playroom one day, he did not react to the complete rearrangement by housekeeping staff of furniture and play material since our last session. I wondered whether what I was observing was related to his mother's hospitalization for six months before he reached his second birthday. At that time in the psychoanalytic camp little attention was paid to the significance for psychotherapy of the first two years of life, since the focus was on the years beyond the age of 3–4 and how a child resolved her/his oedipal conflict.

Now and then I interrupted my nondirected format, which emphasized dialogue Albert and I exchanged while we "played," and asked him to join me in various activities. For example, we went outside to have a "feeling contest." I closed my eyes and Albert placed my fingers on one of the bricks that made up the wall surrounding the clinic. Then he lifted my hand away and again placed my fingers on a brick. My job was to decide whether I was feeling the same or a different brick. Then Albert took a turn. And whenever Albert stepped out of his robotic mode, I took him outside and set up a series of contests, each requiring a different degree of assertiveness and delay (e.g., hurling tennis balls at a tree trunk and lobbing them into a wastebasket). When I reviewed these sessions with one supervisor, an excellent clinical psychoanalyst who, however, was not into research, he became puzzled and annoyed. I will never forget one of his comments: "I don't know what you're doing; but I *do* know that what you're doing is not psychotherapy." I had not yet learned, nor had my supervisor, about London's (1964) book that appeared at this time. Discovered much later by me, London analyzed "insight" and "action" therapies and argued that therapy that attempts to integrate action and insight might be more effective for a wider range of problems then one that emphasizes only one of these approaches.

In the early adulthood of my professional career I left Colorado and joined the faculty at Clark University, the home of Heinz Werner and organismic-developmental psychology, where I learned more about relationships among body perceptions, cognitive functioning, and development from Seymour Wapner, Bernard Kaplan, and other colleagues. A few years later I joined the faculty of the Boston University School of Medicine where, stimulated by discussions with Louis Sander and Gerald Stechler, psychoanalytically oriented infant researchers, I became interested in how observations of infants provide a way of understanding how experiences that occur in the first two years of life contribute to later development. During my time at Clark University and Boston University School of Medicine, I completed training in adult and child psychoanalysis.

These early research and clinical experiences, and exposure to the organismic-developmental viewpoint and psychoanalytically oriented infant research (along with my own training in psychoanalysis), converged into research conducted with populations of clinical and public school children, concerned cognitive functioning and the relations among action, fantasy, and language as modalities of expression (e.g., Santostefano 1977, 1978, 1986). This work influenced my initial proposal concerning the treatment of children, that is: (1) clinicians should move beyond nosology and diagnose from the viewpoint of development (Santostefano 1971); (2) principles of infant development could be a useful guide in conducting psychotherapy with children (Santostefano and Berkowitz 1976); and (3) therapists should address cognitive functioning within personality and interrelate what a child does, imagines, and says (e.g., Santostefano 1980b).

I next assumed a position as director of the department of child and adolescent psychology, McLean Hospital/Harvard Medical School, where I continued my clinical work and research for twenty years, a phase I consider the middle age of my professional career. I continued studies of the relationships among action, cognition, meanings, and emotion (e.g., Santostefano 1985, Santostefano and Moncata 1989, Santostefano and Rieder 1984), and at the same time focused on constructing an integrative approach to psychotherapy with children. With my first attempt I described treatment guidelines that integrated cognitive development and psychodynamic psychotherapy on the one hand (e.g., Santostefano 1978, 1985a) and guidelines that integrated what a child does, imagines, and says within psychodynamic psychotherapy on the other (e.g., Santostefano 1986, 1988b). I elaborated this integration (Santostefano and Calicchia 1992), emphasizing the importance of the first two years of life and the relationship and enactments between child and therapist rather than interpretation and self talk. I also reported a series of studies (Santostefano 1995b) that illustrated the heuristic value for psychotherapy of integrating embodied meanings, overt behaviors, cognition, and emotion.

This primer integrates, elaborates, and extends these earlier reports. Part I considers the need to desegregate the field of child psychotherapy and obstacles to integration. Part II discusses why and how segregation has been maintained between real and subjective knowledge, body and mind, and cognition and emotion, and the views psychodynamic and cognitive-behavioral therapies hold of these segregated domains. Part III reviews the influence these segregated domains have had on concepts and techniques of cognitive-behavioral and psychodynamic child therapies. Part IV lists issues that should be considered when segregation is dissolved and psychotherapies are integrated. Parts V and VI present a developmental framework for integrating child psychotherapies. This framework articulates principles that emerge from infant studies and extends them into childhood and adolescence by interrelating unconscious meanings a child is negotiating with others using particular cognitive functions and modes of expression as tools. Part VII translates this framework into guidelines for conducting a form of integrative psychotherapy. Here consideration is given to the goal of treatment, diagnostic data required to guide the course of treatment, where therapy could take place in addition to the traditional playroom, the catalysts that promote change, how child and therapist construct an intersubjective world they will share, and whether and when a therapist relies on structured and unstructured interactions. Part VIII describes treatment cases that relied on structured interactions throughout treatment, other cases that relied on a transition from structured to unstructured interactions, and a case that relied on unstructured interactions throughout treatment. Part IX discusses how and why diagnosis from a developmental-dialectical viewpoint differs from the currently prevailing approach of diagnostic categories and how it could be more heuristic for planning child psychotherapy. In addition, a series of research studies are reviewed to illustrate the types of questions raised by the proposed model, and the methods used to answer them—a number of which are innovative, providing observations not usually made available by traditional psychological tests.

    This primer is intended for students learning about psychotherapy with children and adolescents who may not yet have become hardened psychodynamic or cognitive or behavioral therapists and therefore may be more open to integration. This volume is also intended for their teachers and supervisors in the hope that they may become interested in the heuristic value of integration. I am sure that some of my psychodynamic colleagues, when considering this text, will conclude that I have omitted one or another consideration at the heart of their approach, and that some of my cognitive-behavioral colleagues will come to the same conclusion. I very likely have. But my intention is to present enough of each approach to set the stage for a discussion of integration. Therefore, while I present one model of integration, my main interest is in stimulating as much interest in the topic of integration among child psychotherapists as there appears to be among adult psychotherapists.

◈ ◈ ◈

I conclude with expressions of gratitude and appreciation to my wife, Susan, who has gathered much experience and knowledge from her five "in vivo internships," each involving her raising our five children, experience and knowledge she astutely applies in her clinical work and brings to our discussions. I am also grateful to the many colleagues from whom I have learned as I have tried to contribute to their training, notably Dr. Scott Creighton, Dr. Patricia Burke, and Dr. Michael Robbins.

.

1

The Need to Desegregate the Field of Child Psychotherapy and Obstacles to Integration

CONTENTS

HOW MANY FORMS OF CHILD PSYCHOTHERAPY ARE IN USE AND WHICH APPROACHES ARE VIEWED AS MOST USEFUL?

A minimum of 7.5 million children in the United States need help with mental health problems (Weisz and Weiss 1993). While 230 forms of psychotherapy are used to provide this assistance, only three broad approaches are dominant at this time: behavioral therapy, cognitive therapy, and psychodynamic therapy. For the most part, each approach holds that its concepts and techniques are "true" and "worthy" and the others less so or not at all, segregation that has been maintained in mental health fields for decades. In one survey (Kazdin et al. 1990) of more than a thousand child psychotherapists, psychologists reported that they found an eclectic approach most useful, sometimes using behavioral, sometimes cognitive, and sometimes psychodynamic techniques. Psychiatrists on the other hand found psychodynamic techniques most useful.

There are two angles from which this survey could be viewed. First, if we hold to one side those who favored an eclectic approach, psychologists viewed behavioral modification and cognitive therapy techniques as useful, while psychiatrists did not. In contrast, psychiatrists viewed psychodynamic and psychoanalytic techniques as useful, while psychologists did not. From another angle, I focus on the clinicians who rated an eclectic approach as useful. Although psychologists and psychiatrists differed in their view of the effectiveness of behavioral, cognitive, and psychodynamic therapies, they showed strong agreement with regard to the usefulness of an eclectic approach: 72 percent of psychologists and 74 percent of psychiatrists reported that at times they found an eclectic approach useful. That therapists prefer an eclectic approach has a long history. Garfield (1994) reported that E. Lowell Kelly, in his 1960 presidential address to members of the Division of Clinical Psychology, American Psychological Association, described the results of a survey he had conducted: of more than 1,000 clinical psychologists, almost 40 percent declared themselves to be eclectics falling just short of the 41 percent who declared themselves to be psychoanalytic or psychodynamic. Garfield also summarized ten surveys conducted between 1976 and 1990 showing a steady increase in therapists preferring an eclectic approach. In the most recent survey, 68 perent of psychiatrists, clinical psychologists, and social workers surveyed expressed a preference for eclecticism, reflecting that an eclectic approach apparently has established roots in social work and continues to grow in clinical psychology and psychiatry. Should a therapist treat children sometimes using a behavioral, sometimes a cognitive, and sometimes a

3

psychodynamic technique? From the viewpoint of integrating psychotherapies, the answer is no.

CAN YOU GIVE A CLINICAL EXAMPLE ILLUSTRATING HOW DIFFERENT THERAPIES VIEW THE SAME CHILD?

When 9-year-old Sally stuck her hand into an opening of a streetlight pole, she accidentally received an electric shock that left her unconscious, but miraculously did not kill her or result in neurological damage. During the next school year, her academic performance slipped from adequate to well below grade level, and she became very hyperactive and inattentive. She impulsively pinched the buttocks of peers, and on several occasions urinated on the floor of the school bathroom. During an evaluation, she revealed that while lying in bed or sitting on a toilet, she fantasized that a monster would cover her body with hot spit, and that she believed her father yelled at her frequently because she was not as good as her brother. A behavioral therapist would help this girl regulate her hyperactivity; a cognitive therapist would treat her inattentiveness; a psychodynamic therapist would help her deal with the frightening monster-fantasy, providing her with insight that the giant monster, with its hot spit, is a symbol of the pole with its electric current, as well as of father punishing her for being a bad girl. The viewpoint of integrating psychotherapies urges a therapist to address the whole child, rather than select as the target of treatment irrational thoughts, hyperactive behavior, or unconscious dynamics producing conscious fears.

WHAT DOES INTEGRATING PSYCHOTHERAPIES MEAN?

Clinicians who have grappled with the meaning of integrating psychotherapies argue that integration is not an eclectic salad with, for example, a little bit of cognitive therapy, a little bit of behavior therapy, and a little bit of psychodynamic therapy tossed in (Wachtel 1984). They also remind us that various targets of psychotherapy (emotions, behaviors, cognitions, relationships, conscious and unconscious fantasies) exist within the same person. The viewpoint of integration proposes that a therapist should not treat hyperactivity or fears, much as a physician might treat a knee or a cold without giving particular attention to the total person who houses the knee or the cold. Rather, this viewpoint attempts to unify various concepts that in turn give rise to therapeutic techniques that are heuristic and address the whole of a person's psychology (Stricker 1994). While Arkowitz (1992) characterized integration as containing three main directions (theoretical integration, identifying common factors among therapies, and technical eclecticism), Garfield (1994) noted "technical eclecticism is viewed [by many authors] as eclecticism rather than psychotherapy integration since [the] focus is on selecting appropriate procedures and techniques to fit individual clients and not the integration of specific theories" (p. 129). "The goal [of integration] is the development of a new, coherent structure, an internally consistent approach both to technical interventions and to construction of theory" (Wachtel 1984, p. 45). Later I will have more to say about technical eclecticism which I view as an obstacle to integration.

WHAT DOES A THERAPIST SEE WHEN LOOKING AT CHILD PSYCHOTHERAPY?

If child therapists favor either a behavioral, a cognitive, or a psychodynamic technique when conducting psychotherapy, they peer through one lens that permits them to see only overt behavior (such as Sally's hyperactivity), or cognitions (such as Sally's belief that father thinks she is not as good as her brother), or symbols of conscious and unconscious fears (such as Sally's fantasy that a monster will cover her with hot spit). Some therapists peer through "bifocals" and see only the concepts and techniques of two approaches; some peer through "trifocals," at one moment using cognitive, at another, behavioral, and at still another, psychodynamic techniques. The important point is that whichever lens a therapist peers through at any given moment, the lens brings into view the "correct" concepts and techniques of one approach while those of others are segregated and pushed out of view.

IS ECLECTICISM THE GREATEST OBSTACLE TO INTEGRATING PSYCHOTHERAPIES?

Eclecticism, or using a trifocal lens, is perhaps the greatest obstacle to integrating psychotherapies. Since a majority of psychologists and psychiatrists surveyed reported that an eclectic approach is useful, we should consider an example. Lazarus (1995), although describing adult patients, provides us with an excellent illustration of an eclectic at work. With his 2:00 P.M. patient, Lazarus applied a psychodynamic approach he characterized as saying little, listening attentively, and dwelling on childhood memories. At 3:00 P.M. he applied cognitive therapy techniques with another patient by being "active, disputational, energetically parsing dysfunctional beliefs . . ." (p. 36). At 4:00 P.M., with still another patient, he applied behavioral techniques using role playing and social skills training to help her cope with two tasks: with one, she is to make remarks to an audience when she receives her firm's annual award; with the other, she is to approach her mother assertively rather than timidly in order to address an unresolved issue.

After sketching these clients, Lazarus (1995) made a statement reflecting one reason why an eclectic view presents an obstacle to integrating psychotherapies.

"The techniques I selected were in keeping with *my perceptions* of the client's specific needs and experiences . . ." (p. 36, my italics). But what guided Lazarus's perceptions? At 2:00 P.M. he was peering through a psychodynamic lens that brought into view techniques of listening and reflecting; at 3:00 P.M., through a cognitive lens that brought into view cognitive restructuring techniques; at 4:00 P.M., through a behavioral lens that brought into focus rehearsing how one should handle a situation. But Lazarus was firm in the opinion that he was not peering through theoretical lenses, rejecting the proposal offered by others mentioned earlier that integrating concepts from different theoretical viewpoints is a necessary condition to technical integration. "I strongly favor technical eclecticism and regard theoretical integration with considerable suspicion and disdain" (p. 37).

Yet other clinical examples Lazarus (1995) described illustrate that from patient to patient he is peering through one or another theoretical lens that brings into focus what he perceives in his patients. For example, he described an anxious young man who negotiated a business merger that significantly compromised his partner. Initially this patient "denied having feelings of guilt and proceeded to rationalize that because of his partner's alleged hostility towards him, he had done nothing improper . . . [later] he got past certain rationalizations and denials and gained insight into possible motives behind his behavior . . ." (p. 33). When Lazarus sees "rationalizations," he is referring to the observation that the patient justified his cheating by explaining that his partner had always been hostile toward him. But where do rationalizations come from? Did the patient invent this behavior? He certainly did not. Rationalizations, as behaviors, appear when we look at behavior through a psychodynamic lens that conceptualizes the mind as using a variety of strategies (mechanisms of defense), which from the psychodynamic view avoid painful anxiety, relocating one's "bad" feelings and motives. Along the same line, Lazarus perceived and understood behaviors he termed "denials" and "insight" by peering through a psychodynamic theoretical lens.

The point I am emphasizing is that whether Lazarus was selecting techniques in keeping with his "perception" of the needs of each of his clients, he was peering through different theoretical lenses (cognitive, behavioral, and psychodynamic) that brought particular phenomena into view. Lazarus disagrees with my position. "Technical eclecticism," he stated, "permits me to select techniques from any discipline without necessarily endorsing any of the theories that spawn them" (1995, p. 31). Lazarus must also disagree with Kuhn's (1962) now famous thesis that at every level of science and observation, paradigms, or points of view, that already exist in the mind of the scientist or therapist influence what is observed. Lazarus would argue that if you perceive that a patient needs a wheel, you borrow a wheel and use it. Kuhn would argue that unless you have seen a stone rolling down a hillside many, many times, and from these experiences evolve the concept of objects capable of circular motion, you would not see a wheel even when it is before your very eyes. The goal of integration, as we noted earlier, is to develop a coherent theory, or point of view, from which techniques emerge (Wachtel 1984).

WHAT IS A PSYCHOTHERAPY KALEIDOSCOPE AND HOW COULD IT BECOME AN OBSTACLE TO INTEGRATION?

The reader may have already embraced an approach so that when "looking" at child psychotherapy, she/he peers into a kaleidoscope that holds a particular design. If the reader is a psychologist, it is likely that her/his kaleidoscope contains designs of cognitive and behavioral methods, and if a psychiatrist, designs of psychodynamic techniques. Counseling and school psychologists, along with social workers, have very likely been introduced to one or another kaleidoscope by the particular school of therapy that dominated the setting in which she/he was trained. Others may have been introduced to the merits of an eclectic approach. Moreover, in many cases the reader may be certain that the design in her/his kaleidoscope, is the "right" one. Kelly (1965) recognized this phenomenon as "hardening of the categories." Or, as Colby and Stoller (1988) noted: each sect has its truth, and every truth has its sect, and out of all delusions we select one which matches us best, and we proclaim it the truth. When considering the same patient then, therapists frequently see different problems and the need for different techniques because they look into different kaleidoscopes. For example, when a psychodynamic therapist peers through her/his kaleidoscope at Lazarus's 4:00 P.M. appointment, she/he would not see the need to engage the patient in rehearsing a speech, but would attempt to resolve "an underlying conflict" with aggression by making conscious the connection between being afraid of approaching mother assertively and speaking to a crowd.

WHAT STEPS SHOULD WE FOLLOW TO SHAKE A PSYCHOTHERAPY KALEIDOSCOPE SO WE SEE A DIFFERENT DESIGN?

To disrupt the familiar pattern in one's psychotherapy kaleidoscope requires that several preliminary issues be considered: (1) how psychotherapy is defined by therapists using different approaches; (2) what psychotherapists do; and (3) what we learn when we compare these definitions and techniques.

HOW IS PSYCHOTHERAPY DEFINED BY THERAPISTS USING DIFFERENT APPROACHES?

Psychoanalysts and psychiatrists (e.g., Hammer and Kaplan 1967) often define psychotherapy in terms of helping a child advance from early psychosexual stages to later ones: from experiencing and representing interactions with others in terms of the need for nurture (oral stage), then in terms of control (anal stage), then in terms of ambition and achievement (phallic stage), and then in terms of triangular relationships, competing with an authority figure for the love and preference of another (oedipal stage). Yet one child psychoanalyst (Coppolillo 1987) made no mention of helping a child move through psychosexual stages, defining therapy as a process that enables a child to use self-knowledge in the service of achieving self-regulation. Another (Spiegel 1989) also proposed that psychotherapy enhances a child's self-esteem, enabling the child to view herself/himself in more realistic ways and become aware of her/his feelings.

In contrast, a psychologist (Reisman 1973) defined psychotherapy broadly as "communications of person-related understanding, respect, and the wish to be of help" (p. 10). Others who use cognitive and behavioral techniques defined psychotherapy as teaching thinking processes that help children slow down and cognitively examine their behavioral alternatives before acting (e.g., Kendall and Brasswell 1985). Others defined psychotherapy as all encompassing, "an interpersonal process designed to bring about the modification of feelings, cognitions, attitudes and behaviors which have proven troublesome to the person . . ." (Strupp 1973, p. 3); or as "any intervention designed to ameliorate psychological distress, reduce maladaptive behaviors, or enhance adaptive behavior through counseling, structured or unstructured interventions and training programs" (Weisz et al. 1987).

Shirk (1988), attempting to integrate cognitive-behavioral and psychodynamic kaleidoscopes, distinguished between psychotherapy that is concerned with changing the meaning of behavior and that views overt behaviors as forms of representation on the one hand and, on the other, psychotherapy that is concerned with changing behavior itself and views behaviors as skills. He defined child psychotherapy in terms of three dimensions: (1) structure (i.e., the degree to which activity is directed by the therapist or by the child); (2) medium (i.e., a continuum of exchanges between child and therapist from conversation to play); and (3) communicative functions (i.e., a continuum of communications by the therapist ranging from verbal interpretations that analyze the meaning of a child's behavior to communications that provide a corrective, emotional experience in a supportive environment). I will return to the heuristic value of Shirk's definition in Part VII.

WHAT DOES A CHILD PSYCHOTHERAPIST DO?

Typically, psychodynamic psychotherapists allow a child to engage in whatever play activity and discussions she/he chooses to change how the child thinks, feels, and behaves. Change is facilitated as the child gains insight into mental conflicts that are outside of awareness. The child is expected to learn that her/his thoughts, feelings, and actions are generated from within her/his personal world rather than activated by persons and environments. This learning is brought about as the therapist employs several tools described by Coppolillo (1987): (1) inquiry; (2) empathy; (3) introspection (the therapist teaches the child to look at her/his own private thoughts and fantasies); (4) associations (the therapist uses the child's associations to decode unconscious motives); (5) help so the child understands why she/he is in therapy; (6) help so the child understands that there is an unconscious; (7) countertransference (the therapist uses her/his own thoughts and feelings, activated by the child's behavior, as a source of data about the child's difficulties); (8) interpretation and pressing the child to express her/his thoughts, feelings, fantasies, and conflicts in words; and (9) understanding (analyzing) the transference.

Typically, cognitive-behavioral therapists ask a child to engage in various tasks designed and directed by the therapist. Change is facilitated as the child develops social skills to solve problems using behavioral strategies in particular contexts (e.g., coping with a classroom or fear of darkness). This learning is brought about as the therapist employs several tools described by Meichenbaum (1977) and Meyers and Craighead (1984): (1) help the child define and understand her/his problem; (2) self-instructional training (the child is taught to instruct herself/himself while coping with problematic situations); (3) behavioral contingencies (rewards are provided to reinforce the desired behavior); (4) homework assignments; (5) modeling (the child observes a demonstration of some behavior to be learned, provided by the therapist or film); (6) affective education (the child is trained to recognize and label her/his emotions and those of others); (7) role playing (the child plays roles in imaginary situations that eventually replicate aspects of the child's environment); (8) training tasks (the child completes a series of tasks initially consisting of simple, impersonal cognitive games and then more complex, interpersonal, emotionally evocative cognitive games).

> **WHEN PSYCHODYNAMIC AND COGNITIVE-BEHAVIORAL THERAPIES ARE COMPARED, WHAT ARE SOME OF THE DIFFERENCES AND SIMILARITIES IN WHAT A THERAPIST SEES AND DOES WHEN LOOKING THROUGH A KALEIDOSCOPE?**

Several elements are shared by each approach: (1) psychotherapy is a method of learning designed to decrease distress and maladaptive behavior and to improve adaptive functioning; (2) self-knowledge and self-awareness are necessary for self-regulation; (3) a child needs to become aware of and label his/her emotional experiences. Other elements are also shared if not in content at least in form. A cognitive-behavioral therapist uses modeling and extrinsic rewards in formal, structured interactions. A psychodynamic therapist continuously models an attitude of inquiry and introspection, and is likely to reward the child with smiles, facial expressions of approval, and verbal compliments. In addition, each approach assigns a central position to verbalizing. Psychodynamic therapists emphasize helping a child verbalize her/his motives, emotions, and fantasies, while verbally interpreting these behaviors. Cognitive-behavioral therapists emphasize self-talk and the role of words in regulating behaviors.

A comparison of the kaleidoscopes of each approach also brings into view patterns that are quite different. A cognitive-behavioral therapist focuses on some unit of behavior (e.g., restlessness) viewed as rooted in particular environments. This behavior becomes the direct target of therapeutic intervention (e.g., the child is trained to be less restless by performing a graded series of tasks while using self-talk). In contrast, a psychodynamic therapist looks beyond the child's restlessness and directs interventions at some presumed, unconscious, mental conflict (e.g., between the wish to be aggressive and internalized prohibitions against this wish). This conflict, with its anxiety and guilt, is seen as the cause of the child's difficulties and is frequently interpreted until the conflict becomes part of the child's conscious awareness.

CAN YOU DESCRIBE OBSERVATIONS OF CHILDREN IN TREATMENT, AND THE QUESTIONS THEY RAISE, THAT REQUIRE US TO SHAKE UP THE PSYCHODYNAMIC AND COGNITIVE-BEHAVIORAL KALEIDOSCOPES AND CHALLENGE THE VISION AND METHODS OF EACH?

An aggressive-impulsive child tries to act upon the person of the therapist by winding a rope around him. Should the psychodynamic therapist interpret this action in terms of some presumed unconscious motive; for example, "Is this the way you would like to stop your mother from picking on you?" Should the cognitive-behavioral therapist explain to the child that the rope is not part of the steps in self-instructional training that they are working on? Some therapists have proposed that it is "absurd" for a therapist to allow herself/himself to be bound while playing some game. Another child sits sullenly in the playroom, ignores the therapist, and makes clear that she/he wants to go outside. Should the psychodynamic therapist interpret to the child that she/he is running away from the problems they are trying to solve? Should the cognitive-behavioral therapist introduce a program of self-assertion training? Some therapists are firm in the opinion that psychotherapy "appropriately takes place behind closed doors." Another child takes home the materials being used in some task the therapist introduced, and then does not return them. Should the therapist ask for them? Another brings an item from home to the treatment room and insists on using it instead of the skills-training material the therapist has been using. Should the therapist allow this? And an impulsive, distractible 7-year-old child rejects self-talk training and interpretations. Should the therapy be postponed until the child is older?

To illustrate other observations that require us to shake up traditional kaleido-scopes, consider the following. When I entered the waiting room to greet a 10-year-old boy for an initial appointment, he was not there. I found him standing at the entrance to the building. His jacket was pulled over his head, so I could not see his face, nor could he see mine. Father, who was kneeling by the boy, was trying to coax him with soft, reassuring comments to remove his jacket. The boy did not budge.

On another occasion I greeted a 5-year-old girl, Jane, and her mother in the waiting room for an initial consultation. After chatting with them for a minute, I invited the child to accompany me to the playroom. In response, she anxiously clutched mother's body. The more mother reassured her that she would "have fun," the more the child clutched her mother in fear and desperation.

I greeted Louis, a 7-year-old boy, sitting by his mother in the waiting room, happily sharing pictures of a magazine. A second after I introduced myself and invited him to join me, he leaped up and rushed into the treatment room. He im-mediately darted about, handling at least a dozen items. Then he began tossing several of them across the room, sometimes clearly aiming at a window.

In my last example, Ellen, a high school student, slouched in a chair located as far away from her parent as the room permitted. She returned my greeting with a long stare. I noticed her army jacket and boots, as well as four earrings on one ear and three on the other. When I invited her to join me, she grunted that she would not go "in the office to talk" but would go outside.

When responding to each of these behaviors—which are quite typical in one's work with children and adolescents—what does the therapist do? Should she/he say anything, and if so, what? These children would not be receptive to verbal com-mentaries proposed by either psychodynamic or cognitive-behavioral therapies ("You sometimes have scary feelings. We will try to find out the reasons why" or "As I understand it, you came here because you are having trouble . . .").

CAN YOU GIVE AN EXAMPLE OF WHAT DIFFERENT THERAPISTS SEE WHEN LOOKING AT THE SAME CHILD?

Imagine four practicing psychotherapists who have been asked to observe inter-views with a child and parents from behind a one-way mirror. One is a cognitive therapist, another a behavior therapist, another a psychodynamic therapist, and the fourth an integrative therapist. In addition, a developmental researcher has been asked to serve as a consultant. They understand that after the observation each will share opinions about how the child should be helped.

The parents of 5-year-old Harry enter the office. They are obviously distraught as they describe that Harry has been expelled from preschool, not only because he has been hyperactive, but also because he has been hitting, biting, and spitting at teachers and peers. These behaviors persisted even though teachers tried various strategies at the suggestion of a consulting psychologist. For example, at the start of a day they showed Harry five Hershey's Kisses (which he loves) and explained that he could eat them at the close of school but would lose one each time he slapped or bit someone. In spite of such strategies, Harry's inappropriate behavior continued. Sharing details of his early history, parents noted that at home he displayed the same behaviors, occasionally hitting, biting, or spitting at his parents, younger sister, and grandparents without provocation.

After the parent interview, Harry darts into the adjoining playroom. He does not look at the examiner and engages in several activities at a frantic pace—scribbles on paper, makes balls of play dough that he hurls against the wall. Reminding Harry that he should not throw clay against the wall, the examiner invites him to hurl clay into a wastebasket. Harry flings a ball of clay in the direction of the wastebasket but misses by a good distance. Then, without hesitation, he hurls another ball of clay against the wall, quickly followed by another. He stands before a window, stares outside for several minutes, and begins to yank on the curtain. The examiner puts his arms around Harry, gently reminds him that he cannot hurt anything in the room, and urges him to try the game of flinging the clay balls into a box. But Harry continues pulling on the curtain. At this point the session comes to a close as Harry races toward the waiting room and his parents.

The behavior therapist speaks up first, pointing out that Harry's hyperactive, impulsive behavior and inattentiveness must be brought under control. The cognitive therapist enthusiastically agrees and proposes that, following a point of view that derives from the Soviet psychologist Luria, if Harry could internalize verbal commands with the help of self-instruction training, he could then exercise voluntary control over his behavior. Speaking in unison, the cognitive and behavioral therapists conclude that Harry does not have self-verbalization to regulate his behavior, and verbalizations of others seem to have no influence on his actions. What Harry needs is to be taught to slow down and cognitively examine his alternatives before taking action. To begin treatment a therapist could use a "copycat game" in which Harry imitates the therapist who is trying to figure out, with the help of self-statements, which geometric designs printed on a sheet of paper should be colored in. Tasks would then be gradually increased in cognitive complexity, and also in terms of containing stimuli that are emotionally evocative and related to interpersonal issues. As one example, Harry could look at pictures of children and adults in different situations and identify the emotions they are displaying. Later he would be asked to describe what is going on in a picture, the different actions a key person in the picture could take, and the consequences of each action. In the last phase of treatment Harry and the therapist would enact behaviors depicted in the picture and then behaviors related to particular contexts in which Harry has had difficulty. For example, Harry's parents had noted his impulsiveness when he and his sister are watching TV. Harry could play himself and the therapist his sister, and then they would reverse roles.

When Harry gets the urge to hit the therapist, he would be encouraged to use self-instruction steps he had already learned.

The psychodynamic therapist listened to the cognitive and behavioral therapists in disbelief and with some irritation. She points out that she has a very different view of Harry and how therapy should help him. She begins by describing therapy as a journey the child and therapist share as the therapist is led by Harry through his personal world, a terrain the therapist has never seen before. The psychodynamic therapist also points out that if treatment begins with tasks, one runs the risk that Harry would not invite the therapist into his personal world.

While listening to the psychodynamic therapist, the attention of the cognitive and behavioral therapists drifts away and their eyes take on a glassy stare. They have heard this type of poetic formulation before but they do not understand what the psychodynamic therapist is talking about. Noticing their expressions, but undaunted, the psychodynamic therapist continues, determined to get them to understand why the underlying dynamics of behavior are important.

First, Harry should be provided with a relationship in which he could gradually discover the unconscious motives and fantasies that are the source of his biting, spitting, and hyperactivity. One possible unconscious motive is that Harry has not yet resolved his rage over being replaced by a younger sister. When he slaps a peer, he is expressing rage toward his sister. Another unconscious conflict could stem from his relationship with his parents. As his mother seems to pamper and cling to him, Harry could be struggling with the fact that he had to surrender his "Queen" when sister was born. And Harry's father seems aloof and distant. Therefore, he does not have a strong authority figure with whom he can identify and internalize, enabling him to develop a superego that controls impulses. When he becomes conscious of these issues, the biting, spitting, and hyperactivity should diminish.

When the psychodynamic therapist completes her comment, everyone sits in silence, lost in private thoughts. At this moment the developmental consultant steps in. Because she is not a therapist, and still uncertain whether she belongs, she addresses the others in a didactic tone. Searching for reconciliation and integration, she points out that each therapist is committed to promoting change in Harry's behavior and relieving him of his suffering. The cognitive and behavioral therapist believe that it is important to choose a specific target that is on the surface and overt, namely Harry's aggressiveness and impulsivity. To change this behavior, they recommend tasks that will teach him to use verbal statements to regulate himself and to benefit from modeling others. The psychodynamic therapist believes it is important to choose a target that is inside, or covert, namely unconscious meanings, wishes, and urges. Harry's behavior will change as he gains insight, as he becomes aware of those conflicted wishes and fantasies in his unconscious. The developmental consultant concludes that cognitive, behavioral, and psychodynamic views of therapeutic targets and change are different, and developmental research and theory could provide an approach to integrating them. For example, it is important to understand Harry's status in terms of different lines of development, such as the relationship between his cognitive and emotional functioning and the relationships among what he does, imagines, and says. In recent years, the consultant reminds the therapists that infant research has been learning a great deal about how knowledge and meaning given to experiences are constructed during the first two years of life, as infant and caregiver engage in continuous dialectical interactions, and how this knowledge and related representations influence what a child expects from others and what a child does, imagines, and says in future interactions and negotiations. Research stresses that from the first months of life and beyond, actions lead to representations and representations lead to actions and that behaviors, whether actions, fantasies, or verbal statements change as the organization they form progresses from global and inflexible to differentiated and flexible levels.

At this point, as if to avoid a debate, the group turns to the integrative therapist who has remained silent but attentive throughout the discussion. She accepts the invitation and begins, "Let's ask ourselves, would we be better able to help Harry if we integrate cognitive, behavioral, and psychodynamic viewpoints using developmental-dialectical concepts?" The three therapists and developmental consultant respond in unison, "Oh, you propose we take an eclectic approach? We should take from cognitive, behavioral, psychodynamic, and developmental techniques, whatever would be of help to Harry." The integrative therapist replies with a firm, "No! I do not mean take a little of this and a little of that. I mean an integration that results in a model of therapy that addresses both outside and inside behaviors, cognition and emotion, body and mind, and their relations." The four seem puzzled and declare they do not understand. At this point the integrative therapist relies upon a metaphor. "Well, I believe Nietzsche once said something like, 'Mankind seems not to be able to hear new music when it is first played.'"

At the close of Part I, I assume the voice of the integrative therapist and devote the remaining parts of this primer to discussing the root-causes of segregation in child psychotherapy, issues and needs that should be addressed when this segregation is dissolved, and the form of integrative psychotherapy for children I propose as one approach to addressing these needs.

2
Segregation in Psychology: The Tendency to Construct Boundaries

CONTENTS

WHY DO DIFFERENT VIEWPOINTS OF PSYCHOTHERAPY EXIST, AND WHY IS IT DIFFICULT TO SEE ANOTHER?

As noted in Part I, Nietzsche once said something like, "Mankind has a bad ear for new music," or maybe he said something like, "Mankind seems not to be able to hear new music when it is first played." Referring to the psychotherapy kaleidoscopes we discussed previously, when looking at a child, therapists become accustomed to seeing a particular pattern of concepts and techniques. The pattern they have learned becomes very familiar, so that it is difficult to see a different pattern, much like persons to whom Nietzsche is referring who have difficulty hearing new music. One reason why therapists have maintained segregated views is that, for decades, American psychology has divided the discipline with boundaries, for example, child and adult psychology, clinical practice and research, normal and pathological, conscious and unconscious, verbal and nonverbal. Boundaries have also segregated child and adolescent psychotherapy into three main camps: cognitive, behavioral, and psychodynamic, with cognitive and behavioral sometimes joining forces. By understanding the reasons for human psychology's segregation and polarization, one can more readily move beyond segregation and engage in the process of integrating psychotherapies.

WHAT IS THE AIM OF SEGREGATION IN PSYCHOLOGY?

Ken Wilber (1979) convincingly argued that in Western thinking, when we attempt to understand and give meaning to experiences, knowingly or unknowingly, we immediately draw mental boundaries that cast the experience as one of a pair of opposites: good versus evil, beautiful versus ugly. Once a boundary is drawn, one side of the divided territory is viewed as true and worthy, the other as less worthy. He also discussed how the Eastern way of experiencing is characterized more by a process of forging holistic meanings. For example, the Chinese convey the meaning of *crisis* by combining two brushstrokes. One conveys the meaning of *danger* (phonetic pronunciation "WAY"); the other, the meaning of *opportunity* (phonetic pronunciation "GEE"). By combining these brushstrokes, the meaning of crisis unites being aware of danger and recognizing opportunity.

Why is Western thinking different, drawing boundaries rather then uniting meanings? According to Wilber, beginning with Greek philosophers, we have been oriented to construe experiences as containing either pleasure or pain. The boundary the mind draws serves to renounce the part that arouses pain, freeing us to pursue pleasure. In my example, then, instead of experiencing a crisis as unifying the pain of danger with the excitement of opportunity, Western thinking splits off what is construed as the cause of pain and pursues what is presumed to avoid the crisis.

WHEN DID AMERICAN PSYCHOLOGY BEGIN TO PRACTICE SEGREGATION?

When the discipline of American psychology was taking shape, the Western tradition of constructing boundaries was already exerting considerable influence. But one of the founding fathers of psychology seemed to be unhappy with this tendency. In perhaps the first discussion of personality assessment, published more than a century ago, Sir Francis Galton had this to say in 1884 as he surveyed what students of human behavior of that day were doing. "There are two sorts of [investigators] . . . those who habitually dwell on pleasanter circumstances . . . and those who have an eye but for the unpleasing ones" (p. 180).

Some years later, in 1911, Frederick Lyman Wells provided an explicit example of how investigators were dwelling on "pleasanter circumstances" in order to avoid "unpleasing ones" (Santostefano 1976c). He had just published his extensive experiments with the "free association method," a procedure already familiar to psychologists: the examiner spoke a word to which the subject replied with "the first word it suggests to you" (Santostefano 1976c, p. 174). Investigators examined reaction times to stimulus words, and the content of associations, as a way to study a person's "emotional life." The method had been reported in Europe in 1883 by its originator, Sir Francis Galton, and introduced into the United States in 1887 by James McKeen Cattell. In the twenty years that followed, the free association test method captured the interest and enthusiasm of psychologists who reported numerous studies. Reviewing these studies, Wells noticed a trend that disturbed him. He believed that too many investigators had been avoiding the unpleasant goal of learning about a person's emotional life by hiding themselves in more "pleasant" studies of the grammatical and intellectual connections between stimulus words and associated responses. Wells made clear his frustration with the division between pleasant and unpleasant studies: "The psychology of today is very much a science of looking for the truth and hoping you won't find it . . ." (Wells 1912, p. 436).

Since the work of Galton and Wells, American psychology has continued to draw boundaries, three of which have particular relevance for integrating child and adolescent psychotherapies. One segregates "real knowledge" from "subjective knowledge," another "body from mind," and another "cognition from emotion."

Segregation between Real and Subjective Knowledge

> **SINCE PSYCHOTHERAPY INVOLVES LEARNING, IS KNOWLEDGE LEARNED OBJECTIVE OR SUBJECTIVE?**

In philosophy and the history of science, there have been two views of knowledge, reflecting two opposing camps that have engaged in revolutions and counterrevolutions for centuries. One view is usually referred to as "objectivism" or "realism" and the other as "interpretationism" or "rationalism." The discussion to follow draws heavily from the illuminating writings of Overton (1994a,b, 1997a,b, Overton and Horowitz 1991). Each view leads to one of two pathways that eventually result in fundamentally different therapeutic concepts and methods (Table 2–1). The starting point of each pathway (Level I) involves epistemology, namely, the study of knowledge and how it is acquired. The position of objectivism holds that the external world contains knowledge that already exists independent of a person's cognitive and perceptual activity. In contrast, interpretationism holds that there is no knowledge as such in the environment. Knowledge does not exist independent of the knower, but is constructed by a person's perceptions, cognitions, and actions.

> **WHAT STRATEGIES OF KNOWING DO OBJECTIVISM AND INTERPRETATIONISM PROPOSE RESULT IN KNOWLEDGE?**

The next level (II, Table 2–1), concerns strategies accepted as providing scientific approaches to determining what knowledge is and how it is acquired. Since objectivism holds that knowledge already exists in the environment, independent of the observer (Level I), this view accepts the strategy that neutral, direct, and well-controlled observations will discover that knowledge, observations that must be made before formulating interpretations. One example of the objectivist position is found in diagnostic and statistical manuals. These manuals are presented as free of any theory and based solely on empirical research findings. The clinician is asked to collect "neutral" observations of a patient's presenting problems and history and then determine whether a required number of behaviors that would qualify her/him for a diagnostic label are observed. For example, the clinician must determine that six or more of the following behaviors have persisted for at least six months to qualify for the diagnosis of attention deficit/hyperactivity disorder, predominantly inattentive type:

TABLE 2–1. The Pathway and Ladder of Objectivism and Interpretationism

Levels	Objectivism	Interpretationism
I What is knowledge and how is it acquired?	Knowledge exists independent of the knower.	Knowledge is constructed by activity of the knower.
II Strategies of knowing	Neutral, controlled observations result in knowledge that is independent of the knower.	All knowledge is determined by the observer's assumptions and pre-formed concepts.
III Metatheoretical assumptions	Boundaries can be set between the observer and the observed, the observed and the environment, the real event, and the subjective experience.	Observer and observed are two poles on a continuum, each defining and defined by the other and engaged in a dialectical process.
IV Metaphors of human functioning	Machine metaphor: person is a machine; inputs (stimuli) activate the machine to produce outputs (responses) that are mediated by internal stimuli and responses (cognitions).	Organic metaphor: person is a cell embedded in an organization of cells and engaged in an active dialectical exchange with them.
V Change and growth	Growth results from accumulation of behaviors and representations that correspond with what is adaptive in the real world or from elimination of behaviors and cognitions that are maladaptive.	Growth results from repetitive cycles of differentiation and integration of one's behavior and that of others participating in the relational matrix.
VI Approaches to psychotherapy	Cognitive-behaviorial therapies.	Psychodynamic, interpersonal, humanistic therapies.

1. Makes careless mistakes in schoolwork
2. Has difficulty sustaining attention in tasks
3. Does not seem to listen
4. Fails to finish schoolwork
5. Has difficulty organizing tasks
6. Avoids tasks that require sustained mental effort
7. Loses task-related items such as pencils
8. Easily distracted
9. Often forgetful

The strategy followed by interpretationism is quite different. This view holds that there is no knowledge as such in the environment; the position taken is that all observations, including those controlled in some experimental way, are influenced by what the observer already thinks, believes, and assumes. To explain and understand observations, the investigator searches for patterns or organizations. Observations of patterns have resulted in explanations and concepts such as "mental schemas," "attachments," "cognitive style," and "representations of interactions generalized." Since this type of explanation involves constructing a metaphor that symbolizes the pattern observed, metaphors are accepted as scientific interpretations. Applied to diagnostic evaluations of presenting problems, the interpretationist would look not for a set number of predefined behaviors, but for patterns of behavior that reveal, for example, some aspect of a child's body image (e.g., when approached by a depressed parent, the child's body slumps and the head turns away), aspects of the child's cognitive activity (e.g., the child looks away each time the parent looks at the child), and indications of how the child represents interactions with others and what the child expects from others (e.g., the child displays these behaviors when interacting with an adult who is not depressed).

WHAT ARE THE METATHEORETICAL ASSUMPTIONS OF OBJECTIVISM AND INTERPRETATIONISM?

Strategies of knowing are based on metatheoretical assumptions, Level III on each pathway (Table 2–1). Given the position that well-controlled observations will uncover knowledge that already exists, objectivism assumes that the observer can maintain several boundaries that enable her/him to gather this knowledge. One boundary is set between the observer and the person being observed, another between the individual and environment in order to observe how the individual responds when the environment stimulates her/him and how it responds when she/he acts on it. A third boundary is set between some event or phenomenon ("the real") and what the person being observed reports ("the subjective").

In contrast, interpretationism assumes that the observer and person being observed cannot be divided. Rather, each is viewed as two poles on a continuum, or two sides of a coin, forming a relational matrix. Each person is engaged with the other in a continuous, dialectical process, and each is defined by the other and defines the other. When entering this dialectical process, each person introduces an organization of activity that transacts with the activity presented by the other.

As metatheoretical assumptions become elaborated, they are organized around a metaphor, Level IV on each pathway. The metaphor depicts fundamental images that guide the type of questions asked and the concepts and methods constructed to address these questions. Metaphors construct different images of what happens between two or more persons (interpersonal issues), what happens within an individual (intrapersonal or intrapsychic issues), and the meanings a person gives to experiences.

WHAT METAPHOR DOES OBJECTIVISM USE TO SYMBOLIZE HUMAN FUNCTIONING?

The metatheoretical assumptions of objectivism have been represented by a metaphor that symbolizes a human as if she/he were a machine (Table 2–1, Level IV). The machine used as the referent for the metaphor has changed as various machines have taken turns dominating our culture; for example, the telephone switchboard, hydraulic pump, and most recently the digital computer. Following this metaphor, observations are guided by a set of images: behaviors can be separated into parts, the parts can be added or subtracted, the whole can be defined by adding the parts, behaviors are aroused by stimulation, relationships between stimuli and responses are linear, the machine receives "inputs" (stimuli/information) and delivers "outputs" (responses or behaviors).

How the machine metaphor images the space between inputs and outputs (i.e., the inside of the machine or person) has changed over the years. In the 1920s the work of John B. Watson, which led to initial behavioral approaches to therapy, focused on inputs and outputs and paid no attention to the inside of the machine, rejecting concepts such as consciousness, mind, and imagery. A few years later a shift occurred when B. F. Skinner conceptualized the organism as active in that it exhibits behavior from which the environment selects and reinforces particular responses. But Skinner continued Watson's position that the inside of the machine or person should be ignored, and proposed that a person does not act on the world; rather, the world acts on the person. This position framed principles of operant learning that exerted, and still exert, a significant influence on behavioral approaches to therapy. These principles are referred to as the ABC model; that is, antecedent conditions (A) evoke behaviors (B) that will occur again if the consequences (C) contain positive reinforcement or will dissipate if consequences contain negative reinforcement. The A-B-C of behavioral therapy relies on the metatheoretical assumption that a boundary separates individual and environment and the causes of behavior are found *outside* the person.

Bandura's (1977) social learning theory revised the interior of the machine or person, introducing the image that between antecedent stimuli (A) and behaviors they evoke (B) are internal stimuli and responses that mediate between them as well as between behaviors (B) and consequences (C). These internal stimuli and responses were referred to as "symbols," and "representations." Since the same terms are used by interpretationism, it is important to note that with the machine metaphor a representation is considered in terms of whether cognition distorts or accurately represents an external event as it exists outside the person. In addition, Bandura's social learning theory added the image that behavior could be learned by observing behaviors of other people who serve as "models." By revising the inside of the machine with images of cognitive mediators and the influence of observing models, it was possible to conceptualize stimuli and responses contained in a person's private thoughts and vicarious reinforcement that derived from imitating desirable behavior.

As cognitive research mushroomed in the '70s and '80s, the digital computer became the metaphor of the machine or person. The space between external stimuli and overt responses was viewed as "information" that is "processed." Now the inside of the machine or person is imaged as consisting of stations, each performing a particular step in the processing of information. For example, one model proposes five stations arrayed in sequence, each playing a role in producing appropriate social behavior: (1) searching for and attending to a message, (2) interpreting the message using available mediational units, (3) listing possible responses, (4) deciding which response is the most effective, (5) enacting the response selected.

> ## HOW DOES THE MACHINE METAPHOR IMAGE INTERPERSONAL RELATIONSHIPS, INTRAPERSONAL PROCESSES, AND THE MEANINGS A PERSON GIVES TO EXPERIENCES?

Each person in a relationship exerts an independent, direct, causal influence on the other. Therefore, relationships are acquired by a schedule of environmental reinforcements and by observing the behaviors of others. Interpersonal difficulties are understood as being under the control of discrete environmental or neurobiological factors or some combination. Anxiety is viewed as resulting from conditioning a response to a specific stimulus. These views of interpersonal processes have led to an emphasis on techniques such as training in relaxation, modeling, and imaging scenes or events that cause personal distress. Intrapersonal processes are imaged as responses snapped onto stimuli in a linear fashion to form chains called "mediators" or "symbols." These mediators express attitudes, feelings, and expectations. Experience is viewed as something that happens to a person and is cast as a "cognitive representation" that is evaluated in terms of whether it corresponds with the "real" happening. From this linear view, cognitive representations are considered to be either distortions or accurate reflections of the "real," and problem behaviors are defined as "cognitive distortions" of what an environmental event really means.

HOW IS CHANGE VIEWED BY OBJECTIVISM AND INTERPRETATIONISM?

For objectivism, and its metaphor of a person as a machine, change (Table 2–1, Level V) takes place as a person accumulates behaviors and representations of experiences (symbols, beliefs) that correspond to what the "real" world requires and eliminates or replaces behaviors and those representations that do not correspond to the real. Change is also defined in terms of whether mediators become more efficient in processing representations and behaviors required by others. For interpretationism, with its organic metaphor, change takes place as a person, participating in a dialectical process, revises and renders more flexible meanings assigned to experiences that have been coconstructed with another. Earlier meanings are not replaced but are integrated within new ones to form a new organization of cognitive/affective understanding. Revised meanings are not evaluated in terms of what is considered to be "real" or desirable according to others, but in terms of whether the meanings are agreed upon and coordinated within the particular relational matrix in which the person is participating.

WHICH FORMS OF THERAPY RELY ON THE MACHINE METAPHOR AND ITS IMAGES?

Cognitive therapies, behavioral therapies, and cognitive-behavioral therapies (Level VI) rely on the machine metaphor. In these approaches, psychological problems are defined in terms of the absence or deficiency of cognitive skills (mediators) that distort "real" external events. The emphasis is on treatment techniques designed to provide the cognitive skill or mediator that is absent and/or techniques that adjust, correct, or modify the mediator that is distorting the opportunities and limitations presented by the real world.

WHAT METAPHOR DOES INTERPRETATIONISM USE TO SYMBOLIZE HUMAN FUNCTIONING?

Interpretationism has been guided by images that depict a person as, for example, an embryo or cell (Table 2–1, Level IV). While the particular growing organism used as referent has varied, several interrelated images are retained. With one, the image of holism, the cell or person along with other persons, and the atmosphere (environment) that surrounds them form a totality. This image focuses attention on the organization formed by a person and others, including the environment. As with the growth of organisms *in utero*, the organization initially has a ground plan, and out of that ground plan the parts arise to form a functioning whole (Erikson 1980). Moreover, each part is determined by the total context in which it is embedded. Therefore, two behaviors that appear identical may be understood to be different, while two behaviors that are manifestly different may be understood to be identical; for example, a 5-year-old injures the family's pet kitten and also breaks the rattle of his baby brother.

Another organic image sees a person as inherently and continuously engaged in a dialectical relationship with other parts that make up the whole within which the person is functioning. This notion, called dialectics, has its roots in the philosophy of Hegel, who proposed that any entity inherently brings with it a contradiction. As the original thesis (or concept) and its paradox differentiate, the difference between them is negotiated and becomes the ground on which a new concept is formed that integrates them. Once integration is accomplished, this new unit becomes a new concept that brings with it another paradox; again, the difference between them is negotiated, resulting in another concept with its paradox, and so on. This cycle of differentiation and integration is repeated and repeated. From the image of dialectics, a person's thoughts, emotions, and actions are never perfectly matched with those of others or with the environment's opportunities and limitations. Each defines and is defined by the thoughts, emotions, and actions of the other, and as the paradox between them is negotiated, the system moves toward an integration to form a new matrix or relationship.

Another image (dynamics) emphasizes that when embedded in an organization that includes others, a person does not experience stimulation passively. Rather, from birth she/he makes use of modes of functioning, such as sensory thresholds, and cognitive/emotional responses, that enable her/him to actively approach, avoid, select, and organize stimulation. Behavioral structures, and the functions they perform, are always two sides of the same coin; the organization of behavior is activity and activity is organized.

Another image (directiveness) emphasizes that as behaviors engage in a dialectical process, the totality formed moves from initial states that are global and undifferentiated to states of increasing differentiation and hierarchic integration.

As cycles of differentiation and integration are repeated, each previous "old" behavior is not replaced by a new one but becomes integrated within the next level of organization.

One more image emerges when holism, dialectics, dynamics, and directiveness are combined. The image of self- and mutual regulation concerns the notion that as behaviors within an individual or between individuals differentiate, the organization becomes unstable. To reestablish stability, the organization attempts to regulate itself by evolving new, more differentiated and integrated behaviors within an individual (self-regulation) and/or between individuals (mutual regulation).

HOW DOES THE ORGANIC METAPHOR IMAGE INTERPERSONAL RELATIONS, INTRAPERSONAL PROCESSES, AND THE MEANINGS A PERSON GIVES TO EXPERIENCES?

As noted above, each person is imaged as defined by and defining the other. The infant and caregiver are frequently used as an illustration. The initial unit they form eventually differentiates into me and not-me, infant and mother. Piaget (1952) used this image to formulate cognitive development. He pointed out that experiences are not attached to a personal consciousness sensed as a "self" or to persons external to this self. These opposing poles only gradually become differentiated. Once differentiation has taken place, a dyad is formed between mother and infant that contemporary psychodynamic theorists term *attachment* and *object relations*. From this image both infant and mother create their relationship. The infant (or mother) does not move toward autonomy from the other or attachment to the other. Rather, each always moves simultaneously toward being both autonomous from the other and attached to the other.

The images used to portray developments within a person (intrapsychic processes) are the same as those used to portray interpersonal processes. The images of holism, dialectics, differentiation, and integration define a person's "internal relations" (Overton and Horowitz 1991, p. 15), conceptualized as mental organizations that determine the ways in which a person knows, feels, and gives meaning to experiences with others. In Piaget's (1952) cognitive theory, these internal relations are termed *schema*s, which represent actions a person has taken, define what the person expects, and guide actions the person takes in the present. In psychodynamic theory these intrapsychic processes are referred to as, for example, "psychic reality," "ego functions," "mechanisms of defense," and "internal world." To illustrate the processes of intrapsychic development, a child could consciously think that "everyone in school is better than I am." This thought forms an antithesis with a fantasy the child frequently entertains: "I am as powerful as Superman." The space between the thought and fantasy defines a paradox, an organization of internal relations that is unstable. As experiences with others are assimilated, involving both successes (e.g., winning a race) and failures (e.g., receiving a grade of D), the paradox is negotiated, and the thoughts and fantasies in question are integrated to form a new organization of relationships (self-regulation). Meanings a person gives to experiences are at the heart of the organic metaphor. Unlike the machine metaphor, meanings are not evaluated in terms of whether they correspond to the "real" meaning of an event. All meanings are coconstructed by both a person and another as each participates in reciprocal exchanges.

WHAT FORMS OF THERAPY RELY ON THE ORGANIC METAPHOR AND ITS IMAGES?

Within the organic metaphor, the image of meanings forms the foundation relied on by various psychodynamic approaches to therapy (e.g., traditional psychoanalytic, interpersonal, humanistic). These approaches define psychological problems in terms of "conflict" between one meaning (e.g., a wish or desire) and another opposing it (e.g., the wish is bad). Anxiety is seen as arising from conflict between meanings that are in opposition and/or from the loss of relationships. Conflict between meanings also includes whether or not meanings operate inflexibly within a relational matrix. Inflexible meanings are nonadaptive since they fail to benefit from both novel interpersonal and intrapsychic experiences. Therefore, from the view of the organic metaphor, as Overton and Horowitz (1991) pointed out, the aim of treatment is to facilitate the development of adaptive meanings that promote further differentiation and integration and not to adjust inaccurate representations so that they conform with something viewed as real.

Segregation between Body and Mind

HOW HAS PSYCHOLOGY VIEWED THE RELATIONSHIP BETWEEN BODY AND MIND?

Body and mind have been segregated by a boundary in western thinking from the writings of Greek philosophers to those of the twentieth century (Fisher 1990). All have grappled with the dualism of mind and body and the need to segregate the body because it was viewed as the source of passion and pain. Adopting this view, American psychology split off the body as a psychological concept and held it in the shadow until the 1980s (Cash and Pruzinsky 1990).

This was not the case when neurology and psychoanalysis were beginning to take shape at the turn of this century however, probably because their methods relied on a patient's close scrutiny of experiences that inevitably revealed preoccupations pertaining to the body. Neurological reports appeared describing, for example, patients who experienced a limb as present when it had been amputated. Within this climate, in 1926, the neurologist Henry Head proposed an unconscious "body schema" to conceptualize how body perceptions are integrated to form a picture of the body-self that integrates body experiences (Fischer 1990). Although giving little attention to how body experiences are tied to personality, early neurologists legitimized the study of body-image phenomena.

Paul Schilder (1935) is credited with being the first to construct a bridge connecting body and mind (or personality). He conceptualized body image as ever-changing, as having roots in early experiences and current interactions, gaining expression in everything from one's clothing (e.g., adding jewelry, tattoos) to the ability to empathize or become angry (when we are angry the body becomes "firmer"; when we feel friendly the body "expands"). In addition, he proposed that body image had relevance for experiences in everyday life as well as pathology, and anticipated the emergence of body therapies and studies of the effects of exercise and dance on body image.

HOW DO PSYCHODYNAMIC CLINICIANS VIEW THE RELATIONSHIP BETWEEN BODY AND MIND?

Following Schilder, several psychoanalysts added formulations to the concept of body image. For example, Carl Jung (Fisher 1990) noticed that persons experience their bodies as protective enclosures within which they can find refuge and fend off attack (when frightened, a child pulls bed covers over his/her head). More recently, other psychoanalysts have focused on body experiences that occur during treatment sessions, proposing that the process of repeating gestures in the treatment situation transforms body meanings into fantasies and conscious thought. In one example (Mahl 1987), an adult patient repeatedly rubbed the back of her hand against a nearby, roughly plastered wall during psychoanalytic treatment sessions. From these body experiences a memory emerged of father regularly rubbing his beard against her face, leaving her tingling with excitement. Similarly, other psychoanalysts (Kramer and Akhtar 1992) have discussed how movements, postures, gestures, sweating, and other bodily experiences that occur during treatment are a part of the person's communications, conveying symbolic meaning. Pruzinsky (1990), describing "somatopsychic approaches" to psychotherapy, argued that while all experiences take place in the context of body experiences, most forms of psychotherapy portray the patient as a "disembodied entity."

HOW DO COGNITIVE-BEHAVIORAL CLINICIANS VIEW THE RELATIONSHIP BETWEEN BODY AND MIND?

In spite of this interest in body image within psychoanalysis, the topic received only isolated attention within mainstream psychology until cognitive research freed it from the bondage of behaviorism. At that point the body as a psychological construct entered through the doorway of cognition. For example, several investigators (Wapner and Werner 1965) demonstrated that body attitudes influence perceptions of objects and judgments of one's position in space. And Fisher and Cleveland (1958) illustrated that a person's body-image boundaries correlate with personality traits. But after these programs peaked in the 1960s, interest in body-image research declined (Tiemersma 1989).

Most recently, body image research has resurfaced, focusing, for example, on eating disorders and the effects of plastic surgery (e.g., Cash and Pruzinsky 1990). The conceptualizations of a number of these investigators differ from Schilder's holistic, dialectical view, and reflect the viewpoint of objectivism. In one instance a cognitive-behavioral clinician used the ABC paradigm and proposed that stepping on a scale (A) leads to the belief, "I'm too heavy" (B), which triggers an emotional response of disgust from others (C). Another investigator proposed that body image be segregated into parts: "body schemas" (perceptions of one's own body), "body concepts" (knowledge about the body expressed with verbal labels), and "body values" (emotionally charged attitudes about the body).

The influence of objectivism can also be seen in the methods employed by more recent studies. Unlike earlier attempts, the methods do not engage the body in producing responses but segregate the body and mind by using inventories and interviews that elicit conscious knowledge about body image rather than unconscious symbolic representations as emphasized by Schilder and psychoanalytic investigators. For example, of the more than forty popular methods used by investigators (Thompson et al. 1990), nearly half ask a person to respond to questionnaires or to choose between statements such as, "I like my looks just the way they are" and "I am physically unattractive." The second most widely used method asks an individual to rate satisfaction in a series of silhouettes that vary in body size/weight. I believe the popularity of questionnaires as stimuli for assessment, rather than body experiences, keeps embodied meanings at a distance and segregates the body from conscious thoughts and beliefs.

Segregation between Cognition and Emotion

HOW HAS PSYCHOLOGY VIEWED THE RELATIONSHIP BETWEEN COGNITION AND EMOTION?

In Western thought a boundary has also segregated cognition and emotion since the essays of early Greek philosophers (Kagan 1978). Although some argued that thought and emotion should be unified, the boundary was maintained to preserve thought as right and rational and to protect it from passion and the irrational. Curiously, little or no attention was paid to the relationship between cognition and emotion in the first decades of this century because behaviorism dominated with its taboos against mind and imagery. Behaviorism provided scientific justification for splitting mind and emotion, segregating what Galton earlier called the "more pleasant" from "unpleasant" things. Then along came the studies of Jean Piaget, which legitimized cognition and provided one way of understanding the forbidden mind. American psychologists quickly embraced this viewpoint, cast aside the boundary between the mind and behavior, and produced a flood of research resulting in a sophisticated, cognitive science (Gardner 1985). As cognitive science grew to the size of a giant, a boundary between cognition and emotion, dormant during the era of behaviorism, was established. Investigators began to locate themselves on the side of either cognition or emotion. When those who stood on the side of emotion peered over the boundary, they became upset because the cognitive giant was neglecting emotion. Skirmishes between cognition and emotion were soon launched, reflected in a series of conferences convened over a ten-year period (Santostefano 1986).

In 1975 the Social Science Research Council promoted a conference because an understanding of emotion appeared meager when compared with the growing knowledge of cognition. Shortly thereafter another conference was convened by the Educational Testing Service, again because emotional development was being ignored in contrast to cognition. A year later still another conference was sponsored by Wheelock College and Bank Street College because investigators were maintaining an exclusive focus on cognitive phenomenon. In 1981 the Annual Carnegie Symposium was devoted to the role of emotion in cognition. "As people we delight in art and music. We fight, get angry, have joy, grief, happiness. But as students of mental events, we are ignorant of why and how" (Clark and Fiske 1982, p. ix). And in 1983 the Piaget Society decided to focus its annual conference on the issue of the segregation of thought and emotion (Bearison and Zimiles 1986). Throughout these conferences the boundary between cognition and emotion was not questioned but accepted as something "real" rather than as a conceptual convenience. Because the boundary was experienced as real, investigators raised an increasingly complex tangle of questions: "Is a feeling state a special type of cognitive process?" "What is the difference between cognition about emotion and cognition that is a component of emotion?" "Is cognition the result of emotion or the cause of emotion?" (Izard et al. 1984, pp. 3–6). Regardless of their theoretical orientations, investigators tended to define and measure emotional variables and cognitive variables separately.

Curiously, Jean Piaget, who was credited with freeing American psychology from the ethos of orthodox behaviorism, was also held responsible for the division that developed between cognition and emotion and the emphasis given the former (Bearison and Zimiles 1986). But Piaget recognized that the boundary between cognition and emotion was imaginary, serving research, and he seemed clear about why he had chosen one over the other. Piaget acknowledged that Freud focused on emotion while he chose intelligence. In his autobiography (Campbell 1977) he gave the reason. He preferred the study of the intellect over that of the "tricks of the unconscious" and "departures from reality" (Campbell 1977, p. 116) because his mother's poor mental health had a profound impact on him when he was a young child. Recognizing that the boundary between cognition (intellect) and emotion (tricky unconscious) is a conceptual convenience, Piaget was still able to make significant contributions, which we review later, to our understanding of unconscious mental activity. I believe cognition and emotion will remain segregated as long as investigators view the boundary as real and the domains as opposites—independent of each other, parallel and interacting with one another, or with one dominating the other.

Concluding Comment to Part II

From its earliest days, the study of human behavior has divided functioning into domains segregated by boundaries, three of which we discussed: objectivism versus interpretationism, body versus mind, and cognition versus emotion. Recall that Francis Galton (1884) felt that students of human behavior set boundaries in order to separate pleasant circumstances from unpleasant circumstances. I believe there is another possible reason, reflected by the images of objectivism and interpretationism. Who decides what is real, adaptive, normal, and expected? Who decides what is to be done to change things? Woven together, these questions form an issue that concerns who is in control. This cord of control plays a part, I believe, in how we segregate and handle what is pleasant and unpleasant. If emotions and the tricky unconscious are experienced by therapists as unpleasant, then they are more likely to shape concepts and methods that provide them with control over what is real and who decides what is to be done to promote change. If emotions and the tricky unconscious are not experienced as unpleasant, these therapists are more likely to shape methods that share control with a child, enabling the child to share her/his "unpleasantness."

3
How Segregation between Objectivism and Interpretationism, Body and Mind, and Cognition and Emotion Influenced Child and Adolescent Psychotherapy

CONTENTS

An analysis of how each of these boundaries has influenced child psychotherapy would require its own volume, especially since, as noted earlier, more than 200 types of child psychotherapy have been described. Therefore, I have selected two major, current approaches to child psychotherapy for my discussion: cognitive-behavioral and psychodynamic. As we shall see, cognitive-behavioral therapy has been influenced more by the images of objectivism: psychodynamic therapy, by those of interpretationism.

Cognitive-Behavioral Therapy Is Grounded in Objectivism: The Body as Overt Activity and the Mind as Conscious Products

Reviews of the origin and development of behavioral therapy describe how, in the 1970s, cognitive therapy emerged and exerted a significant influence on behavioral therapy (e.g., Arkowitz and Messer 1984, Corsini and Wedding 1989, Wachtel 1987). As behavioral and cognitive therapies interacted, they came to share a common set of propositions about child psychotherapy. Whether the child to be treated is socially withdrawn, aggressive and hyperactive, learning disabled, experiencing a specific fear, suffering from anxiety, or a juvenile delinquent, four broad propositions guide the cognitive-behavioral approach to diagnosis and treatment: (1) a child's problem behavior is carefully delineated; (2) the events or stimuli that trigger this behavior are carefully determined; (3) mediators that connect events with maladaptive behaviors are established; (4) a treatment program is designed that actively and directly corrects or replaces the targeted behavior and its mediators.

> ### HOW IS THE BEHAVIOR TARGETED FOR TREATMENT IDENTIFIED AND EVALUATED IN COGNITIVE-BEHAVIORAL THERAPY?

Hollin's (1990) application of the cognitive-behavioral approach in assessing young offenders provides an example. Following Skinner's ABC model (see above), assessment is concerned with discovering the antecedents of a particular behavior, carefully defining this behavior, and logging the consequences it produces in the environment. Hollin considered whether some antecedent event/situation existed recently or long ago; involves a particular place (e.g., classroom), particular time of day (e.g., mealtime), particular words or actions of an individual or group, or a unique feature of the physical environment (e.g., high or low temperatures). In terms of the problem behavior, careful attention is paid to articulating whether the behavior is public (e.g., violating property) or private (e.g., personal thoughts, emotions), and the number of times the behavior occurs within a given time interval. Emphasis is also given to determining a child's history of consequences since these outcomes play a critical role in determining how the behavior was reinforced and how it can be extinguished. For example, consequences are evaluated in terms of whether they occurred soon after, or long after, the problem behavior; whether they were delayed until a particular number of behaviors had been performed; and whether consequences were "social" (e.g., a reaction from another person or group) or "physical" (e.g., a physical change in the environment, such as vandalizing property).

The assessment methods Hollin (1990) recommended also show the influence of objectivist images, segregating real from subjective. "Direct measures" are more desirable because they assess a person's overt behaviors, which can be cross-checked by different observers. In contrast, "indirect measures," such as self-observation and interview, are not "authentic" since they cannot be as carefully recorded and cross-checked by different observers and "it is impossible" to determine the authenticity of thoughts and feelings a person expresses. In short, the "real" should be observed as much as possible, while the examiner keeps a wary eye on the subjective. The image of objectivism is reflected in still another way. Hollin devotes only one paragraph to the diagnostician doing the observing, his comments reflecting the view that knowledge that already exists can be obtained if the observer makes well-controlled observations. Observers are trained so that they do not become victims of the phenomenon of "observer drift," that is, the examiner gradually shifts her/his observational criteria.

From this illustration the influences of objectivism are apparent: (1) diagnostic data about the child's problem exists in the child's behavior and in her/his environment independent of the diagnostician (knower); (2) neutral, well-controlled observations produce these data and the child does not collaborate with the diagnostician in constructing the data; (3) to make neutral observations, boundaries are set that separate the diagnostician and child on one hand and the child and her/his environment on the other; (4) a child's problem behaviors (outputs) are understood as due to particular responses from the environment; and (5) a child and environment are separate entities: either the child acts on the environment or the environment acts on the child.

WHAT ARE SOME OF THE ADVANTAGES AND DISADVANTAGES OF THE COGNITIVE-BEHAVIORAL APPROACH TO EVALUATING A CHILD'S PROBLEM BEFORE TREATMENT?

The therapist is reminded of the importance of making careful observations of a child's behaviors and the circumstances surrounding them, and cautioned not to draw premature inferences. However, the ABC paradigm also raises questions when viewed in terms of the tendency to separate "real" from "subjective" in order to maintain control over what is viewed as "unpleasant" versus "pleasant." The child does not have control over defining what is a problem behavior for her/him, nor does the child define whether a particular behavior has been followed by positive or negative consequences. If a child is split off from the assessments made, much information of value to a therapist could be lost. For example, what the cognitive-behavioral therapist assumes is behavior typically followed by negative consequences may be incorrect, and therefore lead to treatment techniques that miss the intended mark. To illustrate, consider the following anecdotes. Jimmy was referred by the state's bureau of child services because he had stolen a number of items from a drugstore (e.g., perfume, a box of chocolates). John stole a baseball bat from a sports store. Mary again broke a class rule and was sent to the principal's office for the eighth time this term. From the view of the store owners, police, teacher, and therapist, stealing and breaking rules were behaviors followed by negative consequences. But when each child participated in defining what for her/him was a positive and negative consequence, the therapist learned that what others defined as negative, the child had defined as positive. For example, when Jimmy stole, he anticipated with excitement his mother's delight upon receiving another "gift." John felt admired and accepted by his gang members when he brought the baseball bat to the vacant lot where they played baseball. As for Mary, whose father had disappeared some time ago, sitting in the principal's office, whether listening to him urging her to try harder or sternly reprimanding her, was an enjoyable experience because he reminded her of her father. What I emphasize here is that if only the adult in control decides what are negative consequences, ignoring what the child's subjective world defines as negative or positive, the treatment program may miss an important part of what needs to be changed.

> ## WHAT DOES A COGNITIVE-BEHAVIORAL TREATMENT PROGRAM CONSIST OF ONCE THE TARGET BEHAVIOR IS IDENTIFIED?

A wide variety of cognitive-behavioral techniques are available to help a child (e.g., Brems 1993). Each technique assumes that a child's problem behavior can be corrected or replaced by behaviors and words, which the child enacts, that the therapist prescribes. Each technique falls within one of two broad categories that define what the therapist does to the child to replace or correct the behavior. One category relies on the principle of contingent reinforcement. Here the child receives rewards contingent upon her/his performing behavior that fits expectations of the environment. As a result of this reinforcement, the behavior becomes an established part of the child's repertoire of behaviors. Various rewards are used, such as verbal praise or providing the child with a model to imitate or some token she/he desires. The second category relies on the principle of punishment. Behaviors not fitting environmental expectations are suppressed or interfered with by repeatedly following the problem behavior with a negative consequence. For example, at the start of a session a child is given ten tokens that can be cashed in for some desired object. A token is taken away each time the child walks away from a task that she/he and the therapist are working on.

Below are several of the more commonly used cognitive-behavioral techniques. They show the influence of several images of the objectivist, machine metaphor:

Inputs stimulate the child to behave in a particular way.

Growth results when maladaptive behavior is replaced by behavior that fits with what the environment defines as desirable.

The child and therapist do not coauthor a technique; rather, each technique involves something the therapist does to the child.

The relationship between the child and therapist receives relatively little attention except for discussions held to help the child feel comfortable and to understand the behaviors required by the particular technique being used.

Self-Instruction Training

This technique follows several steps. The therapist works on a task that addresses the child's problem behavior. She/he talks aloud, articulating several problem-solving skills: (1) define the problem—"Let's see, what am I supposed to do?" (2) focus on the task and response required—"I better concentrate and focus in, and think only about what I am doing right now"; (3) select a response required by the task—"I think this is the right one"; (4) reward herself/himself—"Not bad, I really did a good job!" The child imitates these steps while working on a task. The therapist then repeats the steps with a similar task, now whispering the self-instructions, and the child again imitates the therapist. Last, the therapist performs another task, now using gestures and expressing the same comments in private thought, a performance that the child imitates. Self-instruction training is frequently used to help inattentive and hyperactive children.

Modeling

Along with self-instruction training, the child is exposed to behaviors to be learned, usually demonstrated by the therapist but sometimes displayed by videos. The therapist models some behavior, which the child imitates. The child then models some behavior, which the therapist imitates. Frequently, a distinction is made between modeling "mastery" versus "coping" behaviors. With the former the therapist demonstrates some ideal behavior, such as handling a series of math problems rapidly and correctly with a minimum of difficulty and frustration. In contrast, with the latter, the therapist occasionally makes mistakes and shares any difficulties encountered while completing the task. Typically, the therapist models mastery behaviors during early stages of treatment, and coping behaviors in later sessions. Kendall and Braswell (1985) provided an example of modeling coping behaviors to demonstrate that skills the child is learning can be applied to everyday living. The therapist intentionally opened his briefcase upside down so that materials spilled out onto the desk and floor. "Heck, why am I dumb? No, wait. I'm not dumb; I just didn't think . . . I didn't remember which is the top and which is the bottom of the briefcase . . . let's see; how can you tell which is the top?" As the child watched, the therapist examined the briefcase, and pointed out that a label is on the top. "If I can remember that this goes on the top, then I won't spill all of these things next time." The therapist then whispered the statement. At the start of this segment of treatment, the child noted that his soccer team had won their last game and that he had scored a goal. The meanings and emotions related to winning and scoring in a game were not included as part of the coping skills training the therapist enacted. Modeling has been used to eliminate behavioral deficits, reduce excessive fears, and promote a child's adaptive social behavior.

Modifying Cognitive Mediators

Frequently embedded within modeling, this technique modifies the child's thinking and understanding that take place after the child experiences a situation and before she/he responds. As one example, a therapist stood with a socially isolated child at the edge of a field. While watching soccer players, the therapist said, "Gee, they're really running around. Is it okay to do that? [pause] Oh, this is recess, I forgot, I guess it is okay to run around. No, they're better players than I am. But look there? That wasn't such a good kick, I could do that. I could just run around even if I don't kick it much at all." In providing this example, Kendall and Morison (1984) proposed that the therapist is thinking through the process in a manner consistent with how the isolated child might interpret the situation. It should be noted that the meaning a child gives to an experience is determined by cognitive mediators that the therapist selects.

Correspondence Training

Integrating reward, punishment, self-instruction, modeling, and modifying cognitive mediators, this technique consists of three different procedures. With one, the "say-do" technique, the child is asked to state what she/he is going to do and is rewarded if the behavior corresponds with the stated intention. With the "do-say" technique, the child describes what she/he has done previously and is rewarded if the statement accurately describes the behavior. With the "show-do" technique, the therapist correctly performs some behavior. The child is asked to show the therapist what the behavior would be like if enacted in a particular setting, and is rewarded if the demonstration is correct. In general, with correspondence training, the child learns there are behaviors "out there" that are desired by others and that can be discovered and accurately labeled.

Role Playing

In the first sessions the child is asked to enact hypothetical problem situations; in later sessions, situations that simulate a real problem for the child. Situations are written on index cards; for example, "You are watching television and your mother/ sister changes the channel." After several situations are written down, the child discusses each, following several steps: the problem is described; three or four alternative ways of coping with the situation are pointed out; the consequences associated with each alternative are discussed; one of the alternatives is selected as most desirable; self-reinforcing statements are made to reward herself/himself for demonstrating good problem solving; and the situations are enacted, with child and therapist playing roles.

Systematic Desensitization

This method is intended to reduce fear by repeatedly exposing a child to anxiety-producing stimuli without the child's experiencing the harm she/he anticipates. Several steps are followed: (1) stimuli that evoke anxiety are determined; (2) a hierarchy is constructed of stimuli that evoke little to considerable anxiety; (3) the child is trained to relax; (4) while relaxed, the child is asked to manipulate an item, or imagine a scene representing the low end of the continuum; and (5) when this encounter is accompanied by little or no anxiety, the child is exposed systematically to each item in the hierarchy until the item that arouses the most anxiety/fear is engaged with little stress. For example, to help preschoolers prepare for dental procedures, each child first handles items that produce the least anxiety (e.g., a mirror, X-ray film) and gradually items that arouse higher degrees of anxiety (e.g., a syringe).

The method of systematic desensitization seems to have one foot in objectivism and the other in interpretationism. Rather than modifying behavior, or placing behavior under verbal control, the goal is to reduce anxiety as defined by the child's subjective world. As the child engages physical objects, pictures, or imagined scenes, the therapist is addressing emotions that derive from the child's unique fantasies, providing the child with opportunities to cope mentally with the stress. I recommend Wachtel's (1977) discussion of systematic desensitization as one ground on which cognitive-behavioral and psychodynamic therapies could be integrated.

Tasks Graded in Difficulty

In one of the hallmarks of cognitive-behavioral therapy with children, the therapist administers a hierarchy of tasks beginning with less complex and emotionally neutral stimuli, followed then, in stepwise fashion, by more complex and emotionally evocative tasks. This technique, it seems to me, is a cousin of systematic desensitization, but has two feet in interpretationism rather than one, relying on principles of change that are different from those implied by other cognitive-behavioral techniques. Administering graded tasks implies that change involves building on previous behaviors; in contrast, other techniques view change as resulting from replacing one behavior by another, or controlling behavior with words. In the case of a graded task, each task is a step up a stairwell of cognitive-behavioral growth, enabling a child to keep one foot on the step just mastered while raising the other foot to the next higher step. In my view, the emphasis given to the technique of graded tasks is one of the most significant contributions of cognitive-behavioral psychotherapy with children.

A RECAP

The assessment and treatment approaches typically used in cognitive-behavioral therapy reveal the influence of objectivist images:

1. Knowledge about the child and what she/he should do exists in the environment independent of the child, and neutral, well-controlled observations reveal that knowledge.
2. To obtain this knowledge, boundaries are set between child and therapist, child and environment, and what is considered to be real and subjective.
3. Inputs stimulate the child to behave in a particular way. The child's behavior is defined as maladaptive by the environment because it results in negative consequences.
4. Growth results when maladaptive behavior is replaced by behavior that fits environmental expectations. To help the child achieve desirable behavior, the therapist trains the child in various cognitive and coping skills that manage or inhibit stimuli that evoke the problem behavior and/or change the child's cognitive mediators representing environmental stimuli.
5. Child and therapist do not coauthor techniques; rather, each involves something the therapist does to the child. The child–therapist relationship receives relatively little attention except for discussions to help the child feel comfortable and understand behaviors required by a technique.
6. Change occurs when the child accumulates the necessary coping and cognitive skills. The technique of graded tasks is an exception. Here change occurs as the child's psychological functioning becomes increasingly differentiated and integrated to cope with more complex tasks.

Psychodynamic Psychotherapy Is Grounded in Interpretationism: The Body and Emotion in the Mind

---

WHAT DOES PSYCHODYNAMIC MEAN?

While it is generally recognized that the term *psychodynamic* derives from Freudian psychoanalysis, there is less awareness that the meaning of the term has undergone continuous change. Whenever the term is used, readers typically conjure up notions from psychoanalysis of the early 1900s (e.g., "dammed-up energies," "cathexes"). To articulate an understanding of the influence interpretationist images exerted on psychodynamic concepts and treatment techniques, and compare these with the objectivist concepts and techniques of cognitive-behavioral therapy, it should be useful to sketch revisions that have taken place in psychodynamic theory. (Detailed historical reviews are available; e.g., Lear 1990 and Mitchell 1988.)

Initially Freud (Breuer and Freud 1895) was influenced more by objectivism when he proposed an essentially stimulus–response theory to account for his observations that symptoms (responses) patients brought to him disappeared when they remembered "real" childhood events (stimuli) that had actually occurred. Because these events were unacceptable to the person's conscious sense of herself/himself, the mind intentionally repressed them. In this repressed state these memories remained "split off" from the rest of a person's personality and were never revised in response to feedback from the environment. As the reader may notice, this model is influenced by the objectivist images of "real" environmental events as inputs activating outputs (behavioral symptoms).

In 1897 Freud began to revise this model which he discussed a few years later in 1900. Now he took the position that a person's reports of past disturbing events should not be considered "real" events but rather fantasies representing forbidden wishes that the person harbored during childhood and wanted to express in action but did not. This reconceptualization shifted toward interpretationism in proposing that there is no environment "out there" as such, but environments constructed by the mind that influenced how childhood events were construed and experienced. Freud proposed that different body zones took turns coding (symbolizing) experiences, forming an intrinsically developing hierarchy: experiences with the mouth (oral stage); then, for example, with toilet training (anal stage); and then with genital excitation (phallic stage). How the experiences were construed could become fixated in one of these zones and fail to move to the next. While shifting toward interpretationism, this second model retained emphases of the first, namely, that wishes (inputs or stimuli) causing a person's difficulties (outputs or responses) are found in childhood history. Freud continued to give relatively little attention to the role of present-day experiences with the environment.

In 1923 Freud again revised his theory, now giving more attention to a person's dealings with the environment. He proposed three psychic agencies. The *ego* was conceptualized as a system of psychological functions (e.g., perceiving, remembering, taking action, maintaining a conscious view of one's self) that transacted with the environment while simultaneously dealing with and coordinating presses from the *id* or *libido*. The id was conceptualized as the energy of impulses and wishes that paid no attention to environmental prohibitions, pressing for expression in action. The *superego* was conceptualized as rules and standards internalized from authority figures with whom a person identified. But the goal of psychoanalytic treatment remained essentially the same: to uncover, tame, and rechannel repressed impulses and wishes that give meaning to experiences (bringing into consciousness what is unconscious). This goal was elaborated with the dictum, "Where id was let ego be."

Although Freud was influenced by interpretationism in developing his second and third models, he also "crossed over" into objectivism. For example, he employed the demarcationist strategy of objectivism that all concepts should be reducible to a physical basis. And he proposed that the system—ego—and the energy for that system—id—are separate, and that a person as a system is active only in response to stimulation (energy). Thus the ego was conceptualized as an organization of behaviors without energy, and the id as a source of motivating energy without organization.

But even during Freud's lifetime major interpretationist concepts were added to the psychodynamic position. For example, in 1939 Heinz Hartmann presented what was then a major shift in emphasis—the notion that adaptation to the environment was as critical as unconscious meanings and that person and environment each act on and influence the other. Hartmann's ideas influenced a surge of interest in the 1940s and '50s in interpersonal relationships and what came to be called "object relations theory." Harry Stack Sullivan, for example, made an explicit commitment to interpretationism, emphasizing relationships and the view that the organization of behavior is activity and activity is organization. W. R. D. Fairbairn emphasized that the organization of activity we call a person is always directed toward evolving relationships with others. Bowlby emphasized "attachment"; Winnicott, the matrix formed by an ongoing relationship between persons (Masling and Borstein 1994, Overton 1994a, Overton and Horowitz 1991). These contributions and others resulted in a "revolution" within psychoanalytic theory that gave central importance to dialectical relationships as the foundation of personality development and difficulties. This revolution, summarized and elaborated by Mitchell (1988), revised the meaning of psychodynamic as involving cyclical events between persons and environments (Wachtel 1987).

In summary, over a span of 100 years, major revisions took place in what psychodynamic means: from Freud's models of repressed memories of real events and dammed-up unconscious energy to the focus on organizations of behavior and interpersonal relations. However, the meaning a person constructed and assigned to experiences and the importance of unconscious mental processes have remained at the center of the psychodynamic position. As we turn to consider the influence of interpretationism on psychodynamic approaches to child therapy, the reader should be aware that we will have in mind psychodynamics as outlined in the last decade, not as characterized in the 1930s.

HOW IS BEHAVIOR TARGETED FOR TREATMENT IDENTIFIED AND EVALUATED IN PSYCHODYNAMIC THERAPY?

Whether the child to be treated is socially withdrawn, aggressive and hyperactive, suffering from a learning disability, experiencing a specific fear, gripped with generalized stress and anxiety, or a juvenile delinquent, a broad proposition guides assessment. While mindful of the child's presenting difficulties, the therapist looks beyond these target behaviors, or symptoms, and helps the child reveal meanings that have been outside of her/his awareness (unconscious) that are in conflict with each other and the cause of the child's problems. To accomplish this, the therapist initially focuses on establishing a working relationship and alliance with the child because it is assumed that in interactions with the therapist a child's mind will not reveal these unconscious conflicted meanings, nor her/his difficulties, unless she/

he has developed some measure of trust. In terms of psychological tests used to evaluate a child, "projective tests" are preferred. These methods intend to help a child project onto test stimuli unconscious meanings that dominate how she/he construes experiences and relationships, and whether particular meanings are in conflict. Commonly used methods include the Rorschach inkblot test, various picture story-telling tests, and human figure drawings (Siegel 1989). The most popular assessment method with young children among psychodynamic therapists is perhaps the play interview (Conn 1993). Typically, the child is invited to select any of the materials available in the office (dolls, animal figures, games, toy furniture, clay, water) and play with them in whatever way she/he wishes. The therapist observes what the child authors, participates as indicated, and sometimes asks questions to determine whether the child can verbalize the meaning of some play. For example, 7-year-old Sally placed two parent dolls in a bed and a girl doll at the foot of the bed instead of in another bed. The therapist asked the girl doll figure, "What's the matter?" Sally, responding for the girl doll, replied, "I'm afraid someone will kidnap me." With older children and adolescents, a therapist relies more on verbal discussion while paying close attention to the meanings the child expresses rather than to the literal content of the adolescent's comments. For example, while discussing an experience he recently had with his father, an adolescent picked up a small glass vase and absentmindedly commented, "This is cracked," a response the interviewer considered a critical part of the organization of meanings the adolescent was expressing about his father as well as the therapist.

In summary, unlike the cognitive-behavioral approach, little attention is given to the overt form of a child's behavior relative to the attention paid to the unconscious meanings and conflicts a child reveals. Similarly, less emphasis is given to antecedent conditions and consequences that follow a child's problem behaviors. The psychodynamic therapist is primarily interested in how a child sees her/his world of persons and relationships.

WHAT ARE SOME OF THE ADVANTAGES AND DISADVANTAGES OF THE PSYCHODYNAMIC APPROACH TO EVALUATING A CHILD'S PROBLEMS BEFORE THERAPY?

A therapist is reminded of the importance of learning how a child construes her/his experiences with others and is cautioned not to accept only a parent's or teacher's definition of the child's experiences. A therapist is also reminded of the importance of taking the time necessary to establish a trusting, allied relationship so that a child will share personal meanings, conscious and unconscious, and invite the therapist to respond to and learn more about these subjective experiences. However, by remaining selectively focused on possible symbolic meanings a child's behaviors represent, a therapist could miss how overt forms of a child's behaviors contribute to an understanding of her/his difficulties. For example, the subjective worlds of two young boys are viewed as dominated by aggressive meanings and ambivalence about rules and standards. Yet, with one child, this inference is based on the observation that he speaks in an argumentative tone, frequently engaging in verbal confrontations. With the other child, this inference is based on the observation that he frequently pushes and pokes other children and sometimes engages in physical fights. In addition, an exclusive focus on symbolic meanings of behavior could result in a therapist's making premature, incorrect inferences about a child's subjective world. For example, presenting at a diagnostic conference, a therapist centered on the observation, reported by parents, that 9-year-old Jane ritualistically hopped into the parents' bed in the morning, at which point mother arose to wash and dress, while father, with considerable pleasure, made breakfast for the child. This behavior, along with the child's placing a girl doll in bed with the parents during a play interview, formed the center of the diagnostician's formulations: that Jane was conflicted about unresolved sexual, oedipal longings for father and for this reason was constantly antagonistic toward mother. In psychotherapy, however, Jane gradually made clear that she construed father as a nurturing mother and mother as someone who gave only conditionally.

WHAT DOES A PSYCHODYNAMIC TREATMENT PROGRAM CONSIST OF ONCE CONFLICTED MEANINGS ARE IDENTIFIED?

Guided by the assumption that a child's problem behaviors will be resolved when conflicts among unconscious meanings are brought into awareness and clarified, a therapist uses various techniques, some emphasized early in treatment, others later, but all playing a part throughout.

Establishing a Therapeutic Alliance

At the start of treatment the focus is on child and therapist constructing a therapeutic relationship, not on the child's problem behaviors. It may take three or twenty-three meetings to accomplish this important prerequisite. A therapist knows that a good-enough therapeutic alliance has been constructed when the following are achieved: (1) the child attains a degree of comfort, expresses herself/himself as a matter of course, and becomes aware to some degree that her/his behaviors and thoughts are generated from within rather then elicited by others; and (2) child and therapist sense they are allies and begin to share in constructing and representing the child's inner, private fantasies and thoughts with words, images, and symbolic play.

Helping a Child Elaborate Representations (Meanings) of Her/His Experiences

Once child and therapist develop a good-enough alliance, they set out to elaborate various meanings the child uses to represent her/his personal world. Here the influence of interpretationism is apparent: that all knowledge is constructed by the knower, and the knower and the observer are two poles on a continuum, each defining and defined by the other. With one example, Coppolillo (1987) described a 5-year-old enuretic boy who handed the therapist a doll saying, "You be the dad; I'll be the mom." The therapist took the father doll and asked the mother doll where they were going, to which the child replied that they were taking the baby to the doctor. Upon arriving at the doctor's office (they walk across the room), the baby doll reveals to the doctor that he is sad because his parents whip him when he wets the bed. To help a child elaborate meanings, different materials are used (puppets, costumes, games [Schaefer and Cangelosi 1993]) in various formats (fantasy play, storytelling, role playing [e.g., Kottman and Schaefer 1993]). In addition, several tools are used.

1. *Inquiry and empathy.* The therapist maintains an attitude of inquiry and empathy in order to experience what the child is experiencing.
2. *Introspection.* The therapist teaches the child the process of introspection. For example, at an appropriate moment a therapist could say, "You know, when you told me that, a picture of another boy I knew came into my head."
3. *Verbalizing experiences.* The therapist helps the child put into words experiences she/he may not have been able to describe. For example, "Have you noticed when you think of your little sister you get a picture in your head. Look at the picture inside your head and tell me about it."
4. *Searching for patterns in the symbols a child constructs.* The therapist carefully tracks the child's associations in search of patterns.

Discovering and Uncovering Unconscious Meanings

As a child elaborates meanings/fantasies, the therapist pursues a twofold goal reflecting the influence of interpretationism: uncovering a child's unconscious wishes and meanings, and labeling these meanings with words and concepts (interpretations) so they are understood and regulated at a conscious level. To discover unconscious meanings, a therapist relies on the demarcationist strategy of interpretationism, searching for patterns that emerge from her/his interactions with a child and the child's descriptions of past and present events in her/his daily life. Once a pattern is identified, the therapist interprets its unconscious meaning.

Coppolillo (1987) provided an example in his treatment of Teddy, an 8-year-old boy who was in therapy because of aggressive, unruly behavior that began after the death of his father. Since Teddy had not been able to discuss his loss, the therapist speculated that Teddy's aggressive behavior was very likely an expression of unconscious pain that had not yet been expressed consciously. In one session Teddy complained about a teacher, whom he felt was mediocre, with the expression, "He ain't no Harmon Killebrew" (a superb professional baseball player at that time). Later, again referring to the teacher, Teddy responded, "He's not the greatest, like he just ain't no Oscar Mayer." Sensing the beginning of a pattern, and mindful that father had been a butcher, the therapist reflected his confusion in the hopes of elaborating the pattern. Teddy responded, "My father used to tell me that Oscar Mayer was the greatest. The best hotdogs. . . . He [the teacher] ain't no Harmon Caballero." With this Teddy introduced still another ingredient in the emerging pattern—Carmen Cavallero, whom he called "Harmon Caballero," was a very popular pianist at the time. Relying on the pattern of meanings that had emerged, the therapist pointed out that all three were "the greatest." Teddy responded, "Yeah! They are the best. My father used to say that." Then the therapist made an interpretation, lifting an unconscious meaning into awareness. "Teddy, I think you're saying that your father was the greatest, and since he died you just don't see how anyone can be as great as he was for you." At this Teddy began crying softly, now aware of the meaning that had been underground and influencing his complaints of the mediocre teacher. In later sessions, Teddy elaborated this pattern of associations and its meaning by acknowledging that for him the therapist's name (Henry Coppolillo) sounded more and more like the fictitious name "Harmon Caballero" introduced by Teddy earlier. With this, Teddy was transferring an unconscious wish onto the therapist. Teddy unconsciously synthesized the names Harmon Killebrew, Carmen Cavellaro, and Henry Coppolillo, to form the name "Harmon Caballero," thus experiencing the therapist as the greatest. As the pattern and its meaning became elaborated and entered his conscious awareness, Teddy revealed his conflict with wanting to love and be loved by the therapist or someone else as great as father, but feeling guilty about this wish.

Countertransference

The feelings and thoughts a therapist experiences in response to a child's behavior are examined by the therapist for clues about possible patterns that might reveal unconscious meanings. Here the therapist is obligated to be aware of her/his personal, cultural convictions and whether and how they differ from those of the child.

Constructing a Common Language

Guided by the dialectical image, child and therapist invent symbols during their communicating, making the therapeutic relationship a unique experience for each.

Interpreting (Labeling) Unconscious Meanings and Wishes

Considerable attention is given by psychodynamic writers to how and when a therapist verbally interprets a child's unconscious meanings. With an interpretation, child and therapist exchange something of such great conceptual importance that this interaction has been referred to as a "sacred moment" (Winnicott 1971). At this moment a therapist hopes to promote change by dismantling and rendering powerless a child's neurotic conflict: an unconscious wish, plan, conviction, or fantasy that, if carried out in action, or recognized consciously, would produce painful anxiety and guilt. Teddy, discussed above, provided an example. He harbored an unconscious wish to love and be loved by someone like his father. But this wish collided with his allegiance to his father, resulting in considerable guilt and anxiety. To manage this anxiety he was consciously critical of a "mediocre teacher" as a way of defending against the anxiety generated by the love and admiration he felt for the teacher.

Terminating the Relationship

Interpretationism, with its emphasis on dialectical relationships, influences the care psychodynamic therapy takes in deciding when and how this special relationship is concluded. Criteria for terminating include whether the child shows she/he is free from internal oppressions, relates productively with others, responds to the environment in more flexible ways, and is free of symptoms. Also reflecting the dialectical image, attention is given to developments *within the therapist* that signal the therapeutic relationship can now be terminated gradually. For example, the therapist feels less need to provide support and less responsible for carrying the relationship because the child is more spontaneous and secure.

A RECAP

Psychoanalytic treatment as typically practiced, including elaborations introduced by interpersonal perspectives, reveals the influence of interpretationism: (1) a child's knowledge about her/his world does not exist outside the child but is constructed by the child; (2) to gather this knowledge, a therapist establishes a special relationship with the child and in this way enters the child's personal world; (3) the child shares with the therapist motives, meanings, and fantasies that are unconscious and in conflict; (4) the therapist searches for patterns of meanings that are in conflict as revealed by the child's fantasy play and discourse; (5) change results when the child becomes aware of these previously unconscious meanings and integrates them into conscious motives and wishes.

CAN YOU COMPARE OBJECTIVIST AND INTERPRETATIONIST INFLUENCES ON CHILD PSYCHOTHERAPY?

In cognitive-behavioral therapy a specific problem behavior is targeted for treatment and viewed on the one hand as determined by particular environments and on the other by consequences that occur in the environment in response to the problem behavior. Here we see the influence of objectivism in that a boundary is drawn between child and environment and between "real" events and the child's subjective experience. To help the child, she/he is asked to perform tasks designed to change the behavior directly, change the environment, or correct the way in which the child is misrepresenting the environment. The child gains control over the problem by accumulating skills. The child's subjective experience—both in and out of awareness—and the child's relationship with the therapist are given relatively little attention.

Psychodynamic therapy, influenced by interpretationism, virtually ignores the child's overt behavioral problem and the environment in which the problem occurs. There is almost exclusive focus on the child's subjective experiences, meanings, and fantasies both in and out of awareness. Whatever the child's problem, the therapist uses fantasy play and discourse to help the child become aware of unconscious meanings and motives. Growth and change result when the child integrates these previously unconscious meanings into her/his conscious thoughts and fantasies.

Since our goal is to integrate psychotherapies, when lifting the boundary between objectivism and interpretationism we are faced with several questions. Should the behavior selected for treatment be on the outside and surface (i.e., overt) or inside and deep (i.e., an invisible meaning)? How can we join what a person says with what a person imagines and does? What is cognition? Does it involve surface or deep behaviors, and how does it relate to emotion? Are unconscious processes more important than conscious processes or vise versa? And should we ignore or emphasize the relationship between patient and therapist? What should a therapist do to help a child—administer tasks, play anything the child wishes, talk, or interpret the child's motives and meanings?

4

Issues to Consider When Dissolving Boundaries and Integrating Child Psychotherapies

CONTENTS

To this point we have considered the boundaries dividing real and subjective, body and mind, and cognition and emotion, along with how the assumptions of objectivism and interpretationism have influenced psychotherapy with children. As we continue our discussion, we should remind ourselves that nature does not produce individuals who have a mind and no body or individuals who neither imagine, speak, nor act. To integrate these domains, it is first necessary to remove the boundaries, a recommendation made by the 1986 workshop on psychotherapy integration sponsored by the National Institute of Mental Health (Mahoney 1993).

Boundaries dissolve when we accept the proposition that what appear to be opposites share a fundamental unity. The notion that opposites share an identity, while prominent in Eastern thought, has also been advanced in Western writings. For example, Alfred North Whitehead's philosophy proposes that events usually considered irreconcilable are actually like the crest and trough of a single wave. The unity of opposites found its way into the writings of Ludwig von Bertalanffy, the theoretical biologist who proposed an "organismic" viewpoint that in turn became a central feature of Gestalt psychology in the 1930s and '40s, proposing that real and subjective are two poles of an inherently relational field. The organismic perspective was extended to a developmental psychology by Heinz Werner (1948), who argued that the study of organizations of behavior (holism) that develop toward increasing differentiation and integration should be preferred over the study of segregated elements.

But if body and mind, cognition and emotion, and images of objectivism and interpretationism are taken as organized wholes rather than detached pieces, what fundamental unity do they share? If one is the trough and the other the crest, what is the wave? An approach to this question is provided by Schacht's (1984) cogent discussion of models that have been followed by investigators interested in integrating psychotherapies.

WHAT MODELS HAVE WRITERS FOLLOWED TO INTEGRATE PSYCHOTHERAPIES?

With the first model (Schacht 1984), therapists take the position that two or more approaches to therapy are fundamentally incompatible, and only one is valued. The article by Lazarus (1995), considered earlier, provided one illustration of a position that renounced the use of psychodynamics. When Schacht's second model is followed, therapies that oppose each other solve the problem by attempting to reduce one to the other, translating the language of one approach into that of the other. Illustrations of this model were first introduced in the 1930s when, for example, Franz Alexander translated psychoanalytic concepts into the language of Pavlovian conditioning. A decade later, Dollard and Miller translated psychoanalytic concepts into the language of learning theory (Arkowitz and Messer 1984, Marmor and Woods 1980).

When therapists follow Schacht's (1984) Model III, two therapies are viewed as complementary and suitable for dealing with separate problems in the same patient. A therapist works with a patient using one approach during one phase (e.g., exploratory psychodynamic psychotherapy to uncover past experiences related to conflicts with parents) and a different approach in another phase (e.g., assertiveness training to cope with anxiety over competing in gym class).

When Model IV (Schacht 1984) is followed, two or more methods address the same problem, but each method retains its identity. With the fifth model, integration takes place within therapeutic techniques, representing some hybrid of two approaches. As one example, authors have integrated the behavioral procedure of systematic desensitization and the psychodynamic technique of uncovering unconscious fantasies. The result is a therapeutic method that desensitizes adult patients to underlying impulses and fantasies rather then desensitizing them to overt stimuli.

With the last model, the goal is to integrate propositions and concepts in an effort to construct a model of human functioning that is heuristically valuable to psychotherapy. These approaches are often expressed in terms of a key metaphor. Schacht (1984) offered as one example the model of "Man as an Information-Processing Machine," a metaphor that we considered earlier. Schacht saw the need for integrating concepts, a position supported ten years later by Stricker (1994) and Mahoney (1993).

Agreeing with these authors, I have attempted to follow Schacht's sixth model in my effort to construct a conceptual scaffold for child psychotherapy that dissolves the boundaries between objectivism and interpretationism, body and mind, and cognition and emotion. But when I turned to the literature on child psychotherapy, I found relatively little assistance. Discussions tend to focus on the pros and cons of integrating adult psychotherapies. Only one of thirty-five chapters in a handbook on psychotherapy integration (Stricker and Gold 1993) is devoted to child psychotherapy, and one to adolescent psychotherapy. In another handbook (Norcross and Goldfried 1992) none of the eighteen chapters is devoted to child psychotherapy. Stimulated by writings concerned with integrating adult therapies and by my own research, I propose that several issues, hierarchically related, should be considered when integrating child psychotherapies (Table 4–1).

Issue I: Are Behaviors to Be Treated Outside and on the Surface or Inside and Deep?

Debates over whether the determinants of human behavior are located "outside" (overt actions, verbalized beliefs) or "inside" (unconscious wishes, fantasies) have gone on since the time of the Greek philosophers (Wachtel 1987). As discussed earlier, cognitive-behavioral therapy, rooted in the machine metaphor of objectivism, tends to circle around the patient, focusing on surface-observable behaviors (e.g., speaking overtly or covertly as in self-instruction training, modeling the actions of others). As Kohlenberg and Tsai (1994) noted, "[I]t is impossible to devise treatment methods that focus on nonbehavioral entities . . . that can not be directly contacted or observed by the therapist" (pp. 194–195). In contrast, psychodynamic therapy, rooted in the organic metaphor of interpretationism, tends to enter the patient, emphasizing inferences about the meanings of behaviors (e.g., when a child waters a plant, the therapist infers the child wishes to be nurtured).

One example of the outside/inside dichotomy can be seen in a popular approach that categorizes the problems of children and adolescents as either "externalized" (outside) or "internalized" (inside) (Weisz and Weiss 1993). Externalized problems include, for example, fighting and vandalism; internal problems include tearfulness and withdrawal. It seems that in the United States "outside problems" are the most frequent reasons why children are referred to clinics (Weisz and Weiss 1993), while in Thailand "inside problems" are the most frequent (Weisz et al. 1987).

TABLE 4–1. A Hierarchy of Issues that Should Be Considered When Integrating Psychotherapies for Children

ISSUES
I Are behaviors to be treated outside and on the surface or inside and deep?
II The need to relate what a person does with what a person imagines, thinks, and says
III The relationship between cognition and emotion
IV The meanings a person gives to experiences
V Conscious and unconscious processes
VI Contexts, environments, and situations
VII Psychological conflict
VIII The relationship between patient and therapist
IX What should the therapist do to help? Reconsidering the importance given to verbal labeling and interpretation
X Developmental principles: The glue for integration

CONCLUDING COMMENT

Why are behaviors such as stealing and fighting viewed as external and feeling unloved and shy as internal? Could surface and deep behaviors be related in some way? Imagine a child standing timidly on the edge of a playground, watching others race about in a baseball game. For a few moments the child spontaneously engages in a vivid fantasy in which he smashes a home run. Since the same child is standing timidly, fantasizing hitting a home run, could the behaviors be related in some way? This question converges with one Mahoney (1993) posed: "[H]ow do changes at one level reflect and reciprocally influence changes at the other?" (p. 6).

Issue II: The Need to Relate What a Person Does (Action) with What a Person Imagines (Fantasy), Thinks, and Says (Language)

HOW DOES COGNITIVE-BEHAVIORAL THERAPY VIEW THE RELATIONSHIPS AMONG MODALITIES?

When focused on modifying a child's overt behaviors, cognitive-behavioral therapy centers on the language mode and conscious cognitions to promote change. If the right words and thoughts are expressed, as in self-instruction training, they can regulate actions. If verbalized cognitive mediators represent a situation correctly, a person would function within that situation with appropriate behaviors. And if the child consciously understands that positive consequences follow the desired behavior, the child will include that behavior in her/his repertoire. A volume (Knell 1995) proposing an integration of play and cognitive-behavioral methods to treat children emphasized the language mode. "While the child is acting out his anger by kicking the play carriage, a punching bag, or a puppet representation of his sister, the therapist can help the child label his feelings. Merely acting aggressively in therapy does not teach the child that there are alternatives. Labeling the aggression . . . can offer the child some other, more adaptive way of dealing with his frustration and anger" (p. 29). But cognitive-behavioral therapy does not provide us with a conceptualization that sufficiently articulates how the words of self-instruction or the verbal representation of a situation (cognitive mediators) are related to a child's fantasies and actions. Nor does this approach give particular significance to the observation that actions vary in form. For example, a boy may kick the door to his brother's bedroom and on another occasion kick his brother.

HOW DOES PSYCHODYNAMIC THERAPY VIEW THE RELATIONSHIPS AMONG MODALITIES?

That spoken words have power to regulate actions, fantasies, and emotions is also a core feature of psychodynamic therapies. Freud set the stage, viewing everything a person did as resisting the task of lifting repression and revealing, with spoken words, some forbidden fantasy or meaning (Mitchell 1994). When the psychodynamic approach gave rise to the treatment of children, this emphasis on spoken words dominated in spite of the use of play and activity. For example, Erikson (1964) noted, "Children . . . need to be induced by systematic interpretation to reconsider, on a more verbal level, the constellations that have overwhelmed them in the past . . ." (p. 265). Anna Freud (1965) held that a child "gains its victories and advances whenever [conflicts] are grasped and put into thoughts or words" (p. 32). The importance of verbalizing continues to the present. Echoing early writers, Coppolillo (1987) noted, "The therapist has a powerful tool in tackling the task of inducing the child to express conflicts in verbal terms" (p. 245). Moreover, in spite of the focus given to a child's fantasies, little attention is paid to the observation that fantasies vary in form. For example, a child may fantasize herself, sword in hand, galloping on a horse through the playground in pursuit of a gigantic dragon; on another occasion the same child may fantasize standing with hands on her hips challenging a playground bully. Similarly spoken words take different forms. A child may shout, "I'll smash your face!" on one occasion and on another, "I'll beat you in a race any day!" In addition, little or no attention is given to conceptualizing how verbal expressions of one's concerns are connected to one's fantasies and actions, and why it is so important "to induce the child" to reconsider her/his conflicts in verbal terms.

For cognitive-behavioral therapy, verbalizing is given importance because conscious thoughts are viewed as having power to control actions. For psychodynamic therapy, verbalizing is given importance because words shift a meaning from an unconscious to a conscious level. Given the emphasis on verbalizing, and the tendency to equate verbalizing and self-talk with cognition, a related question emerges.

WHAT IS COGNITION? IS IT SURFACE OR DEEP BEHAVIOR?

The term cognition is used in many ways and appears to have no generally accepted referent, probably because two "cognitive revolutions" occurred during past decades, each defining cognition differently. A sketch of these revolutions should help us evaluate how cognition is viewed and applied in psychotherapy.

In the decades prior to the 1950s, cognition was essentially ignored because behaviorism "glorified the skin" on the one hand and psychoanalysis was preoccupied with unconscious motivation on the other. But the situation soon changed. Three symposia convened between 1948 and 1955 sparked the first cognitive revolution, which became known as the "New Look" (Santostefano 1991a). What was it that was new? Investigators abandoned the search for universal laws that explained cognitive activity as a self-contained entity and set out to integrate cognitive functioning (surface behaviors) and personality (deep behaviors).

The stage was set by Heinz Werner's (1949) introduction to a symposium in which he noted that while studies of perception were flourishing, psychology had done little to integrate perception and personality. Responding to this need, Werner and Wapner (1949) offered their sensory-tonic field theory of perception, forecasting the importance of locating the individual within the environment. Klein and Schlesinger (1949) asked psychologists to consider that the perceiver, who was absent in cognitive theory and research, could be understood as employing perceptual attitudes. Witkin (1949) conceptualized the importance of individual differences in the body's perception of the upright. And McCleary and Lazarus (1949) discussed perception without awareness.

Reflecting the rapid momentum of the New Look approach, a second conference was convened the next year, guided by the view that "the study of perceptual activity provides a basic approach to understanding personality and interpersonal relations. Perceptual activity supplies the material from which the individual constructs his own personally meaningful environment" (Blake and Ramsey 1951, p. iii). Hilgard (1951) discussed how perception may be influenced by "the realities outside and by the realities within ourselves" (p. 95) and now the individual attempts to maintain a state of "dynamic equilibrium" (p. 95) between these influences. Frenkl-Brunswik (1951) proposed that the best way to capture a person's dynamic equilibrium was to study her/him in a natural, cultural habitat. Elaborating his concept of perceptual attitudes presented the previous year, Klein (1951) viewed cognition as coordinating an individual's subjective world and environment, and emphasized individual differences in this function. Bruner (1951) urged investigators to define concepts that forged cognition and personality as one entity. Another theme received prominent attention at this conference. Recognizing the dominance of behaviorism at the time, Bronfenbrenner (1951) attempted to desensitize the aversion of U.S. psychology to the concept of unconscious.

The issue of unconscious cognitive processes became the focus of the third symposium that launched the New Look movement (Gruber et al. 1957). Behaviorists and psychoanalytically oriented researchers and clinicians articulated three motifs: (1) cognition is at the center of a person's adaptations to the environment; (2) the environments to which a person adapts are cognitive representations or symbols rather than actual things as they are; and (3) unconscious cognitive structures code or determine what pictures a person takes, so to speak, of environments. The thrust then of the New Look revolution was influenced by interpretationism.

Cognition was defined as (deep) unconscious structures that equilibrate environmental stimulation with stimuli from a person's subjective world in the service of adaptation. This notion provided one way of connecting action (adaptation), fantasy (personal world), and cognition. Research influenced by this view flourished in the 1960s and 1970s (see Santostefano 1978 for a review).

But the New Look approach was eclipsed by a second revolution (Gardner 1985) that was influenced by objectivism. In sharp contrast to the interpretationist view of the first revolution, research shifted the focus away from cognition as unconscious structures coordinating meanings related to environmental stimulation and personal motives toward cognition as "processing of information." Recalling his participation in the first revolution, and reviewing developments in the second, Bruner (1990, 1992) argued that the introduction of the computer as the ruling metaphor was responsible for this shift and that investigators should return to the interpretationist image of cognition as unconscious structures.

HOW DOES PSYCHODYNAMIC THERAPY VIEW COGNITION?

As the New Look elaborated its concepts and observations, psychodynamic therapists were informed that cognition was emerging as a powerful point of view and were urged to consider how cognition could influence their clinical work (Holt 1964). Apparently this suggestion was not followed by many; writers pointed out that the field of cognition was being neglected by psychodynamic therapists. It is interesting to note that those who did address cognition relied on Piaget's cognitive psychology rather than on the concepts of the New Look (e.g., Anthony 1956, Lewis 1977, Wolff 1960). Since these early studies, however, volumes have appeared that address cognition and psychodynamics (e.g., Colby and Stoller 1988, Horowitz 1988) and describe forms of cognitive-psychodynamic psychotherapy for adults (e.g., Weiner 1985) and children (Santostefano 1995a). Unlike earlier clinicians who relied on Piaget, these attempts, by and large, maintain the motifs of the New Look approach. In spite of these contributions, cognition continues to receive relatively little attention by psychodynamic therapists. For example, two volumes on psychodynamic psychotherapy with children (Coppolillo 1987, Spiegel 1989) do not list cognition in the index, and a handbook of child psychoanalysis (Wolman 1972) gives cognition spotty attention.

HOW DOES COGNITIVE-BEHAVIORAL THERAPY VIEW COGNITION?

As one might expect, cognition has been and is being given considerable attention in cognitive-behavioral therapy. However, many different behaviors are proposed as cognitions to be treated and changed. Various investigators reporting in one volume (Emery et al. 1981) define cognition, for example, as "sleeping cognition," (p. 288) "dream content," (p. 231) "helplessness-anxiety," (p. 231) "discussing perceptions of an event," (p. 57) "a person's tendency to drift from topic to topic," (p. 88) and "distortions of one's physical appearance" (p. 71). Some authors propose a broad definition such as "thoughts that pass through a person's mind," while others propose a more circumscribed one: "dysfunctional ideation." To make matters more confusing, other behaviors have also been proposed as cognition in cognitive-behavioral therapy: attributional styles (inferences a person draws to explain why an event occurred), role taking or perspective taking (how a person assumes the point of view of another), cognitive problem-solving skills (how a person thinks of alternative solutions to a problem), and belief systems.

This confusion was clarified to some degree more than a decade ago by Arnkoff and Glass (1982) with their excellent critique. They pointed out that there is an overwhelmingly narrow focus on self-statements and beliefs, that a belief may have several meanings, and that several statements may convey a single meaning. Converging with our earlier discussions of outside and inside behaviors and the first cognitive revolution, these authors suggested that what a person says may be the tip of the iceberg, and therefore there is a need to consider "deep" as well as "surface" cognitive structures in order to learn the meaning underlying a particular verbalized statement. Noting that self-statement therapies set out to help the client identify "bad thoughts" and replace them with "good ones," they also proposed that: (1) an "irrational" thought could sometimes be adaptive, a rational thought maladaptive, depending upon the meaning the thought holds for the individual and the function it serves; and (2) some experiences may not be amenable to self-report because of their inaccessability to verbal language.

Two years later Hollon and Kriss (1984) also attempted to clarify the concept of cognition by proposing two types: cognitive products and cognitive structures. Cognitive products are conscious beliefs and self-statements that one can observe directly. This definition is employed by both cognitive-behavioral and psychodynamic therapies. Cognitive structures are defined as *underlying unconscious organizations* (converging with the emphasis of the first cognitive revolution) that operate outside awareness, assigning meaning to experiences. The content of cognitive structures cannot be observed directly, but are inferred from cognitive products. Examples include Piaget's concept of schemas and the psychoanalytic concept of mental mechanisms of defense (discussed later).

CONCLUDING COMMENT

The motifs of the symposia that launched the first cognitive revolution, when combined with the critiques discussed above, give rise to several questions that should be addressed when integrating psychotherapies:

1. How can we connect the meanings and fantasies a person assigns to experiences with overt behaviors and verbalizations?
2. How can we operationalize the notion that unconscious cognitive structures equilibrate environmental stimuli with stimulation from a person's subjective world?
3. How can we operationalize and relate different expressions that occur within each of the different behavioral modes (action, fantasy, and language), and how can we relate expressions in one mode to those in another?
4. What is the cotter pin that links actions to fantasies and fantasies to words so that if one mode moves or turns so do the others?

Issue III: The Relationship between Cognition and Emotion

We noted earlier that a boundary has been maintained between cognition and emotion, with considerable attention devoted to how the two are interrelated. This issue continues to capture considerable interest as illustrated by the appearance of a journal, *Cognition and Emotion*, devoted to this topic. Some researchers have proposed that cognition and emotion are independent of each other; others, that they interact, with one dominating. When cognition is viewed as dominant, thinking and reasoning are considered "good" and emotion "bad" and in need of control. Sidestepping whether cognition is good and emotion bad, several researchers have attempted to relate cognition and emotion in some way. For example, Izard (1978) conceptualized affective-cognitive structures as traitlike characteristics that form stable personality orientations resulting in, for example, a person tending to be either passive, hyperactive, or anxious. Mandler (1982) focused on how a person "appraises" stimulation, conceptualizing "descriptive cognitions" (judgments based upon stimuli that are "out there") and "evaluative cognitions" (judgments that do not depend on stimuli in the environment). Referring to our previous discussions, descriptive cognitions are surface behaviors, or cognitive products, while evaluative cognitions are deep, cognitive structures.

These formulations leave unattended an issue central to child psychotherapy. Cognition is not operationalized as mobile organizations that shift and change in response to changes in stimulation. Mandler (1982) acknowledged that his notion of appraisal failed to address this issue when he noted that a horse could be judged as beautiful at one time and ugly at another when the person has had no experiences with horses that could account for this change in appraisal. But psychodynamic child therapists are familiar with this issue. How should we understand that in one session a child may experience and express disgust while shaping "long BM's" of clay, and in the same session experience and express pride and pleasure while shaping "a rocket" from clay? How therapists consider cognition and emotion is not influenced to any appreciable degree by these research programs. Rather, cognitive-behavioral and psychodynamic therapists are influenced more by the concepts of Freud and Piaget.

HOW DID FREUD VIEW THE RELATIONSHIP BETWEEN COGNITION AND EMOTION?

Freud's initial view of the relationship between cognition and emotion is represented most vividly perhaps by his famous metaphor that depicts emotion (the id) as a galloping horse and cognition (the ego) as a rider struggling to maintain control over galloping emotions and urges (Freud 1923, p. 25). Three years later he made clear that he had changed his mind, taking the position that cognition had more power. Now he proposed that the ego (cognition) exerts power and control in dealing both with the environment and with representations of drives. "Just as the ego controls the path to action in regard to the external world, so it controls access to consciousness . . . it exercises power in both directions, acting in the one manner upon the instinctual impulse itself and, in the other, upon the representative of the impulse" (Freud 1926, p. 95). This comment anticipated the concept, articulated by the New Look, of cognitive revolution described earlier: that cognition controls and coordinates information from environments and emotions.

HOW DID PIAGET VIEW THE RELATIONSHIP BETWEEN COGNITION AND EMOTION?

Piaget (1981) proposed two hypotheses. With one, cognitive and emotional aspects of behavior are always present simultaneously in all situations, and one does not result from or cause the other. With the second hypothesis, cognition and emotion are functionally parallel, each following its own developmental course. From 0–2 years (sensorimotor period) the infant engages in reflexes and "circular reactions" that coordinate visual, auditory, and bodily experiences that form the first mental schemas of experience. This is paralleled by the first stage of emotional development in which "affective reflexes" occur, as when the infant loses balance, and "elementary feelings" are experienced, such as pleasure and unpleasure. From 2 to 7 years (preoperational period) symbolic thinking gradually emerges. Information is engaged through the manipulation of symbols of objects rather than objects themselves. But judgments are strongly influenced by perception so that, for example, two events appear related because they occur together in time. With emotional development, emotions such as sympathy, obedience, and defiance are guided by schemas deriving from reactions to objects and persons. But as with cognitive stimuli, the child can attend to only one emotion at a time and cannot deal with two emotions that appear contradictory. During the next period of concrete operations (7–11 years) the child conserves information in images and deals simultaneously with two pieces of information that appear contradictory. And the child understands that although an object may be transformed, certain properties do not change (e.g., the child knows that the amount of water doesn't change when poured into a differently shaped vessel). Emotional development parallels these achievements. The child now conserves two emotions (e.g., the parent loves me and is angry at me, but remains the same parent), and moral values are conserved such as honesty and cowardice. In the final stage of cognitive development (11–15 years) information is gathered not only from existing reality but also, in particular, from possibilities, abstractions, and propositions. This cognitive stage is paralleled in emotional development by the emergence of ideological emotions such as freedom, charity, and justice.

HOW IS THE RELATIONSHIP BETWEEN COGNITION AND EMOTION VIEWED BY PSYCHODYNAMIC THERAPY AND WHAT ARE MECHANISMS OF DEFENSE IN THIS RELATIONSHIP?

Psychodynamic therapists have relied almost exclusively on Freud's revised view, and have elaborated how cognition attempts to regulate emotions activated both by environments and by a person's subjective world. The main goal of this regulation concerns preventing painful emotions from entering conscious awareness. The starting point is defined by what is termed a *psychodynamic configuration* (Horowitz 1988), which concerns (1) how the self wants to relate to others; (2) what the self wants to obtain from or give to others; (3) wishes and fears associated with what one wants; (4) emotions associated with what one imagines are the aims of others toward the self; and (5) cognitive mechanisms used to manage these emotions and information. Psychodynamic configurations are not static but change continuously as a person copes with different environments. The elements of configurations are presumed to operate outside awareness and are viewed as "dynamic" relationships. That is, when a conflict exists between opposing wishes/urges, the disturbing ideas and their associated emotions are warded off in some way from being experienced directly in one's awareness. To accomplish this, cognition is conceptualized as making use of several "mental mechanisms of defense," which are inferred from aspects of a person's behaviors and contexts in which they occur.

One mechanism (see Knapp 1988) involves selective inattention. Here, cognition excludes a disturbing idea and its emotions by focusing elsewhere. This cognitive activity constitutes "repression" enabling a person to deny or avoid some emotion. As one example, a child sat calmly, with a blank facial expression, upon hearing that his mother had died. With another defense mechanism, an idea with its emotion is admitted into consciousness in symbolically disguised form. For example, a child may represent an urge to be angry by symbolically playing that lightning strikes a doll figure. With this process, termed *sublimation*, an emotion/ urge is experienced in consciousness although in disguised form. With the cognitive mechanism termed *intellectualization*, the emotion is detached from the wish or urge to which it belongs and only the idea enters awareness with the disturbing emotion isolated. For example, a child who entered treatment because he enjoyed torturing the family pet kitten eventually became interested in learning more about torture methods used during the Spanish Inquisition. In this way potentially disturbing ideas were engaged with well-rationalized and dispassionate thinking and curiosity. With the mechanism termed *reaction formation*, a disturbing feeling is replaced in conscious awareness by an equally strong or stronger feeling that is "acceptable." For example, a 6-year-old girl expressed "love" for a newborn sib in exaggerated ways—proclaiming her love dozens of times each day, assisting mother in bathing and feeding the infant, and guarding the infant's safety. Here, anger and envy directed toward the infant were inverted and replaced by love and caring. With the last cognitive mechanism we consider, a disturbing feeling is managed by segregating persons as either good or bad and assigning the disturbing feeling to someone designated as bad, a process referred to as *projection*. For example, a boy who harbored intense hate toward a sib became preoccupied with his belief that a classmate hated him.

In addition to the concept of psychodynamic configurations, some psychodynamic therapists have also relied on Piaget's concept of conservation in order to help a child resolve ambivalent feelings (hate and love of each parent) (Lewis 1977). As Nannis (1988) proposed, without conservation it is difficult for a child to know that mother still loves her/him when she is yelling and scolding. While some authors rely on Piaget's theory, the conceptualization of psychodynamic configurations dominates psychodynamic therapy, conceptualizing cognition as mental activity outside awareness, as a mobile system that equilibrates emotions aroused both by environments (as symbolized by a person) and a person's subjective world of wishes and fantasies.

HOW IS THE RELATIONSHIP BETWEEN COGNITION AND EMOTION VIEWED BY COGNITIVE-BEHAVIORAL THERAPY?

It seems to me that the relationship between cognition and emotion implied by the content of many cognitive-behavioral interventions relates to Freud's initial formulation of cognition (the rider) struggling to control or stop stronger emotions and urges (the horse). For example, Kendall and Braswell (1985) characterized their methods as "teaching children to slow down and cognitively examine their behavioral alternatives before acting" (p. 1) and providing the child with "an opportunity to practice self-instructional skills while grappling with problematic situations that pull for a more impulsive, emotional type of responding" (p. 135). In discussing the behavioral technique of role playing, Kendall and Morison (1984) noted that some children become quite excitable when participating. While an increase in "emotional arousal" is desirable, this arousal may occasionally take the form of "silliness" which impedes the conduct of meaningful role playing. At such times the therapist could hold up a "stop sign" or ask the child to "freeze as though he/she were a statue" (pp. 140–141). With this suggestion, cognition (the rider) is recruited to stop galloping emotions (the horse). Another example is provided by a volume describing cognitive-behavioral therapy with children in schools (Hughes 1988). In discussing hyperactivity, this author noted that self-controlled children have skills that "inhibit inappropriate responding" (p. 110). In other words, these children are blessed with a rider (cognition) that can control the horse (emotion). Accordingly, with one technique the child is trained to verbalize a set of self-directives before responding (e.g., "I must look and think before I answer"), statements intended to enable cognition to hold the horse still, if even for a moment. Other cognitive-behavioral therapists rely on Piaget's model and emphasize, as do some psychodynamic therapists, the process of conservation. For example, Knell (1995) proposed that without conservation of emotions, a child may be unduly influenced by a single environmental event: a popular boy not selected by peers for a ballgame on one day may believe he is always unwanted.

CONCLUDING COMMENT

The relationship between cognition and emotion elaborates the questions raised earlier when we considered the relationship between what a person does, fantasizes, and says. On the one hand we have Freud's initial view that conscious cognitions (products) struggle to control emotional surges from gaining expression in action. This notion seems to be represented in cognitive-behavioral techniques designed to strengthen cognition's ability to block or control emotions so that the child does not act before thinking. On the other hand we have Freud's revised model that unconscious cognitive mechanisms (structures) operate to disguise emotions in some fashion so that painful anxiety does not enter conscious awareness, and so that these emotions do not gain direct expression in action. We also have the Piagetian notion that how emotions are conserved in images enables a child to experience emotions as autonomous from actions they require, and to acknowledge that opposite emotions could be felt toward the same person. There is a need to integrate these notions heuristically, providing child therapists with guidelines defining when, and with which techniques, a child could be helped to improve how she/he regulates what she/he does, fantasizes, and says.

Issue IV: The Meanings a Person Gives to Experiences

When assigning meaning to some experience, a person constructs a symbol that represents the experience in some way. It is generally accepted that when a symbol is constructed (as well as its close relatives, simile and analogy), something is described or expressed in terms of properties that belong to something else (Santostefano 1988b). For example, consider a 3-year-old who, while walking along with his parent, spots a jogger. The boy immediately leans his body forward, and with each exuberant "choo-choo!" vigorously thrusts his right arm forward and back, providing an example of a symbol consisting of actions, fantasies, and language. In exclaiming "choo-choo!" and in thrusting his arm forward and back, while apparently fantasizing a train, he is saying, "The man is a powerful train engine!" At an older age, with language more fully developed, this same child could make use of a simile ("That man is running like a powerful engine!") and an analogy ("That man runs as if he is a powerful engine!").

HOW IS MEANING VIEWED BY PSYCHODYNAMIC THERAPY?

As discussed previously, meanings given to experiences became a major cornerstone of Freud's approach, and have continued to hold a central position in various extensions of psychodynamic therapy. When Freud observed that many of the memories patients presented proved to be, from his point of view, fantasies expressing wishes, he explained the origin of these fantasies by conceptualizing that "instinctual drives" produce meanings that form a person's "psychic reality." Instinctual drives are not states of hunger, for example, but involve a process that joins the body and mind as one, conceptualizing a connection between "psychical representation," that is, cognitive meanings representing experiences, and actual bodily experiences. By conceptualizing a close connection between body experiences and the construction of meaning, Freud forecast the emergence years later of embodiment theory, to which I return later. The meanings constructed form a person's psychic reality that includes wishes and fantasies, accompanied by emotions, that a person injects, usually without awareness, into day-to-day experiences.

Following Freud, writers modified this concept so that psychic reality became synonymous with distorting reality and with psychopathology. If a child feared school, the child was viewed as dominated by "psychic reality," and when free of this fear, functioning in "objective reality." This modification resulted in two types of meanings: "real," and therefore normal, and distortions of the real, or "imagined," and therefore abnormal. This modification also shifted away from Freud's interpretationist position toward objectivism. One consequence of this dichotomy was the view among psychodynamic therapists that different symbols are used to construct meanings: images construct meanings in one's psychic reality, while words construct meanings in objective reality. More recently, psychodynamic investigators, especially those influenced by observations of infants, have advocated that the original, more heuristic concept of psychic reality be retained (Barratt 1984). From this view the reality with which a child negotiates consists of all that the child experiences and understands, whether or not it fits with the conventions of family/community. Moreover, the same processes are applied whether a child is judging a sausage-shaped piece of clay as the same or longer than another, or whether the child is pretending to eat the clay as a hotdog or flee from it as a snake. What the child knows, does, and feels is what the child represents.

Gill (1984) argued that the issue of meaning distinguishes psychodynamic and cognitive-behavioral therapies: the former attempts to change the meaning of behavior while the latter attempts to alter the behavior directly, ignoring its meaning. In a similar vein, Shirk (1988) noted that psychodynamic therapists consider overt behaviors as important primarily because of the meanings they reveal rather than because of their contingencies. In the next section we find that the picture has changed to some degree from that portrayed by Gill and Shirk.

HOW IS MEANING VIEWED BY COGNITIVE-BEHAVIORAL THERAPY?

Initially ignoring this issue, cognitive and behavioral therapies gradually gave some attention to the issue of meaning. For example, Thompson (1981), in a provocative article that asked the question, "Will it hurt less if I can control it?" took the position that therapy should focus on changing the meanings a person gives experiences. Similarly, Mahoney (1985), questioning the emphasis on techniques that replace maladaptive thoughts with realistic ones and employ self-instruction, proposed that the heart of change is found in how meanings change. And Arnkoff (1980) proposed that the meaning given to an experience is the "ultimate issue" that needs to be considered in treatment. While not considering meaning to be the ultimate issue, Kendall and Morison (1984) seemed to approach meaning through "cognitive mediators" a child uses when given a reward. They pointed out that an adult may provide social praise, but the child's cognitive processing of that experience may render the praise "nonrewarding." Although they do not use the terms *unconscious* and *meaning*, they do seem to be saying that a meaning the child gives to some praise may render the adult's statements as having meaning other than praise.

More recently, Bohart (1993) elaborated the issue of meaning in terms of "experiencing and knowing." Converging with Freud's instinct theory, he pointed out that experiencing meaning relies less on conceptualizing and more on bodily perceptions, sensations, and actions that form the foundation for thoughts and concepts that later label experiences in relationships with others. Experiencing meaning, then, occurs from embodied, nonverbal to conceptual, verbal levels. Because cognitive-behavioral therapies focus on changing beliefs and cognitive mediators, how a person experiences, Bohart suggested, tends to be neglected.

CONCLUDING COMMENT

Psychodynamic therapy has always viewed meanings given to experiences as the main focus of treatment. But meaning has been inferred primarily from the words spoken by the patient. Cognitive-behavioral therapy, while initially ignoring the issue of meaning, has gradually paid more attention to it, although the essence of meaning is still found in spoken words. If we accept Freud's view, echoed by Bohart (1993), that experiencing meaning is holistic and contextual—involving sights, smells, sounds, and actions as well as spoken words as a person interacts with others—the importance of interpersonal interactions comes into view, which we consider below.

Issue V: Conscious and Unconscious Processes

Our discussions thus far have implied the notion that mental and behavioral activity takes place both within and outside a person's subjective awareness. However, the importance of addressing unconscious as well as conscious processes in treatment continues to divide mainstream cognitive-behavioral and psychodynamic therapies.

WHAT IS THE VIEW OF CONSCIOUS AND UNCONSCIOUS PROCESSES IN PSYCHODYNAMIC THERAPY?

The importance of unconscious processes predated Freud by several centuries, but it took Freud to drive it home (Colby and Stoller 1988). Freud consistently maintained the view that we are not aware of many of the motives, wishes, and attitudes that guide our behaviors and that we actively keep these motives and attitudes outside awareness to spare ourselves the anxiety they generate. That unconscious processes exist, and are of central importance in therapy, is taken for granted, a view that is perhaps the distinguishing feature of the psychodynamic approach (Wachtel 1984; see also Knapp 1988 for a particularly useful discussion of the psychodynamic view of the unconscious). Although most take unconscious processes for granted, some pause to articulate their view of its importance. For example, in a volume (Colby and Stoller 1988) devoted to the interface between cognitive science and psychoanalysis, Stoller stated, "No other field [psychoanalysis] has tried so hard to find the form, dynamics, purposes, origins, and effects of unconscious forces . . . and no other field has had the enthusiasm, nerve, arrogance, and at times, courage to try to systematize these unconscious aspects of subjectivity" (p. 35).

WHAT IS THE VIEW OF CONSCIOUS AND UNCONSCIOUS PROCESSES IN COGNITIVE-BEHAVIORAL THERAPY?

The notion of unconscious processes has continued to be invisible within cognitive-behavioral therapy, or at best at the edge of its stage. This is not surprising since, as we noted earlier, the heritage of this approach initially eliminated feelings and mental activity and anything else that seemed subjective. Thus we are not surprised to find the concept of unconscious processes conspicuously absent from descriptions of cognitive-behavioral therapy prior to 1980 (e.g., Bedrosian 1981, DiGiuseppe 1981, Feuerstein 1980, Kendall and Hollon 1979, Meichenbaum 1977). Since then, the scene gradually changed as several developments exerted an influence. With one, when therapists attempted to identify aspects of stimulation that accounted for positive or negative reinforcement, they noticed that some outcomes could not be attributed to the direct effect of the procedure. To account for this, therapists formulated what were conceptualized as "nonspecific effects" (e.g., what a person expected of some stimulation; encouragement provided by the therapist). Another development involved introduction of the notion of cognitive mediators, mental activity that occurred after a person perceived a stimulus and before she/he enacted some response. Mendelsohn and Silverman (1984) argued convincingly that phenomena conceptualized as nonspecific effects and cognitive mediators refer to many of the same phenomena that psychodynamic therapists conceptualize as unconscious fantasies.

Another turning point was reached when two critiques of cognition (discussed earlier) appeared. Arnkoff and Glass (1982) criticized the focus on conscious self-statements and drew attention to the possibility that a conscious thought may be the tip of an iceberg. Hollon and Kris (1984) conceptualized the tip of the iceberg as cognitive products (conscious self-statements) and the rest as cognitive structures (unconscious organizations constructing meaning). Perhaps because of these influences, the notion of unconscious processes has been slowly easing itself toward the center of the cognitive-behavioral stage. As one example, "radical behaviorism" (Kohlenberg and Tsai 1994, Jacobson 1994) proposed that strengthening provided by reinforcement occurs at an unconscious level. Yet despite these developments the importance of unconscious processes appears not to have found its way into mainstream, cognitive-behavioral treatment of children and is still noticeably absent, failing to appear in the index of several volumes (e.g., Hughes 1988, Knell 1995, Matson and Ollendick 1988).

CONCLUDING COMMENT

If we accept the importance of including unconscious processes when integrating psychotherapies for children, how should we conceptualize the unconscious? Is the unconscious sóme dark cave in which reside thoughts and fantasies that have been previously formed and then pushed into the cave? If we shine a light into the cave, will we discover these preformed thoughts and fantasies? How can we operationalize unconscious processes in a way that serves the treatment of children?

Issue VI: Contexts, Environments, and Situations

The psychology of environments and situations received a surge of interest in the early 1980s (Magnusson 1981, Shapiro and Weber 1981, Zimmerman 1983), emphasizing that behavior is dependent upon the context in which it occurs and that situations are holistic, experienced as unified wholes rather than as discrete stimuli.

WHAT IS THE VIEW OF THE ENVIRONMENT IN PSYCHODYNAMIC THERAPY?

The importance of the environment was ushered into psychodynamic theory in 1939 by Heinz Hartmann when he introduced "autoplasticity and alloplasticity" to conceptualize the reciprocal relationship between an individual and environment and that a person both changes and is changed by the environment. He also conceptualized environments in terms of whether stimulation was usual or unusual, given a person's history. Wachtel (1984, 1987) has been perhaps the most active psychodynamic theorist concerned with reciprocal influences between person and environment, which he conceptualized as "cyclical psychodynamics." While a person's behavior is influenced by an unconscious meaning (e.g., he discussed a young man anxious about being swallowed up by his girlfriend), a person also seeks relationships and situations that behave in terms of that meaning (e.g., the young man chose female companions who dominated him). In terms of research, I (e.g., 1978, 1986) made central use of the concepts of usual and unusual environments in studies of cognition and emotion conducted in molar environments (e.g., adults preparing for a parachute jump; children preparing for surgery) and in molecular environments (e.g., test stimuli designed to evoke different fantasies/emotions). In spite of contributions since Hartmann's early emphasis on the environment, psychodynamic therapists still pay less attention to the environment, both in the community and in the treatment room, than they do to a child's inner world of unconscious fantasies and motives.

WHAT IS THE VIEW OF THE ENVIRONMENT IN COGNITIVE-BEHAVIORAL THERAPY?

The environment has been, and continues to be, a cornerstone of this approach. Initially the environment was viewed as consisting of discrete events resulting in responses. Then Bandura (1977) introduced his social learning theory and the concept of "reciprocal determinism." With this concept, according to Hughes (1988), "Bandura turned Watson's brand of behaviorism on its head. Rejecting an undirected view of the effects of the environment on the individual, Bandura viewed the person–environment relationship as a reciprocal, influential process" (p. 6). While similar to Hartmann's auto- and alloplasticity and Wachtel's cyclical psychodynamics, the concept of reciprocal determinism, influenced by the machine metaphor, maintains a boundary between the person and environment. Either the person constructs the environment and acts accordingly or the environment constructs the person and acts accordingly, defining a linear relationship (Overton and Horowitz 1991). Knell (1995) provided illustrations of techniques that are used to deal with problems framed within discrete environments (e.g., toilet; divorced parents). Using one of Knell's illustrations, an encopretic boy, initially treated with the behavioral technique of shaping, was encouraged to play with a toy bear near the toilet, then sit the bear on it, and then pretend it made a bowel movement. Next the child was coached to have the bear repeatedly fall into the toilet as the therapist verbalized the child's actions. When the bear kept his pants clean and used the toilet, the therapist gave the bear verbal praise and stickers, and trained the bear to use positive self-statements such as "I feel good when I use the toilet."

CONCLUDING COMMENT

In the example provided by Knell, the child–environment relationship is linear, and the direction of the influence is from child to environment (i.e., the child, through the bear, acts upon the toilet in various ways). From the view of cyclical psychodynamics, what is missing is the meaning the toilet holds for the child and how the meaning guides the child to seek particular experiences with toilets that, from the child's point of view, act upon her/him in particular ways. Another example of a boundary between child and environment, and a linear relationship between them, is found in Hollin's (1990) cognitive-behavioral therapy with young offenders. He pointed out that a youth may invent or exaggerate some offense, complicating what a therapist could choose as the target of therapy. To cope with this, he recommended comparing the youth's self-report with police records, which are taken as the "truth." In contrast, the concept of cyclical dynamics would explore the interplay between two dynamics: (1) the meaning for a youth of some antisocial behavior that she/he exaggerates or invents and the role this exaggerated behavior plays in guiding the child to act on police in particular ways; and (2) the ways in which the police construe and act upon the child in terms of that behavior.

Both cognitive-behavioral and psychodynamic therapies acknowledge the importance of the person–environment relationship, which is viewed as linear by the former and dialectical and cyclical by the latter. If we are committed to the previous issues described (including both surface, conscious, and deep, unconscious behaviors), then the relationship between child and environment (including the environment of a therapeutic situation) should be conceptualized in terms of cyclical and dialectical concepts: that a person and environment continuously influence and define each other, negotiating a fit between them. The linear concept, in which the therapist either changes the behavior the child applies to the environment or changes the way environments act upon the child, seems less heuristic.

Issue VII: Psychological Conflict

Psychological conflict implies that some behavior, idea, or emotion is opposed by another behavior, idea, or emotion. The view therapists take of these opposing forces relates to the position they assume in terms of surface and deep behaviors, the relationship between cognition and emotion, the significance of conscious and unconscious mental processes, and the role of environments.

HOW DOES COGNITIVE-BEHAVIORAL THERAPY VIEW CONFLICT?

Although concerned with relieving a person's stress, cognitive-behavioral therapy has not emphasized the importance of conceptualizing conflict. As Wachtel (1987) pointed out, Bandura's influential volume (1969) does not contain any references to "conflict." I have noticed that other early, influential volumes also do not list conflict in the index (e.g., Beck 1979, Meichenbaum 1977). Similarly, the topic of conflict is conspicuously absent in later volumes (e.g., Emery et al. 1981, Guidano and Liotti 1983, Kendall and Hollon 1979, Knell 1995, McMullin 1986, Meyers and Craighead 1984).

Yet several authors have given attention to the concept of conflict. For example, Hoffman (1984), in presenting the foundations of cognitive therapy, addressed the issue of conflict in terms of Piaget's concept of equilibration. From this view, conflict concerns the degree to which the organization of a particular mental schema (cognitive structure) is mismatched with behaviors and information available for assimilation from a person's environment. If this discrepancy continues over time, "Frustration will be accumulated as the cognitive structure tries to relate to these particular situations [and] will be loaded with negative feelings" (Hoffman 1984, p. 32). He described the hypothetical example of a toddler whose needs were regularly met by the actions of others, resulting in schemas anticipating that all needs will be met. Then, when any future environment does not present the same degree of nurturing activity, the child's cognitive structures would be in conflict with environmental stimulation. Arkowitz and Messer (1984) and Wachtel (1987) conceptualized the view cognitive-behavioral therapy holds of conflict as involving competition among different thoughts and/or behavioral responses that have been reinforced in different ways by the environment on the one hand and as involving opposition by the environment to particular thoughts or behaviors on the other.

From a cognitive-behavioral viewpoint, then, conflict is determined for the most part by the environment, and is eliminated either by replacing or controlling conscious thoughts/actions with techniques such as self-instruction training and modeling or by techniques that modify environments opposing a person's thoughts/behaviors (e.g., modifying the demanding ways of parents, or an unstructured classroom).

HOW DOES PSYCHODYNAMIC THERAPY VIEW CONFLICT?

Conflict is a core feature of psychodynamic therapy. A person is seen as inherently locked in a struggle among "inner forces" (fantasies/urges, meanings, internal prohibitions, mechanisms of defense) that are inferred from constellations of a person's psychological activity. In assessing conflict, particular attention is paid to whether unconscious mental mechanisms of defense (see Issue III) are efficient so that unconscious wishes and urges do not result in maladaptive action. Since psychodynamic therapists view conflict as inherent in human functioning, they hold that conflict cannot be eliminated but only alleviated. Treatment focuses on bringing wishes and fantasies into awareness and restructuring inefficient mechanisms of defense. As a person becomes aware that she/he is angry at a parent for some reason, the person also changes the degree to which she/he projects this anger onto other authority figures, such as a teacher, a maneuver that previously resulted in stress and experiencing the teacher as angry at her/him.

When conceptualizing conflict, cognitive-behavioral therapists have focused on conscious thoughts (cognitive products) while psychodynamic therapists have focused on unconscious fantasies and mechanisms of defense (cognitive structures). A link between these positions was suggested by Lewis (1977), who integrated Piaget's theory of cognitive development into psychodynamic therapy for children. Pointing out that psychoanalysis usually considers stresses stemming from intrapsychic conflicts, he proposed that stress could also stem from a mismatch between a child's stage of cognitive development and the complexity of information the child is attempting to master, a position similar to Hoffman's (1984) noted above. Consider a 9-year-old child who has not yet developed the capacity to conserve information (see Issues II, III). Because of this lag, the child has difficulty in appropriately distancing from events and emotions surrounding her/him, resulting in anxiety. The importance of a child's cognitive development, especially in terms of whether a child's cognition efficiently equilibrates emotions, wishes, and environmental demands, plays an important role in the integrated model of child psychotherapy proposed in this volume.

Issue VIII: The Relationship between Patient and Therapist

The relationship between patient and therapist has been assigned different degrees of importance by cognitive-behavioral and psychodynamic therapies. This is not surprising if we remind ourselves of the assumptions of objectivism and interpretationism that have influenced each approach. Recall that, from the viewpoint of objectivism, to gather neutral observations of knowledge that exist "out there," a boundary is set between therapist and patient, subordinating the relationship between the two. From the viewpoint of interpretationism, the therapist assumes that a patient's knowledge will be constructed by her/his activity *within* the therapeutic relationship. Since the therapist proceeds by joining the patient in a dialectical process to construct this knowledge, the relationship is considered crucial.

In his first writings Freud (e.g., 1904, 1905) assigned a central position to the patient–therapist relationship. He used the term *alliance* to conceptualize how patient and therapist construct a mutual commitment to engage in the task of resolving conflict. He used the term *transference* to conceptualize another quality of the relationship. Freud noticed that when a patient interacted with him during treatment sessions, the person gradually relived and repeated behaviors she/he had already developed to conduct her/his emotional and cognitive life, behaviors that took shape during experiences with significant others. He proposed that a person cannot escape repeating (transferring) or acting out these behaviors in the treatment situation instead of remembering their origin. In the beginning of treatment, for example, one of Freud's patients did not remember being defiant and critical with his parents as a child, but instead behaved in this way with the therapist. Freud assumed that a patient's way of knowing or remembering was to repeat the behaviors in the relationship. He also conceptualized that the compulsion to repeat an action instead of remembering served as resistance to change. He assumed that if a patient transfers feelings onto the therapist—as if the therapist were mother or father—it follows that the patient would find it very difficult to admit knowing of wishes or impulses, since in doing so they would have to be revealed to the very person to whom they relate. For Freud, a person's difficulties were resolved when she/he relived and worked through her/his resistance to change in the relationship with the therapist during in vivo experiences. "[W]e must [eventually] treat his illness not as an event of the past but as a present-day force . . . and while the patient experiences it as something real and contemporary [in interaction with the therapist], we have to do our therapeutic work on it . . . " (Freud 1914, p. 151).

While the patient–therapist relationship remained at the center of psychodynamic therapy, almost immediately after Freud developed his position psychoanalysts began to debate the question, What is the proper stance a therapist should take in the therapeutic relationship? (see Messer and Winokur 1984 for a review). Some therapists, emphasizing one of Freud's notions, argued that the therapist should remain a "blank screen" and "neutral" so that the patient could more readily experience her/him as someone else. The therapist could then point out how these behaviors "distorted" experiences with the therapist and therefore with others.

On the other side of the debate, as interpersonal concepts received increasing attention other therapists argued that the "real relationship" between patient and therapist was more important, and that transference behaviors were not so much symbols of the past but experiences occurring within here-and-now transactions between patient and therapist. From this position the concept of transference was revised. Gill (1984), for example, proposed that while the patient in the here and now repeats ways of behaving that originated from past experiences, the behaviors of the therapist also exert an influence on how the patient behaves, and in this sense "co-determines the transference" (p. 169). In addition, some writers have attempted to integrate the concept of the therapist as a "blank screen" with that of "participant." Greenson (1977), addressing adult psychotherapy, noted, "This [integrated] kind of listening requires that analysts have the capacity to shift from participant to observer, from introspection to empathy, from intuition to problem-solving thinking, from a more involved to a more detached position" (pp. 100–101) (quoted in Messer and Winokur 1984, p. 68).

WHAT IS THE VIEW OF THE PATIENT–THERAPIST RELATIONSHIP IN COGNITIVE-BEHAVIORAL THERAPY?

The relationship between patient and therapist has received little or no attention (Arkowitz 1984) except for cooperation required on the part of the patient so that she/he can engage in various tasks introduced by the therapist. Bandura (1969), who introduced the concepts of modeling and cognitive mediators, viewed the patient–therapist relationship as a friendship or as a substitution for some lack in the patient's life, and discounted the importance psychodynamic therapy gave to the relationship and to "transference." Several years later, Rhoads (1984) pointed out that there is little interest in a person's relationship with the therapist unless something in the relationship interferes with the therapy.

More recently, there has been a shift—at least among those who represent an approach called "radical behaviorism"—that views the patient–therapist relationship in ways that resemble that of psychodynamic therapy. Kohlenberg and Tsai (1994) proposed that a therapist should "watch for clinically relevant behaviors (CRBs)" (p. 185), defined in much the same way that Freud defined transference behaviors eighty years earlier. CRBs, behaviors occurring in the treatment session, represent and repeat behaviors that "clients complain about in outside relationships" (p. 185). However, this approach departs from traditional psychodynamic therapy in proposing that, in addition to watching for CRBs, the therapist should "evoke" these behaviors during a session. Whether these behaviors are generated by the patient or evoked by something the therapist says or does, the therapist provides the patient with opportunities to develop behaviors that correct or improve the CRB. For example, the authors referred to a patient who complained that he withdraws when people don't pay attention to him during conversation. If this client showed withdrawal behaviors when interrupted by the therapist, the therapist engaged the client to be "assertive" and direct the therapist back to what the client was saying, reinforcing the desired behavior. Echoing Freud, then, these authors urged therapists to observe clinically relevant behaviors, or what psychodynamic therapists call "transference reactions." But, unlike psychodynamic therapists who focus on exploring the meaning and origin of these behaviors, the authors proposed that if the therapist recognizes CRBs beforehand, she/he is "more likely to naturally reinforce, punish and extinguish these behaviors in ways that foster the development of behavior useful in daily life" (Kohlenberg and Tsai 1994, p. 186).

HAS THE DIFFERENCE IN THE VIEWS OF THE PATIENT– THERAPIST RELATIONSHIP HELD BY MAINSTREAM PSYCHODYNAMIC AND COGNITIVE-BEHAVIORAL THERAPIES CHANGED RECENTLY?

The proceedings of a 1993 panel discussion (Gaston et. al. 1995) suggested that the difference still exists. Therapists from each of three persuasions were invited to discuss the patient–therapist relationship: one psychodynamic therapist, two cognitive-behavioral therapists, and two experiential-humanistic therapists. The psychodynamic therapist presented a view reflecting Freud's early formulation. For example,

> Usually in dynamic therapy, we talk more about the alliance and transference; the alliance refers to the collaborative and realistic aspects of the relationship, and transference and countertransference to the more distorted reactions from both the patient and therapist . . . in long term therapy, the therapist makes sure that the transference neurosis develops so that the therapist can access the patient's inner world of transactions with others in distorted views of the world. [p. 8]

The cognitive-behavioral therapists stated that the concept of alliance "simply does not exist or has not until recent years" (p. 4). They elaborated, however, that while the emphasis has been on technique rather then on the relationship, "more and more cognitive-behavior therapists now recognize [the importance of the alliance]" (p. 4). For these therapists the alliance serves to facilitate the work with cognitive-behavioral tasks.

> [T]he alliance functions to encourage clients to carry out various forms of homework; increase the positive reinforcement value of therapists . . . facilitate any modeling that may occur by virtue of therapeutic self-disclosure . . . keep up the client's hope . . . and overcome any resistance or noncompliance that may exist. [p. 4]

These comments reflect an emphasis on techniques and a view that the therapist has "procedures" that must be performed on the person of the patient, with the relationship viewed only as facilitating techniques. This view was graphically illustrated when the cognitive-behavioral therapists cast the relationship within a metaphor of surgery and anesthesia.

> When we conceptualize the alliance from within a cognitive-behavioral point of view, we think of it as akin to anesthesia that occurs during major sur-

gery. Somebody goes into the hospital for surgery because there are certain procedures that need to be implemented. In order for these procedures to take place, the person must be under anesthesia; the anesthesia facilitates what is really important (i.e., the procedures) . . . similarly, within a cognitive-behavioral point of view, a good alliance is necessary and often crucial. Without it, you can't proceed. . . . [p. 5]

The experiential-humanistic therapists pointed out that for them the relationship is the core vehicle for change, converging with the psychodynamic panelist and with others we noted earlier. Moreover, the relationship is necessary to achieve the goal of experiential-humanistic therapy, namely, experiencing meanings, a goal that converges with Bohart's position noted earlier. The relationship is necessary if the patient is to engage in the task of experiencing problem behaviors, discovering the meanings of these behaviors, and increasing "the capacity to symbolize these felt-meanings in order to strengthen the self" (p. 6).

CONCLUDING COMMENT

Decades ago, Freud proposed that when interacting with a therapist, a patient repeats behaviors that cause problems in everyday living, and that it is these very behaviors that the therapist must address within the relationship to effect change. This proposal is also held important by radical behavioral therapists, but given little attention by mainstream cognitive-behavioral therapists. Psychodynamic therapists, who revised Freud's original position, bring attention to the notion that a patient identifies with and attaches to the therapist in much the same way that a child identifies with and attaches to her/his caregivers. They also emphasize a dialectical position: while the patient construes the therapist, the therapist also construes the patient, so that together they construct a relationship that is unique to them. These revisionists propose that transactions within this unique relationship promote change as much as, or perhaps more than, what the therapist says (interpretations). This view is also held by radical behaviorists who propose that how the therapist responds to "clinically relevant behaviors" determines whether the patient will evolve more adaptive ways of behaving. Experiential-humanistic therapists emphasize that when reliving some issue within the therapeutic relationship, what is most important is that the patient discover and experience the meaning of what is being relived and then cast the experience in some symbolic form. The integrative model outlined in this volume attempts to integrate these conceptual ingredients and translate them into therapeutic techniques suitable for work with children.

Issue IX: Reconsidering the Importance Given to Verbal Labeling and Interpretation

As discussed earlier, both cognitive-behavioral and psychodynamic therapies seem to deify the spoken word. Yet Bohart reminded us that meanings fuel the process of experiencing, which is contextual and body based. There has been a surge of interest in revising the view that the spoken word has ultimate power in promoting change. The surge comes from an unlikely source, given that psychodynamic therapy from its inception viewed verbalizing and interpretations by the therapist as the "holy grail" of treatment. Revisions actually started in the 1940s when a few psychodynamically oriented therapists expressed the opinion that the spoken word should be dethroned (for a review see Shirk 1988). For example, Axline deemphasized verbal interactions and emphasized helping a child express emotions, attitudes, and thoughts through play. And Winnicott proposed that the purpose of a therapist's communications is to create a supportive "holding" environment for a child.

HOW COULD A CHILD EXPERIENCE VERBALIZING AND INTERPRETATIONS BY A THERAPIST?

In recent years Mitchell (1994), a psychoanalyst, has become one major voice calling for the need to reconceptualize the role of language behavior in treatment. He reminded readers that in traditional psychodynamic treatment, "The patient is expected to stop acting and instead speak about his conflictual feelings and thoughts . . . and the analyst is expected to stop acting and instead use her/his experience to fashion appropriate interpretations" (p. 98). He also pointed out that, in spite of the therapist's best intentions and preparation, the patient could experience an interpretation, and other verbal comments by the therapist, as "assaults," presenting the therapist with "a dilemma." Although Mitchell is discussing adult psychodynamic therapy, his comments could also apply to child therapy. From my observations, a child could also experience an interpretation as an assault, and may do so more often than an adult does, and more often than a therapist might realize.

A child therapist typically uses verbal labeling and interpretations when experiencing and expressing meaning, probably because her/his language mode is well developed and practiced. In addition, an equally strong influence comes from the therapist's training. The psychodynamic therapist typically has ascribed to guidelines such as the one we noted by Anna Freud, that a child overcomes conflicts whenever they are put into words. The cognitive-behavioral therapist typically ascribes to the assumption that self-talk guides action, and that a child benefits from expressing maladaptive behavior in "language-based ways" (Knell 1995).

But if we look at the mode of "talking" from the viewpoint of a child, the meaning a verbal statement captures, while perhaps correct and suited for the adult, may not be the mode the child prefers because she/he is experiencing meaning primarily in the modes of fantasy and action, whatever her/his age. To illustrate this point consider a clinical vignette described by Coppolillo (1987), a psychodynamic therapist. For a number of sessions a boy had been "guarded, reluctant to reveal anything about himself and showed little inclination to explore the significance of anything he said" (p. 215). In one session this boy began to play a game of solitaire with a deck of cards he had brought with him. The therapist interpreted this behavior: "Do you suppose that by playing solitaire, you're showing me how it feels to be ignored?" The boy replied, "No solitaire. Just sit here and talk to this old, shithead son-of-a-bitch." With this the boy walked away and handled some items in a disinterested way (p. 215). The boy's response makes clear that he experienced the interpretation as an assault, placing the therapist in a dilemma.

WHAT ARE ENACTMENTS AND HOW DO THEY SERVE AS ALTERNATIVES TO VERBAL INTERPRETATIONS?

In the vignette just described, playing solitaire and walking away are examples of enactments. Mitchell (1994) pointed out that, because of recent changes in psychodynamic theory, some therapists now see enactments different from the way Freud did. Freud stressed that a patient should stop acting and verbalize his feelings and thoughts, a position also held by cognitive-behavioral therapy (see Issue III). The notion of enactments conceptualizes verbalizing, fantasizing, and taking action as "continuously interpenetrating each other" rather than as inversely related. This position, the reader may notice, converges with our interest in interrelating what a child does, imagines, and says. To illustrate, I return to the clinical vignette described above and consider it from the view of enactments. When the boy began playing solitaire with cards, instead of verbally interpreting this behavior, Coppolillo could have taken a deck of cards, sat at the far end of the room, and preoccupied himself with a game of solitaire. By using an enactment, he would be speaking to the child in the child's mode of the moment, namely, the action mode. Without using words, this enactment would say, "I know what it feels like to be ignored." By speaking in a child's mode, the child usually produces other enactments to elaborate the meaning and issues with which she/he is grappling without anything being said.

Spiegel (1989) provided another example. He described Daniel, a 10-year-old who entered treatment because of encopresis. One day, when he walked into the playroom, Spiegel, smelling feces, said, "It smells like you had an accident in school today" (p. 32). Daniel replied that he did not have an accident and that accidents don't happen anymore. Spiegel let the matter drop. Unlike the Coppolillo anecdote we considered earlier, Spiegel's words apparently were not experienced by Daniel as an assault, perhaps because the meaning of these words was denied by him ("No, it doesn't happen anymore"). Daniel continued to play with a car he had constructed that was designed to be propelled by an inflated balloon expelling air. Spiegel thought to himself that "[a]t some level, the propulsion by air from the balloon could have represented flatulence or the expelling of feces" (p. 33). At one point, enacting, Daniel placed a chunk of clay at the end of his nose. Spiegel verbally interpreted this behavior, "You look like Pinocchio? Pinocchio lied to Geppetto about school. Sometimes telling the truth is just too difficult and embarrassing" (p. 33). Daniel ignored this comment and continued to play. Spiegel did not pursue the matter.

When Daniel placed clay on the end of his nose, Spiegel assumed that since Pinocchio lied to Geppetto about school, Daniel was expressing the meaning that he also had lied to Spiegel about not having an accident at school. I believe that by placing clay on the end of his nose, Daniel was enacting and expressing one of several possible meanings, and the therapist needed to set out with Daniel to discover which meaning Daniel was experiencing at the moment. To mention only a few possibilities, the clay could have symbolized feces on the end of the therapist's nose, behavior that could have been a retaliation against the therapist ("Take that!") for commenting about the odor in the first place. Or the clay could have symbolized the child's recognizing that he smells. Or the clay could have symbolized that Daniel believed that the therapist thinks he (Daniel) stinks.

From the view of enactments, Spiegel could have responded with some action symbol, thereby matching the child's mood in order to help him continue elaborating the meaning. For example, Spiegel could have become very involved with Daniel in locating pieces of clay in the car to ensure that the car was "perfectly balanced." Or he could have placed a piece of clay on the end of his nose by way of saying, within the action mode, "I hear you, tell me more." In other words, the integrative model to be outlined proposes that the therapist refrain from making verbal interpretations, at least while a meaning is being constructed and elaborated by a child, and speak as much as possible through action metaphors. That action metaphors should be the focus of therapy with children converges with the opinions of a growing number of psychodynamic therapists who have criticized the emphasis on verbal interpretation. Joining Mitchell, for example, Valenstein (1983) proposed that understanding and insight are driven home by persistent action and interaction as patient and therapist engage in a prolonged repetitive process of testing and learning. Similarly, for Gill (1984), the main sources of change come from persistent interactions between patient and therapist and from new experiences and meanings the patient encounters and constructs with the therapist.

Enactments also concern whether a child engages in a task. Beginning with Freud's (1912) position that "it is wrong to set a task before the patient," (p. 119) many psychodynamic therapists (e.g., Messer and Winokur 1984) cautioned therapists not to ask the patient to perform some task because to do so decreases opportunities to explore the patient's inner conflicts and resolve them through interpretation of transference behaviors. Yet cognitive-behavioral therapists do not hesitate to introduce tasks the child is expected to manage. We consider later how an integration of the psychodynamic view of enactments and the cognitive-behavioral view of introducing problem-solving tasks benefits child psychotherapy.

Issue X: Developmental Principles: The Glue for Integration

Recalling our discussion of the boundary that divides objectivism and interpretationism, a therapist is typically committed more to assumptions that derive from one side or the other. When making a commitment to one of these positions instead of its counterpart, a therapist probably feels she/he is standing on solid ground, and experiences anxiety when asked to step over the boundary, because the other side appears to be quicksand. Thus, asking a therapist to think about integrating these polarities places her/him in a dilemma. If a cognitive-behavioral therapist keeps one foot on the solid ground of objectivism, where could she/he plant the other foot to avoid the quicksand of interpretationism? And if a psychodynamic therapist decides to step over the boundary, keeping one foot on the solid ground of interpretationism, where could she/he plant the other foot to avoid the quicksand of objectivism? I propose that if therapists place both feet on a platform constructed of particular developmental principles, they will discover there is solid ground that integrates both points of view. To set the stage for this proposal, we consider first how development is viewed in cognitive-behavioral and psychodynamic therapies with children.

> ## WHAT ROLE DO DEVELOPMENTAL PRINCIPLES PLAY IN COGNITIVE-BEHAVIORAL THERAPY?

Traditionally, developmental considerations have not been of central importance in cognitive-behavioral therapy. For example, the term *development* does not appear in the index of Meichenbaum's (1977) early influential volume, and is absent from the indexes of more recent volumes (e.g., Hollin 1990, Hughes 1988). However, several cognitive-behavioral therapists have given attention to developmental considerations. Kendall and Morison (1984), noting the importance of taking into account a child's "developmental level," pointed out, for example, that before the age of 5 or 6, self-instruction training may not be a desirable technique. Instead, young children should get a "heavy dose" of adult praise and coping models. For these authors development equals chronological age. "Developmental level (or simply age) is an important consideration that is directly implicated in the proper execution of a training procedure" (p. 286). That a child's chronological age should be considered when selecting a technique, especially self-instruction training, was expressed again by Kendall (Kendall and Braswell 1985) and echoed by others (e.g., Matson and Ollendick 1988, Meyers and Craighead 1984, O'Connor 1993). Other cognitive-behavioral therapists have defined development not as equal to age but in terms of Piaget's theory of cognitive stages. The relevance of this theory for clinical practice has been discussed by several writers (e.g., Cohen and Schleser 1984, Shirk 1988, Sollod and Wachtel 1980). Reviewed elsewhere (see Issues II and III), at the foundation of Piaget's model of development is the concept of schemas, mental structures by which a person represents, adapts to, and organizes experiences with things, and that undergo intrinsic change from birth to early adolescence. In Piaget's theory the concept of schemas is supplemented by two processes that are developmentally invariant: organization and adaptation. Organization assumes that cognitive structures are organized into a totality and interrelated so that a change in one part produces changes throughout the cognitive system. The concept of adaptation assumes that new experiences are assimilated into and become a part of already existing cognitive structures. As new stimuli are encountered, existing schemas reorganize, accommodating to the properties and demands unique to these stimuli. The relationship between assimilation and accommodation defines what Piaget termed "equilibration" and determines growth. When assimilation and accommodation are in a state of balance, equilibrium exists; when in a state of imbalance, disequilibrium exists. Piaget proposed that cognitive functioning inherently strives to reduce states of disequilibrium and to achieve equilibrium. A number of cognitive-behavioral therapists have made use of Piaget's theory of schema development when planning treatment programs for children (e.g., Guidano and Liotti 1983, Knell 1995, McMullin 1986).

WHAT ROLE DO DEVELOPMENTAL PRINCIPLES PLAY IN PSYCHODYNAMIC THERAPY?

Almost from the beginning, psychodynamic therapy was formulated by Freud in developmental terms. Unlike Piaget, Freud focused on cognitive regulation of representations of drives rather than on cognitive activity involving encounters with external stimulation. Because many revisions of this theory were introduced by Freud and others over a span of fifty years (e.g., Kay 1972, Rapaport 1960, Wolman 1972), I will mention only particular concepts that have relevance from my thesis.

As we discussed earlier (see Issue III), Freud's initial theory was devoid of developmental considerations, conceptualizing behavior in terms of a stimulus–response model. He then switched to a developmental perspective, proposing in 1897 that reports by patients did not refer to real experiences as such but to childhood fantasies, and that these fantasies represented wishes that gratified innate, progressively maturing, unconscious representations of "instinctual drives" (urges, emotions). Freud considered instinctual drives as "constitutional factors" interacting with environmental stimulation, or "accidental factors," in determining behavior.

> [T]he constitutional factor must await experience before it can make itself felt; the accidental factor must have a constitutional basis in order to come into operation. To cover the majority of cases we can picture . . . "a complemental series" in which the diminishing intensity of one factor is balanced by the increasing intensity of the other. [1905, pp. 239–240]

As the reader may notice, Freud's conception of development at this point seems to be similar to the one Piaget formulated some years later. Representations of instinctual drives maturating intrinsically (independent of prior experience) are similar to Piaget's concept of cognitive schemas maturating intrinsically. And the notion of a "complemental series" between constitutional and environmental factors is similar to Piaget's notions of cognitive assimilation and accommodation involved in a process of equilibration.

While Freud (1923, 1930, 1932) thought that a number of relatively independent instincts derived from various bodily zones, he eventually settled on two major instincts. One concerned the notion of "libido" or love and construction (usually referred to as the sexual instinct). When he could not explain why people sometimes wish to destroy others and inflict pain, he postulated a second major instinct, aggression or destruction. He drew an analogy between the sexual instinct, sometimes referred to as *Eros*, and the physiological process of anabolism. The aim of the sexual instinct is to create and preserve life, to bind elements of life together, "by bringing about a more and more far-reaching combination [a more complex-differentiated organization] of the particles into which living substance is dispersed" (1923, p. 40). Similarly, he drew an analogy between the aggressive instinct, sometimes referred to as the *Death Instinct*, and the physiological process of catabolism. The aim of the aggressive instinct is to destroy things by undoing connections of the particles into which living substance is dispersed.

The sexual instinct became the focus of the first major elaboration of his developmental theory. In 1905 he conceptualized that the maturation of the sexual instinct moved through several invariant "psychosexual" stages during the first five years of life. Each stage was defined in terms of experiences with a particular body zone that dominates as the vehicle symbolizing the self and interactions with others. From birth to about the age of 18–24 months (oral stage), experiences such as eating, sucking, and body/tactile sensations shape the first symbols of self and others. Primary identification, or the wish to be like another person, is an early emotional attitude that emerges at this time. The infant swallows what it loves and loves what it swallows.

After the age of 2 (anal stage) experiences with the anus that expels and retains dominate in the construction of symbols, experiences involving pleasure with urinating and defecating. In addition, the toddler now is required to accommodate to the environment's opposition to these pleasures by prescribing when and where the toddler is to relieve her/his bladder and bowels. Meanings such as rebelling, defying, and submitting are organized now. Feces could take on the meaning of a gift to parents, or a part of one's body that one does not want to give up. In the phallic stage of development (3–5 years), experiences with genital organs dominate in producing symbols, now emphasizing meaning such as power, ascendance, and anxiety over losing power.

The Oedipus complex emerges from the phallic stage. While the child loves both parents, erotic fantasies are experienced involving the parent of the opposite gender (e.g., the 4-year-old boy tells his mother he wants to marry her and the 4-year-old girl asks father to take her with him on a trip, noting that mother is too old and may die). These fantasies are accompanied by others representing the parent of the opposite sex as competition, a threat, and someone to hate—emotions that conflict with the love the child has already evolved. How this configuration is resolved by a child plays a pivotal role in whether and what type of behavioral symptoms and conflicts emerge later.

Following the phallic stage, with its Oedipus complex, psychological development enters the "latency phase" (6–11 years). Sexual tensions are sublimated and eventually subside, and a sense of self identity is stabilized. Then, in adolescence, with its biological changes, the same dynamics involving receiving, giving, resisting, submitting, ascending, and so forth erupt again and are renegotiated with parents, sibs, peers, and teachers.

Freud's view of development included another closely related concept. As representations of instinctual drives mature, they are restrained and regulated by other intrinsic factors. The emphasis Freud gave to factors that restrain and regulate representations (schemas) is one major feature distinguishing psychodynamic and Piagetian developmental theories. Freud conceptualized these restraining factors as the "ego," which consists of various cognitive processes such as perception, thinking, and memory. The task of the ego is to distinguish between, manage, and coordinate stimuli from representations of drives and environments and restrain the push for action that emerges from representations of instinctual urges. These urges are restrained when cognition shifts from "primary process" to "secondary process" thinking. Primary process thinking ignores logic, is guided by the wish for pleasure (Freud's "principle of lust," or "pleasure principle"), and demands immediate satisfaction in action. Secondary process thinking is guided by the requirements of efficient adaptation (Freud's "reality principle"), and takes into account the consequences of actions and environmental prohibitions and opportunities. When actions are delayed, a "hallucinatory"(mental) image is constructed that substitutes for the need-satisfying event. The notion that images substitute for actual things forecast Piaget's concept of "internalized imitation" and Stern's concepts of "representations of interactions" and "evoked companion" (discussed in Part V).

Freud proposed another cognitive development that restrained the urge for action. Conceptualized as the child's conscience, the "superego" begins to develop during the anal phase and continues developing thereafter. Motivated by the fear of punishment and the need for affection, a child gradually "internalizes" (assimilates) the demands and expectations of parents and eventually constructs mental representations (superego) that consider these rules as her/his own. The superego functions as a self-observer, and this organization of internalized standards confronts the ego with its own demands.

With another elaboration, Freud proposed that an "ego ideal" develops that also tames and restrains the demands of the id. He conceptualized an aspect of the superego (parental values) as an ideal to give special attention to the phenomenon that a child idealizes particular attributes of parents. The representations that make up the ego ideal serve as a source of "self love" (or what others refer to as self-esteem) whenever a standard has been met successfully. If the ego ideal is not fulfilled, a sense of guilt (social anxiety) derived from the fear of loss of love is experienced.

Various aspects of Freud's developmental theory were elaborated by others. For example, Anna Freud (1946) described mechanisms of defense (see Issue III) that the ego uses to coordinate the demands of representations of instincts and environments. Heinz Hartmann (1939) elaborated a psychology of the ego in terms of the issue of adaptation (see Issue VI). And Erikson (1950) proposed stages of psychosocial development to elaborate Freud's psychosexual stages. In the past two decades psychodynamic researchers have focused on infant development. In contrast to Freud's position that the Oedipus complex shapes a child's personality, these investigators have elaborated how experiences in the first two years of life contribute significantly to the formation of personality (e.g., Lichtenberg 1983, Mahler 1979, Sander 1969, 1975, 1989, Stern 1985). We consider infant research in Part V.

The concepts of psychosexual stages and mental structures such as id, ego, and superego have played a major role for years in how psychodynamic therapy is planned and conducted when treating children (e.g., Cangelosi 1993, Coppolillo 1987, Faust 1993, Hammer and Kaplan 1967, Pearson 1968, Wolman 1972). Moreover, the developmental concept of regression and progression in functioning is considered critical. A major goal of psychodynamic therapy is to facilitate the emergence of developmentally early forms of behavior (e.g., wishes, behaviors, fantasies) that, if expressed by a patient, provide the therapist with opportunities to access disturbances in a person's development that contribute to her/his present problems.

CONCLUDING COMMENT

Cognitive-behavioral therapists have considered skills that a child must already have developed in order to benefit from some intervention. Others have turned to Piaget's concept of the intrinsic unfolding of mental schemas representing cognitive actions on things. Psychodynamic therapists have turned to Freud's psychosexual stages; the development of ego, id, superego, and ego ideal; and the notion that therapy should permit developmentally early forms of behaving to emerge so that disturbances in development can be addressed.

Earlier I proposed that a developmental platform would prevent a therapist from stepping into the quicksand of either objectivism or interpretationism and provide the glue for integration. But where would we find such a theory? Here we reach an impasse. Choosing a developmental theory is complicated, given that the concept of development is a protean one (Kaplan 1959, Nagel 1957, Reese and Overton 1970, Wohlwil 1973). Development is variously taken to refer to growth, achievement of a new response, attainment of an ideal end-state, change occurring over time, or any observation employing children of different ages. No single, generally accepted theory of psychological development exists. Rather, several schools have emerged, each offering various concepts. Among these are social-learning theory; the developmental theory of psychoanalysis; the cognitive-developmental theories of Jean Piaget, Heinz Werner, and Jerome Bruner; the field theory of Kurt Lewin; and the biological-systems theory of Ludwig von Bertalanffy.

The child psychotherapist, then, finds that developmental concepts do not live in a single house but in many varied houses. When we look inside one we find thinking and cognition with emotion absent, social learning with unconscious fantasies absent, interpersonal transactions with cognition and emotion absent, or differences in terms of chronological age, with infant development residing in one, childhood development in another, and adolescent development in another. The field of life-span developmental psychology has emerged to counter this compartmentalizing, emphasizing that the same developmental principles can serve the study of behaviors from birth to old age (e.g., Baltes and Schaie 1973, Goulet and Baltes 1970). In my view, because integrating child psychotherapies requires a single model of development, I found it necessary to construct a conceptual scaffold. But which planks of the many offered address the various issues we have considered? We answer this question in Part V.

WHAT NEEDS SHOULD BE MET WHEN INTEGRATING CHILD PSYCHOTHERAPY?

The ten issues we have considered give rise to the following needs that should be met when integrating child psychotherapy:

1. Define how developmental principles synthesize therapeutic concepts and their operational definitions, integrating child psychotherapies.

2. Design treatment techniques that connect outside/surface behaviors with inside/deep behaviors and that interrelate a person's actions, fantasies, and verbalizations.
3. Embed cognition within personality and operationalize cognitive functioning so that cognition and emotion, and cognitive products and structures, are integrated as one organization, serving a child when coping with opportunities and limitations of changing environments.
4. Operationalize how meanings given to early experiences contribute to the construction of meanings assigned later.
5. Operationalize conscious and unconscious processes.
6. Operationalize the environment in terms of a dialectic between child and therapist.
7. Operationalize psychological conflict as occurring both within the child's subjective world and between the child's subjective world and her/his environment.
8. Operationalize how interactions between child and therapist relate to interactions the child has experienced since infancy, and how the child–therapist relationship plays a role in the treatment process.
9. Operationalize what the therapist should do to help a child, in addition to verbal labeling and interpretation.

5

A Developmental Framework for Integrating Child Psychotherapies: The First Two Years of Life

CONTENTS

begin with the proposition that processes that take place between a child and therapist are fundamentally the same as those that take place between an infant/ child and her/his caregivers, a position expressed by some (e.g., Blatt and Behrends 1987, Kruger 1990) and implied by others (Mahoney 1980, Orlinsky and Howard 1987, Schneider 1990, Sechrest and Smith 1994). In typical development, a child and caregiver define a two-person field within which both coauthor a relationship and the experiences they share, and within which they negotiate whether the child is left free to do whatever she/he chooses or is asked by the caregiver to meet some demand. Similarly, child and therapist define a two-person matrix within which both coauthor a relationship and the experiences they share, within which they negotiate whether the child plays freely or is asked to imitate self-instructions the therapist has delivered. This view of therapy, then, does not ask what knowledge the therapist should provide a child to help her/him resolve problems and grow psychologically. Rather, this view asks how should a troubled child construct knowledge with another person, and continually revise that knowledge, to promote psychological growth (see Lear 1990 for a similar position). To translate this point of view into therapeutic techniques, I have constructed a developmental model cast within a metaphor of a three-story house (Table 5–1).

The Foundation: Integrating the Concepts of Sigmund Freud, Jean Piaget, and Heinz Werner

Why did I select the concepts of Freud, Piaget, and Werner for the foundation of my conceptual model, omitting, for example, social learning therapy? More than three decades ago two leading developmental researchers and theorists, D. B. Harris (1957) and A. L. Baldwin (1967), evaluated major developmental theories and recommended that any model should contain the following:

1. Conceptualize individuals as active systems, maintaining some degree of integrity, stability, and self-regulation.
2. View change as involving a transition from behaviors that display undifferentiated organizations to behaviors that display differentiated organizations, defining psychological functioning at several levels.
3. Include intrinsic development (i.e., maturation) as well as change due to external stimulation.
4. Account for how new behaviors are acquired for the first time.
5. Include as equally relevant overt acts, thoughts, feelings, fantasies, drives, and inhibiting behaviors as well as involuntary behaviors.

TABLE 5–1.   A Developmental House Integrating Child and Adolescent Psychotherapies

Third floor	Guidelines for therapeutic techniques that define how child and therapist negotiate and enact the demands of each other, construct knowledge about the self, each other, and others, and facilitate psychological growth
Second floor	Three models of development from age 3 to adolescence: (1) life metaphors that represent past negotiations with developmental issues, construe and give meaning to present stimulation, and prescribe actions; (2) cognitive-behavioral regulators that equilibrate demands from life metaphors and environments; (3) action, fantasy, and language behaviors used to negotiate developmental issues with others in adaptations
Stairway to the second floor	Embodiment-enactment theory: experiences during infancy extend into and influence what a person does, imagines, and says during childhood and adolescence
First floor	Principles of development during the first three years of life from the models of Piaget, Stern, Sander, Beebe, and Lachmann
Foundation	An integration of propositions from the developmental theories of Freud, Piaget, and Werner

An integration of concepts from the theories of Freud, Piaget, and Werner produces a set of developmental principles that satisfy these recommendations. The interested reader is referred elsewhere (Santostefano 1978, Santostefano and Baker 1972) for a more detailed presentation of these principles and a review of research findings that support them.

WHAT IS THE PRINCIPLE OF HOLISM?

The psychological properties and meaning of any behavior are determined by the total context of which they are a part. Two behaviors similar in form may be psychologically different if embedded in different contexts; for example, a 5-year-old hurls a wooden block while playing in his backyard and another while in his kindergarten classroom. At the same time, two behaviors that are different in form could be psychologically the same if embedded in similar contexts; for example, a 5-year-old kicks the family's pet kitten and also breaks his baby brother's rattle.

WHAT ARE THE PRINCIPLES OF PSYCHOLOGICAL GIVENS. AND DIRECTIVENESS OF BEHAVIOR?

Rather than passively experiencing stimulation, an individual makes use of innately given behavioral structures, or modes of functioning, such as motoric rhythm patterns, sensory thresholds, and emotional/cognitive response styles. These modes enable the individual to actively approach, avoid, select, and organize stimulation, and to take action in order to accomplish some intention and/or to effect change in her/his relationship with the environment. A fit usually exists between a person's innately given behavioral structures and the type, pace, and intensity of stimulation provided by others. With a good fit, a person's experiences provide psychological nourishment for growth. When inadequately matched, a person's experiences become obstacles to growth. In an effort to maintain synchrony between self and other, an individual regulates her/his behavioral responses at a pace that ensures coordination and mutuality between her/his evolving psychological structures and ever-changing stimulation in the environment. An individual's attempt to maintain integrity in the midst of changing stimulation is related to the individual's tendency to develop toward relatively mature states under the widest range of conditions. Whenever development occurs, it proceeds in a particular direction: from organizations of behaviors that are relatively global to organizations that are differentiated and hierarchically integrated.

WHAT ARE THE PRINCIPLES OF STAGES OF DEVELOPMENT, MULTIPLE BEHAVIORAL MODES AND GOALS, AND CONSISTENT INDIVIDUAL DIFFERENCES?

When functioning at a developmentally early stage, the individual uses one, or a few, behavioral modes, and her/his responses show little delay and require physical contact with the environment. Gradually the individual differentiates from the environment and functions with several differentiated modes that are capable of operating in contact with, or in the absence of, related environmental stimulation. For example, in Piaget's model the infant initially gathers information about the texture of objects by mouthing and touching them (sensorimotor mode). With development, the infant constructs mental schemas representing these physical activities and is now able to determine the texture of some object by surveying it from a distance (perceptual mode) as well as by touching it. Progression from one stage in a sequence to the next results in the individual's having available multiple means to achieve the same goal. For example, a child may either fantasize her/his baby brother being frightened by a monster or perform some action to frighten the infant. Similarly, progressing from one stage to another results in multiple goals that can be used to serve the same mode of behaving: when frustrated by mother, a child may use the fantasy mode and imagine retaliating against an older sister, and when lonely in mother's absence, imagine receiving affection from a teacher. The availability of multiple modes and alternative goals frees the individual from the demands of the immediate situation so that behaviors may be expressed in more delayed, indirect, and stage-appropriate ways. In addition, a child is able to discover alternative ways of behaving that acknowledge opportunities and limitations in the environment. When combined with the principle of psychological givens and holism, the principle of differentiating behavioral modes proposes that individuals display consistent differences from birth throughout the life span. Last, early forms of functioning are not replaced by new behaviors. Rather, early behaviors become subordinated by and hierarchically integrated within later developing forms. Although subordinated, these early forms of behaving remain partially active. For example, a fifth grader had long since been appropriately controlled in the classroom and focused on academic tasks. Then his teacher, with whom he had a strong attachment, became ill and a substitute teacher replaced her. In this context the boy became hyperactive and defiant again, behaviors he had not shown since the first grade.

WHAT IS THE PRINCIPLE OF MOBILITY OF BEHAVIORAL FUNCTIONS?

That subordinated behaviors have the potential to become active relates to the principle of mobility of behavioral functions; that is, regression and progression of behavioral systems. When operating at a developmentally early stage, an individual does not shift easily from one behavior or level to another in response to changes in stimulation, opportunities, and limitations. In contrast, the individual operating at developmentally later stages is characterized by greater flexibility: now shifting easily, in response to changes in opportunities; sometimes operating at a level characteristic of earlier development (regressing), at other times operating at a more advanced level (progressing).

When a fourth grader gets up from her/his seat and enters the playground during recess, she/he "regresses" to the action mode—running, pushing, and wrestling in a vigorous game of King of the Mountain. Upon returning to the classroom, the same child shifts "progressively" to modes of functioning characteristic of higher levels of development. Now motility and action are delayed/

subordinated, and thinking/fantasizing dominate as she/he completes a page in a workbook. Progressive and regressive shifts are presumed to result in a "good fit" between the individual's adaptive intentions and needs (both emotional and cognitive) and limitations and expectations presented by the environment. Shifting among levels of functioning is presumed to foster development and ensure adaptive success.

WHAT IS THE PRINCIPLE OF MOTIVATING FORCES AND REGULATING STRUCTURES?

Long- and short-range motivating forces stimulate the individual to make use of innately given, motoric, cognitive, and emotional functions. Long-range forces correspond to representations of instinctual drives or embodied experiences (see Part IV, Issue X). Representations of drives continually push for immediate expression in action and are inherently directed toward particular persons, objects, and interactions. At the same time, psychological structures that regulate and restrain long-range forces also develop. Long-range forces are usually regulated by substituting one goal for another, and by making use of alternative modes of behaving whenever the sought-for object, or preferred mode of expression, is unavailable because of intrapsychic or environmental circumstances.

Consider, for example, a 3-year-old longing to be cuddled by mother who is away on a trip. This toddler may cuddle mother's wool sweater as an alternative goal that substitutes for mother's body and permits the toddler to continue expressing, in the action mode, the representation of the instinctual drive of affection. Now, at age 6, with the fantasy mode and representational thought more differentiated and mature, the child does not resort to action, but mentally entertains a scene, imagining mother's return and caress. Regulating mechanisms, then, redirect and modify the representations of long-range forces, enabling the individual to coordinate various forms of behavioral expression with changes created by the environment.

Short-range motivating forces include, for example, curiosity and the need for change and complexity. The psychodynamic concept of "stimulus nutriment" (Rapaport, cited in Gill 1967) and Piaget's concept of "alimentation" (Flavell 1963) define the process of short-range forces. These concepts propose that individuals must "nourish" their cognitive schemas by repeatedly assimilating environmental "nutriments" that sustain them. Recall that Piaget conceptualized that whenever schemas are in a state of moderate disequilibrium with existing stimulation that is slightly more complex in organization than the schemas, cognition is motivated to repeatedly assimilate the more complex information and to gradually accommodate (reorganize) the schema to fit the complexity of the stimulation. In normal cognitive development, then, cognitive structures are motivated to seek a level of complexity of information that is only slightly greater than the complexity of the organization of existing schemas.

Rapaport elaborated this concept to address the derailed cognitive development that patients typically present. His concept of "stimulus nutriment" elaborated Piaget's concept of "alimentation." Cognitive structures may lag in assimilating and differentiating, or may remain fixated in organization, whenever they become part of an organized mental defense or coping strategy. In these cases the "nourishment" for a cognitive structure comes from the avoidance of stress and anxiety rather than from more complex information in the environment. Unlike long-range forces, short-term forces are not directed inherently toward particular interactions with persons or things. Rather, they seek and avoid particular organizations, qualities, degrees, and tempos of stimulation, and are motivated to maintain a state of equilibration between cognitive structures and information contained both in the environment and in a person's subjective world.

WHAT IS THE PRINCIPLE OF ADAPTATION?

Adaptation involves a reciprocal-dialectical relationship between the individual and her/his environment (e.g., parent, teacher, peer). Each defines the other and each is defined by the other, becoming poles on a continuum that inherently forms a paradox concerning the intentions of each. To deal with this paradox, person and environment negotiate with each other, in continuous cycles of interaction, to achieve a mutually agreed-upon degree of coordination. The individual acts on the environment, making use of an evolving series of average and expectable behavioral organizations (cognitions, actions, fantasies, spoken words) that more or less match environmental expectations and opportunities. At the same time, the environment acts on the individual through a continuous, evolving series of average-expectable organizations of stimulation that more or less fit the behavioral modes available to the individual. In this dialectic, then, the individual has available behavioral modes that are preadapted to handle expectations from the environment, while the environment usually provides opportunities and limitations that suit the individual's stage of development.

Demands from the individual and environment are never perfectly matched, however. In adapting to these mismatches the individual shifts from a more recently acquired level of responding to earlier levels, or evolves a new, differentiated mode. Consider a 4-year-old who enters a preschool classroom for the first time, an environment that requires him to share and wait more than he does at home. At first the child responds to this change, and the frustration it arouses, by regressing to behavior he used earlier, withdrawing to a corner of the room. Gradually, as the child negotiates with teacher and peers, he transforms his withdrawn behavior into helping the teacher distribute crayons. Although the adaptive process occurs continuously at certain critical periods within the life span, particular behavioral systems are especially ready to deal with and assimilate particular classes of stimulation. If the critical experience is not made available, the behavioral system assumes a deviant line of growth. Considering the 4-year-old again, if the teacher is not active and creative in engaging the child to join the group, the child's use of withdrawal may persist as a way to manage a prohibition.

Last, the individual and environment, in their dialectical process, determine which behaviors and stimulation are adaptive. One individual may experience a particular context as average and expectable, for example, an inner-city child and a rural child each playing in her/his community. But if an inner-city child is transferred suddenly to a rural street and the suburban child to an inner-city street, each would experience stimulation that is not average and expectable for her/him, and the behavior each displays could be viewed as a developmental failure. Thus behavior viewed as adaptive in one situation may be a developmental failure when resorted to by the same individual in other contexts.

CONCLUDING COMMENT

The proposed foundation does not play a significant role in current approaches to treatment with children except for psychodynamic therapies in which one or another principle can be found. There are exceptions, and one is represented by Brems's (1993) volume, which provided excellent summaries of several developmental models. However, she did not connect developments during the first years of life with those that occur later and have relevance for psychotherapy integration. Instead, from a discussion of infant development she described development in 4- and 5-year-old children and in middle childhood (6–10 years old) as a separate topic, because "infants are never and toddlers are rarely seen in psychotherapy" (p. 57). I take a very different approach. In the next sections, principles of development of the first two years of life that derive from the foundation we have just considered are extended into childhood and then into guidelines for treatment. At this point we leave the foundation and climb to the first floor, where we begin at the beginning and consider how knowledge is constructed during the first two years of life.

The First Floor: How Knowledge about Self and Others Is Constructed during the First Two Years of Life, and How Cognitive Behavioral Modalities Are First Organized

Following the pioneering research of Piaget, infant investigators, many influenced by psychodynamic views, have gathered observations that articulate how an infant constructs knowledge about herself/himself and others, and how an infant gives meaning to experiences, whether touching the fringe of a pillow or mother's hair. These investigators take the position that knowledge an infant constructs, and environments with which the infants negotiates, are shaped by the infant's representational activity so that an infant's subjective world and environment become one. What the child knows, does, and feels is what the child represents. This position converges with Bohart's (1993) proposal, discussed earlier, that the construction of knowledge and meaning is embedded within all experiencing and occurs at various levels from embodied, nonverbal experiences to conceptual, verbal experiences. If we accept the principle, located in the foundation of our model, that early experiences (behaviors) are not replaced by later behaviors but become integrated within them, then the ways in which a child constructs knowledge and meanings during treatment have their roots in the first years of life. Therefore we need to conceptualize how meanings constructed in the first years of life are extended and assimilated into meanings and behaviors that emerge after the age of 3. To address this need I draw upon formulations of five infant investigators (Table 5–2). Each brings into focus a particular set of considerations that, when integrated, provide a particularly useful view when integrating child psychotherapies.

HOW DOES PIAGET DESCRIBE THE WAYS IN WHICH KNOWLEDGE AND MEANINGS ARE CONSTRUCTED DURING THE FIRST TWO YEARS OF LIFE?

Piaget proposed that the processes involved in constructing knowledge during the first two years of life define six stages. In Stage I (0–1 months) the infant experiences various bodily sensations (sucking, tactile and gross body perceptions, sounds) when contacting her/his own body and the environment. These experiences gradually shift from being mere reflexes to "acquired adaptations" that are repeated, resulting in the beginnings of mental schemas or representation of bodily experiences.

In Stage II (1–4 months) acquired adaptations are elaborated into "primary circular reactions." Now the infant repeatedly engages in activity that coordinates schemas representing experiences with different modalities (vision and touch, sound and touch, one body sensation and another). The infant sucks her/his thumb not because of chance contact, but through coordinating hand and mouth, coordination that relies on schemas that derived from previous experiences with each of these body parts.

During Stage III (4–8 months) the infant engages in "secondary circular reactions" and is concerned with consequences in the environment that result from her/his activity. Now the infant repeats behaviors to "make interesting sights last." Since these repetitive behaviors are attempts to sustain interesting contacts with environments, the infant begins to be oriented beyond the self. For example, the

TABLE 5-2. Models of Development in the First Two Years of Life

PIAGET		STERN		SANDER	
Months	Cognitive Development	Months	Self-Development	Months	Infant (I)—Mother (M) Negotiations
(0–1)	Acquired adaptation	(0–2)	Emergent self: relate diverse experiences (emotions, bodily events) in interactions with caregiver and things	(0–3)	Initial adaptation: I's cues and M's activity become coordinated
(2–4)	Primary circular reactions: rhythmic cycles of activity coordinating schemas (experiences) with different modalities			(3–6)	Reciprocal exchange: organizing crescendos of emotional/behavioral exchanges
		(2–7)	Core self: construct first representations of interaction that summarize and conserve repeated experiences with others, including constellations of actions, sensations, and emotions	(6–9)	Early directed activity: I actively controls stimulation and anticipates some response; M accommodates by remaining passive and/or responding to direction
(4–8)	Secondary circular reactions: provoking responses from the environment and making interesting sights last			(9–15)	Focalization: I's directions to M more differentiated in having needs met, including protection from danger; I explores unknown; M unconditionally available
(8–12)	Coordinate secondary circular reaction: imitate action of others			(12–20)	Self assertion: with newly formed autonomy, I asserts self in opposition to M; M gives permission and sets limits
(12–18)	Tertiary circular reactions: discovering new ways of accomplishing goals, performing actions that become play rituals	(7–14)	Subjective self: sense and understand motives and intentions of others that lie behind and guide physical actions	(18–24)	Testing aggression: I's assertions become explicitly aggressive behaviors; I attempts to "make up"; M punishes, permits, and provides alternatives
				(24–36)	Modifying aggression: I develops multiple modes for expressing aggression; M continues to provide alternatives
(18–24)	Experimenting with mental representations of things: imitate persons who are absent—deferred imitation	(15–24)	Verbal self: verbal symbols shared in language as well as actions, facilitated by deferred imitation	(12–36)	Inventing symbolic behaviors that are shared: in sharing and inventing symbols, I and M increase their understanding of other's intentions and of alternatives available for mutual regulation
				(0–36)	Consolidate body image

infant deliberately imitates a movement performed by another so that the other will continue to perform that movement, each participating in a cycle of interactions and sharing "intentions."

In Stage IV (8–12 months) the mental schemas of secondary circular reactions become coordinated to form a new totality that deals with new situations. For example, the infant sets aside an obstacle (e.g., a sheet of cardboard) in order to reach a desired object (e.g., a rattle), and does so repeatedly, frequently with laughter. In addition, the infant is now able to imitate actions of others with behaviors that are structurally analogous. When Piaget opened and closed his eyes, for instance, the infant first opened and closed his hands, and then his mouth.

In Stage V (12–18 months) secondary circular reactions give rise to "tertiary circular reactions," behaviors the infant uses to actively experiment with the environment in order to discover new ways of accomplishing goals. To obtain a toy placed under a blanket, the infant repeatedly explores different ways to pull the blanket away. In another significant development the infant transforms the behavior of a tertiary circular reaction into a play ritual. For example, Piaget described his infant daughter, who one day pressed her nose against her mother's cheek, forcing the infant to breathe much more loudly. "This phenomenon at once interested her . . . she drew her nose back . . . sniffed and breathed very hard (as if she were blowing her nose) then again thrust her nose against her mother's cheek, laughing heartily" (quoted in Flavell 1963, p. 128). The infant repeated these actions at least once a day for more than a month "as a ritual."

In Stage VI (18–24) the infant continues to invent new ways of accomplishing things, but now relies more on mental experimentations rather than on trial and error actions. Thus the infant is able to acquire new knowledge prior to taking action. For example, a carriage is set against the wall. Instead of tugging and pushing in trial and error experimentation, the toddler looks over the situation, walks to the other side, and pushes the carriage away from the wall. With another important development the infant shows the capacity for "deferred imitation." When an important person or thing is absent, the toddler reproduces the person or thing, showing that she/he is capable of true pretending. As discussed earlier (see Part IV), the child is now symbolizing by transferring properties from one object to another. For example, upon observing mother put on a hat and leave the room, the toddler places a napkin on her/his head, pretending that it is a hat.

HOW DOES STERN DESCRIBE THE WAYS IN WHICH KNOWLEDGE AND MEANING ARE CONSTRUCTED DURING THE FIRST TWO YEARS OF LIFE?

Stern's model (1985) elaborates Piaget's, emphasizing the role of emotions and interpersonal interactions in the construction of knowledge and meaning. The infant's experiences with things and persons are unified wholes (the principle of holism) that include sensations, perceptions, actions, cognitions, "categorical emotions" (anger, joy), and "vitality affects" (surging, exploding, fading). Stern emphasized that all knowledge and meanings are constructed within subjective experiences that always involve other persons and may involve inanimate things. Instead of using one of Stern's examples, an observation Piaget used to illustrate primary circular reactions serves as an illustration.

> [The infant] scratches and tries to grasp, lets go, scratches and grasps again . . . this can only be observed during feeding time when the infant gently scratches his mother's bare shoulder. [Then, a few days later when in the cradle, the infant] scratches the [bed] sheet, then grasps it and holds it a moment, then lets it go . . . [now Piaget places his fist against the back of the infant's right hand] . . . [the infant] scratches and grasps my fist. . . . [in the next few days] I note . . . regular, rhythmical activity, scratching, grasping, holding and letting go and finally progressive lost of interest. [Flavell 1963, pp. 93–94]

Piaget focused on the infant's rhythmic grasping, holding and letting go of a bed sheet. Stern would focus on the infant's rhythmic scratching of mother's shoulder and father's fist as well as the bed sheet. He would also emphasize the emotions involved during these moments; for example, the infant's interest and emotions surged when grasping the shoulder and sheet, and then faded when letting go. As constellations of sensations, perceptions, emotions, and actions are repeatedly experienced with persons and things, these elements are integrated and conserved as "*Representations of Interactions* [that have] *Generalized*" (RIGs), or prototypes that prescribe what the infant expects and how the infant performs.

When an experience is similar but not identical to previously repeated experiences, the already established RIG is activated as an "evoked companion." Consider a mother who plays peek-a-boo in a different way because she is now depressed. In response, the infant uses the evoked companion from an already established RIG as a standard against which to check whether mother's current emotional tone is a variation of the past or an entirely new type of self–other experience. If mother's depression endures, a new RIG is constructed by the infant. Evoked companions also operate when the infant is alone. Consider a toddler who, while alone, stacks one block on another, bursting with exuberance. The child's exuberance is not due solely to experiencing success with objects, but also relates to the evoked memory of stacking blocks while an enthusiastic caregiver cheered. The process of constructing RIGs and evoked companions results in the emergence of four "senses of self."

Emergent Self (0–2 Months)

The infant relates diverse experiences in interaction with caregivers and things that result in emotions, sensorimotor experiences, and the first global meanings.

Core Self (2–7 Months)

The infant constructs the first RIGs summarizing repeated experiences with persons and things that include constellations of sensations, actions, and emotional tones. The infant is now equipped to anticipate what should be expected in interactions with others, and whether a given experience is the same or different from previous ones. Further, the infant begins to sense that she/he and the caregiver are different agents with different emotional experiences.

Subjective Self (7–14 Months)

Self and others are defined by more than the physical presence of infant and caregiver, each sharing actions and emotions. This new sense of self includes subjective mental states in that the infant senses and understands the motives and intentions that lie behind and guide physical happenings.

Verbal Self (15–24 Months)

Interactions between infant and caregiver are organized by the perspective that each of them contains personal knowledge that, in addition to action symbols, is expressed and shared in language symbols.

HOW DOES SANDER DESCRIBE THE WAY IN WHICH KNOWLEDGE AND MEANING ARE CONSTRUCTED DURING THE FIRST YEARS OF LIFE?

Sander (1962, 1964, 1976, 1989) elaborates the contributions of Piaget and Stern, emphasizing that infant and mother are involved in a continuous process of give and take, with each attempting to influence and accommodate to the other in mutual adaptations. He conceptualized this process as mother and infant "negotiating" particular "issues," negotiations that contribute to the organization and development of the infant's cognition, motility style, expressions of emotions, and meanings. The manner in which mother and infant negotiate one issue influences the success with which they negotiate the next. While Sander describes infant and mother negotiating, other persons who are significantly involved in the infant's care (e.g., father, aunt, grandparent) would also be viewed as partners in these negotiations.

Issue #1 (0–3 Months): Period of Initial Adaptation

In the first months, mother and infant negotiate a fit between the baby's states (alert inactivity, various cries, smiling) and mother's behaviors (type and timing of stimulation—rapid, delayed, consistent), which she provides when feeding and bathing the infant. Success in negotiating this issue is reflected by the degree to which the infant develops a predictable, organized rhythm of feeding, eliminating, sleeping, and wakefulness. In addition, the infant responds to the caregiver in a discriminating way, quieting for her more readily than for others. Success is also reflected by mother's developing a subjective sense that she "knows" her child and maintains a balance between her empathy for the infant's needs and her objectivity.

Issue #2 (3–6 Months): Period of Establishing Reciprocal Exchange

Negotiations now emphasize back-and-forth, active-passive exchanges between infant and mother. Sander gives special importance to exchanges that take place around the infant's rapidly developing smiling response. Mother smiles and pauses, allowing the baby to respond. Then mother moves her smiling face closer, waits for the infant to react, and then makes another presentation, now adding a new stimulus such as a touch or vocalization. Throughout this back-and-forth process the infant gradually elaborates her/his response, beginning with a localized smile, then including arms, legs, trunk, and voice in "exuberant, wiggling, infectious, joyful play." The quality, crescendo, and organization occurring in this reciprocal activity is crucial. Reciprocal exchanges occur during various child-care activities (feeding, changing, bathing). An important related issue concerns whether mother can allow the child to pursue some solo activity.

Issue #3 (6–9 Months): Period of Early Directed Behavior

Up to this point, interactions are largely due to mother's initiative. Now the baby begins to use smiling to initiate and direct social contact with mother. Several behavioral dimensions become important. The infant intends to engage a person and some form of stimulation, and anticipates in turn some response. Further, the baby begins to show preferences for types of stimulation while attempting to control or avoid other stimulation. These qualities are seen in the well-known stranger anxiety that appears during this stage. In crying and fussing when a stranger appears, the baby is attempting to control and direct stimulation. At the same time, the infant becomes more active, reaching out to manipulate and avoid physical objects. The major accommodation required of mother during this period is that she remain passive more often than was required previously. In response to the infant's direction, mother should honor her/his preferences for particular experiences and objects that she removes or brings within the infant's reach.

Issue #4 (9–15 Months): Period of Focalization

The infant's directed activity now becomes increasingly more differentiated as she/he sends explicit cues to mother, focusing on her as someone who is unconditionally available, an important ingredient in the infant's developing autonomy. Since the child is able to explore larger space, she/he sends cues to mother that concern the need to be protected from danger and also to enter the unknown. If mother responds adequately, while maintaining the reciprocity already negotiated, she makes available a stable base from which the child can move away from her and explore increasingly larger geographies where the toddler experiments with competence and curiosity.

Issue #5 (12–20 Months): Period of Self-Assertion

As the child experiences autonomy, her/his assertion in opposition to mother becomes the focus of their negotiations. With curiosity and motor skills growing, with a secure feeling that she/he can separate from mother yet have her available, the toddler begins to show negativism ("No!"), possessiveness ("Mine!"), temper outbursts, and exhibitionism (e.g., when naked, the toddler dashes into the living room filled with company). In response, mother sets limits and gives permission. Toilet training introduced at this time becomes one arena in which these negotiations take place, along with getting dressed and mealtime. Mother's responses could vary in terms of consistency and the imagination she uses in suggesting alternatives. For example, if a child insists on exploring a potentially dangerous kitchen utensil, mother could offer another that is relatively safe. To make further gains in autonomy, a child should sense that her/his victories when being assertive can be accepted by mother. If mother's behaviors are severely limiting, the child could surrender the push for self-assertion. As a result, the child's explorations of the environment, curiosity and learning, and interactions with others become inhibited.

Issue #6 (18–24 Months): Period of Initial Testing of Destructive Aggression

The child's assertiveness gradually gives rise to explicit, aggressive intentions—destroy some object, scatter materials, injure another child. In addition, the child is often aggressive toward household items that are especially valued by mother ("He knew that was my favorite vase! I told him not to touch it!"), and shows a sense of triumph when performing acts of aggression. The child may attempt to "make up" with mother by initiating an activity that pleases her or undoing the aggressive act (e.g., sticking Scotch tape on pieces of a broken vase). To contribute to the successful negotiation of this issue, mother should distinguish among various destructive intentions (biting in play versus anger) and coordinate her responses accordingly (severe limits, physical punishment, threats of loss of love). A related consideration involves whether mother can allow alternative aggressive behaviors. For example, if the toddler is banging a toy hammer against the refrigerator, the mother could set an old pan beside it and invite the child to hammer the pan instead. The mother could also initiate a making-up process by, for example, providing the child with the opportunity to repair, or witness the repairing of, some damaged object.

Issue #7 (24–36 Months): Period of Modification of Aggressive Intentions

The child's aggressive behavior gradually becomes modified as the child accommodates to and internalizes the standards of caregivers and develops multiple modes for expressing aggression and alternative goals (e.g., the child shifts from pounding a souvenir ashtray valued by mother to pounding wooden pegs into a form board). It is important that mother provide a flexible range of opportunities for aggressing. The successful negotiation of this issue is associated with several outcomes. The child (1) shapes expressions of aggression that fit household standards; (2) modifies and renders more realistic her/his sense of omnipotence; (3) internalizes parental standards for asserting and aggressing ; and (4) begins to test these standards with other persons and environments.

Issue #8 (12–36 Months): Sharing Symbolic Behaviors Invented during Interactions

During these negotiations child and caregiver invent and share symbolic behaviors that solidify their relationship. Among the factors involved are (1) mother's ability to understand and respond to the child's symbolic behaviors and stimulate symbolic play, and (2) the extent to which the child internalizes symbolic communications invented in the process of interacting with mother.

Issue #9 (0–36 Months): Consolidation of Body Image

Throughout the first three years, the child negotiates and constructs a body image and psychosexual identification. The child expresses curiosity in her/his body, and the bodies of parents and sibs, through exhibitionistic, seductive, and autostimu-lating behaviors. Caregivers respond with interest, stimulation, and prohibitions, and child and caregiver communicate about each other's body and body parts. Throughout these transactions, the child develops perceptions of body sensations, cognitive schemas of body parts, and a sense of body self or body image.

HOW DO BEEBE AND LACHMANN DESCRIBE THE WAYS IN WHICH KNOWLEDGE AND MEANINGS ARE CONSTRUCTED DURING THE FIRST TWO YEARS OF LIFE?

Beebe and Lachmann (1994) proposed three developmental principles to concep-tualize how interactions during infancy become the foundation for the first sym-bolic representations, and how an infant gives meanings to experiences. These prin-ciples overlap conceptualizations proposed by Piaget, Stern, and Sander, but also integrate their concepts in ways that are useful in articulating techniques for child psychotherapy.

The Principle of Ongoing Regulations: The Dialectic between Self-Regulation and Mutual Regulation

Ongoing regulations consist of two interrelated systems: self-regulation by the infant and mutual regulation by infant and caregiver. With self-regulation the in-fant gradually recognizes what she/he can expect in her/his interactions with a caregiver and makes motoric and emotional adjustments in response to changes in stimulation. As these patterns of interactions are repeated, the infant constructs mental schemas that represent them. Stern's concept of "representations of inter-actions generalized," discussed above, is an example. With mutual regulation the infant and caregiver gradually develop a system of shared rules that regulate the actions of each. They develop expectations that each is affected by the other, and each affects the other in predictable ways. These expectations are also represented with schemas. Sander's concept of issues negotiated by infant and caregiver is an example of mutual regulation.

　　Ongoing regulation involves a dialectic between self-regulation and mutual regulation. A study reviewed by Beebe and Lachmann provides an illustration. During face-to-face social play between infants (2–6 months) and their mothers, the investigators recorded when the infant looked away (sometimes the mother "chased" the infant with intense stimulation) and also when the infant looked back at mother (sometimes mother lowered her stimulation). They also recorded the infant's heart rate five seconds before the infant looked away, and observed a sharp increase suggesting that the infant was stressed by the level of interaction taking place. During the five seconds just after the infant looked away, heart rate decreased sharply. When viewed in terms of mutual regulation, looking away was a strategy that was successful in avoiding stimulation that was too intense. At that same time, looking away served self-regulation since the decrease in heart rate indicated less stress. As the authors pointed out, "[T]he very same behaviors through which the infant regulates her/his arousal [e.g., looking away] function at the same time as interactive regulators" (p. 140). This study illustrated that the success with which an infant establishes self-regulation depends on whether infant and caregiver are successful in establishing mutual regulation.

With this first principle, then, Beebe and Lachmann emphasized that the construction of knowledge and representations of experiences require a dialectic between mutual and self-regulation. If the construction of knowledge and representations is viewed only in terms of the infant's self-regulations, pretty much as Freud and Piaget did, then the contribution of dyadic interactions is neglected. Or if the construction of knowledge and representations is viewed only in terms of dyadic interactions—pretty much as social-learning theory does—in which the environment molds the child or the child molds the environment, then the contribution of self-regulation is omitted. Knowledge about experiences, and meanings given to them, is constructed by both self-regulation and mutual regulation occurring at the same time.

The Principle of Disruption and Repair

Inevitably, some interactions violate the system of rules infant and mother have shared to regulate their actions with each other. Apparently, expectations of ongoing regulations are violated often. Studies show that as early as the second and third month of life infants and mothers match their behaviors (such as facial expressions, body movements, smiling) only about 30 percent of the time. However, this situation is not as bad as it appears at first glance. When mothers and infants enter a state of disruption, they return to a matched state of mutual regulation within two seconds about 70 percent of the time. Infants use various behaviors to cope with disruptions of what she/he expects when interacting with caregivers. Some strategies are adaptive (the infant continues to signal mother, or focuses on something other than mother, or engages in self-comforting behavior). Other strategies are maladaptive (the infant withdraws, or gives up postural control, or displays a disorganized state). Further, an infant's experiences with repairing disruptions correlate with cognitive-emotional development. Gradually, repairing disruptions becomes an interactive skill, as the infant constructs schemas representing a sense of hope, of being effective, feeling secure in attachments with others, and a view that repairing interpersonal disruptions is possible. For example, in one study, infants 4 to 6 months of age who had more experiences repairing disruptions also showed more secure attachments to their mothers at 12 months of age than did infants who had fewer opportunities to repair disruptions.

If repeatedly experiencing success in repairing disruptions results in schemas that represent hope and competence, it follows that repeated failure results in the expectation that there is no hope and that one is incompetent. One major source of data about chronic disruptions comes from studies of depressed mothers and their infants. These infants expect that disruptions cannot be repaired. Even when engaged by a responsive adult, these infants still respond by remaining disengaged or by protesting. In addition, they become preoccupied with self-regulation (self-stimulation) and with managing negative emotions.

The Principle of Heightened Affective Moments

While emotions accompany ongoing regulations as well as disruptions and repair of regulations, Beebe and Lachmann proposed that intense emotional experiences play a sufficiently unique role in the construction of representations to justify their being considered a separate principle of organization. Some supercharged moments during the daily rhythm of interactions between infant and caregiver exert an influence on the representation of a particular exchange that is greater than what could be attributed to timing. Examples include when a caregiver and infant coo back and forth, echoing their tones. (Recall that Sander observed infants and mothers exchanging a crescendo of emotions when negotiating reciprocal exchange.) Other highly emotional moments occur only once, or a few times, which relates to the issue of trauma. Reviewing clinical data as well as research findings, Beebe and Lachmann (1994) gave as one example an adult patient who remembered a physical sensation he termed a "stick in the tushie" (p. 149). Later it was learned that this sensation referred to a lumbar puncture the person experienced at 6 months. Another therapist described a child who had experienced multiple invasive medical procedures as an infant. During treatment, this child expressed the wish to be hurt. As one way of looking at single, heightened moments, Beebe and Lachmann referred to Stern, who proposed that while RIGs are formed by averaging a repeated pattern of interactions, sometimes one experience can exert unusual influence and give shape to a salient representation because it cannot be averaged with other similar experiences.

The Three Principles and Bodily Experiences

The three principles provide a more differentiated conceptualization of how bodily experiences are organized. Converging with Sander's proposal that body image is negotiated throughout the first years of life, Beebe and Lachmann noted that the body is involved in all interactions, since perceptions, emotions, and arousals are all bodily experiences. They also pointed out that the crucial role of body experiences is self-evident in the principle of heightened affective moments, because research has shown that heightened emotions are simultaneously heightened bodily states. That individuals form unique representations of bodily states can be inferred from the treatment of children and adults. Recall the child whose experiences were organized and represented by a heightened, negative, bodily state that prescribed the expectation that painful bodily events should occur during psychotherapy.

The Three Principles and Internalization

The main thrust of Beebe and Lachmann's critique is to show how observations of infant researchers support the view that, during the first years of life, transactions between infant and caregivers become located within the infant's mind (e.g., "internalized") as organized expectations or schemas. The process of internalization has been of central interest to psychodynamic theorists since Freud and concerns the phenomenon that a person transforms real or imagined interactions with the environment into inner regulations. Infant researchers have made two particularly significant contributions to the concept of internalization. In the first year of life, interactions that are internalized depend on the actual presence, actions, and emotional tones of others with whom the infant is transacting, a view amply demonstrated by the observations of Piaget, Stern, and Sander. Of special importance to us, there is continuity between interactions that are represented and internalized in the first years of life and those that are represented later in life. As Beebe and Lachmann (1994) pointed out, "The presymbolically represented experiences of the first year bias the developmental trajectory in transformational ways. When these experiences are later encoded symbolically, they retain the impact of the first year" (p. 155). This position converges with that of a number of authors who have articulated embodiment theory, a set of concepts to which we turn next.

Concepts from Embodiment–Enactment Theory: A Stairway to the Second Floor

I consider embodiment–enactment theory as a stairway leading from the foundation and first floor to the second floor, which concerns development after the age of 3 and beyond. This theory provides a bridge connecting experiences during the first 2 years of life with those occurring later and defines psychological change in a way that is helpful to child therapists.

WHAT IS EMBODIMENT THEORY?

Embodiment–enactment theory (Johnson 1987, Overton 1994a,b) proposes that "the mind emerges out of embodied practices that both construct and are constructed by the phenomenological world" (Overton 1994a, p. 231), and conceptualizes the mind as a relational concept, including both a person's body-self experiences (self-regulation) and experiences with others (mutual regulation). This notion is reflected by several models we have already considered. For example, Freud proposed that the first ego (that is, the first mind) is a "body ego." Piaget proposed that "action is primary" in the development of the mind, and Stern and Sander conceptualized how the infant's bodily interactions with others produce mental representations and shape modes of responding. If the mind is relational, involving the body self and behaviors/emotions of others, which should become the focus of observation, the self or the other? Embodiment–enactment theory dissolves this boundary, addressing how the individual's embodied mind develops while interacting with others and the environment. By way of contrast, a sociological theory could focus on how the environment develops while interacting with individuals.

HOW DOES EMBODIMENT THEORY CONCEPTUALIZE PSYCHOLOGICAL CHANGE?

Converging with a principle that contributed to the foundation of our developmental model, human activity is conceptualized as inherently organized. Change in this organization occurs when the activity of a person "bumps into" the activity of others who oppose or resist it. A mismatch between the organization of one's activity and that of another (i.e., "failures") is one necessary condition for change. Another condition occurs when organized behaviors of others affirm and match the organization of a person's activity (i.e., "successes"). Change, then, always occurs through partial successes and failures, forming complementary processes. The reader may notice that these two conditions embrace concepts we discussed earlier, such as Freud's notion of factors that inhibit the expression of representations of drives in response to environmental prohibitions, Piaget's concept of the accommodation of mental schemas in response to mismatches with environmental stimulation, and Beebe and Lochmann's notion of disruption and repair.

As the individual (or body self) engages in continuous interactions with others, cycles that both affirm and resist the individual's organized activity, the whole self-other system moves toward greater complexity (the principle of directiveness of behavior in our foundation). Complexity means that organizations of activity within the individual, and between the individual and others, increase in number of elements, the degree to which these elements are integrated, and the degree to which the resulting integration is flexible. Cycles of change, or what Overton (1994a) called "the arrow of time," occur in spirals simultaneously involving two interrelated domains. In one, a person's mind differentiates from that of others, forming organizations of interactions with others that are increasingly complex, integrated, and flexible. Simultaneously, and converging with the principle of multiple modes and goals, differentiation and integration also occur within the individual, resulting in multiple behavioral modalities that become interrelated and flexible. Accordingly, activity could be represented by another activity, by an image or fantasy, or by spoken words. As the individual develops different modes of expression, optimal functioning requires the flexible interplay among these spheres of expression as well as among levels within a sphere. Johnson (1987) convincingly argued that years after infancy "the body is in the mind" and that meanings verbalized by a child or adult are not independently contained in sentences but are forever influenced by early body experiences. He proposed that "embodied image schemas" constructed during the first years of life are "metaphorically projected" into higher levels of functioning that develop later, serving as principles around which meanings are organized later in life. What one experiences in the first two years of life spirals into what one does, imagines, and says later in life.

CAN YOU GIVE AN EXAMPLE OF HOW EXPERIENCES IN THE FIRST TWO YEARS OF LIFE SPIRAL INTO WHAT A PERSON DOES, IMAGINES, AND SAYS LATER IN LIFE?

John, a tenth grader, first pulled hair from the top of his head at the age of 20 months and continued to do so throughout childhood and adolescence, despite the fact that he functioned relatively well. During his first session John talked about his accomplishments as a gymnast, that he had attained good grades except for the past two terms, that his social life with both male and female friends had been going OK, but recently he lost enthusiasm for gymnastics and guitar lessons. He eventually introduced one difficulty as he saw it: daily fights with his sister, 17 months younger. At the last minute John introduced another problem that the parents had already described when they telephoned for an appointment. Now struggling to express himself, he shared that he has been pulling out hair from the top of his head "for a long time." He pushed aside his wavy hair to reveal an area, about two inches square, totally devoid of hair.

In the next session John shared details about his hair pulling. Each day he ritualistically went into the bathroom, carefully felt the bald area with his fingertips, and plucked out any stub he detected, acknowledging that the pinch of pain "felt good and exciting." He believed he started pulling his hair during kindergarten. In one attempt to learn about the meanings unique to John's personal world, I asked him to discuss the greatest person he had read about. John discussed Abraham Lincoln, giving particular attention to his bushy hair and beard. From this he associated to a recent habit. While doing his homework he fondled the furry head of a toy lion from his childhood days. Visibly anxious and embarrassed, he wondered why the activity excited him.

During the following meeting, John announced that there was something troubling him more than hair pulling, and was in fact the main reason he had asked his parents if he could see someone. With much difficulty he described the confused combination of excitement and anger he experienced when interacting with a science teacher and when taking showers with classmates after gymnastics. Bursting into tears, he wondered if he was becoming "gay." After he collected himself, I noticed that he centered on particular details: the teacher in question maintained a beard, and he was most aroused when taking a shower in the presence of a classmate who had already developed considerable body hair. In addition, one observation gradually impressed me. Whenever John talked about his hair pulling, the science teacher, the classmate with body hair, or the toy lion, he arched his shoulders back so that his abdomen curved out ever so slightly. As John and I continued our sessions, I obtained his permission to meet his parents.

John's parents made clear their main concern had always been John's hair pulling, and they agreed on how and when it began. John was 20 months old and showing difficulty accepting his infant sister. One day, while sister's diaper was being changed, John poked her. Mother screamed angrily and slapped him. John crawled under the bed and refused to come out. A short time later father arrived and coaxed him out from under the bed. At that moment both parents noticed hair strands in his fist that obviously were pulled from the top of his head. In the months that followed they observed that an area at the front of John's scalp remained sparse and, with their pediatrician, concluded he was still pulling out hair, although no one observed him doing this. From this beginning the parents carried the belief that mother's scream and angry slap caused the symptom. As John grew older he participated, on three separate occasions, in behavior modification programs that successfully eliminated the hair-pulling for periods of up to several months, but each time the habit returned.

Searching to understand John's hair pulling, and guided by hypotheses suggested by John's interviews and projective testing, I asked the parents during one meeting whether father had ever maintained a beard. Father did before and after John was born, and he enjoyed nuzzling his beard into John's body. Mother added that she also enjoyed bobbing her head back and forth so that her shoulder-length hair caressed John's body. Laughing, both parents guessed they were "ticklers." As both parents added recollections, mother spontaneously asked father an intriguing question. "Remember what happened when you shaved your beard off?" Father decided to shave off his beard sometime after sister was born. Minus his beard, father walked into John's bedroom, with mother following, both parents wondering what his reaction would be. John glared at father and quickly crawled to the corner of the crib, burying his face in the blankets. Father remembered John as "stressed," while mother recalled he seemed "terrified." When mother picked up John, he burst into tears, refusing to go into father's arms. Both parents tried to reassure him. Following this episode, John avoided father for a number of days.

The parents were sure that father had shaved his beard before the incident during which mother slapped John. At this point I organize observations the parents shared in terms of the infant models we discussed earlier.

Primary Circular Reactions, the Emergent Self, and Negotiating Initial Adaptation (0–3 Months)

John fared well during this time, coordinating schemas from various sensory modalities during interactions with both parents (there were no other caregivers present) and with things. One set of experiences could be viewed as heightened affective moments. Both mother and father enjoyed tickling and caressing John's body, Mother with her hair and father with his beard, very likely forming the beginning roots of a RIG involving intense bodily sensations and surging excitement.

Secondary Circular Reactions, the Core Self, and Negotiating Reciprocal Exchange and Early Directed Activity (4–12 Months)

When placed on the changing table, John began to arch his back, offering his belly to father and mother for tickling, a posture that directed their behavior in order to make the interesting hair brushing last. He also tightened his legs when they tried to change his diaper, and relaxed them once he was tickled. Still later he rolled his head back and forth, imitating mother when she swished her hair across his body. John was constructing a RIG we could call "hair tickling— explosive excitement" that gradually became a part of his core self and extended into his subjective self.

Tertiary Circular Reactions, the Subjective Self, and Negotiating Self Assertion (12–18 Months)

Two factors that contributed to a major disruption in their relationship emerged during this phase. Mother became depressed and preoccupied with her new pregnancy, and she stopped participating with John in hair-tickling play rituals. Father and John, however, continued evolving a series of ritualized play during which they discovered new ways of engaging each other in heightened emotional moments. These rituals continued daily until sister was born (John was 17 months old) and intermittently thereafter for at least three months. For example, John arched his back when in the highchair, which regularly resulted in father's nuzzling him with his beard. After dinner, as John and father played on the rug, John flipped on his back, arched his belly upward and rolled his head back and forth, suggesting deferred imitation was operating (mother had rolled her head in tickling rituals until just weeks ago). In response, father nuzzled him. Introducing a new ingredient, John sometimes reached up, clutched father's beard, and hung on while father swung his head back and forth singing "See-Saw Marjory Daw," the two exploding with obvious delight.

Deferred Imitation, the Verbal Self, and Negotiating Aggressive Intentions (18–24 Months)

John invented new meanings. When father entered the house, John scampered behind furniture and father searched for him with considerable fanfare. When he discovered John, both screamed with delight as father carried him to the rug where they engaged in nuzzling and beard-swinging games. Sometimes when father discovered John, he would be holding his "blankee" over his mouth, apparently representing a beard.

   At this point sister arrived. Mother acknowledged that she became more depressed and impatient with John. Father gradually decreased participating in beard-nuzzling rituals, briefly shifting some of this activity and attention to sister. With this, John experienced a major disruption in ongoing regulations with father, and struggled to cope with the appearance of his sister, mother's anger, and preserving his special relationship with father. As if to make up with mother, John covered his sister with a blanket of baby powder, declaring he was helping. If father nuzzled sister, John attempted to interrupt this activity by pulling at father's leg, flopping on the floor and arching his back, or hiding behind furniture, each intended to focus and direct father to initiate their play rituals. If mother scolded John, he immediately ran to father and initiated a beard-nuzzling ritual using one of his prompts. This ensemble of elements continued within John's developing self for about three months, when father elected to shave his beard.

The Origin and Initial Meaning of John's Hair Pulling

We can speculate that John constructed two RIGs within his core and subjective selves *before* father shaved his beard. One condensed and represented experiences with mother that initially included surging excitement and tingling body sensations, a RIG that was disrupted and revised when mother became irritable and depressed and withdrew from John. The other conserved and represented interactions with father that included explosive excitement when father's beard rubbed against John's belly, neck, and cheeks; perceptions of father's surging excitement; John's sense of being at one with father and as separate from him (e.g., when hiding behind furniture); perceptions of father as a protector from mother's angry moods; father as security and well-being. This RIG was disrupted to some degree when father decreased his participation in hair-tickling games.

When father shaved his beard, the "father" RIG within John's subjective self was disrupted to a major degree and represented a traumatic affective moment. The intensity of John's reaction is not surprising given the key meanings represented by father's beard that formed John's subjective self: well-being, excitement, security, protection, separating/individuation, autonomy. When father shaved his beard, John was faced with the task of restructuring this "father" RIG, including father without a beard, while preserving these positive meanings. John could not accomplish this, however, because father decreased participation in their play rituals, limiting John's interactions with him. When mother slapped John, John had not yet had the opportunity to revise the father RIG. Thus he coped with this assault on the integrity of his self by calling on the well-established RIG of "bearded father" as an evoked companion. However, because the evoked father disagreed with the father who was now without beard, John, capable of deferred imitation, pulled hair from his head (as father had from his face) to preserve the already established meanings of well-being and security. In addition, the hair pulling could be viewed as an attempt by John to modify aggressive intention, pulling his hair instead of sticking pins in his sister or mother in response to mother's slap.

Why John's Hair Pulling Remained Impervious to Change: From 20 Months to Adolescence

From this formulation we can address why the hair pulling continued throughout development as a circumscribed activity whereas other lines of psychological development proceeded relatively unimpeded. The psychodynamic model of intrapsychic conflict requires that the onset and continuation of hair pulling represent a neurotic symptom, a solution to a conflict between, for example, superego dictates and unconscious wishes. The foundation of this behavior, however, was constructed during the first seventeen months of John's life and consisted of hundreds of *nonverbal* physical, cognitive, and emotional experiences that took place before the superego is expected to emerge and before he could develop elaborate unconscious fantasies. Instead of resulting from intrapsychic conflict, I propose that John's hair pulling was a coping device, born out of RIGs already established prior to the age of 20 months, and relying on the processes of deferred imitation and modifying aggressive intentions. This position converges with Stern's (1985), who argued that when an infant presents problems, these "are not symptoms of intrapsychic conflict within the infant [but] the accurate reflection of . . . problematic interpersonal exchange, not psychopathology of a psychodynamic nature" (p. 202).

However, if we grant that John's hair pulling began as a coping device, why were the hair pulling and related meanings not translated into a neurotic symptom, symbols (fantasies) and words John could share once he developed the capacity for symbolic thinking? Stern proposed that while the verbal self gradually builds on the nonverbal, unconscious, core, and subjective selves, some experiences contained within nonverbal RIGs are not translated into words as shared symbols. "Such experiences continue underground, nonverbalized, to lead an unnamed (and, to that extent only, unknown) but nonetheless very real existence" (p. 175). Piaget (1973) elaborated, proposing that the "functional utility" the translation serves determines why some bodily, nonverbal experiences become translated into shared symbols, including words, while others are not. Sensorimotor schemas are not translated whenever they are incompatible with, or "in conflict with," conscious ideas already constructed and accepted, and therefore existing at a higher cognitive level than do sensorimotor schemas. Because of this conflict, bodily, nonverbal schemas are actively held in the unconscious.

Applying these ideas to our case, after father shaved his beard John constructed conscious ideas of father without a beard, but these ideas conflicted with a well-established RIG of the preferred intersubjective, bearded partner who defined John's core self as secure and valued. For John there was clearly no functional utility in translating this sensorimotor abstraction of a bearded father into some symbolic/verbal form. But there was functional utility in John's preserving meanings from his original sensorimotor, nonverbal RIG of a bearded father, meanings that enabled him to cope with father's withdrawal from their unique stimulating games and mother's angry rejection of him in preference for sister. For these reasons the original unconscious, sensorimotor meanings of hair pulling remained impervious to change during his toddler years.

I propose that a nonverbal RIG is not translated into symbolic form, even as childhood and adolescence unfold, if major disruptions, accompanied by heightened, emotional, traumatic moments, were not adequately repaired. In these instances some sensorimotor/emotional component of the original representation continues to gain expression in the behaviors of a child or adolescent without the youth's having a conscious sense of "knowing" what the behavior means, and without being able to share these meanings with others in play or discussions. John provides an example. Recall that when I first met him he arched his shoulders back and protruded his stomach ever so subtly, but noticeably, when discussing his bearded teacher, Abraham Lincoln, or the furry toy lion he had begun to fondle. This body posture was clearly an expression of one aspect of the sensorimotor, embodied father-RIG constructed during infancy. In terms of the emotional element of the original RIG, John experienced a sudden surge of excitement when, for example, engaging the teacher or plucking a hair from his head, emotions that derived from the exhilarating excitement he experienced during play rituals with father. Last, while the bearded-father RIG remained underground and unnamed but active, this RIG continued to preserve the original, embodied sense of security, esteem, and integrity, thereby enabling John to function well academically and socially.

John's Adaptive Success Collapsed When His Bearded-Father RIG Was Translated into Words

John's school grades plunged and he lost interest in athletics and music when the bearded-father RIG collapsed, no longer offering security and esteem. This collapse occurred when the bearded-father RIG became translated from an unnamed, unconscious form to a named, symbolic, conscious form consisting of language and fantasy symbols represented by his wondering "I'm gay!" John experienced this translation as an "assault to his body-self" that produced intense anxiety and intrapsychic conflict that contributed to his academic and social decline.

We can speculate why John's psychology constructed this particular verbal/ fantasy symbolic translation. Recall embodiment enactment theory and Johnson's concept of the "body in the mind" that propose that verbalized meanings constructed later in life are shaped and constrained by early nonverbal body experiences. Applied to John, as he coped with typical adolescent biological changes and participated in discussions and jokes about sexuality while negotiating his psychosexual identification, his "mind" began to assign verbal meanings to these adolescent experiences. However, the "body" in John's mind was unique in containing a core nonverbal representation of unnatural, protracted, and excessive body stimulation in play rituals with father, including heightened explosions of excitement. When this "body" became injected into the process of assigning verbal meanings to John's biological and social experiences, John's mind propelled a translation in the form of a particular linguistic symbol, "I'm gay." His verbalized belief was not determined randomly then, but shaped by the unique developmental interferences he experienced in the first two years of life. Given John's intense anxiety over wondering if he was gay, we could speculate that this translation was not synchronized with, but rather in conflict with, other aspects of his personality.

CONCLUDING COMMENT

We have discussed on several occasions that both cognitive-behavioral and psychodynamic therapies prefer translating a child's behavior into verbalized self-statements, explanations, and interpretations. John's case brings to our attention issues about verbalizing that are critical when integrating psychotherapies. His bearded-father RIG was initially translated into a nonverbal action symbol that was nearly identical to its referent, namely, plucking hair from his head. Later, in adolescence, the next translation again consisted of an action symbol (feeling fur of a toy lion). While these translations involved action symbols, the conscious, emotional experience was usually excitement that did not interfere with adaptation. Then the translation took a turn into another modality. John experienced defuse fantasies about a teacher and peers, a translation producing primarily excitement and a moderate degree of anxiety. When the translation took a linguistic form "I am gay," conscious conflict and anxiety became intense, and John's adaptive functioning collapsed. These observations raise several questions we have noted earlier and address in more detail in what is to follow. Should nonverbal embodied representations be translated into words? If so, when? If not, is it sufficient to translate these representations only into the "language" of action and fantasy?

6

A Developmental Framework for Integrating Child Psychotherapies (*Continued*): From Age 3 Years To Adolescence

CONTENTS

U p to this point we have discussed the foundation and first floor of the "developmental house" I propose as a guide for integrating child psychotherapies. We now need to elaborate how the processes of self- and mutual regulation, disruption and repair of interactions, and heightened emotional experiences that occurred during infancy continue to unfold beyond the third year of life. We also need to elaborate how interactions and negotiations with others during childhood build on meanings constructed during the first years of life, resulting in cognitive and behavioral modalities that gradually undergo differentiation and integration, becoming increasingly more flexible and serving a child's adaptations to ever-changing stimulation. As we tour the second floor, we should expect to find elaborations that provide a way of integrating what a child does, imagines, and says at both surface and deep levels. These elaborations should also define the implications for adaptive functioning when the processes of self- and mutual cognitive regulation are derailed, when behavioral modalities remain inflexible, and when what a child does, imagines, and says are segregated experiences. To address these needs, and relying upon laboratory and clinical studies (e.g., Santostefano 1977, 1978, 1988b, 1995b), I have constructed a developmental framework that consists of three interrelated models (Figure 6–1).

Model I. Life Metaphors—From Embodied Representations in Infancy to Metaphors in Childhood

To bridge the previous discussion with what follows, I consider Piaget's sensorimotor schemas, Johnson's embodied-image schemas, Stern's representations of interactions generalized, and Sander's negotiated issues as contributing to the first "nonverbal editions" of life metaphors.

CAN YOU PROVIDE A CLINICAL EXAMPLE THAT ILLUSTRATES METAPHORS AT WORK?

When in the playroom, a child marched with sober, measured steps, holding a stick overhead and posturing strength and determination. When asked what she was playing, she did not reply. In another session she sat on the floor and nudged a pig hand puppet against a doll while narrating an elaborate fantasy about a giant animal swallowing a person. In still another session, slouched in a chair, she laughed

I. Life Metaphors

- Represent past experiences negotiating key developmental issues
- Construe present stimulation
- Prescribe plans of action to negotiate developmental issues in present environments

II. Cognitive-Behavioral Regulators in Self- and Mutual Regulation

- Hierarchy of cognitive functions: from body regulation to conceptual thinking
- Coordinate and equilibrate demands of life metaphors and persons/environments as construed

III. Behavioral Modalities of Action, Fantasy, and Language

- Hierarchy of behavioral modes from action to fantasy to language
- Respond to demands for action from life metaphors and environments as coordinated by cognition

IV. Persons/Environments

- Prescribe/expect various forms of behavior:
- Ever-changing
- Usual/expected and unusual/unexpected

FIGURE 6–1
A Developmental Framework: Age 3 Years to Adolesence

as she described a birthday present her brother received. "His cork gun was a plop." This vignette illustrates that constructing and expressing metaphors could involve multiple modes: action/gestures, fantasy, and language.

HOW ARE METAPHORS CONSTRUCTED?

It is generally accepted that metaphor (along with its close relatives simile and analogy) involves the transfer of meaning. Something is described in terms of properties that belong to something else. The meaning a person experiences, termed the *referent*, is substituted by and dynamically fitted with the behavioral expression of that meaning, termed the *vehicle* (Smith and Franklin 1979). From this interaction a new meaning emerges that goes beyond the objects substituted and that synthesizes present and past experiences with them. In our vignette the girl's brother, as she construed him, interacted with a cork gun and defecation, producing the linguistic metaphor of a "plop," expressing that her brother is feces, a meaning synthesizing past and present experiences with him.

WHAT FUNCTIONS ARE SERVED BY METAPHORS?

A variety have been proposed, beginning with Aristotle's view that metaphors are ornamental, rendering discourse less dull. Later writers agreed with Aristotle but proposed that these ornaments of language distort meaning, since language should convey only facts, or at best serve to coin terms and new concepts. Other writers took the position that metaphors do not distort meaning but are useful forms of communication. However, like Aristotle, they assumed that a word or sentence is the exclusive locus of a metaphor, a position still seen in writings on the use of metaphor in psychotherapy (e.g., Witzum et al. 1988). In sharp contrast, Ortony (1979) proposed that metaphors are "necessary" and serve several important functions. Metaphors condense many facts, depict events that by their nature are not easily described with words, reconstruct experiences, and are vivid, lying much closer to a person's experiences than do words. He also emphasized that metaphor construction involves pretending and imaging, and urged that a broader definition be adopted. Billow (1977) underscored the need to study the relationships between metaphor and the processes of play and imaging, and wondered if metaphor is an example of imaged thinking and not simply spoken language. Along the same line, Verbrugge and McCarrell (1977) proposed that metaphors invite pretending and imagining and "may be basic to all growth and understanding, whether in the playroom, the psychotherapeutic setting, the scientific laboratory, or the theater" (p. 495).

WHAT IS A LIFE METAPHOR?

Stimulated by Ortony's urging that a broader definition of metaphor be formulated, I define a life metaphor as a process that produces all meanings relating to what a child experiences and knows. We noted earlier that experiencing is a way of knowing and of constructing meaning that is immediate, holistic, contextual, and embodied, integrating patterns of sights, sound, smells, and actions as well as spoken words. Phenomenologically, a life metaphor is a persistent, habitual organization (pattern) of behaviors that simultaneously (1) represents past experiences, (2) construes present persons and situations, (3) prescribes various behaviors/emotions as responses. The vehicles used to construct and express the meanings of a life metaphor may include images, words, thoughts, emotions, postures, and physical actions. Each persistent pattern of behaviors serves to negotiate a key developmental issue vis-à-vis the self and others—attachment/ trust/love, loss/detachment, separation/individuation, controlling/being controlled, dependence/autonomy-independence, initiating/reciprocating, deference/ ambition/dominance, assertiveness/aggressiveness/competitiveness.

HOW DO LIFE METAPHORS ORIGINATE?

The first edition of a life metaphor emerges when a nonverbal play ritual, organized from 8 to 18 months, serves to negotiate a developmental issue. Referring to our previous discussion of infant research, for a play ritual to give rise to a life metaphor, the child should have (1) reached Piaget's fifth stage of cognitive development, discovering new ways of accomplishing goals that become play rituals; (2) constructed the beginnings of Stern's subjective self within which the infant understands the motives of others; and (3) successfully negotiated Sander's issues of reciprocal exchange and directed activity and focalization, when the infant gives more differentiated directions to caregivers.

HOW DOES THE FIRST EDITION OF A LIFE METAPHOR, CONSTRUCTED BEFORE THE AGE OF 2 YEARS, BECOME REVISED IN CHILDHOOD, AND CAN YOU GIVE AN EXAMPLE?

Once a nonverbal embodied developmental issue is successfully negotiated before the age of 2 years, the meaning of this negotiation spirals to another, interpersonal, ritual that continues negotiating the same developmental issue, elaborating it. Throughout childhood, the process consists of a revolving, spiraling series of interpersonal rituals, each expressing a metaphor, negotiating a developmental issue, and building on and elaborating previous issues.

At 18 months a child repeatedly played a ritual in which he sat on his father's lap and gestured so that father buttoned and then unbuttoned his shirt around the boy's body. At this point the toddler slipped off father's lap and scampered away, and father looked for him. With this play ritual, enacted at the dawn of symbolic functioning, the first edition of a metaphor was being constructed and negotiated: attachment (at one with father's body) and separation/individuation (running off with father looking for him). A few months later the child initiated another ritual, elaborating the meaning of attachment-separation to include allegiance and identification. Now the child insisted he sit immediately next to father at mealtimes, gradually extending this seating arrangement to the family car, restaurants, and homes of relatives. During the first months of his third year the child introduced still another ritual, now including the negotiation of self-assertion while retaining a positive identification with father. The child requested that during mealtimes he use a glass identical to father's and that the liquid poured into each be exactly the same height. After drinking, child and father placed the glasses side by side and carefully judged which glass contained "bigger" or "smaller" amounts. A few years later the child engaged father in playing checkers, now negotiating aggression and competition against the idealized parent (while relying on the previously success-fully negotiated issues of separation, individuation, and identification). Still later the child engaged father in debates over the relative merits of the Boston Celtics versus the Los Angeles Lakers.

Illustrating Overton's (1994a) notion of change as "the arrow of time," each cycle of negotiation did not return to the original starting point but spiraled, mov-ing the system of child and father toward greater complexity, differentiation, inte-gration, and flexibility. Each negotiation built on the previous one, resulting in a progressive, integrated series of self–other relationships: from "I am in you and also separate from you" to "I am by your side"; from "Who is bigger/smaller?" to "Who is the greatest?" In addition, following embodiment–enactment theory, the child's bodily negotiations with father also resulted in the child's mind differentiating into different modalities of experiencing and representing. Initially, the vehicles the child used to construct metaphors primarily involved gestures and actions (the shirt game); gradually, imagination (fantasy) differentiated as a mode, assimilating actions and gestures (the glasses were fantasized as the persons of child and father). Still later, language (linguistic metaphors) emerged as a system of expression that assimilated fantasy and action (the debate over the merits of two basketball teams, each repre-senting one of them). Another example is provided in Figure 6–2.

HOW ARE NEW LIFE METAPHORS CONSTRUCTED?

A new life metaphor is constructed whenever new behavioral modalities that code (symbolize) experiences emerge intrinsically as a function of maturation. In Piaget's model a maturational shift occurs at about 2 years when the mind relinquishes coding experiences with sensorimotor schemas and emphasizes coding experiences with mental schemas that copy and represent actions on things. In psychoanalytic theory shifts occur in how experiences are coded as different body zones mature, influencing the meanings given to experiences: from the mouth that emphasizes meanings of nurture to the anus that emphasizes meanings of being controlled, withholding/giving to the genitals that emphasize meanings of ascendance, com-petence, and achievement. The environment plays a nonspecific role relative to maturational influences in the construction of new life metaphors. Consider the following example in which a child experienced the same interaction through dif-ferent life metaphors, constructed early or later in development. In treatment she

Age: Years	Example: Negotiating Dominance–Deference	Arrow of Time	Maturating Behavioral Modalities that Participate in Negotiations

12	• "I decide when we
	  play soccer."
	• "You decide when
	  we play soccer."
		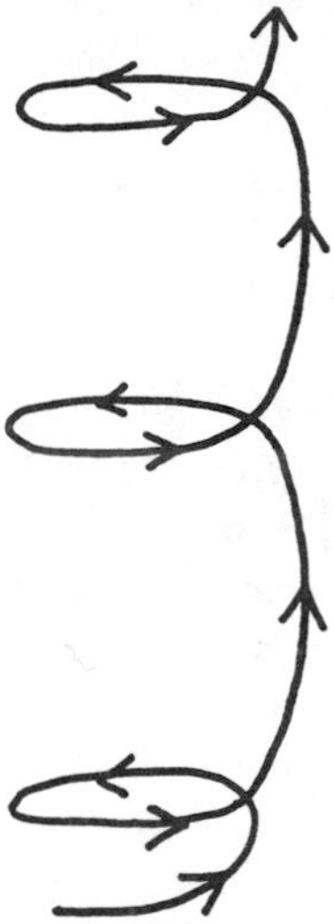	• Organizations of
			  language expressions

8	• Capture playmate's toy
	  pieces of war game
	• Surrender toy pieces of
	  war game to playmate
	  without complaint
			• Organizations of fantasies

3	• Grab toy of preschool
	  playmate
	• Allow playmate to take a
	  toy
			• Organizations of action

FIGURE 6–2

The Development of New Life Metaphors that Evolve as Modalities Emerge in
Maturation: Spiraling Revolutions

revealed that while listening to mother read her a story, she construed the experience at one moment as mother giving her as much milk as her baby brother was receiving; at another time she construed the experience as mother controlling her since she had to go bed after the story was read; at yet another she construed mother as jealous, reading to her as a way of keeping her away from daddy's lap and the "special times" she spends with him. The life metaphors and developmental issues revealed by these experiences are, respectively, reading is milk and being nurtured by mother, reading is mother controls what I do with my body, and reading is mother keeps me from the man I love because she wants him for herself.

HOW ARE EXISTING LIFE METAPHORS REVISED?

The process involved in revising existing life metaphors is represented by the image of a continuous series of revolutions on a horizontal plane, a process that integrates Mounoud's (1982) model of revolutionary periods in development, Piaget's (1977) concept of equilibration, and the psychoanalytic concept of internalization. When existing life metaphors are revised, the behaviors of others play a major role, while maturational influences play a nonspecific role. As illustrated in Figure 6–3, while negotiating dominance-deference, this metaphor "bumps into" the demands and expectations of others, construes each situation, and prescribes actions, fantasies, and spoken words in response to the context at hand. In daily living, of course, the child uses dozens of encounters with persons and contexts during a given week to negotiate an issue. These cycles of interaction, assimilating and accommodating to the demands of some, revise the organization of elements that make up the life metaphor (gestures, fantasies, words, emotions), resulting in a more differentiated and flexible organization. In addition, as the child engages in repeated revolutions in negotiations with others, she/he and others construct an increasingly elaborated pool of shared symbols. Recall the toddler who initiated a "shirt game" as a play ritual. As this game cycled on a horizontal plane, father and boy elaborated the symbols they invented and shared to negotiate separation-individuation. Father wore dif-

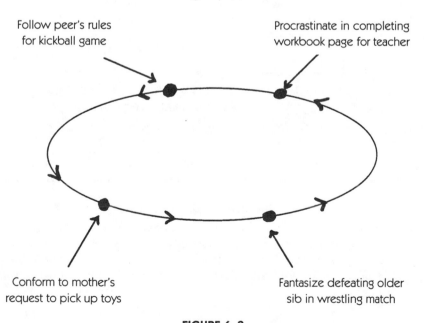

FIGURE 6–3
Negotiating the Same Life Metaphor with Different Persons and Contexts:
Horizontal Revolutions

ferent shirts from day to day and on occasion a sweater into which the boy crawled to engage in still another cycle. As the child runs off, he invented ingenious hideouts while father elaborated techniques he used to search for him: using a small flashlight and then a large one and sometimes pursuing him with a toy airplane.

WHAT INTERPERSONAL INGREDIENT IS ESPECIALLY CRITICAL IN CONSTRUCTING AND REVISING LIFE METAPHORS?

The availability of other persons whose standards the child idealizes and internalizes is essential. These standards do not represent what one ought to do, but what one wants to be. In contrast to the superego (internalized standards that control impulses and prevent wishes from gaining expression in action), the ego ideal is primarily concerned with stimulating a person to take idealized action that emulates an idealized figure. If experiences with others result in heightened, positive emotional exchanges, then the standards and expectations of these persons become woven into the child's developing ego ideal. If a child idealizes a parent, teacher, or therapist, the child is more likely to identify with the permissions and prohibitions of that person and also internalize (accommodate to) the behaviors this idealized figure displays when negotiating with the child.

HOW ARE LIFE METAPHORS RELATED TO THE ISSUES OF PAST, PRESENT, CONSCIOUS, AND UNCONSCIOUS?

Life metaphors may or may not be at work when an individual is experiencing some situation or reliving the past. For example, if a child describes a trip the family took last summer, sharing details that form a photocopy of the event, no metaphor is at work. But if the same child describes the trip while knocking hand puppets together, a metaphor of family conflict could be emerging. Similarly, metaphors are not synonymous without conscious processes. A person could be aware or unaware of a metaphor at work. The boy who placed a piece of clay at the end of his nose, discussed earlier, probably was not aware of the metaphor he was negotiating with his therapist.

WHAT CRITERIA DEFINE THE SUCCESSFUL NEGOTIATION OF LIFE METAPHORS?

Success is a function of several interrelated factors.

1. A child's cognition is capable of perceiving opportunities and limitations of persons and things and recruiting them as vehicles to construct and express symbols (see Model II below).
2. A child is free to take action, fantasize, and verbalize what she/he means or intends (see Model III below).
3. A person with emotional responsiveness, whom the child idealizes, and materials present opportunities for enacting play rituals.
4. The idealized person physically participates with the child in play rituals and negotiations, displaying a wide range of relevant emotions, for as long as the child prescribes.
5. The idealized person does not interfere with the child's revisions and does not introduce stimulation that is excessive or too muted given the child's temperament.

WHEN IS A LIFE METAPHOR VIEWED AS MALADAPTIVE, AND CAN YOU PROVIDE EXAMPLES?

When a child shows, for example, excessive fears, inappropriate aggression, hyperactivity, and inhibition in completing schoolwork, it is assumed that one or another life metaphor, and the developmental issue it represents, has remained rigid. A life metaphor is maladaptive whenever

1. The child's behaviors do not fit with developmental expectations in terms of cognitive and behavioral coding systems that should have emerged through the process of maturation. *Example:* A 30-month-old repeatedly smears the bathroom wall with play dough, finger paints, and sometimes feces. This behavior would not necessarily be viewed as prescribed by a pathological life metaphor because this child is at a stage in development dominated by a coding system psychodynamic theory terms *anal.* Influenced by this coding system, the child is negotiating the issues of testing and modifying aggressive intentions, and control versus relinquishing control. The responses of caregivers would influence the success with which the child negotiates these issues as cycles of interactions are repeated. But if such behaviors

are displayed by an 8-year-old boy, a pathological life metaphor is operating. This child would be expected to have available, through maturational development, other behavioral vehicles to symbolize the issue of aggression and control, reflecting more indirectness and delay. For example, having been required, against his strong protest, to wear a particular pair of pants to school, the child returns with mud splashed on one trouser leg, "It was an accident."

2. The child's behaviors have failed, over an extended period of time, to assimilate and accommodate to available experiences that contain ingredients suitable for restructuring a life metaphor. *Example:* Since infancy, an adopted third grader had not negotiated reciprocity adequately with her adoptive parents, who expressed considerable ambivalence over giving unconditionally. This child constructed a life metaphor that prescribed a sense of emptiness. At the age of 10, while in treatment, she discussed experiencing herself as an "empty basket" that others passed by, refusing to put something in it, resulting in her becoming sullen and withdrawn. In a restaurant with her family she happened to be waited on last; at a party she received a balloon containing, she believed, less air then the balloons given to other children. Instead of assimilating other elements of these situations, the maladaptive metaphor dominated in shaping the same meaning. For example, she recalled later that in the restaurant father allowed her to have her favorite dessert.

3. The child's behaviors are inappropriate for, and/or rejected by, the child's usual environments, producing conflict with significant others (interpersonal conflict). *Example:* A 12-year-old is content to spend endless hours at the computer playing interactive games involving battles between mythical figures. He is in conflict with his parents because he gives little time to homework and has not cultivated relationships with peers. While his excessive fantasy life is meeting the demands of a life metaphor, involving asserting and aggressing, it is at odds with the demands of his environment.

4. The child's behaviors meet the demands of her/his maladaptive metaphor, but are at odds with the demands of standards of others whom the child has already internalized, resulting in anxiety/guilt (intrapsychic conflict). *Example:* From his toddler years a 10-year-old failed to negotiate self-assertion, with its autonomy, in many negotiations with parents who consistently exercised control over what the child ate, played, and wore. As a result, he constructed a life metaphor that construed situations and prescribed behaviors that required him to be passive and submissive. At the same time, since his toddler years, the child had many interactions with an aunt and uncle who had been quite accommodating when the boy negotiated self-assertion. Consequently, the boy internalized experiences with these idealized adults, resulting in a life metaphor that prescribed self-assertion and autonomy. Now, when assigned to a soccer team by the fifth grade gym teacher, the boy is gripped with anxiety and conflict as the metaphor of passivity, born out of his negotiations with parents, collides with the metaphor of autonomy and self-assertion, born out of his negotiations with aunt and uncle.

Model II. Cognition in Self- and Mutual Regulation

The model of life metaphors interacts with, and is elaborated by, a model that defines cognition as unconscious "deep" structures that determine which stimuli are selected and avoided by an individual, influencing meanings given to experiences, and that define how cognition and emotion are one, playing a role in self- and mutual regulations (Figure 6–1). The model derives from the research of George Klein (e.g. 1951, 1954), which took place within the "New Look" approach to cognition (see Part IV). Klein conceptualized that individuals use cognitive strategies he termed *cognitive controls* to equilibrate information and meanings/emotions so as to maintain adaptive control over situations/information. As Klein stated, cognitive controls are mechanisms that "bring into harmony needs, impulses and wishes and buffer the turbulence from within against limitations from without, by selecting, avoiding, integrating and organizing information from the two worlds" (1951, p. 36).

Taking Klein's formulations as a starting point, I embarked on a program of research to explore the concept of cognitive controls with both normal and pathological children (e.g., Santostefano 1978, 1986, 1995b). This program extended Klein's initial formulations along several lines: (1) cognitive control mechanisms were defined to include body image and activity, and body image was linked to cognitive activity at higher developmental levels that did not require the direct participation of the body; (2) cognitive control mechanisms were observed to operate in children as well as adults, from the age of 3 through adolescence; (3) each cognitive control mechanism followed a particular developmental course; (4) clinical groups of children showed deviations from these developmental lines; (5) assessments of cognitive controls predicted learning disabilities and adjustment problems; (6) regressive and progressive changes occurred in the organization of these cognitive mechanisms in response to changes in a person's environment and emotional states. Because my research supported a hierarchy of cognitive functions that integrate body and mental activity, I use here the term *cognitive-behavioral regulators*.

> **HOW DOES THE CONCEPT OF COGNITIVE-BEHAVIORAL REGULATORS OPERATIONALIZE LEARNING THAT TAKES PLACE IN PSYCHOTHERAPY AND CAN YOU GIVE EXAMPLES?**

Given that all schools agree that psychotherapy is a learning process, we need a definition of learning that serves psychotherapy. Piaget (1977) provided one that meets this need. "To know [to learn] . . . is to . . . reproduce the object (information) dynamically; but to reproduce it, it is necessary to know how to produce (copy) the information . . ." (p. 30). This definition articulates two steps in learning:

(1) copying and producing information and (2) reproducing the information by translating it into symbols. Cognitive-behavioral regulators are continually enveloped in this two-step process, simultaneously copying information from external situations and one's personal world and integrating the two to translate the information into symbols/meanings. To illustrate, consider children during moments of psychotherapy.

Case A

John, a 15-year-old, flopped into a chair he usually used, only to pop up and sit in another chair farther away from the therapist, commenting, with a chuckle, "that (the chair he vacated) is hard on my back today." His right hand clenched his left; he glared at the therapist, looked away, and sighed, "Since we met last . . ." He paused, handled an ashtray on the table next to him, glared at it, and seemed to be miles away. Shifting restlessly, he turned his attention to the bookshelves and wondered how many books they held, then recalled a vacation the family took this time last year. The books and vacation faded as he commented, "Yesterday I was late for school. My father blasted me and made me put tools back in the garage. I felt like shit. I can't seem to do anything right . . ." His attention shifted to a homework assignment. He ignored this thought, fingered the ashtray again, edged it toward the therapist, and said with a tone of irritation, "Your ashtray is cracked like my father." Then he laughed anxiously.

   During these moments John regulated his body motility (moved farther away from the therapist, shifted about in his chair, sat still). He visually and tactually scanned and copied information from his external environment (books, ashtray) and his subjective environment (an encounter with father, a memory of a family vacation, a homework assignment). Integrating information from these two environments, he organized a constellation of symbols that defined a theme, very likely without awareness: the office chair is hard on his back; an incident in which his father blasted him, causing him to feel demeaned; a cracked ashtray symbolizing father and therapist and associated with anger and anxiety. This theme, offered to the therapist for examination as a source for learning (he pushed the ashtray toward the therapist), resulted from cognitive structures that (1) copied and selected information from the environment and thoughts, fantasies, and emotions related to life metaphors; (2) coordinated and integrated these two pieces of information, transforming them into symbols that represented and expressed one of his conflicted life metaphors, that is, authority is on his back, is cracked (flawed), and makes him feel impotent and angry; and (3) enabled John, while dealing with the issue, to pretend that the therapist is father and at the same time a source of assistance. During these moments, then, John's cognition was engaged in efficient learning as defined by Piaget, serving the process of psychotherapy.

Case B

Mary, an 8-year-old, lived with her mother, who had separated from father. Moments after entering the playroom, Mary placed a girl hand puppet on the table along with other doll figures, at first randomly, then gradually forming a ring around the girl puppet. She interrupted this activity to discuss that the father of a friend of hers had died. She continued locating other doll figures around the girl puppet, interrupting this activity again to make an "exact" drawing of the home from which she had moved, taking much care to locate the correct number of windows and so on. Satisfied that she had made a good reproduction, she asked the therapist to draw "a mother" in the front yard while Mary busied herself drawing gravestones. Then she continued locating more dolls around the girl puppet, saying, "All of these are her mother and father," then, with a burst of laughter, "That's impossible!"

Mary's cognition selectively produced information from her external world and from personal metaphors as she shifted between pretend play (locating many "parents" around a girl doll), drawing an exact copy of her house, and recalling an event (the death of a close friend's father). As her cognition symbolized this pattern of information, a theme emerged, providing her with an opportunity to learn about the way she has construed the separation of her parents, which was probably the main reason why she refused to leave mother and attend school.

> ## HOW MANY DIFFERENT COGNITIVE-BEHAVIORAL REGULATORS ACCOUNT FOR THE WAYS IN WHICH INFORMATION IS COPIED AND TRANSLATED INTO SYMBOLS?

Of the several cognitive mechanisms identified, five have withstood the test of numerous experiments. Each follows a developmental course, and together they form a developmental hierarchy (Figure 6–4, righthand column).

   1. *Body image–tempo regulation* concerns the manner in which a person uses images/symbols to represent and regulate the body and body motility. The young child registers vague body perceptions represented in global images. In addition, body motility is poorly regulated. With development, differentiated images represent body perceptions, and body motility is regulated in terms of many differentiated tempos.

   2. *Focal attention* concerns the manner in which a person surveys a field of information. The young child typically scans information slowly and directs atten-

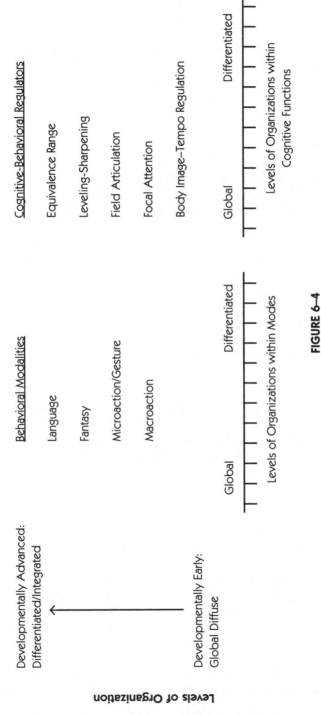

Levels of Organization

FIGURE 6–4

Hierarchies of Behavioral Modalities and Cognitive-Behavioral Regulators that Serve to Negotiate Developmental Issues throughout Childhood and Adolescence

tion only to narrow segments of the available field. With development, the child scans more actively and sweeps attention across larger segments of the field.

3. *Field articulation* defines the manner in which an individual deals with a field of information containing elements both relevant and irrelevant to the intention at hand. The young child attends equally to relevant and irrelevant information. With development a child gradually sustains attention on what is relevant while withholding attention from what is irrelevant to the ongoing intention.

4. *Leveling-sharpening* concerns the manner in which a person constructs images of information that changes or remains stable over time and compares these with present perceptions. The young child typically constructs fuzzy images of past information and fuses these with present perceptions so that subtle changes in information are not recognized. With development the child constructs sharper, more differentiated images and distinguishes them from present perceptions so that subtle similarities and differences between past and present information are noticed.

5. *Equivalence range* concerns the manner in which information is grouped and categorized in terms of a concept. The young child groups information in terms of a few narrow, concrete categories ("These go together because they are all round"). With age the child constructs increasingly broader categories conceptualized in terms of more differentiated, abstract concepts ("These are tools").

WHAT IS THE ORIGIN OF COGNITIVE-BEHAVIORAL REGULATORS AND THE RELATIONSHIPS AMONG THEM?

These mechanisms become fully structured by the third year of life, although the cognitive activity of infants suggests these mechanisms begin to organize during the first years of life (Cohen and Salapatek 1975; see Santostefano 1978 for a review of selected studies). Moreover, the process of each remains the same throughout development, but the organization changes. For example, information is surveyed with the focal attention function whether the scanner is 3 or 13 years old, but the organization changes: the younger child scans with narrow-passive visual sweeps, while the older with broad-active visual sweeps. Cognitive-behavioral mechanisms are also interdependent and "nested one within the other." When functioning adequately, the process of one mechanism relies upon and integrates the processes of other mechanisms lower in the hierarchy. Consider a child who was asked to group various objects that share something in common. The child grouped a bottle of glue, a hammer, and a roll of Scotch tape, because they are "things to fix with." While performing, the child regulated motility, scanned available objects, articulated attributes of each, compared perceptions of these objects with images of similar objects and past experiences with them, and then united a particular cluster of objects in terms of a functional attribute they share (fixing).

HOW ARE COGNITIVE-BEHAVIORAL REGULATORS RELATED TO NONVERBAL AND VERBAL ACTIVITY?

Words, thoughts, and beliefs are part of the process of only one mechanism, equivalence range. However, when a verbalization is constructed to explain why a set of items belong together, for example, this verbal belief is nested within deeper nonverbal and sensorimotor activity. Paraphrasing the critique by Arnkoff and Glass (1982), discussed in Part IV, words, conscious thoughts, and beliefs are the tip of the cognitive iceberg below which is a larger base of images, unconscious fantasies and meanings, and sensorimotor activity. Applied to the model of cognitive regulations, the mechanism of equivalence range is the tip of the cognitive iceberg. Below are the mechanism of leveling-sharpening, field articulation, focal attention, and body-image/tempo regulation.

ARE DIFFERENT LEVELS OF COGNITIVE-BEHAVIORAL REGULATORS "GOOD" OR "BAD"?

One of the most common errors made when considering levels of behavioral organizations is to view one level as "good" and another "bad." Recall that cognitive therapists tend to view logical beliefs as good and illogical beliefs as bad (see Part III). In contrast, while one cognitive-behavioral regulator is conceptualized as developmentally higher (leveling-sharpening) or lower (field articulation), and one level within a mechanism (e.g., narrow scanning) as developmentally less mature than another (e.g., broad scanning), these levels do not define what is adaptively good or bad. Discussed in more detail below, any cognitive-behavioral regulator, and any level within it, could be adaptive or maladaptive depending on the developmental status of the child, environmental conditions and expectations, and requirements of the child's life metaphors.

WHAT ROLE DOES ADAPTATION PLAY IN THE OPERATION OF COGNITIVE-BEHAVIORAL REGULATORS?

Cognitive-behavioral mechanisms, and levels within them, become operative depending on an individual's "adaptive intention," that is, the fit a person intends to negotiate, consciously or unconsciously, between the demands of environments and those of her/his life metaphors. For example, a teacher sends a child to the supply closet to obtain a particular workbook, "like this one." Guided by the unconscious intention of a life metaphor prescribing opposition, the child compares a fuzzy image of the workbook the teacher displayed with inefficient perceptions of workbooks in the closet, and returns with the wrong one.

WHAT IS THE RELATIONSHIP BETWEEN COGNITIVE-BEHAVIORAL REGULATORS AND CONSCIOUS/UNCONSCIOUS PROCESSES?

The adaptive intentions that guide cognitive functioning are typically outside of awareness unless experiences, such as those made available in therapy, bring them into awareness. A child about to undergo surgery may be conscious of coping with surrounding stimulation and her/his anxiety and fear. At the same time the child may be guided by an unconscious intention to avoid information in the surrounding environment because it is construed as threatening, and to focus on private thoughts and fantasies. A later section discusses research studies that illustrate the influence on cognitive functioning of unconscious intentions.

WHAT IS THE RELATIONSHIP BETWEEN COGNITIVE-BEHAVIORAL REGULATORS AND MECHANISMS OF DEFENSE?

Cognitive-behavioral regulators are viewed as mechanisms that are separate from, but function in concert with, mechanisms of defense. The effective functioning of mechanisms of defense requires the effective functioning of cognitive-behavioral regulators and vice versa. Each has a defensive purpose. Mechanisms of defense are organized to deal with conflict between representations of wishes/urges and the rules opposing them. Cognitive-behavioral regulators are organized to deal with conflict between the demands of life metaphors and those of environmental stimulation as construed by the individual. Each has an adaptive purpose. Mechanisms of defense disguise and displace wishes. Cognitive-behavioral regulators seek and avoid information to maintain a level and pace of stimulation and emotion that serves learning and adaptation.

WHAT ARE THE RELATIONSHIPS BETWEEN COGNITIVE-BEHAVIORAL REGULATORS, IQ, ACADEMIC PERFORMANCE, PERSONALITY DISPOSITIONS, AND GENDER?

Studies have demonstrated that the process of each cognitive-behavioral regulator is unrelated to IQ, underlies performance with various academic tasks, predicts learning disabilities, and accommodates to various personality dispositions and life experiences (e.g., Cotugno 1987, Rieder and Cicchetti 1989, Santostefano 1978, 1986, 1988a, 1995b, Wertlieb 1979). Last, while these mechanisms appear to operate independent of gender, they correlate with the degree of match or mismatch between psychosexual identity and gender. When psychosexual identity is discordant with gender, individuals tend to function at less mature levels of cognitive-behavioral regulators (Santostefano 1978, Santostefano and Rieder 1984).

HOW DOES THE CONCEPT OF COGNITIVE-BEHAVIORAL REGULATORS COMPARE WITH PIAGET'S CONCEPT OF MENTAL SCHEMAS?

A cognitive-behavioral mechanism, like a schema, conceptualizes a pattern of behaviors that include overt actions, perceptions, mental images, thoughts, and words. However, several important differences distinguish the two. The processes of schemas change throughout development from actions on objects to mental imitations of these actions, classifications, and logical-hypothetical thinking. In contrast, each cognitive-behavioral process, while undergoing differentiation from infancy through adolescence, maintains its essential organization and function. Further, all cognitive-behavioral regulators are viewed as operating simultaneously throughout development, although one may dominate the manner in which a person manages information in a particular situation. Finally, and of particular importance, cognitive-behavioral regulators, unlike Piaget's schemas, are conceptualized as assimilating and accommodating to information both from contexts and from life metaphors, coordinating requirements of the two domains so that the associated emotions and representations are balanced to permit efficient functioning.

WHAT ROLE DO COGNITIVE-BEHAVIORAL REGULATORS PLAY IN SELF- AND MUTUAL REGULATIONS, AND WHAT IS COGNITIVE ORIENTATION?

The role cognitive-behavioral regulators play in self- and mutual regulation is conceptualized as "cognitive orientation" and involves the "coordinating function" of cognitive-behavioral regulators. The concept of cognitive orientation defines whether a person's cognition is focused on the calls for action from life metaphors or those from contexts as construed, or flexibly shifts between and coordinates the two. As diagrammed in Figure 6–5, when coordinating and integrating calls for action from each domain, cognitive-behavioral regulators reorganize regressively or progressively. Once some degree of coordination is achieved between the two calls for action, the person responds with a thought, spoken statement, fantasy, physical action, or some combination, always including emotions. After a response is rendered, cognitive-behavioral regulators perceive and assimilate the outcome of the response. This feedback contributes to changing the related life metaphor and its prescriptions, and/or the situation/person with which the child is negotiating.

WHAT IS THE NORMAL DEVELOPMENTAL COURSE FOLLOWED BY COGNITIVE ORIENTATIONS?

In normal development, cognitive functioning is autonomous both from fantasies/drives/motives and from environmental stimulation. Cognitive functions are guaranteed autonomy from the influence of fantasies by virtue of the fact that from birth these functions are inherently preadapted to and "fitted with" reality stimulation. On the other hand, cognition's autonomy from the environment is guaranteed by the human's constitutionally given ability to transform stimuli into symbols and fantasies. A person's capacity for representing (symbolizing), then, is viewed as protecting her/him from becoming stimulus-bound and a slave to environmental requirements (Rappaport in Gill 1967).

Consider a 36-month-old toddler who shows he has emerged from the first 3 years of life with a solid capacity to exercise cognitive autonomy. He surveys a large number of toys and then focuses on a three-inch plastic figure of a space man. He rubs the head of the figure saying, "No helmet." He continues surveying, takes another plastic spaceman, which now has a helmet, and carries it back to his table, setting it next to another, identical figure. At another time the same child crawls slowly across the floor, each forward movement of his arms and legs suggesting power and determination. He scans an array of toys, crawls up to a

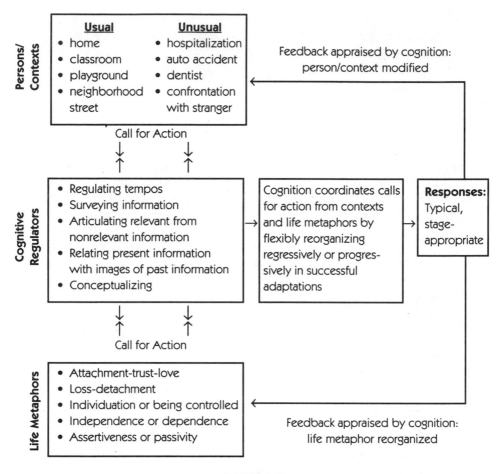

FIGURE 6–5
A Model of Cognitive-Behavioral Regulators Coordinating the Demands
of Life Metaphors and Contexts in Normal Development

stick, picks it up with his teeth, and drops it from his mouth next to a six-inch wooden figure of a man (the stick and figure are the same length). He raises his head again, growls ferociously, and says, referring to the stick just dropped, "Me killed him, too." Both vignettes would be viewed as moments of play. In the first, play involves cognitive functioning that deals with information as it exists. In the second, play involves cognitive functioning that deals with information as it is transformed or imagined. What is crucial for us is that *the same cognitive-behavioral regulators are operating in both episodes; in one they function relatively autonomously from fantasy and in the other, relatively autonomously from reality stimulation.*

Studies (Santostefano 1978) have suggested three phases in the developmental course of cognitive orientation. Before the age of 4 years, cognitive-behavioral regulators are oriented more toward information from life metaphors so that information in the environment is typically experienced in highly personal terms. During the first half of latency (ages 5 to 9), cognitive-behavioral regulators become oriented more toward information presented by contexts and persons. In this orientation coordination provided by cognitive-behavioral regulators enables the child to keep a distance from, and limit the interference of, emotionally laden fantasies and wishes. During the second half of latency (age 9 to early adolescence), cognitive regulators shift to an orientation that is flexibly both outer and inner oriented.

HOW ARE COGNITIVE ORIENTATIONS STRUCTURED DURING LONG-TERM ADAPTATION?

During dialectical exchanges between child and contexts, a child's cognitive orientation becomes organized and fitted to the complexity and pace of stimulation characteristic of the child's usual environments. If a 5-year-old has been engaged for years in a dialectic with a caregiver whose pace of stimulation is rapid and emotionally intense, the orientation of this child's cognitive regulators would be different from that of a 5-year-old child who has been involved in a dialectic with caregivers whose pace of stimulation is slow and emotionally low key. Along the same line, a cognitive orientation that becomes structured while a child is engaged in dialectics within a small inner-city apartment and street life would be different from that structured to manage stimulation typical of a rural community. In one study (Santostefano 1978) 120 African-American and Caucasian boys from different socioeconomic levels, living in a large midwestern city, showed that differences in the cognitive-behavioral regulator, leveling-sharpening, correlated with, for example, the degree to which the child's housing was dilapidated and the extent to which conversation took place at dinner. The configuration of results, which converges with discussions of infants in Part V, suggested that if a child is to construct stable representations of interactions, these interactions should be consistent in organization and repeated many times. If there is little conversation at dinnertime, the child does not experience consistent, predictable interactions with others, nor does he experience calling up memories and giving them meanings in terms of the discussion at hand.

WHAT CAUSES A PERSON'S COGNITIVE ORIENTATION TO CHANGE DURING SHORT-TERM ADAPTATIONS?

Cognitive orientation could shift temporarily whenever contexts and their meanings, which the child is negotiating, change the pace, intensity, and complexity of stimulation in ways that are *unusual* given the child's long-term experiences. Children differ in the flexibility with which cognition shifts to handle short-term changes in stimulation because of various factors—frequency, types, and timing of unusual changes in stimulation the child has experienced in the past and developmental issues the child is negotiating at the time the change in stimulation occurs. In short-term adaptation, then, cognitive orientation reorganizes to equilibrate the requirements of change in stimulation as construed by the child on the one hand and the requirements of the child's life metaphors and emotions (conscious and unconscious) on the other. If this equilibrating is successful, the child continues adequate self- and mutual regulation in the service of continued adaptation and learning.

To illustrate, consider a hypothetical situation involving an adolescent boy brought into an emergency room and presented to the surgeon attending him. At home and school this boy flexibly and actively scanned information in his environments as well as life metaphors. As he is brought into the emergency room, however, his scanning shifts, now limited to narrow pieces of the environment (a picture on the wall) and his cognition directs more attention at private thoughts and fantasies (he should have returned the blade guard on the mower as his father asked him to; it serves him right to get hurt since he failed his history exam, etc.). This shift in orientation toward subjective information insulates the adolescent from an unusual situation over which he has no control and serves to sort out personal meanings he has assigned to the accident. This shift is the outcome of short-term adaptation to an unusual context since the boy has not been in an emergency room before.

For the surgeon the emergency room is a usual environment. Approaching the boy, the surgeon scans actively and broadly, and attends to information relevant to his intention of helping him (skin color, emotional state, location and type of wound). The surgeon withholds attention from personal stimulation that is irrelevant to his present intention (an earlier disagreement with a supervisor; his car did not start easily this morning). At the same time the surgeon coordinates information he registers with thoughts and memories that derive from his training in, and past experiences with, injuries like the one before him. The surgeon's cognitive coordination is the outcome of long-term adaptation in many emergency room situations. Comparing these hypothetical experiences, we have an illustration of what George Klein (1951) meant when he discussed the equilibrating function of cognition. He noted that "[o]ne man's equilibrium is another man's discomfiture" (p. 330).

CAN YOU SUMMARIZE A FEW STUDIES OF COGNITIVE ORIENTATION IN LONG-TERM AND SHORT-TERM ADAPTATION?

A number of longitudinal studies have demonstrated the stability of a child's cognitive-behavioral regulators in long-term adaptation (see Santostefano 1978 for a comprehensive review). In one study kindergarten teachers rated 150 children in their classrooms as "typical" learners and thirty-four as "at risk" learners. All children were administered tests of cognitive-behavioral regulators. Several years later the children, now in the third and fourth grades, were reevaluated. The results showed that kindergarten test scores remained stable and predicted academic difficulties these children experienced in the third and fourth grades more effectively than did teacher ratings.

In terms of short-term changes in cognitive orientation, one study (Faye Shapiro in Santostefano 1978) administered tests of the leveling-sharpening cognitive mechanism and tests of personality on three separate occasions to young boys: at home, in a hospital bed before undergoing surgery for a hernia repair, and again at home thirty days after discharge. Matched comparison groups consisted of boys evaluated at home, in a dentist's chair, and again at home, and boys evaluated only at home at three comparable points in time. When in the hospital (Time 2), relative to the home assessment (Time 1), the surgical group shifted most toward an orientation that addressed life metaphors. While examining a series of pictures presented in succession, they detected fewer changes in different scenes, but especially in the test scene of a hospital room. Moreover, while all of the surgical boys shifted more toward leveling information from Time 1 to Time 2 than did the comparison groups, they showed individual differences in cognitive mobility. These differences correlated with a pattern of changes in personality functioning. On projective tests they expressed more explicit fantasies depicting aggression and body injury (symbolizing and rehearsing the unconscious meaning assigned to the surgery)—the same boys were rated by their mothers as adjusting *best* postoperatively.

Another study (G. Guthrie in Santostefano 1978) illustrated how a temporary cognitive shift away from fantasies toward environmental stimulation contributes to self-regulation and adaptive success. Older adolescent, novice parachutists were administered two leveling-sharpening tests: one depicted a parachutist in free fall, the other a parachutist descending with chute fully deployed. In each scene changes were introduced over sixty-three presentations that were relevant and nonrelevant for parachute jumping. The experimental group was administered the tests at home and again at the airport before executing a jump. The controls consisted of novice parachutists (from the same club), who were tested at home at two comparable points in time. A comparison of tests scores from Time I to Time II resulted in significant differences. When at the airport, the experimentals detected significantly more parachute-relevant changes in the test scene, while controls showed no consistent shift. Moreover, the difference observed with the experimental subjects from Time I to Time II was more pronounced with the free-fall test scene than with the more benign scene of a slow descent. Given that none of the subjects had yet experienced a free-fall jump (in which the jumper opens the chute after falling some distance), we inferred that this scene evoked, to a greater degree, the meaning of danger to body safety. Accordingly, the leveling-sharpening process, when equilibrating in response to the free-fall scene, shifted in orientation to an even greater degree toward environmental, parachute-relevant information (information subjects used to ensure survival).

DO CLINICAL POPULATIONS SHOW COGNITIVE ORIENTATIONS THAT FOLLOW THE SAME DEVELOPMENTAL COURSE AS THAT OF NORMAL CHILDREN?

A course opposite that of normal children has been observed. By age 9, cognitive mechanisms are either excessively occupied with information from fantasies, wishes, and impulses (inner-oriented)—with external information inefficiently copied—or they are excessively occupied with external stimulation (outer-oriented), limiting the contribution of life metaphors and fantasies. Of equal importance, after age 9 cognitive mechanisms maintain these rigid orientations, failing to shift back and forth between contexts and metaphor in keeping with opportunities, limits, and demands. As a result, efforts to adapt are usually limited, whether the task involves learning in school, in psychotherapy sessions, or from experiences.

HOW DO MALADAPTIVE COGNITIVE ORIENTATIONS COME ABOUT?

Two types of mismatch between a person's unique cognitive makeup and her/his environments typically result in a pathological cognitive orientation. With the first, an unusual environment that persists for some time interferes with a child's negotiating key, developmental issues. For example, an 18-month-old requires a hip cast for over a year, limiting motility and physical experimentation with the environment, sensorimotor behaviors that are critical for further cognitive development. In the second type the content of a child's interpersonal environment from infancy is uniquely ill-suited given the child's makeup. As one example, during the second year of life a child's testing of aggression, and physically experimenting with material, is sharply limited by caregivers who are conflicted about their own aggression.

The child copes by solidifying a rigid inner-cognitive orientation that centers on an elaborate fantasy life of aggression, leading to an obsession with computer war games. With another set of circumstances, if caregivers do not pretend, especially with humor, or if caregivers are excessive in requiring the child to be orderly and clean, the child internalizes these standards and develops an orientation that centers on external stimulation as it is and avoids pretending what it could be. In these instances the mismatch is primarily a function of the state of the child's environment within which she/he is required to negotiate life metaphors.

HOW MANY TYPES OF MALADAPTIVE COGNITIVE ORIENTATIONS HAVE BEEN OBSERVED?

Laboratory studies and clinical observations have identified three types of maladaptive cognitive orientations, each characterized by excessive inflexibility and each associated with maladaptations from the toddler years through adolescence.

Type I. Outer Orientation

A pervasive, rigid, outer cognitive-orientation that centers inflexibly on discrete, usually concrete, stimuli, permitting little or no contribution from metaphors and their calls for action.

Type II. Inner Orientation

A pervasive, rigid, inner cognitive-orientation that centers inflexibly on existing meanings from life metaphors, permitting little or no contribution from opportunities persons and situations provide for experimental actions.

Type III. Excessive Shifts in Cognitive Orientation

When the calls for action of a life metaphor are perceived, cognition rapidly shifts to an outer orientation, centering on a reality detail *unrelated* to the metaphor as a way of avoiding its prescriptions. Similarly, when a reality detail and its requirements are perceived, cognition immediately shifts to an inner orientation, centering on a fantasy detail *unrelated* to the situation. By shifting excessively, cognition prevents/avoids integrating meanings and contexts.

Each of these pathological cognitive orientations limits a child's ability to establish rituals of interaction with others that would otherwise permit the cycling and recycling of experiences as well as limiting a child's ability to revise already established rituals. As a result, with each orientation modes of behaving fail to change whether in everyday living or in the treatment situation.

Model III. Action, Fantasy, and Language as Modalities in Self- and Mutual Regulation

When negotiating life metaphors with others, a child takes action, fantasizes, and verbalizes. Some years ago Lindzey (1952) reminded psychologists that fantasy behavior does not always mirror overt behavior, while Brown (1958) noted, "We do not understand the relationships between modes of inner experiencing and overt behavior" (p. 66). A number of years ago, in response to this need, I initiated a program of laboratory and clinical studies with colleagues (e.g., Blaisdell 1972, Eichler 1971, Santostefano 1960a,b, 1965a,b, 1968a,b, 1970, 1977, 1978, 1980a, 1995b, Santostefano and Wilson 1968).

> **HOW DOES A CHILD DEVELOP ORGANIZATIONS OF ACTIONS, FANTASIES, AND LANGUAGE THAT BECOME MODALITIES THAT NEGOTIATE EXPECTATIONS FROM THE ENVIRONMENT AND LIFE METAPHORS?**

As in the case of infant–caregiver negotiations, how parents and other idealized persons respond to a child's modes of expression influence the form and organization these behaviors take. Parents, older sibs, peers, relatives, and teachers permit and oppose a child's modes of expression. As child and others engage in cycles of mutual regulation, they negotiate the paradox between them in a dialectical process. The child attempts to influence what others permit and prohibit in terms of modes of expression, and others attempt to influence what the child prefers as modes of expression. During this process, if the child idealizes and identifies with these persons (see previous discussion of ego ideal), the child's modes of expression accommodate, gradually evolving organizations of actions, fantasies, and verbalizations that satisfy both the child and her/his relational world. Last, the timing and content of permissions and prohibitions, as well as the emotional tones that accompany them, are critical in the child's developing a flexible hierarchy of modalities. In summary, the child's modes of expression "bump into" restrictions and expectations from others. And as the child's modalities accommodate to and assimilate the standards of idealized adults, and as these standards become the child's "own rules of experiencing and behaving," the child's modalities reorganize to satisfy these standards.

HOW ARE THE MODALITIES OF ACTION, FANTASY, AND LANGUAGE RELATED?

Taking action, imaging (fantasizing), and verbalizing are hierarchically ordered, alternative modalities that symbolize experiences (serve as referents) and express meanings (serve as vehicles) as the child engages in self- and mutual regulations when negotiating life metaphors with others (see Figure 6–4, left column).

As an illustration, a 2-year-old child may express aggression and jealousy concerning his infant sib by thrashing on the floor (an undifferentiated response involving the action mode); by 3 he may poke the sib (a more differentiated, yet direct, response). As restrictions and permissions are imposed by parents during many cycles of mutual regulation, the child might, at age 4, express his aggression by smashing the sib's toy (a less direct response). At age 6, as the child participates in cycles of negotiating now including teachers, he may show greater delay and indirectness by kicking the toy wagon of a classmate in kindergarten hours after his sib aroused his anger that morning. By 7, with the emerging capacity to substitute action with fantasy, the child accommodates to the objections of others whenever he expresses aggression in action. Now the child's actions involve pointing his toy gun at his sib and "killing him" in a game of war, enacting macroaction and fantasy. By 10 he may "demolish" the toy troops of a neighborhood friend in a formboard game of civil war, now involving microaction and fantasy. And by 12, with the language mode differentiated and dominating, he may shout vindictives in the playground at a younger child who has recently joined the school.

As the example illustrates, although the three modalities are available throughout the life span, a developmental principle defines the relationships among them as well as the modality that dominates a child's experiences at particular phases in childhood. Younger children (from 2 to about 7 years) tend to represent and express experiences with actions and gestures. With development (from 8 to about 11 years), the action mode is subordinated by and assimilated into the fantasy mode, which dominates. Now images and fantasies are the vehicles used to express meaning—and to rehearse actions—before taking action physically. Still later (12 years and beyond), the action and fantasy modes are subordinated by and assimilated into the language mode, which dominates. While subordinated, earlier modes of symbolizing and experiencing are not replaced by modalities that dominate later, but remain potentially active.

Two other issues should be considered in this developmental progression. With one, the behaviors involved in these alternative modes appear in a child's repertoire long before they are used as effective referents and vehicles. For example, an infant constructs mental representations of interactions long before she/he fantasizes shooting down a peer with whom she/he is playing Star Wars. And a toddler speaks words long before language becomes a differentiated, effective instrument of expression. With another characteristic of this developmental progression, a child differentiates and distances herself/himself from persons and things and also delays or inhibits taking action. When taking action, the child is physically fused with a person or thing and responds immediately, exercising little or no delay. When fantasizing, the child's experience is more distant from the physical environment (indirectness) since she/he "manipulates" an image rather than a person or thing as such, and delays taking action, at least for the duration of the fantasy. When verbalizing, a child's experiencing is least direct in terms of physical contact with persons and things. Words do not *physically* represent their referents, but a fantasy could represent some physical attribute of what is being experienced. And a spoken word bears no physical resemblance to the action or fantasy with which it is connected, and represents the greatest degree of delay and indirectness.

HOW DO ACTIONS, FANTASIES, AND VERBALIZATIONS BECOME CONNECTED AND INTEGRATED?

In negotiating a life metaphor, the child's action experiences are never perfectly matched with her/his emerging fantasies. Language expressions that emerge are never perfectly matched with actions and fantasies, defining a paradox among modes. During many cycles of interactions with others, the paradox between actions, fantasies, and language expressions is gradually negotiated so that fantasies and language increasingly provide more adequate representations of actions. Thus experiences in one mode eventually establish representational roots in the others. Accordingly, a particular action could be represented by a fantasy, or metaphoric statement; conversely, this fantasy or statement could be represented by an action, each substituting for the other. If the paradox among modes has been negotiated successfully, the child is able to shift from one modality to another and back again, each carrying some representation of the life metaphor being negotiated.

ARE THERE DEVELOPMENTAL LEVELS WITHIN MODALITIES AND HOW ARE THEY CONNECTED?

Development within each modality follows the same transition, from expressions that are direct and immediate to expressions that are indirect and delayed. Consider a 5-year-old boy who pokes his younger sib, behavior reflecting directness and immediacy, characteristic of the action mode. At another time the same boy could cover his sib with bath powder from head to foot. This behavior, while still within the action mode, is physically distant (less direct) from the sib to some degree, since the powder, not the person of the child, contacts the sib's body. This action conveys more delay in that it takes time to shake the powder from the can. Here, then, we have two expressions, or levels, within the action mode, one less direct and more delayed than the other. In the same way, alternative fantasies and verbalizations emerge, representing degrees of directness and delay. The same dialectical process that takes place among modes also takes place within a mode. Consider again a child who pokes at his infant sib. As this behavior "bumps into" the prohibitions of idealized adults, a dialectic takes place between this action and other possible actions the child might take (taking the infant's rattle, wanting a drink from the infant's bottle). As the paradox is negotiated among these possible actions, a particular action emerges, enabling the child to continue negotiating a life metaphor while also accommodating the requirements of others. For example, the child could insist on sitting at the kitchen table between mother and the infant's highchair.

HOW DO THE MODALITIES OF ACTION, FANTASY, AND LANGUAGE EXPRESS THE DEMANDS OF BOTH LIFE METAPHORS AND CONTEXTS?

As diagrammed in Figure 6–6, the availability of action, fantasy, and language modes, and of degrees of directness and delay within each mode, provide the child with multiple behavioral means and alternative goals to express the demands of life metaphors while negotiating with different contexts. The more a child has available the capacity for delay to engage in alternative modes of expression and to utilize alternative goals, the more the child can economically manage changes in the environment, at the same time meeting the needs of the life metaphor she/he is negotiating. For example, the parents of a 6-year-old may prohibit vigorous action expressions of a life metaphor. But, when continuing the negotiation of this same metaphor with a peer, the child may engage in vigorous action expressions because the peer has indicated that these expressions are acceptable. A related issue concerns the mobility of action, fantasy, and language expressions in the process of adaptation. Behavioral modes, and levels within each, operate individually or integratively depending on the adaptive intention of the child and the requirements and opportunities of a situation. Changes in environmental conditions, or the emotional-psychological state of the child, could cause her/him to revert temporarily to a developmentally earlier or higher modality or to an earlier or higher level within a modality, representing regressive or progressive shifts. As one illustration, a 12-year-old girl sitting in the classroom looks up from her desk work, peers at a friend, and engages the fantasy mode as she imagines herself to be more attractive and the favorite of a mutual male friend. At lunchtime, in the cafeteria, the same child now engages the action mode as she nudges past her female peer to sit next to a male friend. When lunch is over she exclaims to her female friend, "Don't you think my outfit is the greatest!" now engaging the language mode.

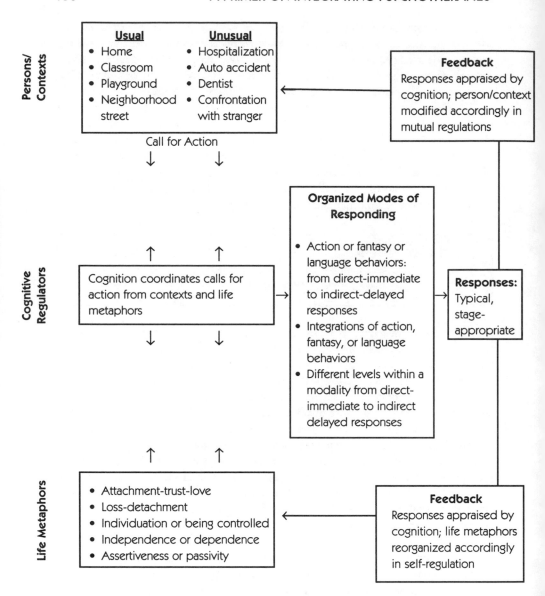

FIGURE 6–6
A Model of Action, Fantasy, and Language as Organized Modalities
Expressing the Demands of Life Metaphors and Contexts in Normal Development

WHAT DERAILS THE DEVELOPMENT OF ACTION, FANTASY, AND LANGUAGE AS MODALITIES IN SELF- AND MUTUAL REGULATION?

Significant unrepaired disruptions of ongoing regulations, with their traumatic, heightened emotions, compromise the modalities of action, fantasy, and language as tools for negotiating. The child manages the disruption by calcifying a modality, so to speak, and segregating it from the others. When this happens, the paradox among modes fails to be negotiated. Therefore, as development unfolds, fantasies do not adequately represent actions and/or verbal expressions do not adequately represent actions and fantasies. What a child does, then, is not integrated with and related to what the child imagines and says. As a result, when engaged in negotiating developmental issues, the child does not benefit from rehearsing actions in fantasy before taking action or verbalizing some meaning/issue that is housed in fantasy. When negotiations among modalities are disrupted, one or more becomes an "independent" world of expression.

The same types of mismatch between child and environment that give rise to pathological cognitive orientations also derail the development of modalities. One concerns a mismatch between the child's developmental stage and "environmental accidents." The other concerns a long-term mismatch between the child's unique makeup/temperament and physical/emotional characteristics of caregivers. As one example of the first, when he was 5 years old and in the "action phase" of development, a child watched his father operate a tractor. Suddenly the tractor tipped over and crushed father, to whom the boy was very attached. While he had been characteristically assertive after his father's accident, he became increasingly inhibited and lost in fantasy play. He was referred for treatment at the age of 9 when teachers became concerned because he regularly stood at the edge of the playground "like a zombie." In terms of the issue we are considering, this boy managed the disruption by constricting and splitting off the action mode and conducting a private life in fantasy. For this boy, taking any form of action could result in disaster, and therefore taking action aroused intense stress. We discuss this boy's treatment in Part VIII.

In terms of a long-term mismatch, consider an example with nearly the same outcome. A toddler was appropriately active, but her parents were excessively concerned with safety and orderliness. As the child negotiated self-assertion, now capable of racing about, her parents regularly "lectured" her. By the age of 7 the action mode was constrained and the child had retreated into fantasy. There was one exception. Having assimilated her parent's lectures, she began to make premature use of language, occasionally stepping out of her fantasy world and engaging her parents in "long arguments."

CAN YOU GIVE EXAMPLES OF STUDIES OF ACTION, FANTASY, AND LANGUAGE AS MODALITIES OF EXPRESSION?

Eichler (1971) administered tests evaluating action, fantasy, and language to 6-, 8-, and 10-year-old boys of average intelligence from both high and low socio-economic families and who had no history of psychological problems. Statistically significant age trends were observed. The 6-year-olds performed the most direct and immediate action first (they broke a light bulb, then hammered a nail, and, last, turned a screw into wood with a screwdriver). The 10-year-olds performed the more indirect, delayed action first (they turned the screw into wood and smashed the light bulb last). The 8-year-olds fell in between. Similarly, with a structured fantasy test, 6- and 8-year-olds selected fantasy stories that depicted more direct and immediate expressions than did the 10-year-olds. With a word association test each age group verbalized about the same number of words to each stimulus word (tree and knife). The 6-year-olds, however, verbalized the fewest number of aggressive words in response to the stimulus word *knife*, the 10-year-olds the most. In another part of Eichler's study these same boys were administered a test assessing preference for taking action versus fantasizing versus verbalizing. Statistically significant age trends were observed that support the model. Six-year-olds showed a preference for action, 10-year-olds for verbalizing, and 8-year-olds fell between.

Other studies have explored the modalities of action, fantasy, and language in various clinical populations such as institutionalized delinquents (Santostefano and Wilson 1968) and brain-damaged and orphan children (Santostefano 1965a). Differences these clinical populations showed fit theoretical expectations. For example, orphaned children more often expressed nurture in direct and immediate actions. Stoops (1974) reviewed fifty-five studies by other investigators who compared two or more modes of expression (action, fantasy, and language). While these studies employed a wide variety of assessment techniques, he concluded that thirty-five offered clear support for my developmental model of modalities, nine offered inconclusive support, and eleven reported findings contradicting the model.

WHAT PROPOSITIONS EMERGE WHEN THE THREE DEVELOPMENTAL MODELS ARE INTEGRATED?

In negotiating life metaphors, whenever a child experiences a significant disruption in self- and mutual regulation and related heightened traumatic emotions, and the disruption is not adequately repaired, psychological functioning is compromised:

1. Life metaphors and their calls for action; cognitive regulators and the orientation these functions maintain; and the degree to which the modalities of action, fantasy, and language remain integrated so that what a child does, imagines, and says are not interconnected.

2. A child's negotiations with life metaphors are left incomplete; cognitive orientation becomes excessively centered on external, or internal, stimuli—to avoid information from life metaphors or environments—or shifts excessively between information from the two worlds. And the modalities of action, fantasy, and language become segregated so that actions are used to avoid meanings contained in fantasies, or fantasies are used to avoid taking action, or language is used to avoid taking action and fantasizing.

3. Unrepaired disruptions that occur once, or over a relatively short period of time, (a parent leaves on a trip for several weeks) may have the same impact as those that sustain over a long period of time (mother experiences a bout of depression). Unrepaired disruptions that are distal (an uncle dies of AIDS) may have the same impact as those that are proximal (the child experiences excessive stimulation, witnesses a shooting).

4. Disruptions and their heightened emotional moments are represented in nonverbal embodied schemas as well as in fantasies and language.

5. Whenever an interactive ritual, and the developmental issue being negotiated, are disrupted, some element of the nonverbal embodied representation of this ritual may be translated into symbols, but an action element, with its emotional tone, remains unconscious yet active long after the disruption has dissipated, appearing in various derivative forms (gestures, noxious skin sensations, unexplainable aggressive actions). In these instances the embodied representation remains segregated from fantasy and language symbols, facilitated by a pathological cognitive orientation.

6. Whenever an embodied schema representing a traumatic disruption has not been translated into shared symbols, the demands of this schema are not readily available to cognitive regulators and modes of expression in ways that serve growth. Therefore, treatment should emphasize translating action/sensorimotor elements of an embodied schema into shared symbols so the meaning becomes available to cognitive regulators and modes of expression and therefore benefits from cycles of dialectical negotiations with others.

7. To facilitate a child's translating embodied schemas, her/his cognitive orientation and modes of expression must be rendered more flexible.

7

Guidelines for Integrating Psychotherapies for Children and Adolescents: A Developmental Dialectical Approach

CONTENTS

Relying on the foundation and the first and second floors of the proposed "developmental house" (Table 5–1), we consider here guidelines for conducting integrative psychotherapy with children and adolescents.

WHAT IS THE GOAL OF TREATMENT?

The goal of treatment is to assist a child in reorganizing maladaptive life metaphors, cognitive orientations, and modes of expression, rendering each domain more differentiated and flexible. If this goal is accomplished, a child's cognitive orientation adaptively coordinates the calls for action from life metaphors and environments: her/his modes respond flexibly, assimilating and accommodating to opportunities and limitations presented by changing situations and relationships. Empowered by these tools, a child is equipped to continue a growth-fostering developmental course during day-to-day encounters with family members, peers, teachers, and others. Each of the models we discussed in Part VI provides a doorway through which a therapist could enter to facilitate change in a child's functioning. As diagrammed in Figure 7–1, a therapist could enter the doorway leading to a child's life metaphors, or to a child's cognitive orientation, or to a child's modalities of expression. In the discussion that follows we clarify which doorway a therapist should enter first and what she/he should do.

HOW DOES ASSESSMENT HELP IN SELECTING A DOORWAY TO ENTER WHEN BEGINNING TREATMENT?

Typically, to plan treatment, therapists rely on intake interviews with child and family; cognitive, intellectual, and projective tests; and questionnaires (Brems 1993, Coonerty 1993, Coppolillo 1987, Matson and Ollendick 1988). However, as illustrated by Brems (1993), who proposed a four-hour intake session with child and family, preferably taking place on a single day, data from interviews are given the most emphasis. While I agree with the value of intake interviews, we should keep in mind that parents and teachers peer through a particular metaphor and provide information about how she/he construes a child. Mother's main concern about 8-year-old Laura was that she experienced "weird" fears (without any obvious precipitating event, Laura would not take a shower because she believed large bugs

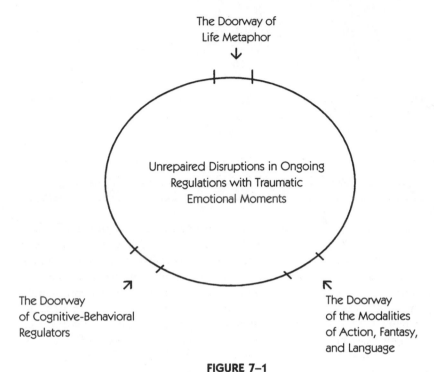

The Doorway of
Life Metaphor

Unrepaired Disruptions in Ongoing
Regulations with Traumatic
Emotional Moments

The Doorway
of Cognitive-Behavioral
Regulators

The Doorway
of the Modalities
of Action, Fantasy,
and Language

FIGURE 7–1

A Paradigm for Integrative Psychotherapy with Children and Adolescents:
Three Doorways through Which a Therapist Could Enter

might come out of the drain). Father on the other hand was concerned about the discrepancy between Laura's obvious high intelligence and lack of motivation with schoolwork. The teacher believed Laura had an "auditory discrimination problem" because she frequently did not follow instructions. The school psychologist wondered if Laura was "borderline psychotic or atypical" because, during a classroom observation, she seemed tuned out and sometimes talked to herself. Similarly, during an initial meeting, a child presents what she/he construes as the reason for seeing a therapist. When Laura was asked why she thought her parents asked her to come for a meeting, she replied probably because she and her younger sister frequently argued. I believe interview data have limited value unless related to data from diagnostic tests.

WHAT SHOULD THE FOCUS BE WHEN INTERVIEWING PARENTS?

In addition to learning how parents define a child's problems, because of the importance assigned to the first three years of life by our developmental-dialectical model I recommend that a therapist devote some of the interview to exploring whether, during the child's first years, disruptions and heightened emotional moments occurred in ongoing regulations, and whether and how these disruptions were repaired. These disruptions might give clues to embodied meanings the child constructed that have remained unnamed yet active, influencing the child's maladaptive behaviors. In many instances parents tend not to attach significance to early events. When asked whether anything upsetting happened in the family or neighborhood during the first three years of a child's life, one set of parents recalled a break-in that occurred when the referred child (now 14) was 3 years old. The family returned from a vacation and found items strewn about. During the next several months (the parents could not agree how long), the child refused to go out to play and cried when left with a sitter. At these times father became angry and noted with relief that the child "soon got over it."

I also recommend that a therapist explore whether a child showed behaviors from 24 to 36 months suggesting that the foundation of a pathological cognitive orientation was being formed ("Do you remember how Sally played during that time? How she handled toys and material?"). Here a therapist is on the alert for observations that suggest a child was beginning to show cognitive rigidity by excessively "patterning" or "dramatizing" stimulation and not combining both cognitive styles (Wolf and Gardner 1979). Similarly, guided by our model, a therapist should explore whether a child showed expressions of a derailed action mode. For example, in the months following the break-in, the parents found animal figures and dolls with heads twisted off, which puzzled them because the child would line them up so neatly during play.

WHAT SHOULD THE FOCUS BE DURING THE FIRST SESSIONS WITH A CHILD?

I recommend that whenever possible the child should be seen first so that the therapist can form her/his own initial impressions without being influenced by the parents' views of the child. In addition, the therapist has a "live experience" to refer to when listening to the parents' concerns. I also recommend that a therapist not conduct an intake interview with the intention of getting the child to talk about her/his concerns in a straightforward manner (for a similar position see Spiegel

1989). With a younger child, a therapist could use the technique of play interview, a favorite among psychodynamic therapists. Excellent discussions of this method are available (Conn 1993, Schaefer and Cangelosi 1993). Inviting a child to select dolls and play any game she/he wishes, the therapist asks questions related to what the child has enacted ("How does she feel?" "Does anything happen during the night?" "Why was she kidnapped?"). But the vivid examples Conn described make clear that a play interview is productive when a child has developed the capacity to construct and enact elaborate fantasies while moving dolls through limited space and to verbalize these fantasies. If a child has this capacity, a therapist learns a great deal about the metaphors that are a source of the child's strengths and difficulties. In my experience, however, a number of children in need of treatment do not have the cognitive capacity to symbolize or the verbal facility to share linguistic meanings through what dolls are thinking, doing, and saying. Moreover, I have found the method to be relatively unproductive with inner-city children who usually have not made use of dolls or toys to express meanings. Last, play and verbal interviews usually provide limited information about a child's cognitive orientation and preferred modes of expression, domains that can be effectively evaluated with psychological tests. For these reasons I devote most of the time to administering psychological tests and only about fifteen or twenty minutes to administering the Life Stressor Interview (see Part IX). This simple method is designed to help a child describe, directly or metaphorically, any disruptions and traumatic emotional moments she/he has experienced. The child's reports are viewed as conscious, verbalized expressions of disruptions that are then related to unconscious expressions elicited by projective tests. A child is asked, "Has anything happened that upset you a lot?"

WHAT SHOULD THE FOCUS BE WHEN USING PSYCHOLOGICAL TESTS?

I view psychological tests as indispensable "X-ray machines" that provide "pictures" of a child's life metaphors, cognitive orientation, and modes of expression not readily observable when one interacts with a child during an interview. Moreover, methods should assess a child's developmental status rather than focus on selecting a diagnostic category, a position that agrees with some (Coppolillo 1987, Spiegel 1989) but disagrees with others (Brems 1993). Because test methods developed specifically to assess these domains are discussed later (Part IX), here I consider how traditional psychological tests could be used to gather the required data.

Life metaphors should be evaluated at three levels: embodied schemas/action, fantasy, and metaphoric language. To assess body-based representations, I have developed the Action Test of Body Image and the Touch Association Test (Part IX). With the former the child assumes various body postures and describes what each body experience brings to mind. With the latter the child feels ambiguous clay objects, placed under a cloth and describes what each brings to mind. With each procedure, then, body perceptions are the stimuli. Projective tests (Rorschach inkblot test, Robert's apperception test) are effective in eliciting representations of life metaphors in the fantasy mode. And the Continuous Word Association Test (see Santostefano 1978) and sentence completion tests are effective in eliciting representations of life metaphors expressed in the language mode. The Life Stressor Interview described above also provides information a child produces at a conscious verbal level about heightened traumatic disruptions the child has experienced at home, in the community, or when watching TV.

Published normed tests (Santostefano 1988a) as well as unpublished methods described in Part IX, are available to assess a child's cognitive orientation. If these procedures are not available, observing how a child responds to traditional psychological tests frequently provides useful information. In general, a child's cognitive efficiency and level of anxiety/stress is compared when she/he is dealing with structured test items that require information to be experienced as it is versus when she/he is dealing with unstructured test items that require information to be imagined as it might be. If a child's performance reflects marked differences, she/he is very likely functioning with an inflexible cognitive orientation.

A pathological, outer cognitive orientation is suggested when a child shows meticulous performance and little anxiety/stress in, for example, copying geometric designs or responding to the Digit Span Subtest of the Wechsler Scales. But when dealing with unstructured items, such as inkblots, this same child shows anxiety/stress ("This is boring!") and detaches from the examiner, engaging in little eye contact. A pathological, inner cognitive orientation is suggested when a child becomes detached, experiences anxiety/stress/fatigue when dealing with structured tests, yet is animated and involved when dealing with projective tests. In addition, this child may take "liberties" with both structured and unstructured tests, assigning personal meanings to stimuli that go well beyond the stimuli and context. For example, while copying Bender-Gestalt Test Design A, the child spontaneously comments, "These are two spaceships crashing!" Pathological shifts in cognitive orientation are suggested when a child rapidly alternates between high and low involvement, shifting from the cognitive orientation required by a task at hand to its opposite. For example, a child abruptly stops copying a geometric design (which requires an outer cognitive orientation, experiencing information as it is) to discuss a movie about "ghostbusters." Then, while responding to a Rorschach inkblot, the child abruptly stops and slowly passes his finger over pencil marks on the tabletop, or asks about a picture hanging on the wall.

In addition to using procedures described in this volume (see also Santostefano 1978, 1995b) that assess a child's preferred mode of expression, a therapist could observe whether, when dealing with traditional tests, a child flexibly engages the mode required by a procedure or regularly shifts to its opposite. For example, while dealing with thematic pictures, a child begins constructing a story and then interrupts to enact some part of it. Or when dealing with the Rorschach test the child says, "It's a fly!" and slaps the card with her hand. Such behaviors suggest that the child is action oriented and has difficulty sustaining expressing herself/himself in the fantasy mode. As another example, while responding to a questionnaire or interview, a child frequently slips into a fantasy using materials in the playroom and/or describes a TV program or movie. Such behavior suggests this child is fantasy oriented and has difficulty sustaining expressing herself/himself in the language mode. Moreover, some children as young as 8 years of age show a tendency to prefer the language mode and to experience difficulty expressing themselves in fantasy or action behaviors. While responding to the Rorschach test, for example, a child frequently interrupts to "talk about," her/his teacher, a school assignment, a trip the family took last week, a younger sib who is a pest, and so on. These "spontaneous" discussions appear "rich" in content and "grist for the therapeutic mill," especially if the therapist is verbally oriented, but they also suggest a rigid use of language and a tendency to avoid other modes of expression.

HOW ARE ASSESSMENTS OF LIFE METAPHORS, COGNITIVE ORIENTATIONS, AND MODES OF EXPRESSION INTERRELATED TO SELECT A TREATMENT PLAN?

The initial task is to evaluate whether a child shows evidence that body-based/action meanings have been translated and extended into the levels of fantasy and language. For example, when assuming various body postures, a child described seeing a tree trunk that had been broken by lightning and a squirrel that had been flattened by a car. Yet, when constructing images when responding to inkblots, pictures, and sentence stems, the meaning of the body-self as deformed and injured does not appear (*when I think about my body* "I think it's the greatest"). In this case the body-based meaning is "unnamed," underground yet active. Treatment with this child would include the goal of translating this embodied meaning into fantasy and language symbols that are shared with the therapist, becoming available for negotiation and revision.

The second task is to evaluate whether one or another of a child's life metaphors disrupts her/his cognitive orientation and modes of expression so that cognition and behavioral modalities have become rigid. After these steps are taken, one of the following broad treatment plans is selected:

1. If a child's cognitive orientation and modes of expression are excessively rigid, treatment would first emphasize structured interactions designed to reorganize them and then emphasize unstructured interactions that translate embodied meanings into shared symbols and revise life metaphors.

2. If a child's cognitive orientation is flexible but modes of expression are rigid, initial treatment would emphasize structured interactions that differentiate and integrate action, fantasy, and language expressions, and then unstructured interactions that translate embodied meanings into shared symbols and reorganize life metaphors.

3. If a child shows stage-appropriate flexibility in cognitive orientation and modes of expression, treatment would emphasize, from the start, unstructured interactions that translate embodied meanings into shared symbols and reorganize life metaphors.

HOW IS CHANGE VIEWED BY THE DEVELOPMENTAL DIALECTICAL MODEL?

Earlier I proposed that the processes that take place between child and therapist are fundamentally the same as those that take place between an infant/child and her/his caregivers. This proposal was nested within a particular view of change: initially the organization of some behavior is relatively global and with development becomes more differentiated and integrated. Change is an inherent characteristic of behavior, and whether occurring over a short or long interval of time, an increase in chronological age is *not* the "cause" of change. Wohlwil (1973) cogently argued, in the language of researchers, that age is not an "independent variable" but a part of the "dependent variable." With age, or time, as part of the dependent variable, a therapist traces the relationship between the duration of a particular organization of child–therapist interactions on the one hand and changes that occur in some dimension of a child's behavior on the other (inhibition of movement, cognitive or physical impulsivity).

Applying these notions to our model, we could represent a child who comes to a therapist as a rushing river of life metaphors, cognitive regulators, and expressions in action, fantasy, and language. A therapist attempts to change the course of this river in much the same way as does a caregiver. But if we take a closer look at our model, with its levels of functioning, we recognize that this representation of a child needs to be elaborated. A more accurate image would portray a child as bringing a hierarchy of lakes (levels of functioning) connected by a river. The model of life metaphors could be represented by a river connecting a hierarchy of numerous lakes such as attaching to and loving others, separation-individuation, asserting. Cognitive regulators could be represented by a river connecting a hierarchy of five lakes: regulating body tempos, scanning, articulating relevant and irrelevant information, conserving images of past information and comparing them with present perceptions, and categorizing and conceptualizing. Behavioral modalities could be represented by a river connecting a hierarchy of three lakes: action, fantasy, and language. In an effort to facilitate change, where do therapist and child embark on a therapeutic journey—or canoe trip? Do they explore one or another lake, or do they canoe the river connecting them? To address this question we need to consider the processes of change that take place when canoeing a lake versus a river.

HOW DOES CHANGE TAKE PLACE WITHIN A LEVEL OF FUNCTIONING?

Imagine a level of inflexible functioning to be like a stagnant lake and constricted by weeds. To facilitate change in this lake, to make a level of functioning more flexible (whether a life metaphor, a cognitive orientation, or a behavioral modality), a therapist interacts with a child *within the child's maladaptive mode* in ways that promote flexibility. Here therapist and child explore a particular lake and clear it of weeds. I refer to this process as "first-order change," which occurs within a level and primarily involves facilitating change in self-regulation (Watzlawick et al. 1974).

HOW DOES CHANGE TAKE PLACE BETWEEN ONE LEVEL OF FUNCTIONING AND ANOTHER?

Now imagine a river that is constricted by rocks and debris at some point along its course. Because the river's flow is impeded, one lake, or level of functioning, is insufficiently connected to others. To facilitate change, the therapist connects (integrates) one level of functioning with another by removing debris that impedes the river's flow. In these interactions a therapist approaches the child *from outside the child's habitual maladaptive mode* and therefore "bumps into" the level or mode typically used by the child. I refer to this process as "second-order change," which emphasizes negotiating mutual regulation.

HOW ARE FIRST-ORDER AND SECOND-ORDER CHANGE RELATED?

I leave the image of rivers and lakes and elaborate an image of a car and driver used by Watzlawick and colleagues (1974). Imagine a car with a standard (stick) shift, gas pedal, and driver. The performance of the driver and car can be changed in two ways. With one, while the driver is, let us say, in first gear, she/he learns to regulate the gas pedal with increasing differentiation, flexibly depressing and lifting the pedal, quickly and slowly, in many different increments and in harmony with speeds required by traffic conditions. In learning movements required to operate in first gear, the driver is functioning within a level and involved in the processes of first-order change and self-regulation. Applied to our developmental models, changing how the gas pedal is depressed involves three particular "movements" within cognition and modes of expression: *differentiation*, *delay*, and *indirectness*.

But what if the vehicle is operated on a superhighway, not a rarely traveled road? Because of constant changes in the flow of traffic, the driver must now shift back and forth among gears. Each gear has its own range of foot movements coordinated with surrounding circumstances. In learning to change from first to third gear, the driver is responding to a major change in expectations outside herself/himself and is involved in the processes of second-order change and mutual regulation.

CAN YOU GIVE A CLINICAL EXAMPLE OF FIRST- AND SECOND-ORDER CHANGE?

A 10-year-old boy is confronted in the playground by a bully standing in his way. In response, the boy pushes the bully to one side. Later he races him to the top of a mount—interactions representing different degrees of directness and delay or different foot movements within first gear or the action mode. Then the bell rings, bringing recess to a close. In the classroom this boy is surrounded by a very different set of expectations that bump into the action mode, requiring second-order change or the ability to shift to another mode. Accordingly, he shifts gears to the fantasy mode. Glaring at the bully seated at the other end of the room, he fantasizes pounding him in a fist fight, and then beating him in a 100-yard dash at the school Olympics—fantasized interactions representing different degrees of directness and delay or different foot movements within second gear or fantasy mode.

If attention is not paid to differences between first- and second-order change, a therapist might interact in a way that the child experiences as an "assault." Recall a moment of psychotherapy reported by Coppolillo (1987) involving a boy who played solitaire with a deck of cards, behavior the therapist interpreted verbally. In response, the boy angrily insulted the therapist and walked away. From the view of our present discussion, by giving linguistic meaning to the solitaire game the therapist approached the boy from outside his preferred mode, requiring him to engage in second-order change and lifted the meaning of playing solitaire from the level of action to the level of language. The child's reaction strongly suggested he was not yet ready for second-order change. To facilitate first-order change in the meaning of the solitaire game, a therapist could sit at the far end of the room and involve himself in a game of solitaire, "speaking" to the child within his mode and preparing him for second-order change. Heard and Linehan's (1994) notion of "accepting" and "extending" strategies of change is related.

HOW DOES THE DEVELOPMENTAL DIALECTICAL MODEL VIEW RESISTANCE TO CHANGE?

Resistance to change has been considered from cognitive and behavioral as well as psychodynamic viewpoints (Wachtel 1982). Recall that Freud proposed that a person resists changing by "doing" instead of "remembering and discussing." But our developmental dialectical model, emphasizing that children frequently bring a rigid mode of functioning that is the opposite of another, requires that we elaborate this view of resistance. If an 8-year-old rigidly engages in games of checkers and avoids expressing herself verbally, is she resisting change because she doesn't want to remember something? The "interdependence of opposites" adds to an understanding of resistance, a concept that Jung (1952) proposed as a fundamental psychological mechanism. This concept includes the mind's tendency to draw boundaries and experience opposites rather than to engage in a dialectical process (Part II). The interdependence of opposites proposes that the identity of some inflexible behavior is defined and preserved by its opposite, which is avoided. For example, the inflexible meaning of good is persevered by the meaning of evil, the meaning of an inflexible action is preserved by the meaning of a related fantasy, and the meaning of an inflexible verbalized belief by the meaning of actions that could express that belief. To illustrate, recall the 15-year-old (Part VI) who sat still, preoccupied himself with the creases of his trousers and the position of a box of tissues, and seemed unable to share with the therapist meanings and feelings he was experiencing. His cognition sharply divided experiences in terms of things as they are and as he construed them to be, and rigidly focused on the former. This outer cognitive orientation was preserved by its opposite, namely, avoiding things as he construed them to be. His "resistance" to discussing personal concerns and fantasies, then, was not so much the outcome of refusing "to remember" but due primarily to his employing a mode of functioning that avoided its opposite. This outer cognitive orientation may at one time have coped successfully with disruptions, but then became habitual, operating independent of contexts. To help this adolescent, techniques are needed that dissolve the interdependence of extreme opposite cognitive orientations, developing his capacity to integrate meanings/emotions with external stimulation (i.e., symbolize) without being overwhelmed by painful emotions.

WHAT ARE THE CATALYSTS THAT CHANGE A CHILD'S LIFE METAPHORS, COGNITIVE ORIENTATION, AND MODES OF EXPRESSION?

Our model proposes three interrelated catalysts that derive from infant research (Figure 7–2).

1. *Cycles of dialectical interactions* assumes that a person is inherently directed toward evolving relationships with others and that the process of growing with another person itself has power to heal. When engaging in cycles of dialectical interactions, child and therapist negotiate and regulate their respective self-expressions and get to know the way the other walks, moves when excited versus tired, smells, sighs, laughs, glances when disappointed versus when pleased, and so forth. This interactive process is analogous to Stern's (1985) "core relatedness" between infant and caregiver. As diagrammed in Figure 7–2, every interaction between child and therapist does not necessarily involve their participating in a dialectical interaction. Imagine a circle that represents differences in self-expression between child and therapist. In the beginning each is standing outside this circle, although each is engaged in some interaction (Figure 7–2, I, II). But as child and therapist participate in repeated interactions, each eventually steps into the circle with the intention of negotiating one or another of their differences, and "getting to know" and regulating some attribute of the other's overt self-expressions (Figure 7–2, III). By increasingly articulating, recognizing, and regulating each other's self-expressions, a relational foundation is established upon which they eventually coauthor meanings they share, a process that involves the next catalyst we consider.

2. *Enactments* are constellations of actions/gestures, touch, fantasies, words, thoughts, and emotions that are intended to introduce a particular meaning into the intersubjective world child and therapist are constructing and sharing, a process that parallels Stern's (1985) "intersubjective relatedness" (Figure 7–2, IV). When a child and/or therapist enact, she/he assumes the other is also in the circle, shares a meaning related to one or another life metaphor they are negotiating, and expects the other to understand the communication and respond in a synchronous way. Enactments are not necessarily equal to what is conceptualized as discourse and play by psychodynamic, behavioral, and relational approaches to therapy (Brems 1993). A child may be engaged in a discussion, or some form of play, and not necessarily intend to share some meaning that serves negotiating a developmental issue with the therapist. Enactments are gradually elaborated and ritualized over many sessions or may take place during brief moments. Recall Spiegel's patient who, after hearing the therapist ask whether he had soiled himself at school, stepped into the

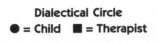

I

Interactions: Discussions of a school trip, playing a game, dealing with a task.

II

Interactions: Child or therapist step into the dialectical circle to negotiate some difference in overt self-expressions; the other does not step in.

III

Dialectical Interactions: Child and therapist step into the circle to negotiate and regulate differences in overt self-expressions, e.g., preferred level of stimulation, emotional tone, body movements. Child and therapist "contour" their self-expressions.

IV

Enactments: Child and therapist step into the circle to share a subjective experience and/or influence a subjective experience of the other; constellations of actions, images, words, emotions communicate and contribute a meaning to their intersubjective world.

Dialectical interactions and enactments require empathy and selective attunement.

V

Idealization/Internalization: Child and therapist idealize and internalize behaviors and meanings of the other devoted to solving the dilemmas they share.

FIGURE 7–2
Catalysts for Change

circle by placing a piece of clay at the end of his nose, enacting a meaning within their intersubjective world.

Enactments and dialectical interactions require the therapist to be empathic, understanding, and selectively attuned. If a therapist has empathically discovered herself/himself within a child's subjective world, and is in tune with the inter-subjective symbolic world constructed thus far, the therapist initiates and/or participates in enactments with the child that, more often than not, serve the treatment process and change. To engage in successful dialectical interactions and enactments, a therapist must shift back and forth from being a participant to being an observer, from introspection to empathy, from intuition to problem solving, and from becoming more involved to becoming more detached (Greenson 1977).

3. *Idealization and internalization.* When dialectical interactions and enactments are accompanied by appropriate empathy and selective attunement, they result in the child idealizing and internalizing the therapist and the therapist idealizing and internalizing the child (Figure 7–2, V). Recall that infant research provides considerable support for the view that enactments between infant and caregiver during the first two years of life become internalized within the infant's mind as organized expectations or schemas. This process continues beyond the third year as a child internalizes interactions with others, as well as caregivers, whose attributes become idealized. These attributes serve as symbolic standards against which a child evaluates her/his behaviors and define what the child wants to be rather than what a child should do. The importance of the therapist idealizing and internalizing the child usually is not given attention. If a therapist gradually discovers herself/himself within the child's subjective world over the course of many enactments, the therapist experiences, as does a caregiver, excitement, fatigue, boredom, pleasure, pride, irritation, and anger. Within these experiences a therapist should, as a caregiver does, idealize and internalize the child. It may seem hard to believe that a therapist sometimes finds herself/himself imitating a verbal expression or gesture the child typically uses or becoming very interested in a child's favorite athletic team, and so forth, as well as experiencing a surge of "therapeutic love" whenever the child makes some gain within or outside the treatment situation (Lear 1990, Orlinsky and Howard 1987).

In the Beginning Child and Therapist Are Foreign to Each Other: Guidelines for Integrating Two Subjective Cultures

Before stepping into a dialectical circle, child and therapist are essentially foreign to each other, bringing different subjective cultures. This issue relates to the growing interest in therapists' becoming sensitive to cultural differences (e.g., Division of Child, Youth and Family 1994, Fischer 1995, Franklin et al. 1993). Johnson's (1993) lucid discussion frames my view. Because child and therapist come from different cultural and ethnic backgrounds, various issues arise, such as the name each expects the other to use, and the potential for child and therapist to experience the other in terms of stereotypes she/he holds of her/his race and cultural and ethnic background.

But when viewed through our model, the issues raised concerning sensitivity to cultural diversity take on a wider significance. Metaphorically speaking, in the beginning infant and caregiver, as well as child and therapist, are *always* of "different cultures" whether or not they are of the same race and ethnic background. In the first months, from the infant's point of view, the caregiver is a "foreigner," and from the caregiver's point of view the infant is a "foreigner." Similarly, in the first months of treatment, child and therapist are foreign to each other. There is an important difference, however. A caregiver has already constructed a subjective world that she/he carries into a dialectical circle; the infant has not. In contrast, both the child who enters therapy and the therapist have already constructed a subjective world that has been and is being shared with others. Thus a number of issues arise as they begin interacting and negotiating in their relationship. Accepting those articulated by Johnson that emerge from race and ethnic and cultural differences, I focus on others that emerge from the developmental-dialectical model.

IF CHILD AND THERAPIST ARE FOREIGN TO EACH OTHER, WHAT CAN A THERAPIST DO TO NEGOTIATE THIS PARADOX?

I recommend that, as opportunities present themselves, a therapist engage a child in negotiating the issues articulated by Sander's model (Part V). Some children may require many negotiations with one issue, others a few negotiations with several issues. Some issues may need to be negotiated only a few times; others, repeatedly throughout treatment. Negotiating these issues operationalizes the catalysts for change described earlier.

1. *Negotiating initial adaptation and reciprocal exchange with cycles of dialectical interactions.* As child and therapist are discovering and contouring each other's overt self-expressions, the therapist is alert to the child's unique postures, gestures, rhythms of activity, and preferences for pace and level of stimulation, especially those involving sound, touch, and temperature, and whether and how these characteristics match her/his own. One child commented that the playroom was "screaming bright"; the therapist lowered the illumination without saying a word. Another child wrapped her arms around herself; the therapist raised the thermostat and obtained the child's jacket, even though for the therapist it was relatively warm. When negotiating reciprocal exchange, the therapist is alert for opportunities to engage the child in active-passive exchanges, especially involving emotions

and body rhythms that match the child's. One child sat outside under a large yew. He reached up and slowly pulled down a branch while lowering his torso, simultaneously singing a long "aaaaah." Then he released the branch; when it snapped back into position he sat up straight and completed his "song" with "choo!" The therapist joined in, rhythmically bowing and singing "aaah-choo!"

2. *Negotiating early directed activity, focalizing, and self-assertion with enactments* requires a therapist to be passive at times, modifying the active response involved in negotiating previous issues even though the meaning of the directed behavior is not yet clear. One child insisted that she and the therapist sit on the floor instead of at a table, and the therapist accommodated. Another ignored the therapist for most of two sessions, "flying" a helicopter throughout the playroom, occasionally mumbling to imaginary characters. The therapist said and did nothing except sit and watch the child, expressing interest with facial expressions whenever the child turned to look at the therapist. As a child experiences the therapist assuming a passive role in response to the child's directions, she/he frequently makes explicit "requests" intended to establish that the therapist is unconditionally available and receptive to sharing a subjective experience. Sometimes a child refers to her/his body or representations of the body-self. For example, while busying herself drawing pictures, a child repeatedly broke the point of her pencil and then glanced at the therapist, who sharpened the pencil each time. If a child adequately establishes that the therapist is unconditionally available, she/he will attempt to negotiate self-assertion both on materials and the person of the therapist. Negotiating self-assertion and aggressive expressions is probably the most difficult task a therapist faces if she/he views these behaviors as "fighting." When engaging in assertive behaviors, a child is developing "interactive tools" *designed to determine whether the therapist is "up to battling" not the child, but the child's difficulties.* The child's expressions of assertion/aggression, and the therapist's ability to survive them, play an important role in helping the child experience the therapist as someone who can be used in the struggle to overcome difficulties (Safran 1993).

This position is different from that of most, who propose that self-assertive behaviors should be controlled by "rules and regulations" (e.g., Brems 1993, Reisman 1973). Prohibiting behaviors, and requiring a child to accommodate to preformed rules, shifts the relationship from a climate of negotiating to one in which a therapist becomes a "probation officer" and the child the "offender." The therapist should be as resourceful as possible in inventing and experimenting with various ways in which the child's expressions of self-assertion and aggression can be permitted in some displaced form, rather than blocked by some rule. And the therapist should find ways to participate in the expression.

To illustrate, Tom, a 10-year-old, had already participated with the therapist in negotiations of reciprocating and directing activity. In one particular session, as he entered the playroom, he pushed the therapist to one side, angrily kicked a wastebasket, and defiantly stated, "This is fucking boring." Then he picked up boxing gloves and invited the therapist to "take me on." The therapist, not comfortable with boxing, challenged Tom to take him on with something else that is not boring. Tom wandered about for a moment, picked up two puppets, and smashed them against each other (very likely an action symbol of child and therapist in battle). This activity quickly escalated as Tom slammed the puppets against toys and shelves. Expressing amazement over Tom's "karate chops," the therapist invited him "to chop these wooden cutouts just like karate fighters do." The invitation worked, since Tom grinned and agreed. The therapist placed eight large, wooden, colored cutouts in a row, commented the cutouts were enemies to be "demolished," and suggested that each be given a name. Tom readily obliged (e.g., "Geek," "Grink," "Retard," "X—the therapist's first name"). The therapist challenged Tom to stand with his back to the cutouts, listen for the cutout named by the therapist, and then turn as quickly as possible and chop it. Tom enthusiastically chopped away, as the therapist timed and recorded how many seconds Tom required to turn, scan the row of cutouts, and chop the one named. Then the therapist suggested that Tom call out a name, and the therapist chop the cutout, while Tom timed him. Intense competition developed between them with the therapist displaying the same vigor and anger as did Tom.

In this vignette, the therapist negotiated that aggression is permitted ("I can take it") within a form and level of vigor that was fitted to his style. Of course therapists vary in terms of the degree and form of assertion/aggression with which they feel at ease. It is as important for the child to *know* this about the therapist as it is for the therapist to *know* this about the child. One child may ask the therapist to engage in a boxing match, while another, without any physical gestures, may quietly yet persistently change the rules of a board game so that the child always wins. Another child may spit on the therapist or hurl a wooden cube at the wall. Negotiating each expression of assertion/aggression enables a child to establish that the therapist has the knowledge and strength to combat the child's difficulties. The therapist facilitates this process by inventing alternative, displaced forms of aggression within the child's preferred mode. This suggestion converges with Heard and Linehan's (1994) use of extending techniques that derive from the martial art of Aikido, i.e., the therapist extends the patient's behavior, rather than blocking it, so that the movement continues in a deflected direction.

WHAT IS THE OUTCOME OF SUCCESSFULLY NEGOTIATING SANDER'S ISSUES?

As child and therapist engage in negotiating each of the issues discussed, they simultaneously construct symbols representing the uniqueness of their relationship and shared experiences: gestures, actions, images, fantasies, emotional tones, and invented language expressions. In addition, following the proposal that all representations initially are embodied, negotiations with each issue result in child and therapist constructing "interactive embodied images" that are gradually elaborated through experiences they share in future sessions. These symbols become the "language" of child and therapist, solidifying their relationship; enabling each to understand, idealize, and internalize the other; and enabling them eventually to enact solutions to the child's pathological life metaphors, cognitive orientations, and modes of expression.

Typical Questions about Child Psychotherapy: Rules and Limits versus Negotiation

The preceding view, that child and therapist should step into a dialectical circle and negotiate various issues in order to activate catalysts for change, relates to questions typically raised about child psychotherapy. These questions concern, for example, where therapy should take place, how involved a therapist should get when interacting with a child, and how a therapist should respond if a child requests a gift, food, some item to take home, or information about the therapist's personal life. When addressing such questions, authors have presented the view that the therapist makes these decisions, establishes rules, and sets limits. Spiegel (1989) devoted a chapter to "limit setting," recommending, for example, that a child should not be allowed to take a toy home, or to bring a peer or sib into the playroom. The therapist should avoid offering food and should not become too involved when interacting, as if she/he is the child's "playmate." *I* recommend that, whenever possible, the therapist step into the circle: questions should be answered, food and gifts should be given, and a child should be allowed to keep an item in her/his pocket. Then the therapist observes gestures, actions, and emotions a child displays moments after, and especially during the next session, to learn what meaning the child is introducing into their intersubjective culture. To illustrate this recommendation I turn to rules and limits typically proposed about the setting in which therapy should take place and the material that should be used.

IS THE PLAYROOM A "SACRED TEMPLE"?

Typically, the view is presented that psychotherapy with children and adolescents must take place in a treatment room. Authors (e.g., Reisman 1973) believe that leaving the playroom for whatever reason decreases the already limited time of a session and that psychotherapy with children appropriately takes place behind closed doors (Coppolillo 1987, Spiegel 1989). Brems (1993) construed a child's leaving the playroom as an attempt to escape. "While play therapy is generally confined to the playroom, it does happen that children 'escape'" (p. 5). She recommended that the therapist find out why the child wants to leave, suggesting that by leaving the playroom, children avoid anxiety, an "unrealistic approach" to life in which no one can always escape from difficult situations. The inference that the child is trying to escape from the playroom, and that such behaviors are "unrealistic," is based on how the therapist, not the child, construes what the playroom means. Moreover, requiring a child to verbalize her/his reasons for leaving may fit the therapist but not the child, who may be "speaking" in a nonverbal language. Brems also discussed strategies the therapist could use to minimize a child's attempts to escape: if a child asks to go to the bathroom, the therapist gives permission to the first request, but in subsequent sessions reminds the child to use the bathroom before entering the playroom; a water cooler could be located in the playroom to prevent the child from leaving to get a drink; and windows could be equipped with blinds "to screen out distractions."

Our developmental-dialectical model presents a view that does not construe the playroom as the only geography of treatment or focus on ways of preventing a child from "escaping" physically by leaving the playroom or cognitively by looking out a window. If we accept the position that child and therapist need to step into a dialectical circle to integrate their subjective worlds, then they should create any number of "geographies" that symbolize the evolving, unique, intersubjective culture they are creating and within which they continually transact to promote change. My colleagues and I have conducted therapy with children and adolescents shifting from one geography to another during the course of treatment. When treating children in the inner city, geographies included the school's gym, hallways, supply rooms, playground, nearby streets, and stores. When treating children in the suburbs, geographies included playrooms, therapist's office, secretary's office, hallways, cellar of the building, nearby streets and stores, and a "therapeutic garden" we constructed as a laboratory to explore a child's use of nature in resolving difficulties. We pay close attention to the issues being negotiated when a child spontaneously moves, for example, from the school building to the street, from the playroom to a hallway, or from the playroom to the therapeutic garden. We have learned, for example, that when a child shifts from the geography of a playroom to the outdoors, this shift frequently facilitates a child's (1) expressing embodied meanings and translating them into symbolic forms; (2) engaging a cognitive orientation different from the pathological orientation within which the child typically functions; and (3) engaging a mode of expression different from the mode the child typically uses.

As one example, a 7-year-old adopted boy, whose functioning had been compromised by traumatic experiences he endured in an orphanage, engaged the therapist in constructing and living in a "village," within which they enacted a common theme: the village and persons of child and therapist were repeatedly invaded in a variety of ways by "bad" people, and child and therapist invented various strategies to fend them off. The child first constructed the village in the therapist's office, using three large plastic containers, four pillows, and an old bed sheet draped over an easel. In sessions that followed, these items were used to construct the same village in (1) the hallway just outside the therapist's office, (2) the playroom, (3) outdoors immediately outside a doorway that leads from the playroom to the therapeutic garden, and (4) finally a cave area some thirty yards from the playroom door. This child used space to negotiate a change from coping with embodied fears within the microspace of the therapist's office to coping with the same fears in the geography "of the larger world."

ARE TOYS THE "HOLY GRAIL"?

Authors typically propose that a playroom should be equipped with care, and they provide detailed lists of various items that have proven productive in therapy: clay, sand, dolls, puppets, graphics, sculpting materials, toys, games, costumes (Brems 1993, Schaefer and Cangelosi 1993, Spiegel 1989). As the clinical vignette discussed above and those to follow illustrate, I recommend that, in addition to a basic set of traditional toys, the playroom should also contain a box of "junk" (rope, assortment of buttons, wooden geometric cutouts, cubes and beads of different sizes and colors, pillows, a blanket or bed sheet). Materials such as geometric cutouts have no inherent or conventional meaning and therefore enable a child to use them as vehicles to invent a wide variety of meanings (a wooden cutout could become a hamburger, a bomb, a magic circle that fends off evil aliens, an ID card). In addition, I recommend that child and therapist accumulate items that belong to their unique "intersubjective culture." For this reason I give each child and adolescent a plastic container (approximately 2 feet × 2 feet × 18 inches) in which she/he keeps materials from session to session.

WHAT SHOULD BE THE FREQUENCY AND DURATION OF TREATMENT?

Mainstream psychodynamic therapy is usually conducted with traditional fifty-minute sessions, one or two sessions per week, for one or two years; child psychoanalysis is conducted three or four sessions per week for three years and sometimes longer. Mainstream cognitive-behavioral therapy is conducted with weekly fifty-minute sessions; the duration may be as brief as ten sessions or as long as one year.

Guided by our developmental-dialectical model, my colleagues and I have been influenced by the degree of a child's cognitive and behavioral rigidity when considering duration and frequency of sessions. We have observed that if a child comes with a severely rigid cognitive orientation and modes of expression, she/he sustains interacting with a therapist for short periods of time, and the longer the session, the more the child tries to avoid stepping into the dialectical circle. If this child is available daily (if she/he is participating in a day-treatment program, or treatment is being conducted at school during the schoolday), and if a therapist is on site, we have found fifteen- to twenty-minute sessions conducted four to five times a week most effective. In one study (Santostefano 1978, Santostefano and Stayton 1967), two fifteen-minute sessions daily were conducted with retarded children by their mothers, who were trained to use structured therapeutic inter-actions following guidelines discussed below. If a child who presents a rigid cogni-tive orientation and modes of expression is available less frequently, sessions should be as brief, yet as frequent, as practical circumstances permit. When children are equipped with flexibility in cognitive orientation and modes of expression, they sometimes generate a vigorous treatment process, so much so that fifty-minute sessions for ten to twenty weeks is sufficient to revise pathological metaphors. Others may require two sessions per week for up to two or three years.

All of this is from the therapist's point of view. What about the child's? Ac-cording to one study cited by Brems (1993), older children and adolescents are more likely to end treatment prematurely. In my experience and that of colleagues, this appears to be the case. But on occasion a younger child may also make a strong bid to stop treatment. Similarly, a child of any age may request that the frequency be changed from, for example, once a week to every other week or to once a month. If a child has successfully stepped into a dialectical circle, contributing to the con-struction of shared symbols, and if a therapist has negotiated to her/his best ability the child's request to stop treatment or change frequency, I recommend that the request be granted. When treatment is terminated before the therapist believes it should be, a follow-up session should be negotiated and scheduled in two, four, or six months to explore the meaning the child's request holds within the unique intersubjective world child and therapist have constructed.

Sometimes a child may indicate she/he prefers to continue. Here too a thera-pist negotiates this request within their intersubjective culture. A child might be correct in recognizing that issues not adequately negotiated need additional atten-tion. And sometimes a child wants to hold on to the idealized therapist, reflecting some absence in the child's environment, an issue a therapist would need to nego-tiate with caregivers and school personnel. Duration of treatment, of course, raises the issue of how to terminate a therapeutic relationship constructively. Excellent discussions are available of the process of termination from different theoretical viewpoints and of various forces that interfere with the proposed frequency and duration of treatment (Brems 1993, Coppolillo 1987, Spiegel 1989). What our developmental-dialectical model adds to these discussions is considered through clinical cases discussed later.

HOW INVOLVED SHOULD A THERAPIST BE WHEN INTERACTING WITH A CHILD?

Picasso has been quoted as saying, "One must get one's hands dirty to achieve anything" (Colby and Stoller 1988, p. 18). Some child therapists, especially those using a psychodynamic approach, remain physically distant from a child, sit in a chair much like Whistler's mother, and interact primarily through verbal discourse while occasionally manipulating toys and dolls. Cognitive-behavioral therapists are more likely to become physically involved in their interactions, especially if live modeling is used (Brems 1993). Following the preceding discussion of catalysts for change, our developmental-dialectical model requires that a therapist step into a dialectical circle and "live" in it as fully as possible while trying to discover and define herself/himself within the intersubjective culture being constructed with the child. A therapist should become as "involved," physically and emotionally, as she/ he is capable of and as required by a child's self-expressions, preferred levels of stimulation, and emotional tone. For one child involvement may include crawling on the floor; for another, sitting in a chair; for another, considerable physical bodily contact such as wrestling, boxing, and chasing and being chased; for another, more subtle touching such as exchanging a "high five," or when a child occasionally leans briefly on the body of the therapist. While touch and various forms of physical contact are the foundation of experience (Barnard and Brazelton 1990), and given the suggestion that a therapist be as physically involved as required by a child, a therapist is also obligated to carefully monitor whether her/his involvement is being excessively eroticized by the child (Brems 1993) and/or is stirring up aggressive tensions the child is not yet equipped to regulate. The involvement recommended by our model requires considerable practice and presents a therapist with a formidable task: enacting a wide range of physical actions, tempos, and emotional tones while remaining ever alert to whether the level of involvement is too little or too much in terms of the particular intersubjective culture child and therapist have constructed and the unique way a child is negotiating some issue.

SHOULD TREATMENT BE DIRECTED OR NONDIRECTED?

This issue has sharply divided cognitive-behavioral and psychodynamic therapies. As discussed earlier, the use of directed tasks is a hallmark of the former and frowned on by the latter. Our developmental-dialectical model does not view directed and nondirected treatment as opposite approaches but as poles defining a continuum. If a child who habitually uses an inflexible cognitive-orientation and behavioral mode of functioning is required to step into a dialectical circle, the child repeats the same rigid behaviors she/he uses in daily living to avoid giving meaning to experiences or to avoid accommodating to and assimilating opportunities and limitations of available environments. This child requires structured interactions that form a handrail, so to speak, that a child could hold onto while stepping into a dialectical circle and negotiating self-expressions and enactments. In contrast, another child, equipped with flexible cognitive orientation and modes of expression, benefits from the freedom to project fantasies, feelings, and issues into the relationship. Therefore, our developmental model prescribes a process that provides whatever degree of direction and freedom is required to enable child and therapist to "live" within their dialectical circle and engage in enactments that promote change in behavioral modes, cognitive orientations, and meanings.

The First Treatment Sessions: Negotiating an Understanding of Why Child and Therapist Are Meeting

The first treatment sessions, which provide opportunities to observe a child's life metaphors, cognitive orientation, and modes of expression, should focus on constructing an understanding of why child and therapist are meeting. This understanding should be conveyed as much as possible with symbolic actions and a minimum of verbal explanation, a position that disagrees with proposals from both psychodynamic and cognitive-behavioral approaches, which emphasize verbal explanations.

> ## WHAT SHOULD THE THERAPIST DO IN THE FIRST SESSIONS?

Ideally, the therapist responds to some symbolic behavior the child expresses that conveys a dilemma she/he is experiencing at the moment, whether or not the dilemma relates to the child's presenting problem. Recall 5-year-old Jane, mentioned in Part I, who, gripped by separation anxiety upon being invited to the playroom, clutched mother. This child would not benefit from hearing, "During our meeting we will figure out why you get so afraid." Responding to the dilemma the child was experiencing in vivo, the therapist left the waiting room and returned with a long rope. Giving mother a reassuring glance, the therapist tied one end of the rope around mother's waist in a playful manner, saying, "Now Mom can't get away," and handed the other end of the rope to Jane. Rope firmly in hand, Jane entered the playroom, with mother in tow, and cautiously explored various items with one hand while clutching the rope with the other. Midway through the session the therapist set two chairs near the doorway to the playroom and invited mother to have a seat. In subsequent sessions mother sat in the doorway, then out of view, while Jane held the other end of the rope, gradually interacting with the therapist. Eventually Jane left the rope lying on the floor and mother returned to the waiting room. This vignette illustrates how the therapist attempted to "clarify" why she and the child were meeting by enacting a solution to a dilemma the child was experiencing in the here-and-now as a present-day force. The enactment (rope) simultaneously addressed Jane's overt behavior (clutching mother) and its meaning (remaining attached to her as one). A minimum of words were used which were embedded in the life metaphor the child was negotiating.

To illustrate this approach with an older child, I return to the adolescent girl, mentioned in Part I, who refused to enter the office but offered to go outside. Ellen shuffled into the therapeutic garden and sat in an area overhung by a canopy of hews. She mentioned several items in a low, slow voice: she liked the outdoors, completed a survival course last year in the West, and complained about two of her teachers. The therapist made only a few comments throughout this monologue. At one point Ellen interrupted herself, stared at the ground, then pointed to ants crawling about. She mumbled, "They're looking for food." The therapist jokingly commented, "We can do something about that," excused herself, and returned with two crackers. Handing one to Ellen and crumpling the other, she carefully located crumbs in the area of the ants. Ellen did the same while continuing her commentary. The therapist enacted a solution to a dilemma Ellen was experiencing in the here and now that bore no direct connection to her presenting difficulty, getting schoolwork done: the ants were hungry and searching for food.

The Process of Psychotherapy from a Developmental-Dialectical Perspective

The topics discussed thus far frame the treatment process defined by our model to address the goal stated at the start and the several issues articulated in Part IV. Using a musical metaphor, the proposed process requires that a therapist orchestrate and conduct the performance of three instruments, sometimes emphasizing *structured* interactions that promote flexibility in cognitive orientation or in modes of expression, and sometimes emphasizing *unstructured* interactions that promote the revision of maladaptive life metaphors. Throughout treatment the three instruments always perform together. The therapist is required to exercise creativity in deciding when and how one of the instruments should be emphasized and how they should be combined. Whether treatment structures interactions or is nondirected, the process contains the same catalysts for change, activated by interpersonal developments between child and therapist. These developments, listed in Table 7-1 and discussed in what follows, are parts of a unified process.

TABLE 7–1. Process during Unstructured and Structured Interactions

I	Circular dialectical interactions: ritualizing experiences	Translate embodied schemas of body-image disruptions into symbolic forms. Child idealizes therapist's efforts to find solutions and internalizes therapist as evoked companion; displays deferred imitation.
II	Interactive metaphor: the need for help	Child symbolically enacts the need for help. Therapist enacts she/he is able to provide assistance required.
III	Interactive metaphor: disrupted, unrepaired life metaphor	Child organizes interactions representing unrepaired life metaphors, projects symbolic characters of the metaphor onto the therapist, manipulates therapist to cope with its demands. Child idealizes/internalizes therapist's solutions.
IV	Interactive metaphor: new editions of disrupted life metaphors	Child introduces new editions of the disrupted life metaphor that elaborate the initial one; projects characters onto therapist, who struggles for solutions, which the child idealizes/internalizes.
V	Interactive metaphor: core pathological life metaphor	Child introduces interactions representing a developmentally basic, unrepaired disruption, with its heightened traumatic emotions, that is at the core of the child's difficulties. Child idealizes/internalizes therapist's solutions.
VI	Here-and-now interactions and concerns	Child focuses interactions on here-and-now interests and concerns and displays more stage-appropriate functioning in her/his environments.

WHAT IS PROJECTIVE IDENTIFICATION?

Whether participating in unstructured or structured interactions, a therapist relies on an interpersonal dialectical process conceptualized as "projective identification" (Ogden 1979). In this process a child eventually projects (transfers) onto the therapist a cognitive orientation, mode of expression, embodied schema, life metaphor, or some combination; manipulates the therapist to experience the dilemma the configuration creates; and observes how the therapist solves it. Over many such interactions a child gradually idealizes, identifies with, and assimilates the ways in which the therapist copes with the dilemma. As a result, the therapist's behaviors and emotions eventually become a part of the child's functioning. This process illuminates the view, paralleling child and caregiver interactions, that child and therapist promote change as they engage in dialectical interactions, experience and repair disruptions in their ongoing regulations, and share heightened emotional moments. But as Mitchell (1994) reminded us, during the process of projective identification a therapist is not "a smooth, clean container" into which a child places her/his projections. Rather, each therapist brings uniqueness (e.g., a preferred level of stimulation and style of expression) that influences what and how a child projects onto the therapist and how the therapist enacts solutions. When child and therapist engage in the process of projective identification, then, they define and organize different aspects of each other and of the subjective world they intend to share. As conceptualized here, projective identification is a basic interpersonal process consisting of several components outlined in Table 7–1.

WHAT ARE CIRCULAR DIALECTICAL INTERACTIONS?

Piaget pointed out that symbols and meanings do not already exist in a dark cave and become known when we shine a light on them. Rather, symbols are gradually constructed as infant and caregiver—and I include child and therapist—participate in many "circular dialectical interactions" organized as rituals (Table 7–1, I). The first symbols constructed with rituals are translations of embodied experiences. For an example of this process in normal development, the reader is reminded of the toddler and father who ritualized engaging in circular dialectical interactions involving the child's body and the father's body and shirt. The significance of circular dialectical interactions for child psychotherapy rests on the view that for every mental knot there is a corresponding embodied knot. Embodied schemas children bring to therapy typically relate to disruptions in body-image experiences that were not repaired: body imbalance, excessive body constriction or assertion, body-image deformation.

As child and therapist become less foreign to each other, the child eventually repeats some constellation of actions/gestures/emotions related to an embodied schema representing a disruption. When the therapist imitates the child's behavior and/or responds by enacting in a relevant way, a circular interaction is launched. The therapist now has an opportunity to join the child in experiencing and expressing the embodied schema and grappling with its dilemma. As these circular interactions are repeated, the embodied schema becomes symbolized cognitively. As with infant and caregiver, if the child values (idealizes) the therapist, the child begins to construct mental representations of the therapist as a "companion" and imitates her/his behaviors, the beginnings of internalization. The need to translate embodied schemas into symbolic form is usually greatest during early phases of treatment.

WHAT ARE INTERACTIVE METAPHORS?

As child and therapist construct and ritualize a world of shared symbols, the child begins to organize interactions around metaphors. With each metaphor the child now projects an organized, symbolic "character" or "voice" onto the therapist and manipulates the therapist to experience and respond to its call for action. As the therapist takes on attributes of this character and struggles to solve its call for action, the child observes, idealizes, and internalizes the therapist's struggle and solution. Typically, several interactive metaphors emerge during this process. The first frequently expresses the need for help (Table 7–1, II). Here a child is establishing whether the therapist is attuned and up to dealing with the expressions of maladaptation that will follow. If a therapist enacts successfully within this metaphor, demonstrating that she/he is unconditionally available, a child follows this experience with an interactive metaphor that expresses the first edition of a pathological life metaphor representing an unrepaired developmental disruption (Table 7–1, III). Again a "character" or "voice" is projected onto the therapist who is manipulated to struggle with the dilemma depicted. The character projected is typically symbolized as some "evil force" that does not exist within the child but in the therapist and environment. Again the child observes, idealizes, and internalizes the therapist's struggle and solution. The first interactive metaphor may be followed by any number of others, each of which is either a "new edition" of the first or a representation of another pathological life metaphor that in some way is connected to the first (Table 7–1, IV).

In some cases, after enacting and revising the calls for action of several editions of a life metaphor, a child eventually organizes an interactive metaphor that expresses a "core, pathological life metaphor" representing a fundamental, unrepaired disruption that has been at the base of most of the child's difficulties (Table 7–1, V). Equipped with interactive tools provided by previous negotiations, the child's functioning "regresses" significantly, making available the roots of her/his difficulty for therapeutic work. Frequently, when a core, pathological life metaphor is negotiated, the therapist is not assigned the role of an evil force that the child battles. Rather, the evil force is projected "out there" as a common enemy. Child and therapist become allies battling this force, displaying strength and confidence against its dictates and demonstrating standards that oppose it. Here too a child indicates that the therapist's strength and respect for rules are idealized and internalized. Once a core, pathological metaphor is successfully negotiated, the child (especially older children and adolescents) will sometimes shift the content of interactions from constructing metaphors to discussions of interests and concerns in the here and now (peers, sports, school) (Table 7–1, VI). These discussions frequently rely on the foundation of shared symbols child and therapist have constructed. At this time a child typically displays more stage-appropriate functioning in her/his environment.

WHAT ARE THE TECHNICAL ISSUES THAT RELATE TO A THERAPIST PARTICIPATING IN INTERACTIVE METAPHORS?

1. The therapist and various materials are available for the child to engage within a treatment room and other areas when indicated (especially the outdoors).

2. The therapist should be aware of his/her emotional/relational world in order to enter the child's and should participate easily in circular dialectical interactions and enactments, whether or not she/he experiences them as uncomfortable, stressful, exciting, or boring. Being at ease with one's world assumes that a therapist is aware of meanings expressed by her/his body images. Awareness of one's body images requires time and effort to develop and is a skill that needs to be learned and practiced (Pruzinsky 1990).

3. The therapist remains alert for ritualized gestures/actions/emotions expressed by the child that reveal some unique embodied meaning, for example, expressions of body disequilibrium (a child repeatedly staggers as if dizzy, or drops material to the floor), excessive or inadequate stimulation (a child repeatedly complains that the temperature is too hot or too cold, or always wears a jacket or coat during the sessions), interference with body assertiveness (a child insists on standing on a table to be taller than the therapist, or insists on using the therapist's pen or chair).

4. When embodied schemas are translated into symbolic forms, and when enactments are organized to express a metaphor, the symbols and metaphors themselves contribute to repairing disruptions since symbols bring order and organization to what has been chaotic and rigid (Beebe and Lachmann 1994, Overton and Horowitz 1991).

5. With each interactive metaphor a therapist enacts characters and solutions, as much as possible following a developmental progression that emphasizes actions, then fantasies, then language. Interpreting and discussing meanings the child experiences, and connecting them to relationships in the child's past and present, are reserved until the last phase of treatment and introduced only if the child's developmental stage indicates she/he would benefit from direct discussions of her/his feelings and motives.

Guidelines for Structuring Interactions

The methods outlined here to structure interactions are intended to help a child step into a dialectical circle so she/he can participate in circular dialectical interactions and enactments. It is important to note that these methods attempt to reorganize *how* a child's cognition and modes construct and express meanings. Guided by the concept of the interdependence of opposites (see above), the tasks initially accommodate to the child's rigid cognitive orientation or preferred behavioral mode, promoting first-order change, and then gradually require the child to employ the opposite orientation or mode. At this point tasks "bump into" a child's habitual cognitive or behavioral mode of functioning and attempt to promote second-order change. As the child's cognitive orientation and modes of expression become more flexible, a therapist gradually relinquishes giving direction and allows the child to guide their interactions. Now equipped with tools to symbolize, and to stand within a dialectical circle, the child invents interactive metaphors. Some children require the use of tasks during most of treatment; others, for brief phases only.

> ## CAN YOU RELATE DEVELOPMENTAL DIALECTICAL TASKS USED TO STRUCTURE INTERACTIONS WITH COGNITIVE-BEHAVIORAL TASKS AND THE OBJECTIONS OF PSYCHODYNAMIC THERAPY?

The tasks proposed here are similar to, yet different from, those used in mainstream cognitive-behavioral therapy, yet they meet the objections of psychodynamic therapy. Unlike self-instructions and correspondence training, for example, the methods are designed to change cognitive structures, that is, unconscious processes that organize and symbolize stimulation. Some cognitive-behavioral tasks decrease or increase behaviors by reinforcing "appropriate" behaviors and ignoring "inappropriate" behaviors. In contrast, the tasks proposed here do not include extrinsic reinforcements delivered by the therapist. Rather, the child's behavior gradually undergoes change as she/he experiences "intrinsic" rewards stemming from her/his idealizing and internalizing the behaviors of the therapist (Santostefano 1978). Last, tasks in cognitive-behavioral therapy are typically designed by the therapist and administered to all children in pretty much the same way. In contrast, *tasks outlined here are coauthored, as much as possible, by child and therapist and framed within a meaning unique to the child's developmental needs.*

Psychodynamic therapy holds that the more the therapist structures interactions, the less the child is able to project characters and voices onto the therapist and bring unconscious meanings and motives to conscious awareness (Gill 1984, Messer and Winokur 1984, Spiegel 1989). From the vantage point of our model, I hold to the opposite position *for some children*. If a child's cognition is rigidly inner or outer oriented, and/or if a child makes inflexible use of one modality of expression that is segregated from others, the child is limited in being able to step into a dialectical circle. During numerous nondirected sessions, one child plays checkers and another plays with a dollhouse, each child doing and saying little that hints they are projecting unconscious meanings and characters onto the therapist.

Rather than enabling these children to avoid unconscious meanings, the proposed methods help them enter a dialectical relationship to construct and express meanings/emotions.

Table 7–2 diagrams guidelines for devising tasks that promote a child's capacity to construct symbols and express them flexibly using various behaviors as vehicles. While the content of tasks may vary from child to child, the form and process of each task follow the same general considerations. As much as possible, tasks should vary along four dimensions: from simple to complex in makeup, from requiring physical actions to requiring mental actions, from requiring little delay to considerable delay, and from ignoring meanings to evaluating meanings. How

TABLE 7–2.   Guidelines for Graded Tasks to Treat Rigid Cognitive Orientations and Modes of Expression

General Guidelines for Graded Tasks

A. Simple to complex
B. Physical actions to mental actions
C. Little delay to much delay
D. No meaning (symbols) experienced to elaborate meanings
E. No emotions aroused to emotions aroused

Treating Cognitive Orientations

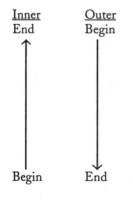

Inner   Outer
End   Begin

Begin   End

A. Engage stimulation as it is with one or more cognitive regulators: body tempo, focal attention, field articulation, leveling-sharpening, equivalence range
B. Engage stimulation as one imagines it to be
   1. Assign usual (conventional) meanings
   2. Assign personal meanings
   3. Express meanings in a progression of nested behaviors (vehicles) (see below)
   4. Shift flexibly among meanings and behaviors (vehicles) expressing them
   5. Shift flexibly among roles (identities) enacted while pretending

Treating Behavioral Modalities

Inflexible
Mode   Begin ──────────────────────────────────→ End

Action   Macroaction—Microaction and Fantasy—Fantasy—Language
Fantasy   Macrofantasy—Microfantasy and Action—Macroaction—Language
Language   Macrolanguage—Fantasy—Fantasy and Microaction—Macroaction

these guidelines are combined depends upon the unique needs of a child (for a more detailed description of these guidelines and tasks see Santostefano 1995a).

WHAT ARE THE GUIDELINES FOR TREATING A RIGID OUTER COGNITIVE ORIENTATION?

If a child's cognitive orientation is rigidly outer oriented, tasks initially accommodate to this orientation and promote first-order change by requiring her/him to engage stimulation as it is, that is, copy or produce stimulation (Table 7–2). With each task the child engages the process of one or more of the cognitive regulators discussed earlier. Since these cognitive functions are viewed as hierarchically related, the notion of first- and second-order change guides which function is emphasized first. If a child shows rigidity in leveling-sharpening, tasks initially emphasize field articulation, the hierarchically lower cognitive function promoting first-order change. Then tasks are introduced emphasizing the leveling-sharpening process, promoting second-order change. Gradually, tasks require the child to shift from copying to transforming stimulation, engaging it as she/he imagines it to be, enabling outer-oriented children to construct symbols while balancing intense associated emotions. The first meanings a child assigns to stimulation are typically conventional. The child is gradually encouraged to invent more personal meanings and to express associated emotions. Child and therapist enact these meanings, assuming roles of various pretend characters and voices. These enactments make use of action, fantasy, and language expressions in a sequence guided by the mode that the child uses in inflexible ways (see below).

WHAT ARE THE GUIDELINES FOR TREATING A RIGID INNER COGNITIVE ORIENTATION?

The child is already freely translating information into highly personal symbols. Accommodating to this orientation, the therapist initially attempts to promote first-order change, entering some aspect of the child's personal world and shifting flexibly among roles defined by the child's fantasy (Table 7–2). These roles are enacted using various action, fantasy, and language symbols, again depending on the mode of expression the child prefers (see below). Gradually, more conventional meanings are constructed and expressed within the child's fantasy, using a variety of vehicles. As conventional meanings are introduced, interactions gradually require stimulation to be experienced as it is, emphasizing the process of copying and producing stimulation.

WHAT ARE THE GUIDELINES FOR TREATING RIGID BEHAVIORAL MODALITIES?

In defining these guidelines, several terms are used (Table 7–2). *Macroaction* indicates that the child moves her/his body elaborately through the total space provided by the area in which the activity is taking place. The actions may be accompanied by fantasy and language expressions, but these modes are subordinate to body actions. *Microaction* indicates that the child's body is more or less stationary as the child manipulates materials within a few square feet of space. Microactions accompany and are dominated by fantasies. *Macrofantasy* designates an elaborate fantasy that is accompanied by little or no physical activity. Although the fantasy is communicated with words and gestures and by manipulating material, these modes are subordinate to, and operate in, the service of the fantasy. *Macrolanguage* indicates that words dominate in expressing metaphors. The conversation may be accompanied by images and actions, but these behaviors are subordinate to, and in the service of, communicating meanings through spoken metaphoric words.

In general, a therapist emphasizes a progression of behavioral expressions during treatment that follows the principle of promoting first-order change and then second-order change. If a child typically makes inflexible use of the action mode, tasks initially accommodate this preference, permitting meanings to be expressed in alternative macroactions. Gradually, task requirements encourage a child to express the same or related meanings with microactions accompanied by a fantasy, and then with macrofantasy accompanied by little or no action. Last, language expressions subordinating fantasy and action are encouraged. In this progression the action mode establishes representational roots in the others. If a child typically makes inflexible use of the fantasy mode, tasks initially require the construction of macrofantasies, then fantasies accompanied by microactions, and then macroactions with little or no fantasy activity. When action and fantasy are integrated to some degree, the tasks require language expressions. In this progression the fantasy mode establishes representational roots in the others. If the child typically makes inflexible use of language expressions, tasks initially emphasize expressing meanings in language followed by expressions in fantasy. Then fantasy expressions are accompanied by microactions. Last, macroactions dominate with neither language nor fantasy playing a major role. In this progression the language mode establishes representational roots in the others.

Guidelines for Unstructured Interactions

When psychotherapy is not structured or directed, several interrelated propositions form the base of developmental-dialectical guidelines: (1) the meanings a child initially constructs are always holistic and contextual, consisting of organizations of sights, sounds, smells, and touch and kinesthetic perceptions, images, actions, and emotions, all rooted in activity taking place at developmental levels below language; (2) to change how a child functions, it is necessary to change the meanings (metaphors) a child has already constructed; (3) meanings are inherently repetitive in that they continually gain expression in evolving cycles of ritualized activity.

WHAT ARE THE GUIDELINES FOR FACILITATING INTERACTIVE METAPHORS DURING UNSTRUCTURED THERAPY?

As a child behaves within the treatment relationship, the therapist should be alert for ritualized activities, representing metaphors, interpersonal dilemmas, and unrepaired disruptions the child projects onto the therapist and their relationship. The therapist should refrain from verbally interpreting (conceptualizing) these behaviors and their meanings. Rather, as much as is appropriate for child and therapist, the therapist should "enter" and "live" the metaphor, experiencing and expressing as much as possible the emotions/actions/meanings that the child has projected onto the relationship. The therapist should respond to the dilemma with embodied meanings/enactments that provide the child with holistic/contextual experiences, and that attempt to find solutions to the dilemma. After emphasizing embodied enactments, the therapist gradually shifts her/his responses, emphasizing first the fantasy mode and then metaphoric language.

As much as possible, the therapist should participate and communicate within the child's mode of expression, drawing upon the intersubjective world child and therapist have constructed and share. The therapist should also be alert for signs from the child that she/he idealizes and is internalizing the therapist's solutions to a dilemma. Typically, after internalizing a solution, a child launches a revision or extension of the previous interactive metaphor. Persistent, ritualized interactions between child and therapist should replicate the developmental process of metaphor construction observed between child and caregiver. In many cases it is not necessary to provide a child with literal knowledge, or conceptual understanding, of her/his difficulties for the child to benefit from psychotherapy and undergo change. But it is necessary to provide the child with experiences that cultivate *how* the child constructs and expresses knowledge. The process of symbolizing in each mode itself has the power to promote change and resolve difficulties.

WHEN STRUCTURED AND UNSTRUCTURED GUIDELINES ARE COMPARED, WHAT KEY ISSUES EMERGE?

In dissolving boundaries, the proposed guidelines prescribe an approach to treating children—whatever their diagnoses and presenting problems—that is framed by two propositions. First, a child's knowledge and the meanings a child has constructed from experiences are embedded in what the child does, thinks, and feels. The second proposition holds that the process of constructing knowledge and meanings is always embedded in the interactions and negotiations that form a relationship, a notion supported by Piaget (1952) and Karl Stern (1965) as well as the infant investigators discussed in Part V. For many children who require treatment, her/his meanings and the network of cognitive functions and modes of expression surrounding them have become rigid, limiting exchanges between her/his subjective world and that of others. When interacting with others, the child attempts to preserve this organization of meanings, cognitions, and behavioral modes, and experiences any threat to this structure as a threat to her/his "reality." Therefore, to help these children grow, guidelines prescribe that a therapist shift back and forth between structured and unstructured dialectical interactions in order to promote flexibility in a child's cognitive orientation and modes of expression and so that pathological life metaphors can be revised. When engaged in this process, the therapist must continually learn who she/he is when entering the child's subjective world, and discover who the child is when she/he enters the therapist's subjective world. Other issues emerge when relating guidelines for structured and unstructured interactions.

The Importance of Rituals

How does a therapist know when some behavior is being introduced into their dialectical circle? If a child ritualizes some behavior, more often than not the child is stepping into the circle. For example, in a case discussed in Part IX, a 5-year-old boy slapped puppets and toy animals from shelves onto the floor, initially sporadically. When he ritualized this action a major interactive metaphor was introduced.

Unifying Overt Behaviors and Their Meanings

In mainstream cognitive-behavioral and psychodynamic therapies, intrapsychic functioning (meanings/emotions) has been split off from behavioral functioning, and words have been split off from actions (Gold 1994). Cycles of dialectical interactions and enactments, whether occurring during structured or unstructured treatment, integrate meanings/emotions (deep structures) with interpersonal interactions (surface structures).

Idealizing/Internalizing the Therapist

During both structured and unstructured processes, a child gradually idealizes and internalizes behaviors the therapist uses to negotiate dilemmas. This process is considered the most critical catalyst for change, the "sacred moment." Thus a therapist should be alert for behaviors on the part of the child that imitate attributes of the therapist, whether a gesture, tone of voice, item of clothing, or verbal phrase. One preadolescent girl began to admire various items of clothing worn by her female therapist. She asked if she could wear the therapist's belt and earrings, a request the therapist granted. Later, requesting that she and the therapist dress alike, child and therapist devoted several minutes at the close of each session to select what they would wear for the next session.

When idealizing and internalizing attributes of the therapist, a child frequently fortifies her/his ability to engage in self-regulation while coping with stress. This is vividly illustrated by the experience of an adult patient described by Gold (1994), an example that forms a bridge to one common way children reflect this process. A woman in her mid-twenties suffered from extreme self-doubt and anxiety whenever she was faced with public speaking. In one session she spontaneously exclaimed to the therapist, "I'm going to shrink you down to the size of a doll and take you along to my meeting this afternoon" (p. 151). This patient, equipped with the capacity to construct vivid imagery, then internalized the therapist in the form of a "doll" that she carried with her in fantasy as an idealized source of strength and companionship.

While some children may have the capacity to take an image of the therapist with them as an idealized companion, more often, at various points in treatment, children ask to take some item from the playroom or the therapist's person. Some clinicians (e.g., Brems 1993) recommend that such requests "must be explored" to learn what they mean and decide how to respond. I recommend that, within reason, the child's request should be granted without discussion.

Transference

Whether treatment is structured or unstructured, transference experiences are co-authored by child and therapist. As they construct a shared culture and engage in interactive metaphors, how the therapist behaves strongly affects what the child experiences within their relationship; similarly, how the child behaves strongly influences what the therapist experiences. Each assimilates and accommodates to the other and each defines the other. While the particular metaphor a child expresses relates to some developmental issue in need of negotiation and repair, the unique form that a metaphor takes is as much a function of the therapist's subjective culture and actions as those of the child. I ascribe to Weimer's (1980) position that continuous cycles of dialectical interactions, in which child and therapist participate, will create new meanings they share, change the meanings of events they experienced, and change the actions each takes toward the other.

8
Case Illustrations of Structured and Unstructured Interactions

CONTENTS

n selecting cases I recognize a number of obstacles. It is difficult to represent how, what, and exactly when a therapist does or does not do something from session to session. It is also impossible to describe fully, for child and therapist, the constellation of tone of voice, emotions, gestures and postures, facial expressions, and words and actions each is displaying during a given interaction and enactment. Along the same line, it is impossible to describe the fleeting impressions, conscious meanings, and intentions each experiences during an interaction, let alone any unconscious meanings that could exert an influence. Last, clinical cases tend to be highly selective. Those presented here were selected to illustrate one or another aspect of the developmental-dialectical guidelines. While acknowledging these obstacles, I hope the treatment cases stimulate the reader to explore and develop her/his ingenuity in using the proposed guidelines when treating children and adolescents.

CAN YOU DESCRIBE CASES ILLUSTRATING THE USE OF STRUCTURED INTERACTIONS THROUGHOUT MOST OF TREATMENT?

Jack: From Tic-Tac-Toe to Geometric Cutouts as Bombs

Jack was described as a loner and "mopey." While managing marginally in the first grades, he seemed almost unable to learn in the third grade, which he was now repeating. At school he frequently rearranged his desk; at home he spent much time lining up, counting, and pasting stickers in a scrapbook. Jack was referred by his therapist because during nearly a year of nondirected therapy, he had maintained control over himself and the treatment process by repeatedly initiating games of checkers and tic-tac-toe. The therapist had introduced numerous interpretations in an attempt to establish trust and dissolve resistance. But Jack clung to form-board games, especially tic-tac-toe, for which he had developed numerous strategies. Psychological test results indicated that he was not aware of representations of violence and cataclysmic happenings that influenced his functioning. The "integrative" therapist who agreed to work with him set as a goal helping him step into a dialectical circle by initially accommodating to his rigid outer orientation and then helping him construct symbols, shared with the therapist, that gradually integrated the inner meaning of cataclysmic violence with external stimulation.

Games of Tic-Tac-Toe to Avoid Aggressive Metaphors

During the first sessions, Jack initiated games of tic-tac-toe and checkers as he had done with the previous therapist. To set the stage for a task that would engage him in the process of symbolizing, the therapist suggested that, in addition to using pencil marks on a sheet of paper when playing tic-tac-toe, each player would locate geometric cutouts on a matrix the therapist had drawn on a large poster board. Jack participated with enthusiasm, expressing relief that he had "something to do" and that the therapist was not "bugging him" with questions.

In the following sessions the therapist increased the complexity of the task, still casting the activity so that information was to be managed as it was without emphasizing what one could imagine it to be. Using a larger matrix, each player now located six cutouts in a row. Jack enthusiastically accepted, challenged by the need to develop more complex strategies. The therapist increased the complexity of the task again, now emphasizing the process of field articulation. For example, during any one game each player had to locate, in a row, six stacks of two particular cutouts: three small red triangles set on medium white squares, two medium yellow diamonds set on large blue circles, and one medium green triangle set on a large black square. In this format, then, particular geometric shapes and colors were relevant in one game but not in another. Before each game Jack and the therapist took turns deciding which cutouts were required to win.

Geometric Cutouts Begin to Growl as Fierce Animals

As the therapist and Jack participated in these ritualized cycles of interaction, the latter occasionally showed signs that he was beginning to imagine the cutouts as animals, displaying the first brief expressions of his repressed anger. When locating a particular stack of cutouts on the poster board, he sometimes growled and pushed it toward one of the therapist's as if to enact one animal growling at another. In an effort to assimilate this fantasy into the task, and to stimulate the process of constructing shared symbols, the therapist suggested that they "make the cutouts be something." Jack responded to this invitation and designated each stack of cutouts as a particular animal (a medium black diamond set on a large black square was a panther). The game continued, and Jack and the therapist took turns designating six animals to be located in a row in order to win (three lions, two panthers, and one gorilla). As symbols were constructed and shared, Jack began to animate the cutouts more often. Sometimes he would have a stack of cutouts stalk or pounce upon the poster board; sometimes one of his stacks would leap and land on one of the therapist's, enacting, for example, a panther attacking a giraffe. When taking his turn, the therapist imitated Jack, moving a stack while growling and stalking one of Jack's.

Tolerating Surges of Emotional Tension

The therapist introduced still another elaboration intended to help Jack develop the capacity to anticipate and equilibrate sudden surges of emotional tension. Each player located two or three stacks of cutouts (joined with tape) on the edge of a table, each stack representing the same animals. Then the player drew on a sheet of paper where the animals would fall (the pattern they would form) after they were pushed from the table to the floor. Jack engaged these sessions with enthusiasm, becoming even more animated in his interactions. In addition, he began to express aggression toward the therapist, sometimes disagreeing angrily with the therapist's opinion about the match between a drawing and a pattern the cutouts formed once pushed to the floor. Then, to structure "interactions" between their animals and symbolize the aggression between Jack and the therapist, another elaboration was introduced. Taking turns, each player held three of his own animals (cutouts) and three of the other player's. With arms outstretched, the cutouts were dropped to the floor. Prior to taking a turn, each player drew a picture of the pattern the cutouts would form, anticipating and imagining which animals would "pounce" on which. During these enactments, Jack showed flashes of intense anger. On a few occasions, when the therapist's animals had pounced on his, he abruptly hurled a cutout across the room.

Geometric Cutouts Become Bombs

At this point Jack's angry tensions were more available in his subjective experiences, benefiting from a more flexible cognitive orientation that symbolized cutouts as fierce animals. Relying on this achievement, the therapist introduced a more elaborate structured fantasy. The fantasy permitted more direct expressions of fantasized aggression and provided opportunities for Jack to enact and control these expressions with different body tempos as well as with cognitive regulators. The therapist asked Jack to pretend a bomb scare had been reported and that he was a member of a special team trained to locate and defuse bombs. Jack accepted the invitation with enthusiasm. Extending the previously shared symbol, the therapist located stacks of cutouts (two in each stack) throughout the playroom floor and on shelves. With each trial, the therapist named the makeup of a bomb and Jack searched for and located it, taking it to a "defusing box" (a cardboard box) where it was dismantled. For example, if a bomb consisted of a medium yellow triangle taped to a large blue diamond, two of the stacks arrayed contained all of the designated attributes. Other stacks contained none of the attributes that made up the bomb; others contained only one or two of the attributes (e.g., a small yellow triangle taped to a large blue diamond; in this instance the shape and color of the yellow cutout were correct but the size was incorrect). As this game unfolded, Jack and the therapist competed in the search for bombs designated by the other. If the wrong stack was touched or removed, the player lost points. If the correct stack was defused, the player was honored by the town's mayor, introduced by Jack.

Gradually, cutouts symbolizing a bomb became more complex (e.g., stacks consisted of three cutouts and then four), requiring Jack and the therapist to engage the process of field articulation at a more differentiated level when examining a stack before removing it. In addition, the therapist introduced regulating various body tempos. With some trials each player searched for bombs as rapidly as possible. Timed scores were recorded to determine who won. In other trials they searched for bombs while each moved as if he were in a slow motion movie. Now the person who took the most time won.

Concluding Comment

Jack's rigid outer cognitive orientation served to avoid its opposite and thereby prevent the construction of representations of rage contained in his personal world. When he entered treatment with the first therapist, his cognition and modes of expression were not equipped to equilibrate these meanings/emotions in interactions with the therapist and required that he control his aggressive meanings by obsessively playing tic-tac-toe. The tasks introduced by the second therapist enabled Jack to step into a dialectical circle, reorganize his rigid outer cognitive orientation, construct symbols that integrated his repressed rage with available stimulation, and experience and express these meanings/emotions in ways that served the therapeutic process. The symbols constructed brought some order and control over the chaos his mind had been avoiding. Following the "bomb game," Jack initiated enacting other "games" of violence as the therapist shifted to a less directed format. In the course of this work Jack associated to father's temper and beatings he had received from father (acknowledged by father). He also enacted disruptions during interactions with the therapist in which he expected the therapist to become angry and "tear him apart." As these disruptions occurred, and as he experienced that they were not followed by beatings, he developed a more affiliated relationship with the therapist, as well as peers, and became more productive in school and less obsessional.

Alice: From a Tape Recorder to the World

Alice's parents reported that she was always lost in fantasy, and was content to spend hours in her room. At school she had no friends and sometimes displayed "peculiar" behaviors. For example, after sitting thirty minutes before a math problem, she had written only a four-letter expletive in the margin. Although she had managed the first school grades, now, in the fifth grade, she had steadily become more withdrawn and "odd." While her behavior suggested to school personnel that she might be psychotic, psychiatric and psychological evaluations produced no evidence supporting this impression. Alice participated in a course of psychodynamic psychotherapy for six months, two sessions weekly. Her therapist became concerned because Alice rarely engaged the therapist, but sat in a corner of the playroom manipulating items she typically brought with her, one of which was a tape recorder. Her therapist tried a number of strategies to promote interactions: e.g., she located various dolls and animals on the table to initiate fantasy play; she pointed out how frightening it must be to share what was on her mind; she offered snacks. When Alice did not respond sufficiently, she was referred for consultation. Tests administered at this time again showed no evidence of psychotic processes, and indicated that she had developed an inflexible, markedly inner cognitive orientation, and that her day-to-day functioning took place primarily within vivid, highly personal fantasies. As a result, the therapist began a program of structured interactions using the guidelines outlined above. The following sketch focuses on those aspects of Alice's treatment that illustrate how the therapist devised tasks embedded within a metaphor Alice brought to the first session in an effort to dissolve her cognitive rigidity and enable her to flexibly engage environmental stimulation.

My World Is a Tape Recorder

Alice arrived with a large, two-reel tape recorder. Removing its cover, she ignored the therapist and interacted with the recorder, fingering wires and gears. On occasion she spoke to her dog, "Cuddles," who, of course, was not present. In an effort to develop characters and voices within Alice's yet unknown personal world, following the guidelines for an inner-oriented child, the therapist began to peer into the recorder, talk with Cuddles, touch and inquire about certain parts, and engage the recorder in conversation ("What's going on in there? Who's in there?"). Alice apparently identified with and accommodated to this behavior since she began to imitate the therapist, addressing the tape recorder ("Hey! Where are you going?"). Over several sessions she referred to parts of the recorder as particular places. A gear at one end of the recorder was Alice's house; a gear at the other end, her school; a red wire became the road connecting them. As Alice imposed more organized meaning to the inside of the recorder, the therapist enacted imaginary persons walking to school, walking home, and shopping in grocery stores by "walking" her fingers over pathways. Alice soon imitated the therapist. This imaginary play took place for a number of sessions with child and therapist quietly sitting and peering into the tape recorder.

Extending Alice's World from the Tape Recorder into the Room

With personal meanings constructed and shared, each referring to some part of the tape recorder, the therapist introduced an intervention that "bumped into" Alice's rigid use of an inner orientation and macrofantasy that arbitrarily and globally expressed the inside of a recorder as the referent for a "world." The therapist invited Alice to extend the world they had created "so we can play it better," by locating various objects around the recorder and over the surface of a large table-top. To promote a more articulate use of materials in symbolizing, wooden geometric cutouts and blocks were used to designate various buildings; rods were used to designate telephone poles; streets were defined with tape; and pictures of buildings were cut out of magazines. Alice now "walked" a doll figure on streets (taped pathways) and through stores (cutouts and pictures) where items were purchased. Initially these items were symbolized by Alice in highly personal terms. For example, candy bars were sometimes represented by paper clips, sometimes by scraps of paper. By enacting characters who entered the store (sometimes using her fingers, sometimes a doll), the therapist showed confusion over which items were what. In this way the therapist encouraged Alice to fit the attributes of items with their meanings. Buttons became hamburgers, pieces of string carefully cut in one-inch lengths became bananas, paper clips became candy bars, and so forth. The therapist also introduced various tempos in the actions the characters performed (one doll, late for school, ran over a pathway; another doll, who was taking a walk after school, slowly meandered along the pathway).

In the next series of meetings the therapist extended the subjective world they had created over the entire floor of the playroom and the corridor just outside the office. Cutouts and blocks were now stacked to represent a school building, a grocery store, home, a friend's house, and other buildings. When constructing these structures, and to emphasize the process of field articulation, the therapist carefully designated cutouts of different sizes and colors for each of the structures; Alice soon joined in. The school became a stack of cutouts with a large blue circle at the bottom, a medium yellow triangle in the center, and a small red circle at the top. Once, when the therapist was helping to set up their world at the start of a meeting, she inadvertently placed a large yellow triangle in the center of the school building. Alice immediately noticed the error, "The school is wrong," reflecting that she was assimilating more articulate fields of relevant and irrelevant information. Also during this phase, Alice and the therapist, each holding a doll, "walked" on pathways while enacting various vignettes, sometimes at different tempos. As one example, Alice walked to a friend's house (the therapist) to play; in another vignette Alice's doll participated in a school race.

Extending Alice's World into the Outdoors

In the next phase the therapist extended the game to the outdoors. During these sessions Alice and the therapist walked about the therapeutic garden, designating various bushes and trees as particular places and enacting a number of the same roles, which now became more elaborated. During the final phase of treatment the therapist and Alice walked to a nearby shopping area, entered stores, purchased items, and talked to clerks—now dealing with information more as it is.

Mary: I'm Trapped in a Straitjacket

Mary came to treatment with a history of difficulty expressing herself verbally and with actions, presenting a special challenge for any treatment program. In terms of our developmental model, not only was Mary handicapped by rigid cognitive functions, but each behavioral mode (action, fantasy, and language) was constricted and barriers segregated each from the others. The creative use the therapist made of developmental-dialectical guidelines enabled Mary to free herself from the straitjacket that imprisoned her psychological functioning in only 14 months of once-weekly sessions.

Mary was referred by her parents at the urging of the pediatrician because she lacked confidence, occasionally overate, frequently slept a lot, and rarely engaged her parents in conversation. She spent weekends at her desk but never got anything done. And despite several tutoring programs over the past years, reading "remains a handicap." Yet when Mary cleaned the kitchen, she did "a great job, but cleans more than necessary." Mary repeated the first grade because she was "nonverbal," which connected with particular developments in her early years. When mother went to work, Mary, then 2 years old, was enrolled in a day-care program, but she had not yet learned to control her bowels. Mother had attempted to train her without success. When placed on the potty, Mary would "sit there very quiet, but she seemed mad for some reason." Mary's lack of bowel control was "embarrassing" for mother, who was reassured by day-care staff that they "deal with this often." As the months passed, Mary continued to require a diaper at the day-care center and mother continued to express her embarrassment to father. One day he angrily sat Mary on the toilet and "yelled at her." From that time she began to use the toilet. It was during this phase of Mary's early life, coinciding with struggles around toilet training, that Mary often refused to speak. Her selective mutism persisted until the age of 6 or 7, which resulted in Mary's repeating the first grade "because she wouldn't say anything." Mary's selective mutism transitioned into baby talk from about 7 to 12.

During the evaluation, when asked to discuss why she thought her parents had requested a consultation and whether she had any concerns she would like to share, Mary noted that her main problem was poor school grades, which she knew concerned her parents. Although she had studied all weekend for a French exam, she got an F. Mary mentioned how stressful she became when called upon to respond in French. Following the Life Stressor Interview, the therapist asked if anything had happened years ago, or more recently, that upset her a lot. Mary shared that when the Gulf War began she became afraid, wondering if the United States would become involved in a war like "the big one." Then she added in a whisper, "My mother bugs me a lot, but I'm used to it; it doesn't bother me."

With tests evaluating cognitive regulators, she showed marked rigidity with two cognitive processes: when focusing attention while information was surrounded by stimuli that evoked emotions/fantasies (field articulation) and when looking at a series of pictures of a scene and reporting any changes that occurred (leveling-sharpening). With the Wechsler Intelligence Scale her full-scale IQ fell in the average range; her performance varied from borderline to very superior. Significantly, given her history of "silence," her lowest scores were with the information and vocabulary subtests.

In terms of her capacity to transform information (symbolize), Mary showed limitations at each of the modalities evaluated, but in particular at the embodied level. When body perceptions served as stimuli (Mary felt objects placed under a cloth and described what they brought to mind), she described physical attributes rather than constructing symbols, suggesting that embodied meanings were segregated, for the most part, from fantasy. With the Rorschach test her responses also indicated that personal meanings were underground for the most part. A number of responses depicted conventional meanings ("bat," "butterfly") while other images (a turtle) suggested a "barrier" blocked personal meanings from gaining expression (Fisher and Cleveland 1968). A few responses did represent meanings that influenced her current functioning. One card she described as follows: "Two people just bumped into each other; they're falling down," representing that interacting with others was associated with body instability and loss of equilibrium. To another card she imaged, "Over here are two ducks carefully sticking their heads out of a hole," representing her fear and caution when entering an interpersonal world. To another she constructed an image of two people arguing, followed by an image of two inchworms, again reflecting her sense of vulnerability in response to aggression and self-assertion. Despite Mary's marginal school performance and history of reading difficulties, she performed well on a standardized test of academic achievement. Reading and math scores fell at about the 75th percentile.

Mary's Treatment

Because of several factors, the therapist elected to conduct treatment with highly structured interactions: Mary's history of elective mutism; her current difficulty initiating and expressing herself verbally; test data suggesting cognitive rigidity; the segregation of embodied meanings from fantasy; and representations symbolizing that interacting and asserting resulted in "collisions," loss of body stability, and emotions of fear and vulnerability. These factors argued against a therapeutic process that emphasized nondirected verbal discussions or that required Mary to initiate activities.

The broad goal the therapist articulated was to enable Mary to develop the capacity to experience flexibility, both cognitively and physically, and to be assertive within opportunities and limitations provided by situations. This goal consisted of several interrelated subgoals: cultivate cognitive flexibility; translate embodied meanings into symbols; connect and integrate action and fantasy expressions of meanings; and then connect action and fantasy with language expressions. The therapist's account of Mary's treatment suggested five phases, each guided by a goal and each using a particular form of structured interactions.

Phase I. Helping Mary Enter a Dialectical Circle (11 Sessions)

During the first session Mary seemed anxious and awkward. She offered that while in French class her mind "went blank" even though she had reviewed the vocabulary words "for hours." She attributed her difficulty to "inheriting" her mother's "brain." Rather than explore this belief, the therapist addressed the dilemma Mary had experienced that day. Reflecting how frustrating it must be to study and then forget it all, the therapist suggested they work on a "concentration and memory game so I can get to know firsthand what happens." Mary accepted the invitation. Placing a number of geometric cutouts on the table, the therapist explained that instead of using French words, the game used cutouts.

With this introduction the therapist engaged Mary in experiencing the cognitive processes of field articulation and leveling-sharpening that the evaluation had shown to be particularly rigid. One task involved a 5×5 matrix of cutouts of different sizes, shapes, and colors. The therapist asked Mary to look for and pick up, as quickly as possible, only one type (e.g., all of the medium green triangles), and timed her so that "we can keep track of whether concentrating gets quicker and better." With the second task the therapist arrayed a 2×3 matrix of cutouts. After Mary studied the pattern, the therapist covered it with a cloth and replaced a cutout with another that shared some attributes but differed in others (e.g., a large yellow diamond was replaced by a small yellow diamond). Removing the cloth, the therapist asked Mary if anything changed in the pattern. Initially Mary noted that something "seems weird," but could not identify the changes, laughing, but clearly upset. The therapist noted, "This must be what happens in French," reassured Mary that these games would help her remember better, and frequently invited Mary to give the therapist a turn. Mary enjoyed watching the therapist struggle to remember the original location of cutouts.

Over the next sessions the complexity of each task was gradually increased. With the first, the matrix eventually consisted of stacks of two cutouts, requiring a more differentiated level of field articulation ("Pick up the small yellow diamonds that sit on medium blue triangles"). With the second task the number of cutouts to be remembered was increased (from six to ten), the length of time available to study the matrix was decreased (from ninety to thirty seconds), and the delay between examining the matrix and removing the cloth was increased (from a few seconds to ninety). In addition to sharing details about school or home, Mary spontaneously showed she was observing her experiences with each task ("You see! This is like when I study for an exam. When I'm in the classroom, things just drift out of my mind").

Mary eventually enacted an interactive metaphor that represented an explicit request for help. As she walked up a flight of stairs with the therapist, Mary complained that her legs hurt and she felt tired. Sitting at the table to begin a task, she commented, "This really tires out your brain, doesn't it?" The therapist pointed out that concentrating is tiring indeed, just like walking up the stairs, but the tasks are making her mind stronger since she can now remember ten cutouts after waiting more than a minute; a few weeks ago she could remember only six and only after thirty seconds had passed. Mary seemed empowered by the review of her progress and continued engaging the tasks.

Phase II. Translating Embodied Meanings into Language Symbols (8 Sessions)

Since Mary had shared personal expressions and asked for help, suggesting she had entered a dialectical circle, the therapist introduced another task that involved remembering patterns of words instead of cutouts. Because it helps to remember something if a person handles it, the therapist explained, words would be connected to tactile experiences. Mary handled a number of objects and expressed a word each object brought to mind. Sometimes she produced a word quickly, at other times she pondered. In response, the therapist suggested Mary could learn when her mind "lets go and is free" and when it is "frozen." Mary and the therapist devised a five-point rating scale ranging from "1" (her mind is "free") to "5" (her mind is "frozen"). Mary's words and associated ratings included *a piece of cloth*—"hide: 4," "scary: 5"; *a mousetrap*—"click: 2," "trash: 5"; *a wooden block*—"cliff: 4"; *a toy tractor*—"farming: 1." Mary became slightly more animated with this task, spontaneously commenting, "I like this game of let your mind go."

Mary eventually generated fifty words, each printed on a card. The words were used, as were the cutouts, to form matrices that Mary scanned to search for particular words ("Find all the words that have to do with the outdoors"). The words were used in a memory task, with Mary again determining whether a matrix of words had changed after she studied it. Significantly, while engaged in these tasks, Mary increasingly shared meanings from her subjective world, hinting at various metaphors that likely interfered with her functioning. As one instance, when she removed the card on which had been printed "cliff," she associated to a trip the family had taken in the mountains of Maine, and that her mother became frightened when they stood on the edge of a cliff. As she demonstrated more cognitive efficiency searching for words and remembering configurations of words, the therapist introduced another change in their structured interactions intended to help Mary connect words to fantasies.

Phase III. Connecting Language Symbols to Elaborated Fantasies (12 Sessions)

The therapist pointed out that, as Mary probably noticed, the searching and remembering games were bringing up different feelings and memories. If more of these "came out for us to share," Mary would be able to concentrate and remember words better, because these memories and feelings "were hanging onto the words." With this, the therapist spread all of the cards they had been working with over the table. Mary's job was to look over the cards, pick two of them, and describe a memory—or "make something up"—that the words brought to mind. Reflecting the gains she had made to this point, she tended to pick up one and then another as she scanned the cards, usually within a few seconds. It seemed likely she was not yet conscious of the story she would eventually construct. Examples of the associations/stories Mary elaborated for each pair of words she selected follow.

Mary/running. Mary described running in a race during gym; she became tired and came in last.

Dog/past. When Mary was about 7 years old, a big dog reared up and put its front paws on her shoulders. Mary screamed. Mother lingered with a neighbor to finish what she was saying before coming to Mary's aid. Referring to mother's seeming lack of concern, Mary commented with noticeable irritation, "I couldn't believe it!"

Noise/car. Once Mary did not want to read. She thinks she was in the fifth grade. Father shook her and yelled at her.

As Mary constructed associations to pairs of words, she expressed thoughts with increasing ease and emotional spontaneity, and shared events that occurred since her last session. Mary also displayed attempts to negotiate self-assertion. At times, for example, occupying herself between trials by "shooting" rubber bands across the room, she playfully warned the therapist, "Be careful, I'm a good shot." Referring to a conference the therapist was scheduled to hold with Mary's parents, Mary joked, "It's fine by me. They'll probably complain that I'm telling them off," and imagined the therapist and her parents in an argument.

Phase IV. Integrating Action, Fantasy, and Language (18 Sessions)

Relying on Mary's gains in constructing fantasies and associations and negotiating self-assertion, the therapist introduced another elaboration that resembled the say-do cognitive-behavioral technique. Mary selected two cards from among many arranged on the table, imagined a scene the words suggested, drew a picture of the scene, constructed a story about it, and then enacted the story. The therapist demonstrated selecting two cards, "car" and "frustration," because they suggested a metaphor representing a sense of being stuck and frustrated. The therapist drew a picture of a car stuck in a traffic jam, and narrated that the person was frustrated because she was late for work. The therapist enacted the scene, pantomiming frustration and irritation.

In the material to follow I describe selected drawings and fantasies Mary constructed and enacted. While I have omitted a number of her productions, those included represent the sequence of meanings that emerged. My intention is to illustrate two issues. As these structured interactions unfolded, Mary gradually expressed metaphors representing her cognitive and physical inhibitions, and the intense anxiety she experienced when asserting. Eventually she constructed and enacted a metaphor that could be viewed as a "core pathological life metaphor" at the root of her difficulties.

Hold back/girl (*Figure 8–1*). Immediately after the therapist performed her "car/ frustration" story, Mary scanned the cards and selected "hold back/girl." Reflecting for a minute or so, she drew a picture and told a story about a girl being restrained by a player on the other team. When enacting this scene, Mary's physical movements were quite muted. She simply stood up, formed a circle with her arms, and then sat down.

FIGURE 8–1

Slip back/sister (*Figure 8–2*). Mary told a story about a girl who shouts for help while slipping down a hill. When enacting this scene, Mary stood up and with arms stretched forward, took a couple of steps backward, spontaneously commenting that her mother contacted the school to find out how Mary was doing and expressing resentment over mother "getting into my business." The therapist chose to respond only to the metaphor of help. With humor, the therapist asked Mary to "do the falling part again." Mary stood up and again took a few steps backward. The therapist, standing behind her, placed her hands on Mary's shoulders saying, "Gotcha— you won't slip back." Mary laughed.

FIGURE 8–2

Disobey/nervous (*Figure 8–3a*). Mary's performance with these words illustrates two techniques the therapist used from time to time. She asked Mary to take each part of a drawing and describe what the part could mean. With the other technique she cultivated Mary's ability to elaborate a fantasy and its enactments by asking Mary to construct a second scene related in some way to the first. When Mary completed the drawing the therapist asked her to list "different things about the teacher." Mary listed, for example, "fed up, annoyed." To the sun Mary listed only "sad," and to the girl, "little green pea, nervous, scared to say anything." When Mary enacted the scene, she first picked up a toy gun, then assumed an erect position as the teacher, shaking her forefinger, and enacted the girl by curling her body into a ball.

FIGURE 8–3a

When the therapist asked Mary if there were other situations that came to mind from what she had just experienced, she drew a student turning in an assignment while the other student, who hadn't finished her work, is thinking, "Oh great, I'm dead!" (Figure 8–3b). Mary spontaneously associated to a similar experience in math class a few weeks before, and at the same time scribbled in the teacher's face, blocking out her eyes and nose.

After Mary enacted the scene, the therapist asked her to draw a picture of how she would like to express herself to the teacher in the story. Mary drew the teacher and then the figure seated at the left (Figure 8–3c). "That's me. I'm as big as the teacher." Then she drew other students, commenting that the chair the student was sitting on is "blocking the smartest kids in class." Relying on previous drawings, enactments, and discussions, the therapist gave her view of the scene. The girl on the left would like to be as smart and confident as the teacher. To accomplish this the big girl has to block competition. But together they would find ways for Mary to be as smart and big as everyone else by getting her mind and body to be free so she "can get in there and take on the competition." Mary listened but said nothing.

FIGURE 8–3b

FIGURE 8–3c

The following session Mary brought in a story she had written and asked the therapist to read it aloud.

> The prison door slammed behind me and silence overtook my cell . . . I couldn't wait to get out . . . I heard someone knock on the wall of my cell . . . A small voice asked if I was all right . . . The voice was nice, and it comforted me to know that I wasn't alone . . . we became the best of friends.

In the therapist's view the prison cell symbolized Mary's "psychological confinement" and the "nice voice in the next cell," the therapist who had become a "best friend." The therapist complimented Mary and commented that she was confident that the friend was going to help "that girl" get out of jail.

High confidence/fence/fat (*Figure 8–4*). To elaborate their interactions, the therapist suggested that Mary select three cards instead of two to make up a story. Mary selected cards that seemed to relate to the comment the therapist had made in response to her written story. Mary pointed out that the person on the left wants to climb over a fat fence and is sure she can make it. The other person is not sure she can, representing Mary's conflict: confidence in being able to achieve is opposed by doubts the wall can be scaled. Mary did not notice she had exchanged the punctuation marks at the end of each statement. While the figure on the left was declaring, "I can do it, I can," Mary wrote a question mark, which belongs to the doubt being expressed by the other figure. The question, "Can you make it," is followed by an exclamation point, which belongs to the quote on the left. This "slip of the crayon" reflects conflict created by two opposing metaphors. Although her mind is declaring she can do it, the declaration arouses anxiety and doubt (question mark); the doubt is expressed with emphasis (exclamation point).

When enacting this scene, using stacked chairs and wastebaskets as a wall, Mary wondered if the person could get around the fence in some way. They concluded that there were "no shortcuts," and the best thing the person could do was

FIGURE 8–4

to prove to herself that she "really could do it." Mary apparently assimilated the notion that obstacles should be confronted. She steadily made gains in cultivating cognitive flexibility and eventually introduced a fantasy that seemed to represent a regression to a core pathological metaphor at the source of her difficulties with asserting. Before introducing this material, we should consider that during previous weeks Mary increasingly expressed anger at her mother because of her lack of nurture and longstanding tendency to control every aspect of Mary's life. Mother was forever commenting about what Mary wears, how she stands, how she holds her silverware during mealtimes, and so on.

Early memory/aggression/baby (*Figure 8–5*). In one session Mary selected three cards, drew a picture, and explained that the mother is remembering and sharing with her child that when mother was pregnant, the child, *in utero*, often kicked mother very hard. Enacting this scene, Mary tied a pillow around her belly and asked the therapist to punch it. They exchanged roles several times.

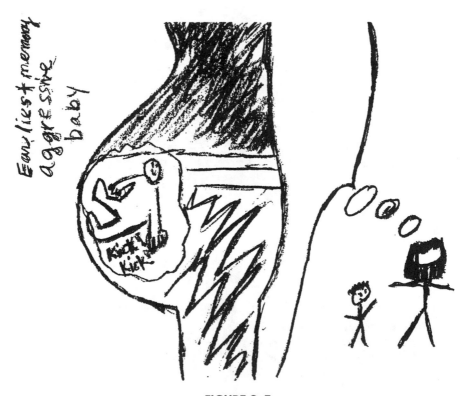

FIGURE 8–5

Risk taking/special/diving in/father (*Figures 8–6a–d*). During the next sessions, Mary selected four cards, puzzled for several minutes, and drew the picture, explaining that a daughter is swimming near a fish "who eats people." Father takes a risk and dives in to save her.

Instead of enacting the scene, Mary drew Figure 8–6b, explaining that while father is saving the girl, the fish is really hungry and wants to attack the people, but freezes, unable to decide what to do. During the enactment, Mary initially took the role of the girl, then, laughing, played the fish, and with mouth wide open moved toward the therapist. Mary paused, sat down, and drew another picture, saying, "There's more to this story."

She drew Figure 8–6c, noting that the fish decided "to go for it and swallow the people." She continued drawing Figure 8–6d, and pointed out that "the fish is so undecided, she swallows the people whole and does not chomp on them . . . The people are kicking inside of the stomach. The fish gets a stomachache and starts coughing."

Then Mary drew Figure 8–6e, continuing her story. The fish coughs up the father and daughter. The children fish, who were introduced in Figure 8–6c, but whom Mary ignored until this point, were very confused about why their mother coughed up the people because they were to be dinner. The baby fish were so angry that they began "to eat her all up."

FIGURE 8–6a

FIGURE 8–6b

FIGURE 8–6c

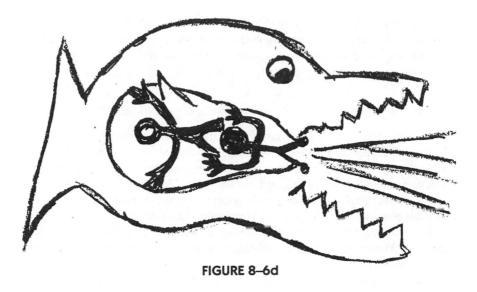

FIGURE 8–6d

FIGURE 8–6e

Mary spent three sessions on this metaphor, during which she shared related associations but apparently was not conscious of their connection. For example, she associated to mother's skimpy meals and said that she identified more with father since mother also nagged him.

Phase V. Discussing Concerns about the Here and Now (8 Sessions)

After enacting the "fish" story, Mary shifted the process to present-day concerns. With summer approaching and school soon ending, she wondered whether she should stop her sessions, discussing her opinion that she was now more able to speak up and handle school work, and that she would like to "try and see how things go on my own." Exploring Mary's wish to terminate, the therapist agreed that she had made gains, and together they set a termination date three weeks after the close of school. During these discussions the therapist was careful to respect and accommodate to Mary's expressions of self-assertion and autonomy and to convey her confidence in Mary.

Mary focused on mother's nagging ways, using her deck of cards to create "stories," although it now seemed apparent she was aware of the issues she was portraying. Sometimes she expressed an issue directly, as illustrated by her drawing of a mother who is a nag even when she is driving a car ("Mom/picky" [Figure 8–7]). Mary revealed that mother constantly blows her horn and "rags" on other drivers. At other times Mary used a cartoon format (Figure 8–8). A mother bear is using "a very relaxed voice to yell at her baby that dinner is ready." Mary did not enact these scenes but engaged the therapist in discussions.

FIGURE 8–7

Yell-animal-relaxing

FIGURE 8–8

Another theme Mary emphasized concerned her feelings that boys are not interested in her (Figure 8–9); her daydreams about boys, which she shares with girlfriends (Figure 8–10); and her hope that the therapist could help her (Figure 8–11).

During the last session before the summer break, Mary and the therapist listed the pros and cons for continuing treatment in the fall. The reasons Mary listed that supported her continuing included how to handle her mother's nagging ways, her anxieties about boyfriends, and her tendency before exams to get sleepy and speak slowly. In terms of why she thought she should not continue, Mary felt that it was time for her to "try to work things out on my own." At the start of the next school year the therapist met with Mary and separately with her parents. Mary seemed pleased to see the therapist, discussing her recent experiences in the tenth grade. She acknowledged that she still became anxious when doing homework, but "it's nothing like last year." She has begun to "hang out" with two female classmates, and this group usually connected with boys in the hallways and at lunch. Mary decided that she would not continue and agreed that she would call the therapist whenever she felt she was "getting stuck again." The parents reported that Mary was "doing well" and were pleased with her progress. She continued to be more outgoing, expressing more clearly what she was thinking and feeling. The therapist engaged mother and father in a discussion of Mary's need to continue testing

Sad - Ignore

FIGURE 8–9

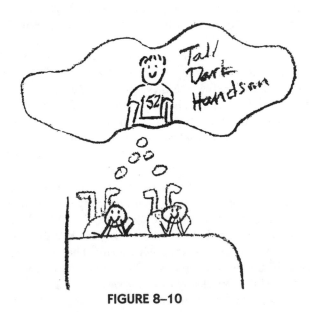

FIGURE 8–10

FIGURE 8–11

self-assertion and aggression, and that at times they—mother in particular—may be irritated by this behavior given that they have been accustomed to her passivity for years.

CAN YOU DESCRIBE CASES ILLUSTRATING A TRANSITION FROM STRUCTURED TO UNSTRUCTURED INTERACTIONS?

John: I'm Devastated by the Loss of a Loved One

John was described by mother and teacher as "in a shell." He began to display this behavior when he was 5 years old, shortly after the death of his father. The G family operated a farm. Mr. G was killed accidentally while operating a tractor that tipped over, crushing him beneath it. John had accompanied father while he handled many of the farm chores. Father had built a special seat for John on the tractor involved in the tragedy, and they frequently rode together around the fields. After the funeral John began to avoid contact with persons outside his immediate family. Reviewing his early history, mother did not recall John's showing any difficulties.

In terms of John's psychological evaluation, he attained a total IQ in the superior range (135), but the examiner had provided considerable support and direction, frequently repeating instructions, refocusing John, and reassuring and coaxing him whenever he blocked or refused to tackle some item. With tests of cognitive regulators, he showed excessive rigidity when scanning a field of information that evoked fantasies and emotions (e.g., pictures of weapons). With an action test of personality, when asked to perform three actions on material in any order he chose, his actions were inhibited and he could not express what came to mind while performing them.

With the Rorschach test John produced images representing violence that was not visible in his day-to-day functioning and that he was struggling to keep under control. In response to one card, for example, he constructed the image of two dead buffaloes that have been shot and "there are blood stains all over." With a sentence completion test John produced responses that symbolized themes that likely occupied his conscious thoughts. One concerned his need to repair his ability to move forward: *What I want more than anything is* "for my go-cart to be fixed." Another concerned his social isolation: *My best friend is* "my dog." On the basis of these data, the diagnostician viewed John as suffering from severe inhibition associated with the death of his father, which extended into cognition as well as the action mode.

John's Treatment

Helping John Step into a Dialectical Circle:
A Formidable Hurdle (10 Sessions)

Upon entering the playroom, John picked up a few objects only to set each back in its place. As he slowly wandered about, I did not mention his mother's concerns or the school's. I waited for some gesture or comment on his part that suggested he was inviting me to enter a dialectical circle. Finally one of these moments occurred. He picked up a football, tossed it a few feet in the air, and caught it. I slapped my hands and held them outstretched, inviting him to throw me a pass. He did. I tossed the ball back, inviting him to play catch. For a moment I felt elated by the possibility that he might begin what could become a circular interaction. But when he caught the ball, he put it back on the shelf. He continued walking about, essentially ignoring me.

During the second hour John behaved in about the same way. Near the close of the hour, I proposed that he could assemble a model of his choosing. Several thoughts flitted through my mind when I made this offer. Recalling his response during the evaluation, expressing his conscious wish to fix his go-cart, I wondered if assembling a model might give this personal meaning an opportunity to express itself in an activity. In addition, it seemed to me that while John was wandering aimlessly about the room, he was experiencing stress as he actively avoided stepping into a dialectical circle with me. By working on a model, I thought he could engage in some focused activity that would help him avoid me. Yet he could engage me whenever he chose. John selected the model of a car and worked with it for the next two sessions, quietly gluing pieces together while ignoring me.

What I chose to do during this time was influenced by test results indicating that his action mode was rigidly held in check, avoiding direct, symbolic expressions, especially of assertion. I initially engaged in activity that symbolized control, order, and repairing disorder, activity I thought was attuned to John's current mode of functioning and might facilitate first-order change. While John quietly studied the directions for assembling the model, I busied myself clearing shelves and organizing materials in the treatment room, commenting a few times, "This place needs to be straightened out." John glanced at me occasionally while working on his model.

In the next sessions I continued my "operation cleanup." I rummaged through boxes of crayons, found broken pieces, lined them up, and searched for other pieces that matched them. Working on the same table on which John was assembling his model, I taped pieces of crayons together. At one point I groaned over the number of broken pieces and commented, "Anytime you want to tape some together, that would be cool." Several minutes passed when John, perhaps responding to my request, complained, with a puzzled look on his face, that he could not figure out a step in the directions of his model. I leaned over, asked which step he was working on, read the directions, and manipulated the pieces, searching for the way they should be glued together. I shared the solution with John, and he glued the pieces. Minutes later he spontaneously reached over and taped two pieces of crayon together. At this point I felt each of us had placed one foot in a dialectical circle.

During the following meetings John worked on his model while I set out other tasks for myself. With each, my intention now was to help John stand in our dialectical circle for a few moments and engage in symbolic microactions representing expressions of assertion. I brought in stacks of paper and old correspondence that needed to be "shredded." I slowly crumpled sheets and tossed each into a wastebasket. With another task I brought in boards, screws, and nails "that had to be screwed and nailed together." During each meeting, I conveyed that any help would be appreciated, and I tried to be careful to move at a pace that resembled John's.

John interrupted his work with the model occasionally and joined me for a few moments in crumpling and tossing sheets of paper, hammering nails, and turning screws into wood. Initially his actions were constricted, as described by the diagnostician. Gradually he crumpled paper with slightly more vigor (imitating me it seemed). At the same time he increased the number of times he indicated he needed help locating and gluing pieces of his model and interpreting some step in the instructions.

During the last two sessions of this phase I chose to use "hammering nails" as a way to further facilitate our participating in a dialectical circle. I brought in a 2 × 4 board, about two feet in length, into which I had tapped seven nails. I invited John to compete with me to see who could drive in the nails with the *fewest* number of blows of the hammer. John accepted. As we engaged in this activity he used slightly more vigor when pounding nails, and showed more affiliation toward me.

At the start of the tenth session John experienced metaphorically what I understood to be his "call for help" and his view of why we were meeting. When we entered the playroom, he turned to me, commenting, "I hurt my finger; I can't bend it." He showed me the index finger of his left hand, which appeared to be only slightly tender. I expressed concern and carefully examined his finger, touching it gingerly. He shared that he was "messing around" in the barn. I offered to put a Band-Aid on it. John accepted and seemed to stand close to me. I carefully bandaged his finger and commented that he could now work on his model better, and grip the handle of the hammer better, when he "takes me on" in one of our hammering contests. John grinned and agreed.

With this interaction, symbolizing John's expression of pain, and accepting me as someone who could help, I thought we had finally stepped into a dialectical circle with both feet, having discovered and negotiated each other's self-expressions, preferred levels of stimulation, and pace of interacting. These negotiations took place while we assembled the car model, crumpled and shredded paper, and turned screws and hammered nails into wood. As it turned out, my hunch proved correct. Our interaction over his "wounded finger" ushered in the first interactive metaphor authored by John.

"I've Been Broken into Pieces and I'm Furious" (1 Session)

In the next session, after showing me that a tooth had been pulled by a dentist (which in fact had occurred some time ago), he engaged me in a game of catch. At one point he hurled the ball at me with intensity. I caught it, grunting "Ugh!" but he made no comment. Then he hurled bean bags at a plastic figure, which tumbled to the floor and broke into pieces. Glancing anxiously at me, he commented, "All the pieces are still good." I examined them, commenting that we could put him back together again. As we busied ourselves gluing the pieces, I noted, "This guy was so mad he exploded into a million pieces." John grinned.

"I Harbor Murderous Wishes": Cultivating Delay and Indirectness in the Action Mode to Displace Aggression Away from the Therapist (7 Sessions)

John's aggressive behaviors escalated rapidly in the next sessions, sometimes expressed in brief, explosive moments of fantasy play and sometimes directly at my person. These expressions occurred, I thought, because the rigidity of his action mode, held tightly since he was 5, was beginning to loosen too rapidly. At the same time, John had not had opportunities, since the death of his father, to develop and practice self-regulation and flexibility, expressing meanings in action with various degrees of directness and delay. I therefore decided to focus first on providing John with experiences cultivating flexibility and self-regulation in the action mode, rather than focus on the content of his aggressive intentions. To this end I introduced two tasks. With one I tapped three nails and three screws into a board, alternating them, and challenged John to compete with me. Each of us was to hammer a nail, then turn a screw, then hammer the next nail, and so on, shifting back and forth between performing vigorous, immediate, direct actions (hammering) and indirect and delayed actions (turning a screw), facilitating self-regulation and delay. To win required the *least* amount of time to embed the nails and screws. Each of us had to aim the hammer carefully, regulate its blow, and carefully regulate the turno of the screwdriver. Each of us timed the other, and we kept a log of our trials.

For the second task I lined up ten wooden geometric cutouts of different sizes, shapes, and colors. A player stood with his back to the array, dart gun at the ready. When the other player called out a designated target, the shooter turned, scanned the row of targets, aimed, and shot the target designated. If a player hit the correct target, he obtained two points; if he missed, he lost one point; if he hit the wrong target, he lost two points. John participated in each contest with increasing enthusiasm. His action mode slipped on only a few occasions. In the nail and screw game he became frustrated on a few occasions and frantically pounded both nails and screws. Once he waved the hammer at my head, and on two occasions he shot at me instead of the designated target, showing the same gleam in his eyes when weeks ago he hurled a ball at me.

Enacting Interpersonal Aggression, Using Dolls and the Therapist as Targets: Cultivating Further Delay and Indirectness in the Action Mode (9 Sessions)

Looking for additional ways to direct John's aggression from my person to representations of humans, I elaborated our dart-gun game to include, as targets, wooden figures of humans instead of geometric cutouts. The figures, each about six inches tall, represented a range of individuals: fireman, policeman, doctor, nurse, mother, father, children. At one point John asked if we could have "a gun fight," shifting the target of aggression from dolls to our persons. I agreed. Initially John expressed appropriate behavioral regulation as we "battled," each of us squatting behind chairs and blasting away. On several occasions, however, John's self-regulation collapsed as he toppled chairs and frantically raced about the room in search of a "better position."

To stem the tide, I introduced two additional structured interactions that maintained our persons as targets, but required different degrees of directness and delay. One game consisted of "pistol duels at fifteen paces." We stood back to back. When one of us gave a signal, we took fifteen steps, turned, and fired at each other. With the other, we took turns timing each other while drawing our dart guns from our belts in two ways. One contest determined who was the "fastest gun." The other determined who was best at drawing and aiming "in slow motion" and delaying squeezing the trigger. On two occasions, during a "slow motion" enactment, John lost total control when he suddenly punched me very hard in the arm. In addition, he occasionally criticized something about the treatment room or the clothing I was wearing.

Did Father Die or Did I Kill Him? (10 Sessions)

During one dart gun game, John set his gun aside, examined boxing gloves, and asked if we could box. I guessed (or wished) that maybe he was now ready to express aggression toward my person in a sublimated form within the sport of boxing, because he had shown he could shift flexibly, to some degree, among different tempos and degrees of delay and directness. I agreed, and decided to represent and enact, as much as possible, symbols of regulation and structure. We taped the floor to mark the boundaries of a boxing ring, placed chairs in opposite corners, set a timer to beep two-minute rounds. I also introduced an imaginary sports arena, announcer, and audience. Initially, John participated within the fantasy, bobbing and jabbing, returning to his corner when the beeper sounded, and obviously enjoying himself. At the close of the session, when we tidied the room, he shared that on his way home, after the last session, he had spotted a squirrel lying on the road, blood coming from its mouth, and wondered if maybe he and his mother had hit it on the way to the clinic. After he left, I puzzled whether this association and its meaning would find its way into the treatment process.

In one session he began to swing wildly and furiously at my body rather than box. As the announcer I commented, "Folks, Slaughter Sam (a name John had selected) is losing points," but my words, spoken within our boxing metaphor, failed to stimulate John's self-regulation. At one point, as John swung away, pounding at my arms and chest, he suddenly began to sob, "Die, die, die." I put my arms around him and held him close to me. He continued sobbing for a minute or two. Then he turned, took a long look at me, and whispered, "Are you hurt?" I said No, and that Bulldozer Bob (a name I had selected) was ready to get back in the ring. I thought I should repair the disruption and convey that John's "murderous onslaught" did not hurt me and that I could go on.

In the following session John boxed for three rounds and made no mention of the previous hour. I decided not to refer to it and waited to see what unfolded. He asked to go outside and play basketball. As we took turns shooting baskets, John ritualized several enactments that elaborated the meaning of the boxing episode when he sobbed "die." Taken together, these enactments represented the death of his father and John's unconscious belief that he was in some way responsible. He called the basketball game he devised "sudden death playoff." In addition, he searched for insects crawling on the pavement and dripped water on them. As he watched each insect struggle, he wondered if he had "killed it."

I Am 5 Years Old Again (9 Sessions)

Our enactments shifted again when John rummaged through a room where nursery school equipment was maintained and pulled out a tricycle and wagon. He rode the tricycle around the treatment room and sometimes in the adjoining playground. He also asked me to give him rides in a wagon. As I pulled him around the playground, John pretended I was a horse. Embracing the fantasy, I tossed my head and snorted, doing my best to imitate a horse. In one session, while riding in the wagon, John mentioned his father for the first time. "My father had a tractor. He wore a red jacket when he drove it." I was struck by this comment, so much so that I asked him several questions about his father, caught up with my eagerness to learn about other memories and to help him address father's death. He climbed out of the wagon, however, clearly upset, saying it made him "sick" to talk about his father. I tried to be supportive, but it became clear that I had erred in asking questions. My inquiries had required John to share meanings about his father verbally and conceptually (second-order change), a process for which he was not yet prepared. John walked away and for the rest of the session busied himself climbing a jungle gym, ignoring me.

During the next sessions John continued "playing horse." I participated, making no further mention of his father. But John eventually referred to his father again in a very interesting way. At the start of one session he walked over to smoking pipes in my office, commenting, "My father smoked a pipe," and asked if he could "play with one." I indicated, "Of course." John rode in the wagon with a pipe in his mouth, urging the horse on, and tugging at the "harness" with a little more exuberance than usual.

I Am Afraid of Losing What I Love and Can Now Discuss My Father (7 Sessions)

John abandoned the game of horse and began to ritualize hiding from me, crawling under a bush outdoors and under tables in the treatment room. When I discovered him, he made comments such as, "I'm coming every day." "I'll sleep here, so I'll be here for my next appointment tomorrow." Each time, I crawled next to him, attempted to reassure him, and made verbal interpretations (e.g., "When two guys become good friends, it's tough to say good-bye and not see each other." "It's scary to say good-bye because we can't be sure I'll be here for our next meeting"). I chose at this time not to literally connect the meaning of his enactments to his loss. In addition to these interpretations, to help John separate, I gave him various transitional objects from my office to take home and return to our next meeting (e.g., a stone from my collection, a book).

I also introduced a structured interaction that I thought might help John cope with his separation anxiety and fear of loss. I suggested that each of us draw a map of "where we live." John complied readily and gradually included drawings of various structures on his farm. During this activity he began sharing details: he doesn't know why, but he has become afraid of walking too far into the woods; he has become afraid of riding the horse the family maintains, unlike his sister and brother. Of special significance, he eventually marked a spot on his map where father's tractor had tipped over. John offered that he often sits on this spot, thinking about his father and the activities they shared, a number of which he described. I suggested he talk to his mother, brother, and sister about planting a tree there. John thought that was a good idea.

We also discussed his new sixth-grade teacher, a male whom he liked very much, and his paternal grandfather, with whom he was now spending a good part of each weekend doing "odds and ends" around the farm. In this context we discussed that while he missed his father very much, and no one could take his place, there are other men like his teacher and grandfather whom he could enjoy and learn from.

At one point John brought in the car model he had taken home at the start of treatment, which at that time was partially constructed. It was now fully assembled, carefully painted, and covered with decals. John displayed the model with pride and offered it to me as a gift "to keep so you can remember us." I thanked him and offered him another model. He selected a battleship.

Concluding Comment

I understood John's giving me the model as a symbol that he had finally repaired his "go-cart," a wish he had expressed during the evaluation. In the course of treatment he developed more flexibility in taking appropriate assertive action, worked through his repressed rage, stepped out of his shell, and eventually addressed the loss of his father—at first acting on my person, then less directly with the wagon game, then by expressing the wish to "live with me," and finally by discussing his father's accident and death verbally. I did not interpret what was suggested by his activities and fantasies at one point, namely, that he may have thought he had killed his father. This metaphor appeared to be resolved without bringing it to a conceptual/verbal level. These gains, coupled with reports from mother and teacher, indicated that John was on a more growth-fostering developmental path and was ready to terminate. John and I selected a date. We spent our last meetings assembling parts of the battleship and talking about daily events.

Laura: Lost in the Deepest Reaches of My Inner Space

Laura was 7½ years old and in second grade when referred by her parents at the urging of school personnel. From the start of the school year she had been tuned out, struggled to complete her work, and constantly needed to be refocused, behavior she had shown during the first grade. She was essentially a nonreader despite considerable tutoring, developed no friendships, and remained withdrawn in the playground and hallways. Because of her inadequate academic performance, she was assigned to a special needs class where she seemed "dreamy" and lost in her private world, causing special education staff to wonder about the possibility of a latent psychosis.

Mother, a computer programmer, and father, a bank teller, were confused by Laura's difficulty handling schoolwork because, from her early years, she showed "exceptional intellectual ability." By the time Laura was about 3, when her parents read to her from storybooks, she spontaneously "read" the words under the pictures, apparently having memorized them. Mother had "tutored" Laura in math almost every night "because math skills are basic to everything and exercise the brain." Father reported with obvious pride that by the time Laura was 4 years old she could count to 100 and correctly perform simple addition problems using wooden blocks.

Laura was evaluated by a team of clinical psychologists. She attained a full-scale IQ of 102 (average range), but showed considerable variability among subtests. Assessments of cognitive regulators indicated moderate to severe lags and an inner cognitive orientation. The metaphors Laura constructed in response to projective tests did not support the possibility of a latent psychosis and provided some information about the fantasies that commanded most of her attention. For example, to one inkblot she imaged two "skeletons running after the same bow" when two angels appear and "order them" to share it. To another she imaged a butterfly trying to fly away from a raging fire. Several of her stories to pictures elaborated the metaphor of nurture, depicting people having "no food" or who "can't find a place to have a picnic."

Laura's Treatment

Helping Laura Step into a Dialectical Circle (4 Sessions)

When the therapist greeted Laura for the first session, Laura returned her greeting with a quiet but firm, "No talking; I'm not here to talk." She drifted about the playroom with the same "floating" movements observed during the evaluation, scanning materials but touching nothing. Looking back at this first session, the therapist acknowledged that she became too eager to help Laura step into a dialectical circle, introducing several structured tasks in the hopes that one of them would serve as a handrail, but the tasks were not yet embedded in one of Laura's fantasies (the therapist set a matrix of geometric cutouts on a table and asked Laura to study it and detect whether the therapist had introduced a change).

In the next session Laura revealed why she was reluctant to enter a dialectical circle and how she was construing the therapist and her activities. The therapist introduced a "search and find" game. Several items were placed in one small pillowcase and a single item in another. Laura was to examine the single item ("It's all alone") and then search through the "family bag" to find "someone from the same family it could belong to." At one point, when she could not find an item, she anxiously asked, "If I get an answer wrong, will you give me time-outs like my teacher does . . . do you think that means I'm stupid?" The therapist recalled to herself that during a previous school conference the teacher had shared that whenever Laura spent too much time wandering around the classroom, she was given a "time-out," acknowledged by the teacher as a "desperate effort" to help Laura focus and get some work done. The therapist understood that Laura was construing her as "a teacher" who held sharp judgments about right and wrong. The roots of these concerns were probably located in the extensive "tutoring" Laura experienced from her parents. The therapist reassured Laura that she did not give time-outs and that she was searching for games that Laura might enjoy and help them become friends.

Laura suggested they play a "drawing game." She would draw a picture and the therapist was to guess what the figure was. The therapist recognized that Laura was negotiating directing their activity and imitating the "search and find game," but now Laura was asking the therapist to search for something. To make her drawing Laura used the wooden geometric cutouts they had used in memory games. This ensemble suggested to the therapist that Laura was placing one foot in a dialectical circle.

Laura arranged five cutouts on a sheet of paper, traced the pattern, colored it with Magic Markers, and announced with a dictatorial tone that the therapist had "only five chances to guess what the drawing is." The therapist struggled to find a solution and hoped that she would not get a time-out, to which Laura grinned. After the therapist made several incorrect guesses, Laura shared that she had drawn "a compass; it shows you which way to go." The therapist commented that she would be happy to go wherever "that compass tells us to go." At this point Laura took the green circle she had placed in the center of her compass, moved it toward the therapist, and said, "This is Ms. Green, my teacher. The lines on it remind me of the wrinkles on her face." With this interaction Laura placed both feet in a dialectical circle and slipped into the deepest reaches of her inner space.

Phase I. A World of Rules and Regulations that Exists in the Deepest Reaches of My Inner Space (16 Sessions)

Laura stared at the green circle, adding that she could see the different faces her teacher makes. Then she wistfully took a large red triangle from the nearby box and set it on the table, "This is Rudolf the reindeer." With the same dreamy quality she placed several cutouts on the table, assigning each an identity (a large black square: "This is the ghost of the night"; a large white triangle: "This is Santa"). "They're [the cutouts] going to be in a play called 'The Show of the Night.'" With the session now over the therapist commented, "That's great! We'll continue next time." Laura responded: "No talking."

Laura's prohibition against "talking" was restated in the next sessions. In an attempt to cultivate their relationship and express interest in Laura's subjective world, the therapist occasionally asked, for instance, "How was school today?" In response to any such comment Laura stated emphatically, "No talking. There's no time for talking!" Recalling these early sessions, the therapist shared with me, "It's as if once the door closed to the treatment room, Laura became totally submerged in the reality of her fantasy. The only conversation Laura initiated outside her fantasy concerned reassurance that she would not be required to read. During the following five sessions she occupied herself with selecting and naming cutouts she fantasized as a "troupe of actors" who were to prepare for rehearsals of "The Show of the Night." To the initial group of five cutouts she gradually added twenty-four.

But Laura did more with these cutouts than name them. From the start she assigned herself the role of teacher and the therapist the role of "teacher's assistant" and ritualized an activity. At each session she carefully lined up the cutouts to which she had already assigned an identity. As new characters were identified, each was carefully placed in line. Laura remembered not only the name of each character, but the character's place in line. The therapist acknowledged that while she prided herself on having a good memory, she had to refer to a written log to keep track of who was who. In Laura's fantasy play these imaginary characters had to "follow rules" in preparation for "rehearsals." She constructed a complex set of rules, directing the therapist to record them in their "rule book"; "You must stay in line"; "You must pay attention." Each time a character broke a rule it received a "warning" and was sent to the back of the line. After receiving five warnings a character could not take part in the play and must "wait until next year" to participate. Laura, totally submerged in her fantasy, rarely made eye contact with the therapist. During each session the therapist waited for directions to log in either a new character or a transgression. Finally, in the last session of this phase, Laura spread the twenty-nine cutouts (characters) over the tabletop in what appeared to be a random array. Then, directing the therapist to "write down the play," she told a long, confused story. Amazingly, each time an interaction was mentioned in the story, Laura manipulated the wooden cutouts involved. The therapist complimented the "characters" on their first rehearsal and told them that she looked forward to future rehearsals, hoping privately that as "The Show of the Night" was repeated, its metaphors would become clearer.

Phase II. A World of Rules and Regulations that Exists in a School (13 Sessions)

Laura made no mention of "The Show of the Night" in the next session. Instead, much to the therapist's surprise, she commented, "These [the cutouts] are all kids in a classroom," designating each of twenty-nine cutouts as a student or teacher. Initially Laura occupied herself with lining up the cutouts by size and alphabetically. Then, as a teacher, she administered spelling and math contests to the "students." When manipulating the cutouts in some fantasy, she displayed a no-nonsense, stern, tutorial style of relating.

During this "classroom fantasy" Laura initiated interesting enactments. She introduced a "spinning game," spinning each cutout (student) to determine who could spin for the longest time before falling, and a "balancing game," setting each cutout (student) on its edge to determine who would "balance the best." The therapist viewed these enactments as representing Laura's body image negotiating control and balance as she struggled to extend her fantasy world into the environment.

During this phase Laura indicated she was idealizing and identifying with the therapist. In the previous phase she addressed the therapist as "assistant" and rarely made eye contact. In contrast, during this phase, Laura increasingly addressed the therapist using the pronoun "we" and equated her person with that of the therapist in highly valued terms: "You know, we have the gift of height." She gradually drew attention to other "gifts" she and the therapist shared: "We have the gift of hair." "We have the gift of teeth" (reflecting embodied representations related to body-image development).

In one session Laura spontaneously decided that all of the children had done well with their spelling, math, and spinning and balancing contests and therefore were ready "to graduate." She spent three sessions carefully arranging the cutouts in rows for a "graduation picture," taking great pains to decide where each "student" would sit or stand. The therapist brought in a camera, and a number of photographs were taken before Laura decided she had obtained "the right one." After the graduation ceremony Laura began to plan for the next group of students. But in one session she interrupted this fantasy and introduced a new edition of her metaphor of rules. Significantly, the vehicles she now used to construct symbols shifted from wooden geometric cutouts to flags of different nations. With this shift Laura assimilated aspects of the environment and coordinated them with the demands of her subjective world while still rehearsing the issue of rules.

Phase III. A World of Rules and Regulations that Exists in Countries (10 Sessions)

Laura announced, "Let's make flags of countries." The therapist readily agreed, gathering cards, crayons, and an atlas containing pictures of national flags. Laura studied the pictures and busied herself drawing flags, each on a 5 × 8 card. Beginning with the first flag she selected to copy (Libya's), she animated each flag and country, assigning a character to it. Libya misbehaved and broke rules as did, for example, Uruguay, Nepal, and Jamaica. Canada was "on the border," sometimes good and sometimes bad. As she produced flags, she manipulated the cards as she had the cutouts, enacting various events representing infractions of rules. Laura eventually drew nineteen flags.

During this metaphor a shift occurred in how Laura construed the therapist. In contrast to the admiring comments of the previous phase, Laura criticized the way the therapist was dressed and made comments with a critical tone: "You look like a grown-up today. You look perfumy today." As these comments increased, Laura declared that she planned to stop treatment. "I have my own brain, eyes, and mouth. I can make my own decisions." The therapist agreed and also suggested that since Laura was no longer going to attend a special needs classroom next year, but would be entering a regular third grade, she should return in the fall for a few meetings to discuss how school was going. Laura agreed to return "only for one meeting."

Phase IV. Negotiating Concerns about My School Environment (12 Sessions)

When Laura returned in the fall, she made no mention of her previous request to stop treatment. Instead, she focused her discussions on third-grade classmates who were "nasty." She also initiated setting up "a regular classroom." She asked for dolls "as big as kids really are." The therapist and Laura went shopping and purchased a thirty-two-inch–female doll, the largest they could find. To represent a classroom, Laura propped up this doll, along with many typical dolls and hand puppets, in rows. Using an easel as a blackboard, she assigned herself the role of teacher, the therapist the role of assistant, and identities to each doll. While these assignments resembled those given previously to wooden cutouts and flags, the imaginary children were now represented by dolls. In addition, instead of focusing on rules, Laura prescribed a series of interactions typical of a school environment, which Laura and the therapist enacted using macroactions. Before each enactment Laura drew a picture of a dilemma that occurs in classroom (e.g., one girl makes faces at another). Significantly, one scene involved a girl who had difficulty spelling. Laura proposed, "I can teach you how to spell," and proceeded to do so.

Enactments of imaginary school situations were interspersed with Laura's initiating playing soccer outdoors, extending their relationship and intersubjective world to a larger environment. Her transference with the therapist during this phase shifted again, from the critical remarks she had expressed previously to displays of idealization and identification with the therapist. Laura initiated a ritual at the close of each session that prescribed the clothing she and the therapist would wear for the next meeting, "We have to dress the same and look alike." Laura gradually shifted from prescribing to negotiating what clothing they should wear, readily accommodating to suggestions by the therapist who also accommodated to Laura's.

Laura's treatment came to a close after two semesters in the third grade. The teacher described her as much less tuned out than had been reported when she was referred for treatment at the start of the second grade. Significantly, not only was her academic performance adequate, but Laura had begun to read in the classroom "for the first time" and appeared to enjoy it.

CAN YOU DESCRIBE A CASE ILLUSTRATING UNSTRUCTURED INTERACTIONS DESIGNED TO TRANSLATE EMBODIED MEANINGS AND TO FACILITATE CYCLES OF ENACTMENTS AND INTERACTIVE METAPHORS AS INTERPRETATIONS?

Harry: My Body Self Is Falling

We first became acquainted with Harry in Part IV. He was referred at the age of 4 years, 4 months after having been expelled from a preschool program because, without provocation, he spit at, bit, and hit classmates and teachers, yet sometimes curled up in a corner of the room, ignoring assistance and preoccupying himself with a record player. Harry displayed the same behaviors at home. In addition, he struggled with mother, refusing to get dressed and following her around the house demanding her complete attention. He also demanded "strange things" to eat for breakfast (e.g., potato chips), which parents tried to negotiate, frequently without success. When father took him to a nearby park, Harry sometimes experienced a "panic attack" when he was about to move down a sliding board.

Early on, because he crawled and walked with a vigorous style, mother thought Harry would benefit from spending time in a playpen so that he could "sit still for a while and play with his toys while I got my work done." From about 12 to 20 months Harry was placed in a playpen for several hours a day. Sometimes he played with toys, and sometimes he rocked on all fours, "chanting" rhythmically. After Harry reached his second birthday he was not placed in the playpen except when he became "too frantic." By the age of 3 Harry had developed a fascination with light switches, turning them on and off many times in succession. He also became fascinated with a record player his parents had given him in the hope that children's music would soothe him. However, he typically sat staring at the revolving record, or moved the arm back and forth, behavior he also displayed at school and that concerned teachers.

I constructed a preliminary formulation from information provided by the parents. By the time he reached his second birthday he had not evolved play rituals with either parent in order to experiment with representing things and interactions. Moreover, he had been confined to a playpen during the time he should have been negotiating directed activity (controlling stimulation and anticipating that others will accommodate), focalizing (establishing mother's unconditional availability), and self-assertion and testing aggression (engaging alternative means and goals provided by others). Each issue was disrupted significantly and left incomplete. As a result, Harry evolved inflexible rituals interacting with light switches and a record player, rituals that directed and regulated stimuli and made interesting sights last.

The results of psychological tests showed Harry to be very bright, to have adequately developed cognitive regulators, for the most part. However, when coordinating environmental stimulation and personal meanings, his cognition shifted rapidly, resulting in frequent slips. The frequency with which he slapped Rorschach cards and waved them about to convey his image, when the task required imaging and not action, is one illustration of these slips. In addition, the action mode dominated and showed little capacity for delay and few alternative means. In terms of the content of his subjective world, two related metaphors emerged: one represented the need for nurture and attachment; the other, the body self as not grounded (to one Rorschach card he imaged a monkey "falling in the sky"; to a picture he told the story of a wind that blows a baby bear and its crib into the sky).

Influenced by these results, I decided that in the first phase of treatment I would emphasize the action mode and macroactions as much as possible. In addition, because his cognition rapidly shifted back and forth between an inner and an outer orientation, I also decided I would try to anchor his cognition for as long as possible within concrete stimuli so that he would use them as vehicles for his symbols and benefit from imaging trial action. One short-term goal, of course, was to help Harry step into a dialectical circle and prepare him for his return to a kindergarten program in the fall.

Harry's Treatment

Chaos: Helping Harry Step into a Dialectical Circle (2 Months)

During the first sessions Harry's activity was chaotic and reflected little or no pretending as he moved about restlessly, chatting almost constantly. Sometimes he did not implicitly invite me to participate: he sat before his record player, moving the arm back and forth; he made balls of play dough, hurling them at the wall and sometimes at hand puppets and toy animals. Sometimes he invited me to play form-board and card games. After initiating a game, however, he remained involved for three or four minutes and then walked away. From time to time, as he walked about in search of something to do, he swatted a puppet or toy animal from the shelf onto the floor.

My first attempts to help Harry step into a dialectical circle failed. As one instance, noticing a Band-Aid on his hand and expressing what I thought was interest, I asked, "What happened?" He responded with irritation, "That's a secret!" and walked away. Other attempts eventually proved successful. Whenever he became occupied moving the arm of the record player back and forth, I tried to set the needle on the same spot of the record, enacting that I was very caught up with the challenge. When either one of us was successful, we cheered. With another strategy, whenever Harry toppled toy animals and puppets from shelves, I set wooden geometric cutouts under them. Looking back, I believe that in doing so I was influenced by his Rorschach images of persons and animals falling. I thought the cutouts might symbolize to Harry, "See, these have ground under them, so they won't fall." Instead, Harry soon limited his swats to toy animals and puppets under which I had placed a cutout, apparently experiencing the cutouts as invitations to topple them rather than as representing stable ground.

Although I did not understand the meaning of his swatting only the toys set on cutouts, I was pleased to find that my response resulted in a ritualized, circular interaction. Eventually, as soon as I set a cutout under a puppet, Harry walked over and toppled it. Harry also began to focus on a hand puppet of a boy wearing a sweater bearing the letter A. If I did not place a cutout under it, he asked me to do so. Toppling puppets under which I had placed a cutout became ritualized, indicating he had stepped into a dialectical circle. This ritual eventually ushered in the first interactive metaphor and marked the close of this chaotic phase.

Metaphor: My Body Is Starving and Has No Control (2 Months)

Harry brought symbolic organization to his chaotic activity when in one session he referred to the puppet with the letter A as "Mr. Fall," simultaneously asking for something to eat. While munching food, he limited his toppling to Mr. Fall. Whether Mr. Fall was toppled from the shelf by a swat of his hand or from the table by a ball of play dough, Harry exclaimed with anxious laughter, "He's going to get spanked. He can't stand up!" Sensing an interactive metaphor emerging, I rushed forward to try to catch Mr. Fall each time he plunged from a shelf. I also surrounded Mr. Fall with toy furniture, my appointment book, and other items to prevent him from being toppled. Harry became invested in my efforts, cheering when I was successful. Occasionally, whenever Mr. Fall landed on the floor, I playfully imitated the puppet and fell to the floor. Here I was guided by the goal of introducing metaphoric expressions in macroaction whenever possible.

Harry assimilated this action and imitated me. He fell to the floor, frequently while holding Mr. Fall in one hand and a cookie in the other. I rushed to place various items (wastebaskets, chairs) around Harry to prevent a fall. Harry sometimes stood still, obviously waiting for me to set up props around him. When my efforts were successful I expressed victory; when they failed, frustration. My enactments and comments conveyed that Mr. Fall needed more than props to keep him from falling, and I puzzled over what else I could do. Harry introduced another interactive metaphor that explicitly called for help.

Metaphor: I Need Help (1 Month)

During one session, while munching a cookie, Harry fell to the floor and dramatically exclaimed, "Help, I'm sinking!" I carefully examined him using the toy doctor's kit. Sometimes he spontaneously reversed roles, assuming the role of the doctor, and asked me to lie on the floor and pretend that I was "a puppy" as he examined me. On one occasion, when Harry fell to the floor "sinking," I quickly spread open a newspaper and pulled him onto the "raft," reassuring him that "we're going to make it." For some reason this enactment in response to his need for help took hold, since Harry initiated it a number of times. During these enactments he cuddled next to me on our "raft." Perhaps stimulated by my conveying that I was prepared to find solutions to "sinking," Harry introduced a new interactive metaphor that elaborated his initial representation of the body-out-of-control.

Metaphor: A Boy Flips Out Unless His Body Is Tied Down (12 Months)

Harry returned to playing form-board games, which he now engaged for longer periods of time. What was particularly conspicuous, Harry held Mr. Fall in one hand while playing a game. I felt pleased, thinking to myself that Harry had experienced me as unconditionally available and developed some degree of self-regulation over his hyperactivity. Moreover, Mr. Fall seemed to have become an idealized companion. But this peaceful atmosphere was short-lived.

While playing Candyland, Harry flipped his wrist without warning, sending Mr. Fall sailing across the room. When he flipped the puppet several times, it dawned on me that another edition of the first metaphor was being authored. Significantly, Harry now began to call the puppet "Alvin," apparently following the letter A on the puppet's sweater. Once it occurred to me that Harry was shaping a new dilemma, I got up and rushed to retrieve it each time he flipped it across the room.

Soon he exclaimed, whenever he released the puppet, "Alvin is flipping out!" While playing form-board games, Harry repeated this enactment during many sessions without revising it, which puzzled me. But then he began to elaborate its meaning. Sometimes, after releasing Alvin, he would announce that Alvin was "lost." In response, I crawled about the room, enacting that I was searching for Alvin, and rejoiced with Harry when I found the puppet. At other times he prescribed that Alvin had "flipped out" and was injured when he hit the wall. At these times I examined Alvin with the toy doctor's kit, administered shots and medicine, and bandaged him. Each time, I expressed concern about Alvin's injuries and wondered what we could do to prevent him from flipping out and getting hurt. I enacted several solutions: I leaned various items (e.g., my appointment book, necktie) on Alvin, representing me as a source of control. And I probed "in the dark," leaning various doll figures on Alvin with the hope that Harry might latch onto one and construct symbols of control. But Harry continued flipping Alvin across the room, pushing to one side the item I had leaned on the puppet.

In one session I tied one end of a string around Alvin and the other around a nearby doorknob so that Alvin's flight was abruptly stopped by the string. Initially I thought the idea "popped" into my head. Later I realized that the string had occurred to me during one session in which I had draped my necktie around Alvin. Although Harry eventually sent the puppet flying, before flipping it he pulled at

Alvin with one hand while holding one end of the necktie with the other, enacting for a second that Alvin could not flip out.

Harry became fascinated with this enactment from the start. He repeatedly threw Alvin in the air and watched the puppet's flight snap to a stop. Then he experimented with strings of different lengths to determine how long the string should be so that Alvin could fly through space and almost, but not quite, hit the wall. Then, in one session, Harry interrupted this ritual and ushered in behaviors that I eventually understood represented a core pathological metaphor.

Metaphor: Bite and Stab; My Brain Is Crazy (2 Months)

Harry roamed about restlessly, a contrast to his previous enthusiasm for experimenting with different lengths of string. If I asked him what the matter was, he shouted, "Shut up!" If I took out string or a deck of playing cards, he walked away. Then he began to attack me verbally ("I hate you!" "I wish you were dead!") and physically (he threw toys at me, punched my arms, kicked my shins, spit at me, tried to bite my arm, and lunged at me with a pair of scissors).

I tried to cultivate alternative goals at which he could direct his aggression (I invited him to stab the scissors into a large ball of clay and to spit at a magazine picture of a man). But these interventions failed as Harry repeatedly attacked my person. On occasion this behavior escalated so that I had to wrap my arms around him while expressing concern. Once he calmed down, I made comments that relied on enactments and meanings we had shared to this point ("You just flipped out and you hit the wall just like Alvin did"). I also enacted a struggle with controlling aggressive impulses. For example, I held a pair of scissors overhead enacting that I was experiencing a struggle between the urge to plunge the scissors into the play dough and the wish to stop my arm ("This is crazy!"). Harry internalized and imitated these expressions, shouting during his outbursts, "My brain is crazy!" "I'm flipping out!"

Then in one session, recalling that string had been a successful symbol of control, I tied one end of a long string around my forehead and the other around Harry's, reminding him how the string "helped Alvin not flip out." This enactment worked. Harry stopped his attacks. For three sessions he and I, with a string connecting our heads, sat and played games. Then Harry made a request that ushered in the next interactive metaphor.

Metaphor: The Police Station (Rules and Standards)
Controls Crazy (2 Months)

Harry announced that a "police station" (the area under a table) needed padlocks. So we went to a hardware store and purchased several. Elaborating what he called the "trapping game," he located items throughout the playroom and carefully leaned a lock on each, with its key nearby, which reminded me of when I had leaned various items on Alvin to prevent him from flipping out. Harry, Alvin the puppet, and I sat under the table. Harry asked me to "be the police station," announcing which item, from among those Harry had distributed throughout the room, was to be used and how. In an "authoritative" voice I announced, for example, "Harry, cut the green sheet of paper with the scissors." After giving a command, I walked over to the item and unlocked the lock leaning on it. Then Harry or Alvin (played by Harry) would perform the prescribed action, following which the lock was secured and leaned on the object. As the police station, I complimented Harry and Alvin whenever they performed well. On several occasions Harry made clear that when a lock was unlocked, his hands still "did crazy things"; for example, he popped a balloon instead of bouncing it in the air. When this occurred, I, as the police station, expressed frustration and puzzled what it was in Harry that had the power to make his hands do crazy things, even when he didn't want them to.

Metaphor: Mr. Bad Is Conquered (10 Months)

Harry decided to transform the area under the table from a police station to "a fort," where we sat behind a barricade of chairs and wastebaskets. He also designated that a cylindrical punching bag was a "mean monster" called "Mr. Bad," who commanded one of us to "do bad things." Harry asked me to make announcements with the same deep voice I used during the police station game ("Harry, throw play dough against the wall." "Alvin, knock down the animals that are on the shelf"). With each command Harry flexed his arms and screamed in defiance, "You can't make us do that!" "Dr. S is stronger than you!" Throughout these enactments Harry draped my necktie around his neck and sometimes whipped Mr. Bad with my belt. Harry brought this metaphor to a close when he crumpled newspapers around the punching bag and pretended to set fire to Mr. Bad, cheering, "Now all the monsters of the world are dead."

Metaphor: I Am Mastering My Aggression, and I Can Discuss Current Problems (6 Months)

Harry returned to form-board games, now engaging them for most of the session. Occasionally he introduced difficulties he was experiencing in school where he was now attending the first grade. While he was concerned, for example, about being sent to the principal's office because he kicked a classmate, he was most anxious when reporting that he had wet his pants at school (confirmed by parents). Gradually he shared that he did not use school toilets because the flushing frightened him and reminded him of thunder. And he was afraid that the water whirling down the toilet would suck him down into the pipe. Harry returned to enacting, flushing paper cups down the toilet, exclaiming "Help, I'm sinking!" We noted that the cup was like Mr. Fall, Alvin, and Harry who sometimes fell and sank. As we had done with Alvin and our heads, we fastened a cup to a string that Harry held as he repeatedly flushed the toilet, confirming that the cup did not "sink away." Harry also displayed behaviors suggesting that his aggressive tensions were beginning to be experienced in terms of intrinsically maturating symbols representing ascendance and power (phallic representations). He played two records numerous times: one about a giraffe who wanted his neck to grow longer, the other about a train that wanted to be powerful enough to climb a big hill.

Critique

Harry's biting, spitting, and striking out were rooted in an embodied metaphor constructed during the first three years of life that construed his body self as lacking nurture and as not grounded and stable. The restructuring of this embodied metaphor required that he and I participate in a series of interactive metaphors. Apparently reassured that I was unconditionally available and capable of finding solutions to our dilemmas—from my pulling him onto a raft, to surrounding him with furniture, to tying a string to Alvin—Harry enacted his core pathological metaphor that called for hate and violence toward others, a state of mind he construed as "crazy." The enactment of string around our heads representing control, which Harry had already experienced as successful in helping Alvin, was also successful in helping him control his violence. From this Harry constructed the first representations of standards of conduct (police station) and control (locks), which he assigned to me. As the police station, I wondered what it was *in* Harry that continued to force him to do "bad things." Internalizing the therapist's (police station) wish to discover this inner force, Harry authored another interactive metaphor that projected an "evil force" (Mr. Bad) that seduced Harry to do "bad things." This force was subdued and conquered by resources Harry idealized and internalized from the therapist. From these experiences his mode of expressing aggression intrinsically spiraled to a higher developmental level of coding (wishes to become bigger and stronger). This developmental climb led to his developing a phobia, projecting the lack of groundedness onto flushing toilets.

Two-thirds of the treatment was devoted to enactments (using wooden cutouts, strings, locks, scissors, a police station, a fort, etc.) that eventually helped Harry develop embodied metaphors of the self as grounded and capable of self-regulation. His biting and spitting were never discussed verbally or interpreted conceptually, but interpreted through action symbols.

The spiraling of interactive metaphors in treatment correlated with positive changes in Harry's behaviors at school and home. He returned to and completed preschool and then kindergarten. Although he slipped occasionally, he showed steady gains in academic readiness skills, and his aggressiveness decreased. No biting or spitting occurred during the last part of the kindergarten year. Moreover, because of his high intelligence and readiness, he was promoted to an accelerated first-grade program that he successfully completed at the conclusion of treatment.

At home Harry had not bitten or spit at family members for months, and he was reciprocating more, no longer insisting on "weird" food or taking forever to get dressed. Six weeks were devoted to negotiating termination, which Harry seemed to manage well. During the last session he asked if he could take "his toys" with him. He selected the ball of string, Alvin the puppet, and the punching bag and departed in a very buoyant mood.

9

Diagnosis and Clinical Research from a Developmental-Dialectical Perspective

CONTENTS

Everyone agrees that to diagnose means to construct an understanding of a child's difficulties in a way that helps a therapist plan and conduct a treatment program. But what strategy does one use to construct that understanding? I believe most clinicians nowadays follow the strategy of objectivism. Accepting that knowledge exists independent of the observer's mental activity, the clinician gathers what she/ he believes are neutral observations of a child's behaviors. Then a diagnostic category is selected, from among those described in the fourth edition of the *Diagnostic and Statistical Manual of Mental Disorders* (*DSM-IV*) (American Psychiatric Association 1994), that best fits the "neutral" observations gathered. In her guide to child psychotherapy, Brems (1993) noted that a "diagnosis is the second aspect of a thorough, all-inclusive conceptualization" (p. 191) and proposed that a therapist achieves this conceptualization by turning to *DSM-IV* categories.

WHAT IS ONE DIFFICULTY A THERAPIST ENCOUNTERS WHEN TRYING TO UNDERSTAND A CHILD'S DIFFICULTIES IN TERMS OF DIAGNOSTIC CATEGORIES?

Recall the difficulties presented by children described previously and consider them in terms of *DSM-IV* categories. In Part I we considered problems Sally developed after she received a severe electric shock. Her hyperactivity and inattentiveness would qualify for a diagnosis of ADHD. Her fears and excessive anxiety concerning fantasies about monsters who cover a person with hot spit suggest a diagnosis of generalized anxiety disorder, and her urinating on the floor, a diagnosis of enuresis. The symptoms presented by Mary, whose treatment was discussed in Part VIII, also suggest several diagnoses: learning disorder not otherwise specified, given her difficulties learning; expressive language disorder, given that her difficulties with expressive language interfered with her academic and social communications; obsessive-compulsive disorder, given the hours she spent ritualistically cleaning the kitchen and her room; and selective mutism, given that in early childhood she refused to speak and later was often not communicative with parents, teachers, and peers.

Similarly, Harry's symptomatic behaviors, described in Part VIII, also suggest several diagnosises: pica disorder, because he insisted on eating nonnutritional substances; ADHD because he did not listen when spoken to directly, avoided school tasks, was easily distracted, and often left his seat; conduct disorder, because he bit and spit at others, and toppled blocks classmates assembled; and Asperger's disorder, because he engaged in repetitive, stereotypic behaviors with record players and light switches.

HOW DOES THE DEVELOPMENTAL-DIALECTICAL VIEW OF DIAGNOSIS DIFFER FROM THAT OF DIAGNOSTIC CATEGORIES?

DSM-IV categories focus a clinician's attention on one or another aspect of a child's functioning. When looking at a child through lenses provided by categories, a clinician frequently peers through the one that brings into focus that aspect of a child's behavior that is causing the most concern in the environment. Sometimes a clinician tends to peer through a lens that has become popular. ADHD at the present time has moved to the top of the best-seller list of diagnostic categories.

In contrast, the developmental-dialectical model proposes that a clinician should strive as much as possible to understand the whole child. Recall the viewpoint of dialectics that assumes that every child is a system of relationships between, for example, cognition and emotion, cognition and interactions, fantasy and interactions, meaning and interactions, and surface (conscious) and deep (unconscious) behaviors. The model also assumes that each of these entities is in a dialectical relationship with the others, creating a difference that is continuously negotiated.

I propose that a developmental-dialectical conceptualization of a child's difficulties is more heuristic than that provided by *DSM-IV* categories, brings observations into focus that are potentially of greater assistance in conducting psychotherapy, and suggests new diagnostic methods. (For similar positions see Coppolillo 1987, Spiegel 1989.) I am aware that this proposal runs against a formidable tide. At this time *DSM-IV* is the "bible" of most therapists in all disciplines as well as of third-party payers. But apparently this bible is becoming unpopular with the lay public. In addition to complaints I have heard from parents when an insurance claim requires that their children be assigned a *DSM-IV* diagnosis, objections to *DSM-IV* have also been expressed by a contributing editor to *Harper's Magazine* who is not practicing a mental health profession. In a provocative article that I recommended everyone read titled, "The Encyclopedia of Insanity: a Psychiatric Handbook Lists Madness for Everyone," Davis (1997) noted that, "According to *DSM-IV* human life is a form of mental illness. We are confronted with a worldview where everything is a symptom and the predominant color is a shade of gray" (p. 62). He creatively examined many of the *DSM-IV* diagnostic categories to illustrate that apparently there is no behavior observed in everyday life that does not fall into a category. "The pages of *DSM-IV* are replete with mental illnesses that have been hitherto regarded as perfectly normal behavior" (p. 63). For example, with regard to diagnoses of children and adolescents, after reviewing the *DSM-IV* criteria for attention deficit/hyperactivity disorder, conduct disorder, oppositional defiant disorder, and disruptive disorder not otherwise specified, Davis noted "A close reading of the text reveals that the illnesses in question consist of failure to listen when spoken to, taking back, annoying other people, claiming that someone else did it, and (among a lot of other stuff familiar to parents) failure to clean up one's room. According to *DSM-IV*, childhood and adolescence is a mental disorder" (p. 66).

WHAT IS THE APPROACH OF NOSOLOGY OR DIAGNOSTIC CATEGORIES?

The model of nosology (or of diagnostic categories) has a long and successful history in medical science, dating back at least to the ancient Egyptians (Temkin 1965). This point of view proposes that to understand pathology it is useful, or even necessary, to locate diseases in separate, independent classifications. These classifications help clinicians and researchers order the morass of phenomena presented by patients, communicate with each other about their patients, provide confidence in the decisions made about treatment, and predict dispositions and plan investigations. Given the success of the nosological model in medical science, it is not surprising that this viewpoint was adopted by psychological practitioners.

WHEN APPLIED TO PSYCHOPATHOLOGY, WHAT ARE THE STEPS FOLLOWED BY NOSOLOGY?

1. First, behavioral traits and symptoms that various patients exhibit are described in as much detail as possible. These traits must be qualitatively different and relatively stable phenomena.

2. These descriptions are clustered whenever they are observed to occur together and used to define a category of psychopathology. For example, the cluster of traits that defines the *DSM-IV* category of ADHD includes does not seem to listen, is easily distracted, often runs about excessively in situations in which it is inappropriate. The cluster of traits that defines the *DSM-IV* category of conduct disorder includes bullies others, deliberately destroys property, stays out at night despite parental prohibition, runs away.

3. In forming categories an attempt is made to cluster traits that are viewed as mutually exclusive. Thus, not listening and running about excessively, which signify ADHD, are viewed as different from ignoring parental prohibitions when staying out at night and running away, which signify a conduct disorder.

4. Once categories are formed, individual differences are subordinated so that children assigned the diagnosis of, for example, ADHD, are viewed as similar to each other and different from children assigned the diagnosis of conduct disorder.

WHEN DID NOSOLOGY GAIN PROMINENCE IN THE PSYCHOLOGICAL SCIENCES?

While the model of nosology received some attention by behavioral scientists in the decades before the 1940s, the perspective gained particular prominence in the field of mental health when, in 1952, the American Psychiatric Association published *A Diagnostic and Statistical Manual of Mental Disorders (DSM)*, the first official manual of mental disorders to contain descriptions of diagnostic categories. In the meantime, the Group for the Advancement of Psychiatry published its own manual in 1966, because classification of childhood disorders had been neglected. Two years later, in 1968, the American Psychiatric Association issued a second edition of its manual (*DSM-II*), now including a section on behavioral disorders of childhood and adolescence. A third edition (*DSM-III*) appeared in 1980, revised in 1987 (*DSM-III-R*), with the fourth edition appearing in 1994 (*DSM-IV*). With the widespread use of these manuals, it is not surprising that the most common way of thinking about psychological functioning viewed behavior either as pathological, and therefore qualifying for membership in a diagnostic category, or as normal and failing to fit a diagnosis.

The domain of child development research and child psychopathology soon became dominated by the perspective of nosology (e.g., Erlenmeyer-Kimling and Miller 1986, Gelfand and Peterson 1985, Gholson and Rosenthal 1984, Wolman 1982). Even journal issues devoted to developmental psychopathology (e.g., Cicchetti 1984) showed that clinicians and researchers were focusing their efforts on comparing diagnostic groups. Kazdin (1989) accepted the model of nosology as a perspective useful for children, taking a position opposite the one proposed here. Yet, significantly, he also recognized that this perspective brings obstacles to studies of development. Examples Kazdin provided included the fact that some behaviors, such as fears and excessive activity, while usually viewed as traits of maladaptation, are relatively common in childhood; and that because children undergo rapid changes, a specific clinical problem and its diagnosis may disappear and be replaced by another.

WAS THE MODEL OF NOSOLOGY ALWAYS ACCEPTED WITHOUT CRITICISM IN BEHAVIORAL SCIENCES?

Although gaining rapid popularity from the start, the viewpoint of diagnostic categories was in fact the subject of intense debate soon after the first diagnostic manual was published. These deliberations, lost in history, appear not to have influenced the construction of subsequent manuals and the approach most clinicians apply when formulating diagnoses. In 1965, three years before the second edition of *DSM* was released, the National Institute of Mental Health invited professionals from various disciplines to discuss the methodology of classification in the mental health field (Katz et al. 1965). The invited guests did more than discuss; they vigorously debated the advantages and disadvantages of diagnostic categories, including the following:

1. Do the virtues of categorizing people outweigh the resulting loss of information about their individuality?
2. Could the mental health field advance more effectively if the characteristics of people are viewed as interacting in a complex manner rather than as fixed diagnostic entities?
3. Could more than one diagnostic category exist in a single person and, if so, how many?
4. Why do some clinical conditions look relatively different at different points in time?
5. What are the limitations inherent in establishing diagnostic types on the basis of self-description, interviewing, and questionnaires?

The remarks of two individuals who attended this conference are particularly relevant. Shakow (1965) cautioned that classifying mental disorders could result in reification—the danger of reifying the abstraction of a diagnostic category rather than dealing with actual behaviors; compartmentalization—taking only a part of the picture and locating a person in a category on the basis of a few behaviors; and simplification—taking a simpler, more easily understood explanation of complex phenomena that may be difficult to grasp in all their intricacies. He also questioned the principle of forming diagnoses by clustering behavioral traits that are observed to occur together and then assuming the cluster has meaning. He cited Jellinek, who as long ago as 1939 raised the same question and drew an analogy to make his point. Jellinek argued that observation would show that pencils of yellow wood have a greater incidence than pencils of any other color (at least in 1939). Yet the question remained whether the color yellow is essential or even relevant to the function of pencils.

George Kelly (1965) pointed out that developing categories of emotional problems "proves itself to be almost completely sterile in suggesting something new to be looked for" (p. 158). He offered his own diagnosis of clinicians who use the model of nosology: "hardening of the categories" (p. 158). To remedy this affliction, Kelly proposed that behaviors should be plotted along each of several basic lines of consideration he termed *key constructs* or *universal reference axes*. Summarizing the conference, Katz and Cole (1965) asked questions we might still raise today. "Are mental disorders really made up of these particular configurations of symptoms and characteristics? And why is it that when we think of diagnosis it is difficult not to think of types?" (p. 563).

DOES *DSM-IV* ACKNOWLEDGE TO SOME DEGREE OBJECTIONS RAISED BY THE 1965 CONFERENCE ON NOSOLOGY?

A section titled "Limitations of the Categorical Approach" (p. xxii), buried in the introduction to *DSM-IV*, refers to some issues raised by the NIMH conference of thirty years ago. The clinician is cautioned not to assume "that each category of mental disorder is a completely discrete entity with absolute boundaries dividing it from the other mental disorders or from no mental disorder" or to assume that all individuals "described as having the same mental disorder are alike in all important ways" (p. xxii).

DSM-IV also informs the clinician that some authors have suggested that classifications should be organized following "a dimensional model rather than a categorical model" (p. xxii). Dimensional models, *DSM-IV* authors acknowledge, communicate more clinical information because, unlike a categorical model, they consider "clinical attributes that are subthreshold" (p. xxii), that is, deep as well as surface behaviors. Kelly's proposal of thirty years ago, that behaviors should be plotted along several basic lines or "universal reference axes," is a dimensional model. But the committees that authored *DSM-IV* rejected dimensional models because they are "much less familiar and vivid than are the categorical names for mental disorders. Moreover, there is as yet no agreement in the choice of the optimal dimensions to be used for classification purposes" (p. xxii).

It seems that these precautions have not been taken into account by clinicians to any noticeable degree. Once an aspect of a child's behavior has been enveloped by a diagnosis, other aspects of the child's functioning fade into the background or are ignored (e.g., the meanings a child assigns to experiences, the dominant modes a child uses to express meanings, how cognition coordinates demands from environments and personal meanings). Moreover, the authors of *DSM-IV* ascribe to diagnostic categories because they are more "familiar," despite being less productive than dimensional models. In other words, these authors believe that clinicians should stick with what they already know. And what do the authors of *DSM-IV* mean when they tell us categories are more "vivid"? I suggest that, in this context, *vivid* relates to Shakow's cautions of thirty years ago: that diagnostic categories are reified because they enable clinicians to deal with the abstraction of a diagnosis, rather than actual behaviors, and with only a part of a person's functioning, providing a more easily understood explanation of complex phenomena.

DSM-IV concluded its comments on the limitations of the categorical approach with a statement that introduces the next topic, "Nonetheless, it is possible that increasing research on, and familiarity with, dimensional systems may eventually result in their greater acceptance both as a method of conveying clinical information and as a research tool" (p. xxii).

IF WE PEER BEYOND NOSOLOGY AND THROUGH THE PERSPECTIVE OF DEVELOPMENT AND DIALECTICS, WHAT DO WE SEE?

Influenced by the deliberations of the 1965 NIMH conference and the precautions noted by *DSM-IV*, I propose that a developmental-dialectical model frees us from the limitations of nosology and suggests ways of searching for new diagnostic methods that could inform treatment. With the developmental house depicted in Table 1, Part V before us, Freud and Piaget offered suggestions that serve as a bridge to the research described below. In 1916, in his introductory lectures, Freud noted, "We seek not merely to describe and classify phenomena, but to understand them as *signs* [my italics] or an interplay of forces of the mind, as a manifestation of purposeful intentions working concurrently or in mutual opposition. We are concerned with a *dynamic view* of mental phenomena" (Freud 1916, p. 67, my italics). Sixty years later Piaget (1975) expressed reservations over the fact that "psychiatry is largely based on the principle of 'syndromes'" (p. vii). He added that the use of diagnostic categories leaves us with the "puzzling observation that some individuals remain normal in situations where others become variously disturbed" (p. vii) and "thus the meaning of a mental disorder can be extremely diverse" (p. vii). As an alternative, he proposed "an analytic approach" by which he meant that the investigator become immersed "in the 'ensemble' of elements that are involved at different levels of functioning" (p. vii). To gather observations of the interplay of mental activities and behaviors at different levels, then, patterns of results across studies are needed. Sechrest and Smith (1994) stated, "Research findings begin to make sense only when they form part of a 'web of evidence'" (p. 15). The series of studies described below, when taken together, are intended to demonstrate how the developmental-dialectical model could serve as a guide in searching for a pattern or web of evidence that is useful in constructing a diagnostic understanding of a child's functioning in ways that serve treatment.

Action, Fantasy, Cognition, and Emotion: Studies Probing How Four Are One

The studies described here supplement those presented previously and are intended to demonstrate the type of questions that arise and the methods designed to address them when boundaries we discussed in Part II are dissolved. I have proposed that when these boundaries are dissolved, body, fantasy, cognition, and emotion are united by conscious and unconscious meanings a person experiences and expresses, a notion employed by other investigators (e.g., Wozniak 1986, Zajonc and Markus 1984).

HOW DO WE ASSESS BODY, FANTASY, COGNITION, AND EMOTION AS DOMAINS UNITED BY MEANING?

Zajonc and Markus (1986) proposed that we should devise methods other than rating scales and questionnaires that create situations in which the body and action serve primarily a representational function. Here they echoed a recommendation by Francis Galton (1884) who more than 100 years ago recommended that investigators devise "traps," forecasting the use of "situational testing" (Santostefano 1968b). To illustrate what he meant, Galton described one of his attempts. After observing that friends who "have an inclination to one another [seem to] . . . incline or slope together when sitting side by side" (p. 182), he devised a pressure gauge that he attached to the legs of chairs in an effort to test this hypothesis. If we look beyond Galton's particular "trap," or test method, he was advocating that assessments and stimuli should be designed to increase the likelihood of observing target behaviors that represent some combination of body (action), fantasy, cognition, and emotion all united by meaning.

CAN YOU DESCRIBE METHODS THAT ATTEMPT TO ASSESS BODY, FANTASY, COGNITION, AND EMOTION, ALL UNITED BY MEANING?

I have been influenced by Galton's recommendation, and for many years have devised and explored various "situational tests" to assess the body, action, fantasy, cognition, and emotion unified by meaning (Santostefano 1960a,b, 1962a,b, 1965a,b, 1968a,b, 1977, 1978, 1986, 1988a, 1995). The design of each method was influenced by the developmental-dialectical model in that the intention was to probe how meanings a person experienced when dealing with test stimuli integrated what the person did, imagined, and said.

The Action Test of Body Image (ATBI) (Santostefano 1978, 1992a)

With this procedure a child is asked to assume various body postures (standing on one leg with arms outstretched, leaning against a wall), perform various body actions (encircle arms, repeatedly open and close her/his eyes), and describe what the body experience brings to mind. Responses are evaluated using several scales: (1) expressions of body imbalance/balance rated on a six-point scale: *1* = cataclysmic loss of balance (e.g., "falling off a cliff"); *6* = differentiated forms of balance (e.g., "ballet dancing"); (2) expressions of body constriction-assertion rated on a six-point scale: *1* = active constriction/inhibition (e.g., "I'm handcuffed"); *6* = high degree of assertion (e.g., "a salmon swimming upstream"); (3) other scales rate the presence or absence of expressions of aggression (e.g., "punching a wiseguy"), fear (e.g., "seeing Freddie Krueger or some wild killer"), fatigue (e.g., "exhausted after school"), body deformed (e.g., "a cripple"), affiliation (e.g., "hanging out with my friends").

The Touch Association Test (*TAST*) (Santostefano 1978)

This procedure is adopted from the Twitchell 3–D Test (e.g., Vanderples and Garven 1959). Ten clay objects are placed one at a time under a cloth. The child examines each with both hands and describes what the object could be or brings to mind: sphere, cube, cone, rectangle, coil-shape; small global shape; a peak; a large global shape; a small (one-inch) twisted fragment; and a shape resembling a human figure. Responses are evaluated as follows:

1. *Typical score.* Responses representing things, persons, and events that fit attributes of the stimulus object in hand. Scores range from *1* (descriptions of attributes; e.g., sphere: "something round and smooth") to *8* (representations of the stimulus; e.g., "the Epcot Center," "A giant balloon I saw on TV that crossed the ocean"). Scores are summed and divided by the number of typical responses, producing the *Body Orientation Index.* This index is conceptualized as reflecting a person's orientation when symbolizing through touch perceptions: from experiencing stimuli as they are (outer/symbolic orientation) to experiencing stimuli in terms of highly personal referents (inner/symbolic orientation). The orientation revealed in response to the humanlike figure is also included as a separate score.
2. *Atypical score.* The number of responses representing things, persons, and events that bear little or no relationship to the attributes of the stimulus object in hand (e.g., cone: "a piece of lint"; cube: "little veins").
3. *Miscellaneous scores.* Three types are defined: (1) *Action taken*—the number of times the child takes some action with the stimulus whether or not the action is accompanied by an image (e.g., sphere, "a marble"—the child bangs the stimulus on the tabletop); (2) *See*—the number of times the child pulls the cloth away to examine the object visually; (3) *Movement*—the number of images representing movement (e.g., cone: "a rocket blasting up"). Each score is treated separately and also summed as a *Miscellaneous Total* score.
4. *Affect score.* The number of responses expressing one or another of the following emotions: aggression toward others (" a rock to hit someone on the head"), nurture ("chocolate candy"), fear ("a giant spider"), noxious texture/temperature ("cold, scratchy"), deformed/disintegrated ("a broken

toy"). These scores are treated separately and also summed, resulting in a *Drive Dominated* score.

Binoculars Test (Santostefano 1995b)

The examiner provides the child with practice to clarify that looking through binoculars from one end magnifies an item and "moves it close to you" while looking through the other end diminishes the size of an item and "moves it far away from you." Then the examiner stands fifteen feet from the child and asks the child to look at the examiner through either end of the pair of binoculars. This procedure assumes that the action of drawing the examiner close, or moving the examiner away, when peering through the binoculars, expresses an embodied meaning representing interpersonal relationships, especially regarding separation-individuation.

Body-Tempo Regulation Test (BTRT) (Santostefano 1978)

The child is asked to move her/his body and representations of the body (i.e., a doll and a pencil) in three tempos: (1) regular ("Walk in your regular way"), (2) fast ("Walk as fast as you can without running"), and (3) slow ("Walk as slowly as you can without stopping"). The child performs each tempo in three dimensions of space.

Floor maze. Regulating body tempos in macrospace. The child walks in three tempos over an S-shaped path, twenty-five feet long, outlined on the floor by a carpet. Time is recorded in seconds.

Table maze. Regulating body tempos in median space. While seated at a table, the child moves a doll of the same gender in three tempos over an S-shaped path, ninety-two inches long, outlined on a board. Time is recorded in seconds.

Paper maze. Regulating body tempo in microspace. While seated at a table, the child moves a pencil in three tempos, drawing a line on an S-shaped path, twenty-two inches long, printed on a sheet of paper (8 ½ × 11 inches). Time is recorded in seconds.

Spiral Test of Impulse Control

The child is given a sheet of paper on which is printed a spiral pathway (170 centimeters long) and asked to draw a continuous line on the pathway with a pencil from beginning to end in each of three trials: (1) "at your regular speed," (2) "as slowly as possible and without stopping," and (3) as slowly as possible without stopping and while the examiner speaks six words at twenty-five–centimeter intervals (father, bad, mother, blood, spanking, bullet). When introducing the trial with spoken words, the examiner explains, "It's okay if you notice the words I say; your job is to move the pencil as slowly as you can without stopping." Time taken to complete each trial is recorded in seconds.

Fruit Distraction Test (Santostefano 1988a)

The Fruit Distraction Test (FDT) evaluates how a child attends selectively to relevant information while subordinating external distractions and internal thoughts and fantasies, a cognitive control termed "field articulation"(see Part VI). Age norms are available as well as studies supporting construct validity and reliability (Santostefano 1978, 1986, 1988a, 1995b). Initially the child is given a practice card with colored bars (red, yellow, blue, green) and trained to name the colors as quickly as possible. Then the child is given Card II (11 × 16 inches) on which are randomly arrayed fifty colored pictures of three fruits and one vegetable arranged in ten rows, five items in each row (e.g., yellow bananas, red apples, bunches of blue grapes, heads of green lettuce). The child is asked to name the color of each fruit as quickly as possible beginning with the fruit in the upper lefthand corner and continuing from left to right and from the top to the bottom rows.

Card III is exactly the same as Card II except that pictures of nurture-related objects (e.g., bottle of milk, ice cream cone) are located next to each colored fruit. The child is asked to try to ignore the pictures and name the colors again as rapidly as possible. After the child completes naming the colors, the examiner removes the card and asks the child whether she/he recalls any of the pictures surrounding the fruit. Previous research has demonstrated that performance with this card assesses a child's ability to focus attention while fantasies/emotions concerning nurture are aroused. The more peripheral items the child recalls, and the more time the child requires to name the colors, the more the child is distracted by external stimulation.

Card IV presents the same items, in the same locations, but now each is colored incorrectly (e.g., a banana is colored red, blue, or green but never yellow). The child is asked to try to ignore the colors and name, as rapidly as possible, the color of each item that should be there. Previous research has demonstrated that performance with this card measures a child's ability to focus attention while subordinating internal thoughts and contradictions.

With Card V, fruit are colored correctly and located in the same sequence as on Card III, but pictures of weapons surround the fruit. Previous studies demonstrate that performance with Card V assesses a child's ability to focus attention while aggressive meanings/emotions are aroused. With each card reading time and naming errors are recorded.

To obtain a measure of the extent to which each type of distraction results in a child's requiring more time to name the colors, Card II reading time and naming errors are compared with those of Cards III, IV, and V. Previous studies (e.g.,

Santostefano 1986, 1988a, Santostefano and Moncata 1989) support the view that errors a child produces reflect cognitive conflict, or "slips of cognition," triggered by unconscious conflicted meanings/fantasies/emotions aroused by test stimuli. Because of this cognitive conflict, the efficiency with which the cognitive mechanism manages information from personal metaphors and environments is momentarily disrupted.

Leveling-Sharpening Shoot-Out Test (LSSOT)
Leveling-Sharpening Friends Test (LSFT) (Santostefano 1995, 1992a,b)

The LSSOT and LSFT assess the manner in which a child remembers visual images of information and compares these images to perceptions of ongoing information, a cognitive control termed *leveling-sharpening* (see Part VI). Age norms are available as well as studies supporting reliability and construct validity (e.g., Calicchia et al. 1993, Ford-Clark 1992, Santostefano 1986, 1995b, Santostefano and Rieder 1984). The LSSOT and LSFT are identical in makeup procedure and task requirement. With each, sixty-three pictures of a scene ($8\frac{1}{2} \times 11$ inches) are displayed in succession, five seconds for each display. Gradually, throughout the series, twenty details are omitted accumulatively from the scene. The child is asked to report changes in the scene she/he notices.

The LSSOT consists of a scene of two cowboys in a shoot-out. The one shot is located in the center of the scene, facing the viewer; he is slumping over, pistol falling from his hand, and blood spots covering his shirt. The other cowboy is located to the left of the scene, with his back to the viewer, so that one sees only his profile and the pistol he is firing. The LSFT consists of two cowboys greeting each other. The cowboy extending a greeting is smiling and faces the viewer. The other cowboy is located to the left of the scene, with his back to the viewer, so that one sees only his profile. Studies support the proposal that the shoot-out scene arouses thoughts/fantasies/emotions concerning interpersonal aggression; the friendship scene, concerning affiliation.

Performance is evaluated with two scores. The *Correct Change Ratio* is the number of correct changes detected and how soon a change is perceived once it is introduced (i.e., the number of scenes displayed before a change is perceived). The greater the number of changes detected, and the sooner changes are detected, the smaller the ratio (cognitive sharpening). Numerically small ratios indicate a child holds a differentiated image in memory of the pattern of ongoing information. The fewer the number of changes noticed, and the greater the lag before a change is noticed, the larger the ratio (cognitive leveling). Numerically larger ratios indicate a child holds a global image in memory of the pattern of ongoing information. The *Incorrect Change Score* is the total number of changes reported that in fact do not occur (e.g., the sun is perceived as shifting location when it does not; bloodstains on the shirt of the cowboy are perceived as having increased, when this does not occur). These errors are interpreted as reflecting slips of cognition triggered by unconscious conflicted meanings and emotions (Santostefano and Moncata 1989).

Two-Person Drawing Test

The child is provided with a sheet of paper (8 ½ × 11 inches) and a pencil and asked to draw "two persons doing something." Drawings are scored on a nine-point scale: 1 is assigned to aggressive forms of interpersonal interacting (e.g., "two kids throwing rocks at each other"); 5 is assigned to forms of parallel activity (e.g., "two girls watching TV"); and 9 is assigned to forms of affiliative interaction (e.g., "two kids shaking hands").

Rorschach Inkblot Test

In contrast to currently popular Rorschach scoring systems that focus on structural determinants of images, we evaluate responses as symbolic expressions of embodied meanings in terms of whether and how interactions between persons and things are depicted and whether a representation of an entity is whole, incomplete, or damaged. (For studies using earlier versions of these scales, see Santostefano et al. 1984, Tuber et al. 1989.) Each unit of motion or interaction is rated along several lines: whether the motion is completed, ongoing, or imminent; whether the agent and recipient of motion is a mythical figure, landscape, inanimate object, animal, or human; whether the motion is vigorous or attenuated/slow; whether the relationship defined by an agent, recipient, and type of motion is conventional (e.g., "two people lifting a box") atypical (e.g., "a frog riding a motorcycle"), or mythical (e.g., "a robot grabbing this alien"). In addition, scales rate whether representations of body self depict humans, animals, landscape, inanimate objects, or mythical figures as complete wholes or as incomplete/disintegrated/disorganized (e.g., "a melted popsicle"; "a man's head, half of it is gone").

Life Stressor Interview (Santostefano 1992b)

After sufficient rapport has been established, a child is asked to "tell me whether anything happened that upset you a lot." The examiner joins the child in discussing the events she/he describes and provides assistance whenever indicated. The examiner is careful not to direct the child's thoughts in a particular direction and limits his/her comments to requests for clarification. As one example, a child responded, "My grandpa died." The examiner asked, "Is there anything else you can tell me about that?" The child responded, "He was drinking beer; his friend said get some beer in the car; when he got back, the friend shot him." Responses are rated in terms of whether they depict a particular type of stressor (e.g., shootings/ fights, arguments, hospitalization of a loved one, parental divorce).

Fears Interview

After the Life Stressor Interview is completed, the examiner says, "Tell me three things you are most afraid of." The fears children report are rated in terms of several scales (frightening movies, insects, fear of bodily harm).

WHAT WAS THE PURPOSE OF STUDIES THAT USED THESE METHODS?

The studies were intended to probe questions the developmental dialectical model raises when boundaries are dissolved rather than prove or disprove hypotheses. These questions share a common denominator. Recall that patterns of bodily experiences and interpersonal interactions are conceptualized as giving rise to organized meanings. In typical development these embodied meanings are eventually extended into higher levels of functioning as the modalities of fantasy and cognition differentiate and become integrated and organized, to form behavioral systems of experiencing and expression. Therefore, each probe described below attempts to explore whether or not, and how, meanings in one modality are extended into another and whether the totality of modalities is flexible or inflexible in some way.

ARE THERE RELATIONSHIPS AMONG EMBODIED MEANINGS CONSTRUCTED WHEN THE BODY SELF IS A STIMULUS, FANTASIZED MEANINGS CONSTRUCTED WHEN INKBLOTS ARE STIMULI, AND OVERT BEHAVIORS? (PROBE I)

Three studies involving clinical and normal populations illustrate our efforts to explore this question.

Study I: The Relationships between Embodied and Fantasized Meanings in a Clinical Population

The subjects consisted of seventy-eight children and adolescents admitted to an inpatient psychiatric facility (age range: 60–204 months; 38 females, 40 males). On admission each youth was administered the Action Test of Body Image (ATBI) and the Rorschach inkblot test.

Results

One factor analysis was conducted with only ATBI responses to explore the embodied constructs this inpatient population defined when the body served as a stimulus. Several clusters or constructs were observed: (1) older children produced more responses than did younger children representing body imbalance-balance, body constriction-assertion and body self as deformed; (2) children who produced embodied meanings of constriction also produced more body-based meanings of fear and fatigue, and children who produced embodied meanings of assertion produced fewer meanings of fear and fatigue; (3) children who produced embodied meanings of balance also produced more embodied meanings of aggression; and (4) females produced more body-based representations of affiliation than did males.

A second factor analysis was conducted with ATBI and Rorschach scores to explore relations between meanings constructed when the body is and is not a source of stimulation. Several factors were observed: (1) children who produced embodied meanings of assertion also produced more Rorschach images representing motion; children who produced embodied meanings of constriction produced a lower percentage of Rorschach images representing motion; (2) children who produced more embodied meanings of fatigue constructed more Rorschach images in which humans were not represented as agents of motion; (3) children who produced more embodied meanings representing aggression and body deformation also constructed more Rorschach images that represented slow, attenuated motion; and (4) children who produced many meanings of the body self as deformed constructed fewer Rorschach images representing entities as penetrated or disintegrating.

Critique

This inpatient population defined embodied constructs that suggest concordance; for example, representations of body constriction correlated with embodied representations of fear and fatigue. They also defined constructs that suggest discordance; for example, representations of body balance correlated with embodied representations of aggression toward others. In terms of the relationship between embodied and fantasized meanings, the second analysis suggested that with this population of troubled youth, a boundary segregates embodied meanings from meanings constructed at the higher level of fantasy and cognition. When embodied meanings represented the body self as penetrated and deformed, the same meaning was not expressed in fantasy as assessed by the Rorschach. In another instance, embodied representations of aggression toward others were associated with fantasized representations of slow motion in Rorschach images. Would a nonclinical population reveal the same or different relationships among embodied meanings and between embodied meanings and fantasized meanings?

Study II: Embodied Meanings Defined by a Normal Population

This study, involving high school students, relates to one part of the question that concluded the previous discussion: Would a nonclinical population reveal the same or different relationships among embodied meanings? The ATBI was administered to sixty-three students attending a public high school serving a predominately rural area (mean age = 16 years; 36 females, 26 males).

Results

ATBI responses were factor analyzed to explore the embodied constructs this population defined. Several clusters were observed: (1) children who produced embodied representations of independence and assertion also produced representations of the body self as safe and balanced; (2) children who produced representations of the body self as valued (e.g., receiving an award) produced more representations of body balance and constructed no representations of aggression; (3) children who produced representations of incompetence produced more representations of body constriction; (4) children who produced representations of fatigue also produced more representations of body deformation; and (5) children who produced representations of body tension also produced representations of aggression toward others. The clusters of body-based meanings produced by the public school children appear to be concordant.

Critique Comparing Studies I and II

A comparison between the clusters produced by public school children and those produced by the psychiatric population of the previous study reveals interesting differences. Recall that the older children of the clinical group constructed more representations of body imbalance, constriction, and deformation. At the same time, representations of body constriction correlated with representations of fear. In contrast, with the high school group the first construct correlated embodied representations of assertion, balance, safety, and independence; in addition, representations of constriction correlated with representations of incompetence, not fear. Further, with the clinical population body balance correlated with representations of aggression toward others. The picture is quite different with the high school students. Representations of aggression toward others correlated with body *imbalance*, devaluation, and tension.

Study III: The Relationships between Embodied Meanings Experienced through Touch Perceptions and Suicidal and Violent Behavior

The Touch Association Test was administered to 207 inpatient youths (age range: 54–212 months, mean age = 154 months; females = 98, males = 101; IQ range: 81–131, mean IQ = 103).

Results

Responses to the Touch Association Test were factor analyzed to explore the constructs this population defined when touch perceptions expressed embodied meanings. Several factors were observed: (1) youth who produced a high number of representations of emotions, especially nurture, also displayed an inner/symbolic orientation (Body Orientation Index) while those who produced a low number showed an outer/symbolic orientation. For this inpatient population, then, tuning in toward one's subjective world results in expressions of highly personalized, emotion-dominated meanings; (2) children who showed an outer/symbolic orientation when touching the humanlike figure also acted upon and looked at it; (3) children who looked at the objects produced fewer representations of fear and of something or someone deformed. With this population, then, looking at stimulus objects, when instructions asked that objects be examined by touch only, avoided experiencing representations of body-based fear and deformation; (4) children who produced many representations of noxious body sensations concerning texture and temperature also produced many representations of aggression.

A second analysis probed the relationship between embodied meanings expressed through touch perceptions and through overt behaviors. A number of youths in this population were admitted because they had attempted suicide or had committed acts of violence against others. A stepwise discriminant analysis explored whether body based meanings obtained with the touch method distinguished these children. Nonsuicidal and nonviolent controls were selected from the same population if histories made clear that suicidal and violent behaviors had not played a part in their functioning. The discriminant analysis accurately classified 70 percent of the suicidal and 69 percent of the nonsuicidal youths. A second stepwise discriminant analysis accurately classified 86 percent of the violent and 79 percent of the nonviolent youth. Different variables predicted who was violent or suicidal. Violent youth acted on and looked at stimulus objects and produced more responses symbolizing aggression toward others and fewer symbolizing noxious textures. Suicidal youth acted less on the stimulus object and showed an inner/symbolic orientation.

Critique

These results illustrate that embodied meanings could also be assessed with the Touch Association Test, a method that holds promise for clinical practice and research. While the findings were obtained from an inpatient population, they raise questions that could guide future studies with nonclinical and other clinical populations. These maladaptive youths, for example, produced an embodied construct that correlated an inner-oriented style of symbolizing with producing emotionally charged meanings. Would nonclinical groups produce the same embodied construct? Referring to another finding, this clinical population defined a construct suggesting that looking at stimulus objects was a way of avoiding embodied representations of fear and body deformation. Would a nonclinical group of children use the same coping device of looking at stimuli, rather than experience them bodily, to avoid experiencing meanings of fear and body deformity?

IS THERE A RELATIONSHIP BETWEEN REPRESENTING THE REGULATION OF BODY TEMPOS IN PHYSICAL SPACE AND THE REGULATION OF COGNITIVE TEMPOS IN MENTAL SPACE? (PROBE II)

This probe explored whether embodied meanings speak through body tempos and whether this voice is metaphorically extended into cognitive tempos.

Study I: The Relationship between Regulating Body Tempos in Three Dimensions of Physical Space and Regulating Cognitive Tempos in Fantasy

The children who participated in this study (N = 45) were hospitalized in a psychiatric facility because of severe adjustment problems and school failure. The group consisted of twenty females and twenty-five males; age range: 6–15 years, mean age = 11.4 years. On admission each child was administered the Body Tempo Regulation Test, the Fruit Distraction Test, and the Rorschach Inkblot Test.

Results

The first analysis explored whether and how the three tempos a child performed within each space dimension were related, and whether and how tempos performed in one space dimension related to those performed in others. The results suggested that these children were characterized by "transmissions" that contained only one "gear." In all three space dimensions, moving fast correlated with the tempo the child used when asked to move "in your regular way."

To explore the relationship between regulating body tempo in physical space and cognitive tempos in mental space, FDT time and error scores were correlated with the time a child took to perform each tempo in each space dimension. The time scores did not result in significant correlations. However, FDT error scores correlated significantly with body tempo scores. In general, the slower the child moved, the *more* naming errors the child made on the FDT. In addition, moving the body *slowly* when asked to move slowly in both macrospace and median space correlated with recalling more of the peripheral figures of Card III. These results suggest that for this inpatient population, unlike nonclinical groups (Santostefano 1978) delaying motion did not help cognition to equilibrate information with emotions/fantasies, suggesting an antagonistic relationship between regulating body tempos and cognitive efficiency.

Another aspect of the study explored whether regulating body tempos in physical space is related to, and extended into, the way in which motion is represented in fantasy. Time scores in each space dimension were correlated with the number of Rorschach images a child produced depicting motion, the number of agents performing the motion and recipients receiving the motion, and the level of vigor represented by the motion. In general, the slower a child moved, whether asked to move at regular, fast, or slow tempos, the more units of motion produced on the Rorschach and the more that motion was represented as performed and received by some agent.

These inpatient children, then, showed a relationship between imaging motion and delaying body tempo similar to that observed in nonclinical populations. At the same time, as noted above, instead of showing a relationship between body delay and cognitive balance/efficiency, they showed that the more they delayed their body tempos, the more cognitive errors they made.

Critique

The youth in this study required hospitalization in part because they presented various difficulties with aggression and hyperactivity, which related to the results obtained. When regulating body tempos in different dimensions of physical space, they did not differentiate tempos but moved fast when requested to move regularly or slowly. In addition, attempts to slow down and to regulate a fast tempo resulted in more cognitive errors or slips of cognition. This finding suggests that the antagonistic relationship among tempos at the embodied level has been extended into cognition.

Study II: The Relationship between Regulating Body Tempos in Microspace While Experiencing Emotions and Fantasies Aroused by Another Person

Teachers of a public school selected children who had not presented learning or adjustment difficulties: twenty (ten females, ten males) in each of three age groups (6, 9, and 12 years). Each child was administered three counterbalanced trials of the Spiral Test of Impulse Control and Cards II and III of the Fruit Distraction Test.

Results

In a preliminary analysis, 6-year-olds showed the slowest tempo with each trial of the spiral test (regular, slow, and slow while the examiner spoke words), 12-year-olds showed the quickest tempo with each trial; and the 9-year-olds fell between.

There was no significant difference between females and males or in the interaction between age and gender.

To explore whether changes in the regulation of movement in microspace express embodied meanings, time taken to move the pencil slowly during the silent condition was subtracted for each child from time taken to move the pencil slowly while hearing the examiner speak emotionally evocative words. No significant relationships were observed between these scores and age and gender. Nearly half of each age group displayed a quicker tempo when hearing evocative words (Emotion/Body Quick Group); the other half displayed a slower tempo (Emotion/ Body Slow Group). An FDT score was calculated for each child. The time a child took to name the colors of fruit without surrounding distractions (Card II) was subtracted from the time she/he took to name the colors of fruit surrounded by distracting pictures of food objects (Card III).

FDT difference scores were entered into an analysis of variance (ANOVA) as dependent variables with Emotion/Body Quick and Emotion/Body Slow groups as independent variables. The Emotion/Body Quick Group used a quicker cognitive tempo when naming the colors of the fruit surrounded by pictures that evoked fantasies/emotions of nurture, while the Emotion/Body Slow Group used a slower cognitive tempo. In addition, the Emotion/Body Quick Group made *more* naming errors than the Emotion/Body Slow Group when coping with the card that contained emotionally evocative pictures of food-related objects.

Critique

These results suggest that with this public school sample changes in body tempo employed in microspace are extended into, and are the same as, changes that occur in cognitive tempo. These results also suggest that children who quicken their body tempos in microspace when dealing with emotions/fantasies also tended to experience moments of cognitive imbalance, resulting in more errors (slips of cognition). In contrast, children who delayed their body tempos experienced more cognitive balance and made fewer cognitive errors. This observation is opposite that made of inpatient children (Study I), for whom moving slowly did not relate to increased cognitive efficiency.

IS THERE A RELATIONSHIP BETWEEN REPRESENTATIONS OF INTERPERSONAL ENACTMENTS AND HOW COGNITION ACTS ON TEST STIMULI REPRESENTING INTERPERSONAL AGGRESSION OR AFFILIATION? (PROBE III)

Study I: The Relationship between Action Taken with Binoculars When Interacting with Another Person and Cognitive Action Taken with Test Stimuli Representing Interpersonal Aggression and Affiliation

Subjects consisted of seventy-five children (thirty-five females, forty males; mean age = 12.5 years) admitted to a psychiatric facility. On admission each child was administered the Leveling-Sharpening Shoot-Out Test, the Leveling-Sharpening Friends Test, and the Binoculars Test.

Results

To form groups, whose performance with the LSSOT and LSFT could be compared for statistical analysis, the children were divided into two age groups (young = 36, mean age = 10.2 years; old = 39, mean age = 14.9 years), and two binocular groups: those who drew the examiner near (N = 62) and those who moved the examiner away (N = 13). No relationships were found between binocular groups and age, or between binocular groups and performance with the Shoot-Out Test. The latter finding suggested that if an embodied meaning was represented by the action of experiencing the examiner near or far, this meaning was not related to cognitive actions taken with stimuli representing interpersonal aggression.

The Friends Test, however, did result in significant differences. The Near Group detected fewer correct changes and later (cognitive leveling) and the Far Group more changes and sooner (cognitive sharpening). In addition, young subjects who drew the examiner near made *fewer* errors than those who pushed the examiner away; older subjects who drew the examiner near made *more* errors than those who pushed the examiner away.

Critique

Children who moved the examiner away when peering through binoculars showed cognitive sharpening when dealing with a scene representing affiliation; children who drew the examiner near showed cognitive leveling. Studies of normal and clinical populations (Santostefano 1978, 1988a) support the view that cognitive sharpening indicates a differentiated, more mature developmental organization than cognitive leveling. Applied to our results, if pushing the examiner away when looking through binoculars represents self–other differentiation, this developmentally more mature stage in self-development was associated with a developmentally more mature cognitive organization when dealing with stimuli representing interpersonal affiliation. Along the same line, if drawing the examiner closer represents self–other fusion, this earlier stage of self-development was associated with a less mature cognitive organization when dealing with stimuli representing interpersonal affiliation.

The number of incorrect perceptions each group produced adds an interesting dimension. Young children who pushed the examiner away when peering through binoculars produced more errors than did young children who drew the examiner near. It seems reasonable to propose that there is more cognitive conflict concerning affiliation in young children who pushed the examiner away than in young children who drew the examiner near. The performance of older subjects converged. Those who drew the examiner near produced more errors, suggesting cognitive conflict in these children who have not yet successfully individuated. Taken together, these results suggest that embodied meanings concerning relationships with others are extended into cognition, revealing themselves in cognitive actions a child takes when constructing and holding in memory images of information that represent interpersonal interactions. The heuristic value of this inference is supported by the observation that no differences were observed with the LSSOT, which contained stimuli representing interpersonal aggression.

Study II: The Relationship between Representing Interpersonal Interactions in Drawings and Cognitive Action Taken with Test Stimuli Representing Interpersonal Aggression and Affiliation

Ford-Clark (1992) asked 185 public school children (grades K to 8; ninety-nine females, eighty-six males) to draw a picture of two persons doing something. They were also administered the LSSOT and LSFT. On the basis of her/his drawing, each child was assigned to one of three drawing groups: Aggressive Drawing Group (scores 1–4; N = 43); Parallel Drawing Group (scores 5–6; N = 56); Affiliative Drawing Group (scores 7–9; N = 74).

Results

LSSOT and LSFT correct ratio scores were entered into a two-way ANOVA with drawing groups. Our interest is addressed most directly by the interaction effect, which proved to be significant. Children in the Aggressive Drawing Group detected more correct changes and sooner when dealing with the scene depicting interpersonal violence (cognitive sharpening) and fewer changes, after some delay, when dealing with the scene depicting affiliation (cognitive leveling). Conversely, children in the Affiliative Drawing Group showed cognitive leveling with the aggressive scene and sharpening with the affiliative scene. In terms of incorrect changes perceived (cognitive slips), the Aggressive Drawing Group produced more errors (showed more cognitive conflict) when managing the friendship scene, while the Affiliative Drawing Group produced more errors (showed more cognitive conflict) while managing the aggressive scene.

Critique

The Two-Person Drawing Test is viewed as revealing embodied meanings concerning interpersonal relations that are constructed at a cognitive level, where body perceptions and enactments play no direct role. We observed that with this normal population representations of interactions depicted in a drawing were extended into, and related to, cognitive actions a child took with two distinctly different stimuli: one depicting interpersonal violence; the other, interpersonal affiliation. Children who represented relationships in drawings as aggressive employed a developmentally higher cognitive organization when constructing images and remembering information representing interpersonal violence, and a lower organization associated with more cognitive conflict when dealing with information representing interpersonal affiliation. Conversely, children who represented relationships in drawings as affiliative employed a developmentally higher cognitive organization when constructing images and remembering information representing interpersonal affiliation, and a lower organization associated with more cognitive conflict when dealing with information representing interpersonal violence.

ARE THERE RELATIONSHIP AMONG EMBODIED MEANINGS CHILDREN REPRESENT, LIFE STRESSORS AND CONSCIOUS FEARS THEY REPORT, AND COGNITIVE FUNCTIONING WITH STIMULI AROUSING DIFFERENT MEANINGS/EMOTIONS? (PROBE IV)

I have noted that from a holistic view a child brings an integrated system of relationships among, for example, embodied meanings, cognitions, emotions, and surface (conscious) and deep (unconscious) behaviors. To probe this viewpoint, children were administered procedures that assess life stressors, conscious fears, meanings represented when body perceptions serve as stimuli, and cognitive functioning when dealing with stimulation that arouses meanings/emotions concerning nurture/affiliation versus interpersonal aggression. The intention was to remove boundaries that separate body from mind, cognition from emotion, and a child's subjective world from environments.

The children who participated in this study, with parental consent, were attending an inner-city public school serving a low socioeconomic population. Those who presented significant learning and adjustment problems were not included.

The final sample (N=93) consisted of eighty kindergartners and thirteen first and second graders: thirty-nine females and fifty-four males; thirty-seven African-Americans; fifty-one Latinos; four Caucasians; and one Asian. Their ages ranged from 56 to 115 months (median age = 76 months). During the school day each child was individually administered the Life Stressor and Fears interviews, the ATBI, FDT, LSSOT, and LSFT.

Study I: The Relationship between Stressors and Fears Inner-City Children Report and Their Embodied Meanings and Cognitive Functioning

Life Stressors

The number of stressors each child reported ranged from one to eight and most stressors fell into one of four groups: shootings/fights (N = 52), physical threats/arguments (N = 51), death of a loved one (N = 33), and illness/hospitalization of a loved one (N = 58). A child could be a member of only one group; another child, a member of more than one group. However, since the types of stressors reported proved not to be correlated, we could compare children who reported a particular stressor with those who did not.

In describing results, I begin "inside and deep," so to speak, and use body-based representations as the point of reference to explore whether and how these unconscious meanings are extended into other domains.

Body-Based Meanings and Conscious Fears

Typically, a child is not consciously aware of the symbolic meanings revealed by her/his associations to body postures, in much the same way as when a child describes what an inkblot could be. A comparison of ATBI and Fear responses enables us to probe whether and how these two domains are related, one embodied and unconscious, the other more cognitive and conscious.

Children who represented body balance reported more fears of being injured by the aggressive actions of others. It seems that with these inner-city children, a sense of body-balance is accompanied by conscious and more accurate appraisals that one could be hurt by others. In addition, children who expressed body-based dysphoric meanings/emotions reported more fears of violence, more fears of mythical figures/frightening movies, and more general states of fear. And children who expressed body-based representations of aggression/hate toward others reported fewer fears of mythical figures/movies. This pattern of results appears concordant. Body-based representations of tension, sadness, and fatigue are fitted with fears of violence and the tendency to project anxieties onto mythical figures and movies. Similarly, if a child's functioning is characterized by body-based representations of aggression/hate toward others, this child is not likely to project anxieties onto mythical figures and frightening movies. Last, a relationship was observed between representations of the body self as deformed/inadequate and fear of violence. Twice as many children who represented the body self as deformed reported fears of violence than did children who did not represent this sense of body self.

Body-Based Representations and Life Stressors

Children who reported shootings/fights as a stressor, when compared with those who did not, produced fewer representations of the body as competent and more representations of the body as deformed/inadequate. Children who reported illness/hospitalization of a loved one as a stressor produced more body-based representations of pain/danger. Although falling just short of significance, they also produced body-based representations of aggression toward others. Children who reported the death of a loved one represented the body as constricted, while those who did not report this stressor represented the body as assertive. These relationships appear to be concordant except for the relation between aggression toward others and illness/hospitalization of a loved one. It is interesting to note that with this population body representations of aggression toward others are not correlated with reporting shooting/fights as a stressor but rather with illness/hospitalization of a loved one.

Relationships between Body-Based Representations and Cognitive Functioning

The Field Articulation Cognitive Control. To explore the relationships between body-based meanings and focusing attention in the face of distractions and contradictions, FDT Cards III versus V and Cards II versus IV were entered into a series of two-way ANOVAs. The children in each of the ATBI groups did not differ in terms of the time they took to name the colors of the fruits on Card III (pictures of food items as distractions) versus Card V (pictures of weapons as distractions). Nor did they differ in terms of the time they required to name the colors of the fruits on Card II (no contradictions) versus Card IV (contradictory colors as internal distractions).

However, when performances with Card III and Card V, and Cards II and IV, were combined, a number of significant differences associated with body-based meanings were observed. For example, children who represented body balance, when compared with those who represented imbalance, named the colors more rapidly whether or not external or internal distractions were present. On the other hand, children who represented body value/competence were distinguished by efficient time scores only in the condition containing internal contradictions.

In addition to these general findings, the number of naming errors made when dealing with internal contradictions as distractions resulted in an interesting significant interaction with body constriction. Children who represented body constriction produced significantly more bursts of cognitive errors when dealing with contradictions than did children who represented body assertion.

The Leveling-Sharpening Cognitive Control. Children who produced body-based representations of aggression toward others detected the first correct change sooner when viewing the shoot-out series of pictures and later when viewing the friendship series; they also detected a greater number of changes in the shoot-out scene and fewer in the friendship scene. They tended to perceive these changes in the periphery, however, thus avoiding the victim. In contrast, children who did not produce body-based representations of aggression toward others detected the first correct change later with the shoot-out series and sooner with the friendship series, perceived fewer changes with the aggressive scene and more with the friendship scene, and tended to look more at the victim.

Another finding raises an interesting question for future research. Children who produced body-based responses representing positive meanings/emotions detected more changes that occurred on the person of the victim. It appears that children who are characterized by positive embodied meanings/emotions show empathy or compassion by unconsciously directing their attention at and remembering more details about the victim.

Relations between Life Stressors and Cognitive Functioning

The Field Articulation Cognitive Control. Children who reported physical threats/arguments as a stressor produced more errors when naming colors of fruit surrounded by pictures of food-related items than when naming colors of fruit surrounded by pictures of weapons. Children who did not report this stressor tended to produce about the same number of errors in each condition. Moreover, errors produced by children who reported physical threats/arguments tended to occur in bursts more so when experiencing emotions/fantasies concerning nurture than when experiencing emotions/fantasies concerning aggression. This finding suggests that of all the stressors, threatening gestures and arguments were associated with cognitive conflict when emotions/fantasies concerning nurture were aroused.

An interesting finding was also obtained when comparing Card II (no distractions) with Card IV (contradictions). Death of a loved one as a stressor resulted in a significant interaction. Children who reported this stressor required *less* time to name the correct colors when dealing with Card IV than did children who did not report the death of a loved one. This finding converged with another result. Children who reported illness/hospitalization of a loved one as a stressor also required less time to name the colors of Card IV than did children who did not report this stressor. Death, illness, and hospitalization of a loved one share several issues, such as coping with the contradiction that a loved one who was once strong and adequate no longer is. The possible dynamics behind the finding that these stressors are associated with handling cognitive contradictions more successfully require further study.

The Leveling–Sharpening Cognitive Control. Children who reported shootings/ fights detected fewer changes and later with the shoot-out scene (cognitive leveling) versus the friendship scene. In contrast, children who did not report this stressor detected more changes and sooner with the shoot-out scene (cognitive sharpening) than with the friendship scene. The makeup of the LSFT and LSSOT provided another source of information about the relationship between type of life stressor and test stimuli that arouse different fantasies/emotions. Children who reported shootings/fights detected fewer changes that occurred on the person of the victim than on the person of the friend. In contrast, children who did not report shootings/fights detected more changes on the victim than on the friend. This finding is elaborated by a significant interaction produced by another type of stressor. Children who reported illness/hospitalization as a stressor also perceived fewer changes on the person of the victim than on the person of the friend. These results suggest that children who report shootings/fights as a stressor are similar to children who report illness/hospitalization in terms of encoding, storing, and retrieving details of ongoing information associated with the person of someone being injured, an issue that deserves further study. However, it also appears that experiencing the stress of harm befalling someone results in a general cognitive defense that levels information associated with danger.

Critique

This probe set out to illustrate a holistic approach to diagnostic assessment by removing boundaries that segregate body/mind, cognition/emotion, and environment/subjective experiences. When these boundaries were removed, various patterns emerged among the domains evaluated. To illustrate the heuristic value of these patterns, I abstracted two from the results, depicted in Table 9-1. These patterns take as a starting point unconscious embodied meanings that dominated a child's representations. Children who represented the body self as constricted when compared to children who represented the body self as assertive reported many types of conscious fears and the death of a loved one as a stressor, showed bursts of cognitive conflict when dealing with information that contained contradictions, and perceived changes later in a scene depicting interpersonal affiliation (cognitive leveling) and sooner in a scene depicting interpersonal violence (cognitive sharpening).

With another ensemble of results, children who did not represent the body self as valued and competent, compared with children who represented body competence, did not report fears of animals and insects but did report shootings and fights as upsetting them a lot. In addition, they took more time to name the colors of fruits surrounded by distractions and embedded in contradictions. They also remembered less information contained in the scene of two cowboys greeting each other and more of the scene depicting two cowboys in a shoot-out. They also remembered more changes that occurred on the person of the victim in the shoot-

TABLE 9–1. Patterns of Relationships among Body-Based Representations, Fears, Stressor and Cognitive Functioning

	Body Constriction	Body Assertion
Fears	Many	Few
Stressors	Death of a loved one	No death of a loved one
Managing distractions	More bursts of errors when dealing with contradictions	Fewer bursts of errors when dealing with contradictions
Remembering information	Perceive changes later in a scene of affiliation and sooner in a scene of violence	Perceive changes sooner in a scene of affiliation and later in a scene of violence

	No Body Value/Competence	Body Value/Competence
Fears	No fears of animals/insects	Fears of animals/insects
Stressors	Shootings/fights	No shootings/fights
Managing distractions	Slow reading time under conditions of distraction and contradiction	Faster reading time under conditions of distraction and contradiction
Remembering information	Remember less information of a friendship scene and more of a violent scene; perceive more changes on victim	Remember more information of a friendship scene and less information of a violent scene; perceive more changes on friend

out scene. Children who represented the body self as competent remembered more changes on the person of the cowboy who was extending a greeting in the friendship scene.

These patterns, or ensembles of functioning, were constructed by inner-city, very young children who, at the time of the evaluation, were functioning adequately, academically and socially. Future studies are needed to determine patterns constructed by nonclinical and clinical children of different ages and living in rural areas and suburbs as well as the inner city. These patterns should be useful in helping a therapist decide whether and how some domain of a child's functioning is discordant with other domains and whether treatment should emphasize, for example, the restructuring of cognition before the revision of conscious fears or of embodied meanings.

Patterns could also be organized from the results of this probe, using as a starting point stressors a child reported as upsetting her/his subjective world. Table 9–2 depicts an illustration in which the number of stressors reported are used as the starting point. Children who reported more life stressors (3–8), when compared to

TABLE 9–2. Patterns of Relationships among Life Stressors and Cognitive Functioning

Life Stressors	Few	Many
Managing distractions	Distracted more by information arousing aggressive meanings/emotions and less by information arousing meanings/emotions of nurture	Distracted less by information arousing aggressive meanings/emotions and more by information arousing meanings/emotions of nurture
Remembering information	Remember more details of information arousing aggressive meanings/emotions and fewer arousing meanings of affiliation	Remember fewer details of information arousing aggressive meanings/emotions and more arousing meanings of affiliation
Maintaining balance between cognition and emotion	More cognitive conflice when information arouses meanings/emotions of aggression and less cognitive conflict when information arouses meanings/emotions of nurture	Less cognitive conflict when information arouses meanings/emotions of aggression and more cognitive conflict when information arouses meanings/emotions of nurture

children who reported fewer (1–2), were distracted less by information arousing aggressive meanings/emotions and more by information arousing meanings/emotions concerning nurture. They also remembered fewer details and experienced less cognitive conflict when dealing with information contained in a scene arousing aggressive meaning/emotions.

This pattern suggests that these children have already developed a cognitive style, or pattern of cognitive controls, that insulates them from the disrupting influences of meanings/emotions associated with interpersonal aggression. This pattern converges with other studies that show that children and adults who are functioning adequately developed a cognitive style within which the relationship among several cognitive processes are supportive and correspondent. In contrast, dysfunctional individuals show a cognitive style that reflects discordant or antagonist relationships among cognitive processes (Cotugno 1987, Ottenson and Holtzman 1976, Santostefano 1978, 1986, Santostefano and Rieder 1984, Wapner and Demick 1991, Wertleib 1979).

I have proposed that the pattern formed by several cognitive processes could be understood as an "organismic" attempt to use a cognitive style that accommodates to and serves a person's unique vulnerabilities when coping with and equili-brating the demands of external stimulation and the demands aroused by fanta-sies/emotions. Since the young children in this probe were functioning adequately, both academically and socially, they appear to have evolved a cognitive style that enables them to maintain successful adaptation while coping with aggressive mean-ings/fantasies aroused by stimulation in their day-to-day living. Future studies are needed to explore whether older inner-city children show the same cognitive style, consisting of correspondent relationships among cognitive processes, and whether those who have become dysfunctional show a discordant cognitive style.

CONCLUDING REMARKS

To explore the heuristic value of the developmental dialectical model and to extend research already reported, I first constructed methods that attempted to invite the body to speak and found them to be promising. Administered to clinical and nonclinical youth, each procedure provided a different window through which one could observe how embodied meanings are metaphorically extended into higher levels, playing a part in how tempos are regulated, motion is imaged, interpersonal relationships and life stressors are represented, and how cognitive organizations change when taking action in response to stimuli representing different interper-sonal meanings. The results obtained in each study support the possibility of as-sessing holistically the relationships among domains of functioning. What are some of the implications of the model, methods, and results for diagnosing children?

When considered as an approach to diagnosis, the model and methods de-scribed here suggest a direction very different from that of the prevailing model of nosology with its questionnaires and behavioral checklists. Relying on the studies described, and recalling the positions articulated by Freud and Piaget, we do not see isolated behaviors such as failure to listen when spoken to, or fear of attending school, or running away, each unrelated to the other. Rather we see an interplay of conscious and unconscious subjective meanings and fantasies, cognitions, actions, and verbal expressions all forming a pattern and each working concurrently or in opposition with the other. We see that these patterns of elements are involved at different levels of functioning. We also see that elements and changes in one part of a pattern or organzation influence other parts of the organization. This obser-vance converges with Piaget's concept of organization as a developmental invari-ant discussed in Part IV, namely, that structures of human functioning are orga-nized to form a totality and are interrelated so that changes in one part produces changes throughout the entire organization. Last, if we look through the lens of the developmental-dialectical model, we realize the need to continue searching for ways of adding to the patterns already observed so that the web of observations steadily includes as many aspects as possible of a child's cognitive, emotional, behavioral, unconscious, and conscious functioning.

Looking beyond stable classifications requires an integration of several developmental principles: holism; directiveness of behavior; multiple modes and levels of functioning; mobility of organizations of functioning; individual differences; and the adaptive process within which an individual and others mutually define, influence, and accommodate to each other, all ingredients of the proposed model. When combined, these principles account for how individual differences observed at higher levels of cognitive processes are linked to individual differences observed in developmentally earlier, embodied processes. This notion of "vicariousness of functioning" was elaborated by Werner (Werner and Kaplan 1963) and applied by others (e.g., Ohlmann and Marendez 1991) to account for the links among body, cognition, and personality.

When looking beyond nosology and through the developmental-dialectical lens, we are also reminded of the need to develop methods that permit observations of the interplay of organizations of symbols operating at several levels. Are we limited to observations in naturalistic environments to meet this need? Can the environment of a desktop provide the clinician with observations of a child's mind and body in action (White 1991)? Are there brief tasks that simulate ordinary environments in which body and mind perform purposeful acts (Neisser 1976)?

I have tried to demonstrate that tasks that provide observations of organizations (ensembles) of symbols operating at different levels, working concurrently or in opposition, can be administered on a tabletop (Touch Association Test, Spiral Test, LSSOT, LSFT, Fruit Distraction Test, Two-Person Drawing Test) or within the confines of an office (Action Test of Body Image, Body Tempo Regulation Test, and Binoculars Test). These methods appear to locate bodily meanings, and their emotions, within fantasy and cognition, and to locate fantasy and cognitive processes, with their emotions, within the body, providing an approach that forges these domains into one when formulating an understanding of a child's difficulties. Although the perspective of nosology may be helpful for certain practical purposes, developing static categories of pathology, as Kelly (1965) pointed out, eventually results in " hardening of the categories" (p.158), a common affliction among clinicians. The methods proposed here, and others stimulated by a developmental-dialectical approach, may provide a remedy for this affliction.

10
Concluding Comments

CONTENTS

In concluding, I emphasize several themes concerning psychotherapy integration that were developed throughout this volume. Fischer's (1995) discussion of myths that prevail in proposals for integrating approaches to psychotherapy included two points that helped me frame these themes. With one he noted, "Throughout the literature authors seem to be selecting theories, or concepts and techniques from theories, for integration in a haphazard, unsystematic way using mainly their own biases or preferences as a guide" (p. 47). With the other he proposed that instead of selecting concepts and techniques haphazardly, investigators should develop ". . . a number of criteria—external to any specific theory—that a theory could or should address or around which it might be constructed . . ." (p. 46).

WHICH MOLD DID YOU CHOOSE TO SHAPE PSYCHOTHERAPY INTEGRATION?

I chose development and dialectics and did my best to avoid haphazardly selecting concepts from different theories, using my biases as a guide. To shape a model for integrating child psychotherapies, I selected two basic, interrelated ingredients: (a) developmental processes of change as differentiation, integration, and flexibility of functioning; and (b) dialectics as negotiations. These ingredients, I believe, remove the barrier segregating objectivism (real knowledge) and interpretationism (subjective knowledge). Once this barrier is removed, the barriers segregating body from mind and cognition from emotion collapse. The dialectical position blends objectivism and interpretationism in conceiving of a world out there with its knowledge, and a world within a person with its knowledge, worlds that forever engage in dialectical negotiations, each defining and influencing the other. Dialectical relationships exist not only between one person and another, but also, for example, between one cognitive function and another, between what a person does, imagines, and says, and between unconscious and conscious processes.

Earlier, we noted that while neither mainstream cognitive-behavioral nor psychodynamic therapies fit into a developmental-dialectical mold, aspects of psychodynamic therapy, such as the importance of meaning and of unconscious processes, do. However, there are encouraging signs of change, especially in the cognitive-behavioral camp, changes that suggest the beginnings of an integration of objectivist and interpretationist images. For example, Goncalves (1995) noted that cognitive and behavioral therapies are shifting: "(1) from a rationalistic toward a more constructivist philosophy; (2) from an information processing model toward a narrative model of knowing; (3) from an emphasis on conscious processes toward an emphasis on unconscious dimensions of experience; (4) from an emphasis on strict cognitive processes toward an acknowledgment of the emotional dimension of experiences; and (5) from logical, therapeutic methods to more analogic and interpersonal ones" (p. 139). At the same time, psychodynamic therapies have also been shifting, giving more attention to overt behavior, interpersonal interactions, cognition, and adaptive processes in addition to unconscious meanings (e.g., Horowitz 1988, Mitchell 1988, 1994, Wachtel 1987). While the shifts occurring in both cognitive-behavioral and psychodynamic therapies converge with aspects of the integrative model I have outlined, in my view, principles of development and dialectics do not yet receive sufficient attention.

In a lucid discussion of integrative child psychotherapy, Coonerty (1993) pointed out that rather than jump from one type of treatment to another (eclectic therapy) when following an integrative approach, a therapist "can conceive of all interventions as coming from an integrative sense of the needs of children . . ." (p. 414). She also noted that intervention in any domain eventually leads to changes throughout others. "Whatever direction the therapist takes, care must be taken to ascertain how change in one area may effect other areas of functioning" (p. 418). After reviewing various spheres in which a child gains experiences (behavioral, cognitive, interpersonal, intrapsychic), Coonerty stated, "whichever focus . . . (therapists) subscribe to, it is essential to child work that not only the area of dynamic conflict, but the interweaving of that conflict with cognitive, behavioral, and interpersonal development, be thoroughly understood" (pp. 420–421).

The model and techniques proposed in this volume provide one way of addressing the several points Coonerty raised. I discussed how and why concepts and techniques of child psychotherapy are segregated into camps and the need to dissolve this segregation before considering a form of integration (Part I). To dissolve the segregation, I proposed that it is first necessary to examine some of its root causes, namely, three boundaries that psychology has maintained for decades, dividing knowledge as either real or subjective, and segregating body and mind and cognition and emotion (Part II). I then attempted to demonstrate how these boundaries influence concepts and techniques that emerged within three of the currently dominant approaches to child psychotherapy: cognitive, behavioral, and psychodynamic (Part III). From an examination of the causes of segregation, and the impact they have had on different approaches to child psychotherapy, I followed Fischer's (1995) proposal and articulated ten criteria that I believe should be considered in any attempt to evolve an integrative approach (Part IV).

Once these issues were articulated, I was faced with the task of deciding how to conceptualize the interrelationships among them in ways that promoted integration. As Fischer noted, "numerous concepts only recently have been proposed as possible key concepts for integration: cognitive schemas; assimilation; balance; self conformation; levels of emotional awareness; the therapeutic alliance; self-experiencing; behavioral enactments; and many other concepts" (p. 47).

Rather than beginning with one of the delimited concepts Fischer listed, I selected a broad proposition: that processes of change and psychological growth which take place in child psychotherapy, as child and therapist interact, are the same as those which take place as infant/child and caregivers interact. Nested within this starting point was another broad proposition. Rather than emphasizing the knowledge a child should be given in psychotherapy to help him/her deal with and resolve difficulties, emphasis should be placed on changing *how* a child constructs knowledge about himself/herself and others when interacting with others.

From these propositions, I constructed a "developmental house," or model, to integrate approaches to child psychotherapy (Parts V and VI). The foundation consisted of principles that integrated concepts from several developmental theories. On this foundation I constructed the first floor which considered how an infant constructs knowledge about herself/himself and others during the first two years of life, and how cognitive-behavioral modalities become organized. This integration placed meanings (representations) an infant constructs from experiences at the center. These initial meanings are embodied nonverbal and unconscious schemas, conserving and representing experiences with others and things and prescribing how the infant responds and what an infant expects from interactions with others. After the second year of life, if an infant does not experience major, unrepaired disruptions when negotiating with others, these embodied schemas are gradually translated into symbolic forms (action symbols, fantasies, metaphoric language) shared with others. To climb from the first to the second floor, I introduced embodiment theory which conceptualized that meanings and modalities formed during infancy are extended into and influence those that develop in childhood and beyond.

The second floor operationalized how the construction of life metaphors (meaning) and the organization of cognitive and behavioral modalities are extended beyond infancy (Part VI). In negotiating and developing life metaphors, a child relies upon two psychological systems. With one, a developmental hierarchy of evolving cognitive functions equilibrate the demands from life metaphors with those of environments. With the other, a developmental hierarchy of evolving modalities (action, fantasy, and metaphoric language) express life metaphors in interactions with others, relying upon delay and multiple means and alternative ends, in order to cope with ever-changing environmental opportunities and limitations.

This developmental-dialectical model was translated into guidelines for conducting integrative psychotherapy with children and adolescents, whatever their presenting problems (Part VII). These guidelines do not provide a series of recipes, each defining how to conduct psychotherapy with children who are viewed as representing one or another *DSM-IV* diagnostic category. Rather the guidelines articulated several interrelated axes that a therapist follows simultaneously when treating all children, an approach that converges with that of others (e.g., Reeve, et al. 1993, Shirk 1988).

Three broad treatment plans were outlined to promote change in how any child negotiates and constructs knowledge when interacting with others. One emphasized revising a child's rigid life metaphors that construe present situations in maladaptive ways and prescribe behaviors that do not serve learning and adaptation. Another emphasized revising a child's rigid cognitive functions which fail to equilibrate information and demands from environments and the child's subjective world. And the third emphasized revising rigid modalities so that what a child does, imagines, and says become interrelated.

I also considered why it is important for a therapist to distinguish between what he/she does to promote change within a level of functioning versus between levels of functioning. I articulated the main catalysts that promote change: cycles of dialectical interactions, enactments, and idealization and internalization. I emphasized techniques that child and therapist could use to negotiate and construct a shared, intersubjective world, and proposed that the playroom and conventional toys should be supplemented by other places (especially the outdoors) and materials. I articulated when and why a therapist should, much as do child and caregiver, sometimes structure her/his interactions with a child, and at other times participate in nondirected interactions. Clinical case illustrations were described in Part VIII.

Lastly, in Part IX, I discussed why the developmental-dialectical model views nosology (diagnostic categories) as limited in providing a diagnostic understanding of a child's difficulties in a way that serves treatment. As an alternative I described several research studies that attempted to demonstrate the kinds of diagnostic questions the developmental-dialectical model raises, especially the holistic question of how functioning at one level, or in one domain, extends into and influences functioning at other levels and domains. The proposed developmental-dialectical model, the issues it raises, and the guidelines for child psychotherapy it prescribes, when taken together, assign primary significance to several domains.

WHY DOES YOUR MODEL ASSIGN A PRIMARY POSITION TO MEANING?

It wasn't too long ago that Skinner (1974) argued, "A small part of one's inner world can be felt or introspectively observed but it is *not* an *essential part* (italics mine) . . . and the role assigned to it has been overrated . . . it is impossible to estimate the havoc [that therapies about internal states and processes] have wreaked . . . [upon] efforts to describe or explain human behavior" (quoted in Mahoney 1985, p. 20).

At the time Skinner stated his position, psychodynamic therapists, of course, disagreed. Since the early 1900s, they had been working on the other side of the boundary, maintaining the opposite view: that a person's internal states and processes are more essential than her/his overt behaviors. But, as discussed earlier, some cognitive and behavioral therapists have abandoned Skinner's view and embraced the position held by psychodynamic therapists, that meanings contained in a person's inner world are primary. For example, after citing Skinner, Mahoney pointed out to his cognitive and behavioral colleagues that "far from being 'vastly overrated' the inner world is probably the least understood and potentially the most revealing frontier in contemporary science" (p. 20).

I could not agree more. In everyday life a child is busy, not so much acquiring knowledge but constructing meanings he/she experiences, altering these meanings, and sharing some of them with others. Since all meanings emerge from interactions with others, a meaning is not evaluated in terms of whether it corresponds to the "real" meaning of an event. The "real" meaning of some experience is what a person and another, present or absent, have negotiated and constructed. I have assigned meaning, and the developmental processes involved in constructing meaning, a primary role in integrating psychotherapies, and have operationalized meanings as life-metaphors that prescribe what is expected from present situations and what one should do to continue negotiations.

It is interesting to note that in the ten years since Mahoney (1985) reminded cognitive-behavioral therapists that a person's inner world is important, a shift can be observed in cognitive and behavioral concepts and methods toward what is being called "constructive psychotherapies" (Mahoney 1995a). According to Mahoney (1995b), in the past forty years there have been significant shifts in cognitive science: from information processing to connectionism and most recently to constructivism. Mahoney reminded his cognitive-behavioral audience that "fundamental to constructivism is an emphasis on the active . . . nature of all knowing. In contrast to the relatively passive models of the mind and brain proposed by information-processing prospectives, constructivism proposes intrinsic self-organizing activity as fundamental to all knowledge processes. Thus, the mind/brain is no longer viewed as a repository (memory bank) of representations so much as an organic system of self-referencing activities . . ." (p. 7). The new cognitive-behavioral paradigm of constructivism reflects a decided shift from objectivism toward interpretationism.

Similarly, Meichenbaum (1995), one of the cognitive-behavioral pioneers, reviewed changes in the ruling metaphors that cognitive-behavioral therapists have followed over the years. Initially, they followed the metaphor of conditioning, then of information processing, and more recently of "constructive narrative." The later metaphor, he proposed, is "guiding the present development of cognitive-behavioral therapies . . . common to (this viewpoint) is the tenet that the human mind is a product of constructive, symbolic activity, and that reality is a product of personal meanings that individuals create. It is not as if there is one reality and clients distort that reality . . . rather there are multiple realities and the task for the therapist is to help clients become aware of *how* they create these realities and of the consequences of such constructions" (p. 23, my italics).

These statements by Meichenbaum represent a complete turn-around from Skinner's position of only twenty years ago, held by mainstream cognitive-behavioral therapists, that a person's inner world is "not essential." However, although Mahoney stated that among cognitive-behavioral therapists "constructive approaches to psychotherapy are increasingly common" (p. 8), and Meichenbaum proposed that constructivism is now the ruling metaphor in cognitive-behavioral therapy, this movement appears not to have reached all of the shores of cognitive-behavioral therapy (e.g., Clark and Fairburn 1977, Dobson and Craig 1996) nor the shores of cognitive-behavioral therapy with children (Reinecke, Dattilio, and Freeman 1996). At least not yet. I believe (hope) that in time it will. What I also hope is that the contributions of the principles of dialectics and development will come to find their way not only into cognitive-behavioral therapy but also into psychodynamic therapy.

WHY DOES YOUR MODEL ASSIGN A PRIMARY POSITION TO THE ISSUE OF EMBEDDING COGNITION WITHIN PERSONALITY AND INTERRELATING WHAT A CHILD DOES, IMAGINES, AND SAYS?

In the preface to their edited volume, Mahoney and Freeman (1985) wondered what is knowledge, how does knowledge relate to what we feel and do, and how are thoughts, feelings, and actions related. They also noted that, "we are committing a costly error of translation if we equate what our clients say with what they think and how they feel" (p. 21). I would add that the error of translation would be more costly if we equate what a child does with what he/she fantasizes, feels, and says. The developmental-dialectical model addressed this challenge in two ways. With one, a set of cognitive functions was operationalized which simultaneously approach, avoid, and select information and calls for action from existing life metaphors (meanings) and environments with which the person is negotiating. With the other, action, fantasy, and language behaviors were conceptualized as modes providing referents and vehicles for expressing these meanings. In the proposed model, cognition is the carburetor mixing the right amount of external stimulation with internal life metaphors, and the modalities of action fantasy and language are the wheels and steering wheels adaptively moving the total person through changing environments.

WHY DOES YOUR MODEL ASSIGN A PRIMARY POSITION TO UNCONSCIOUS PROCESSES AND CAN YOU SAY MORE ABOUT THEIR RELATIONSHIP TO CONSCIOUS PROCESSES?

While unconscious processes have been a cornerstone of psychodynamic therapy from its inception, Mahoney (1985) stated to his cognitive-behavioral readers ". . .

unconscious processes . . . seem to be increasingly difficult to ignore" (p. 21). A decade later he announced, "One of the more surprising developments in cognitive therapy has been the relatively recent acknowledgment of the importance of extensive role played by unconscious processes in human experiences. The surprising aspect of this development derives from the fact that many cognitive therapists have been critical of psychoanalytic theory" (Mahoney 1995b, p. 10). Mahoney noted that some cognitive and behavioral therapists have acknowledged unconscious processes "begrudgingly," admitting that "automatic thoughts" are so habitual that they occur without the individual's awareness, while the greatest degree of acknowledgment is represented by those who have joined the movement of "constructivism." "It is important to note that not all cognitive psychotherapists are comfortable with the above-mentioned rapprochement . . ." (Mahoney 1995b, p. 10). His opinion is supported by the fact that the topic of unconscious processes is still absent from the indexes of recent volumes discussing advances in cognitive and behavioral therapies (Clark and Fairburn 1997, Dobson and Craig 1996), as well as from volumes focusing on cognitive-behavioral therapy with children (Reinecke et al. 1996).

In addition to noticing that interest among cognitive-behavioral therapists in unconscious processes is not widespread, Mahoney stated ". . . more important from a theoretical prospective, cognitive renditions of the unconscious have been distinctly different from those rendered by (psychoanalysis)" (Mahoney 1995b, p. 10). In my view recent cognitive renditions of unconscious processes, to which Mahoney referred, show the influence of objectivism which segregates subjective from real knowledge, body from mind, and cognition from emotion. For example, Muran and DiGiuseppe (1990), in discussing a cognitive formulation of metaphor use in psychotherapy, disagreed with the view that metaphor (meaning) is the language of the unconscious. They proposed that meanings are expressed either literally or metaphorically, the former suited to expressions of "empirical truths," and the latter to expressions of "intuitive truths" (p. 76). For these authors, a client should not be expected to generate her/his own meaning from a metaphor. Rather a therapist should convey the meaning to a client and then ask questions to insure the client has "understood the meaning accurately" (pp. 79–80). This position sets a boundary separating client and therapist, with one imparting meaning to the other, and another boundary separating conscious meanings (literal) from unconscious meanings (intuitive).

This segregation is also reflected by Epstein (1994) in presenting an integration of the cognitive and psychodynamic unconscious within his "cognitive-experiential self-theory" of personality (CEST). He reviewed several theories of multiple processing modes: for example, (a) Freud's notion of the unconscious as operating in terms of principles which he termed primary and secondary process, (b) Paivio's distinction between verbal and nonverbal processes, (c) the distinction made by several authors between tacit, implicit, and explicit knowledge, and (d) the distinction made by social psychologists between two forms of reasoning—a "natural," intuitive mode and an "extensional," logical mode.

With these theories as background, Epstein proposed two systems: experiential and rational. "How we do think, I believe, is with two minds, experiential and rational" (p. 721). Processing within the mode of the experiential system includes several attributes: pleasure-pain oriented; emotionally driven; encodes reality in concrete images; metaphors and narratives; oriented toward immediate action; more crudely differentiated; and experienced passively and preconsciously. Processing within the mode of the rational system includes attributes such as: operates primarily in the medium of language; logical; encodes reality in abstract symbols, words, and numbers; oriented toward delayed action; more highly differentiated and experienced actively and consciously. Also, like psychoanalysis, CEST assumes that "the unaware (experiential) level continuously influences the conscious (rational) level" (p. 716) on a one-way street so to speak, and that the experiential system, as with Freud's primary process, is less suited to serve adaptation.

The view of unconscious and conscious processes held by the developmental-dialectical model proposed in this volume, while converging with aspects of Epstein's two-system model, differs in several significant ways. Rather than thinking with two minds, one experiential (driven by emotions) and the other rational (affect free), my model proposes that we think with one mind which constructs meanings that integrate and coordinate the calls for action (and associated emotions) from life metaphors with calls for action (and associated emotions) from environmental events. My model also proposes that all meanings are constructed by *both* conscious and unconscious processes, viewed as poles on a continuum, each continuously influencing the other on a two-way street so to speak, negotiating the paradox between them, and together serving adaptation. This view of a dialectic between conscious and unconscious processes contrasts with Epstein's that unconscious and conscious processes are independent systems, each with different characteristics. However my proposal converges with Bucci's (1985). Although she conceptualized two modes of information processing, verbal and nonverbal, these modes, when combined by a "referential process," result in new cognitive structures. She also assumed that neither the verbal nor the nonverbal mode dominates and that successful adaptation and effective therapy require an integration of the two modes.

If conscious and unconscious processes are engaged in a continuous dialectical exchange, what does my model say about how each influences the other in the process of constructing meaning? And how do unconscious meanings enter a person's conscious awareness? To set the stage for my response to these questions, I begin by reminding us that in his discussion of the affective unconscious and the cognitive unconscious, Piaget (1973) proposed that the unconscious does not contain already-formed fantasies or ideas which would come into view once we shine a light on them. Rather "The unconscious is furnished with sensorimotor or operational schemata, expressing what the subject can 'do' and not what he thinks" (p. 257). In addition, Piaget proposed that becoming conscious consists of "a reconstruction on a higher level of something that is already organized but differently on a lower level . . ." (p. 256).

I turn next to Lear (1990), a psychoanalyst, who has made a significant contribution to our understanding of unconscious processes and on whom I rely heavily in what follows. Lear reminded us that although Freud tended to treat unconscious thoughts as fully formed and hidden, he sometimes suggested that the way repression is able to contain a wish or meaning within unconscious processes is by preventing it from developing into a fully fledged form. In other words, Freud recognized that the transition from unconscious to conscious levels involves reconstruction and developmental principles. This reminder served as a springboard for Lear's thesis. Converging with Piaget's (1973) proposal that the unconscious consists of "operational" schemas expressing what a person "can do," Lear formulated that the unconscious consists of "disparate orientations to the world" (p. 93). In addition, these orientations ramify in many directions so that one unconscious meaning could become linked to another. Life-metaphors as conceptualized by our developmental-dialectical model are analogous to Piaget's "operational schemas" and Lear's "orientations."

At this point I address how the dialectic between unconscious metaphors and conscious processes gradually result in an unconscious meaning becoming organized and experienced within conscious awareness. Lear elaborated Piaget's notion that becoming conscious consists of a "reconstruction" at one level of something that is already organized but differently at another. This reconstruction, Lear proposed, is a gradual process following a principle of "progressive development." Moreover, the transition from unconscious to conscious levels "does not consist of attaching a word to a thing representation" (p. 106). Rather it involves the incorporation and integration of a concept *at the level of both word and thing*. "The word expresses the concept, the things have been differentiated so as to instantiate the concept, and the concept and thing have been linked together" (p. 107). In this way, the organization of a structure occurs equally and simultaneously at unconscious and conscious levels of mental activity.

Applied to our model, the transition of a metaphor from unconscious to conscious levels consists of the continuous restructuring of a "concept" that is defined by an organization or pattern of actions, images, emotions, and metaphoric language. From this view, while representing a call for action, an unconscious metaphor is also a candidate for becoming a conscious concept with understanding expressed in actions, fantasies, and metaphoric language. The reader may notice that this notion is similar to Bucci's (1985) position, noted earlier, that verbal and nonverbal modes, when combined by a "referential process" produce new structures.

To illustrate the dialectical process that I propose takes place in treatment between conscious actions, thoughts and fantasies, and unconscious life-metaphors, I turn to a clinical case discussed earlier. Recall Harry whose treatment was described in Part VIII. He was surely aware of the difficulties he caused when biting and spitting at others, and of his daily suffering when he sometimes curled up in a corner confused by what it takes to cope with his preschool program. However, at the start of treatment, the unconscious meaning that related to this behavior was not known to him or the therapist. If one looked at Harry's overt behavior when we first met him, it seemed logical to conclude that his biting and spitting were the outcome of disruptions in his early negotiations with testing and modifying aggressive intentions. But as we learned later, this was not the case at all. The unconscious metaphor that prescribed his spitting and biting defined his body-self as not grounded, highly unbalanced, and therefore in constant jeopardy. Tracing how this unconscious metaphor was gradually reconstructed several times, until it entered his conscious awareness, provides one illustration of the dialectic between unconscious and conscious processes as conceptualized by my model.

After a phase of chaotic behavior, Harry engaged in explicit, purposeful, ritu- alistic actions: he repeatedly toppled toy animals and puppets from shelves to the floor. The meaning of this action was not yet clear, although at the time I assumed this behavior was a form of aggression akin to his biting and spitting. In toppling toys, a dialectic started between a yet unknown, unconscious, sensorimotor meta- phor that prescribed the action on the one hand, and his conscious perception of animals, puppets, and toys located on shelves some distance from the floor on the other. (He toppled only materials located on the top shelves.) I joined this ritual- ized, circular interaction by setting geometric wooden cutouts under the toys, be- havior Harry consciously perceived. My conscious understanding of placing geo- metric cutouts under items was that I was providing the toys with solid ground and stability. Harry's conscious understanding was apparently different since he limited his swats to those figures under which I had placed a cutout. As the dialectic con- tinued between the unconscious "orientation" or meaning he was negotiating and his conscious perceptions of my actions and of attributes of the material on the shelves, he eventually centered on a puppet bearing the letter "A" on its sweater. His unconscious and conscious poles reconstructed the meaning being negotiated when he named this puppet "Mr. Fall" and fantasized that it would get "spanked" because "he can't stand up." At this point the unconscious metaphor was on its way, as Lear put it, toward becoming a candidate for a concept or shared meaning. Harry explicitly expressed and shared the meaning of body imbalance, a meaning forged to this point by the dialectic between unconscious and conscious processes.

I tried to prevent Mr. Fall from falling by leaning various items against him. In response, Harry enacted further what the unconscious meaning of body imbal- ance signified and "could do," elaborating both the unconscious meaning and the conscious processes interacting with it. Harry repeatedly fell to the floor and called for help, enacting that he was "sinking." Each time I responded by pulling him onto a raft (newspaper). Harry consciously perceived and assimilated that my body and the newspaper as symbols prevented him from falling and sinking.

At this point, the dialectic between the unconscious meaning of body insta- bility and the newly formed conscious understanding of falling and sinking were pushed upwards developmentally and elaborated in a new reconstruction. Harry flipped the hand puppet, whom he now called "Alvin," across the room numerous times, declaring that Alvin was "flipping out," and expressing concern about its well being. Following Lear's formulation, at this moment, the concept of a "person flipping out" was incorporated at both the levels of conscious language and imaging and unconscious meaning and sensorimotor schemas. In contrast to Epstein's model which reserves words as a characteristic of the rational mode, the vignette we are considering illustrates that the words "Alvin" and "flipping out" became part of a structure which included falling to the floor, sinking, flying through space with no control, and being injured.

Harry eventually assimilated a solution into this organization which prevented Alvin from flipping out and being injured. Harry consciously perceived and understood that if a string is tied to Alvin and also to a door knob, the string controlled Alvin's dangerous flights through space and prevented him from flipping out. As the dialectic continued between this conscious perception and conception of a string as control, and the unconscious meaning of instability and imbalance, another reconstruction occurred. When Harry regressed and bit, hit, and spit at me, the concept of a string as control proved successful in regulating his behavior and in preventing him from flipping out, a concept that had emerged from an integration of conscious and unconscious processes. When one end of the string was tied to his head and the other to mine, without elaborate explanations or verbal interpretations, Harry consciously "understood" that a string could control his imbalance as it had Alvin's. Lear pointed out that a verbal interpretation, by offering understanding and a solution, moves the process of mental development upwards, integrating unconscious and conscious processes. I have emphasized that symbolic actions or fantasies, representing an explicit meaning and/or solution, could also serve as interpretations. As with verbal interpretations, actions and images could enhance understanding, suggest solutions, and further integrate unconscious and conscious processes.

As the dialectic continued between body imbalance versus control, another reconstruction resulted in an elaboration of the "concept" of control and regulation. Harry leaned padlocks on various items and performed the action requested by the "police station" (the therapist). This organization was elaborated further when Harry authored that Mr. Bad (a punching bag) ordered him and Alvin the puppet to perform destructive actions. Harry's refusal signified that the structure of imbalance versus control had become differentiated and solidly integrated at both unconscious and conscious levels. And this structure included Harry's consciously preserving attributes of the therapist which he idealized and construed as strength and power to resist maladaptive actions.

In summary, over the course of treatment, as unconscious and conscious processes engaged in a dialectic, Harry constructed and reconstructed, in a developmental progression, a series of interrelated structures, or concepts, concerning body-self imbalance versus self-regulation/control: from items leaned against Alvin to prevent his falling, to a newspaper as a raft preventing Harry from sinking, to a string as control over "flipping out" and "doing crazy things," to a "police station" that regulated actions, to the therapist being stronger than a "bad force." Throughout this progression, unconscious meanings gradually transitioned into conscious aware-ness in more direct, conventional symbolic forms, e.g., from a piece of string to the therapist as a source of control and strength. Relying on these developmental achieve-ments, which integrated unconscious and conscious processes, Harry eventually initiated verbal, conceptual discussions of conscious difficulties he experienced such as his fear that toilets would suck him down a pipe. During these discussions he relied upon expressions of previously unconscious meanings connected with con-scious perceptions that had been reconstructed and shared with the therapist—he held onto a string tied to a cup so that it could not be flushed down a toilet.

If we consider the clinical example of Harry, we can see that the unconscious is not a maladaptive system distorting reality, as Epstein proposed and as Freud initially formulated. Rather unconscious and conscious processes engage in con-tinuous dialectical interactions. Each influences the other, utilizing the same set of characteristics that were listed by Epstein as related either to the experiential (un-conscious) or the rational (conscious) modes: holistic and analytic; emotionally and logically oriented reasoning; behavior mediated by unconscious meanings/emotions and by conscious appraisal of events; encoding experiences in images, words, and abstract symbols; orientated toward immediate and delayed action; changing slowly with the repetition of rituals and quickly with the use of thought; becoming struc-tured in global as well as more differentiated and integrated organizations of ac-tions, images, and words; dominated by emotion and thought; and relying on evi-dence from physical experiences as well as logic and propositions.

The proposed dialectic between conscious and unconscious processes is also illustrated by research studies described in Part IX. For example, it seems very likely that the young children who looked through binoculars in order to "push the examiner away," while aware that they were looking through binoculars, were not aware of the meaning of this microaction. Nor were they aware that when examin-ing a series of pictures of two persons greeting each other, they failed to notice changes that took place in the scene more so than did children who looked through the binoculars so as to draw the examiner near. Along the same line, the older children in this study, who looked through the binoculars so as to draw the exam-iner near, were not aware that the meaning of needing a close attachment (when they should have already negotiated individuation), influenced the inefficiency they showed when looking at the same picture of two persons greeting each other.

CAN YOU COMMENT FURTHER ABOUT THE PRIMACY OF DIALECTICAL ENACTMENTS INSTEAD OF WORDS AND THE THERAPIST AS AN ACTIVE PARTICIPANT?

We discussed previously that therapists from both cognitive-behavioral and psychodynamic camps have argued that rational conceptual knowing by itself does not appear to be therapeutic. Mitchell (1994), a psychoanalyst, has been a major voice disagreeing with the psychodynamic therapists who rely on the content of verbal interpretation (classical psychoanalysis) to account for therapeutic change, and proposed that enactments and interactions (relational psychoanalysis) are more important. The influence exerted by Mitchell, as well as others who have emphasized a relational approach, has stirred up considerable controversy, reflected by an issue of *Psychoanalytic Psychology* (1995) devoted to debates between the two positions. Along the same line, from his review of published reports by child psychoanalysts, Altman (1994) argued that, in recent years, while child psychoanalysts have been moving toward a relational theory and practice, "the lingering influence of drive theory and associated analytic technique is evident in a common tendency to ignore the impact on the patient of what the analyst does and says in the analytic interaction" (p. 383).

While cognitive-behavioral therapists initially ignored the patient–therapist relationship, they have been giving increasing attention to its importance. As one example, Safran (1990 a,b) "refined" cognitive therapy in light of interpersonal theory. "One's interpersonal schemas shape the perception of the interpersonal world and lead to various plans, strategies, and behaviors, which in turn shape the environment in a manner which confirms the working model. There is, thus, a self-perpetuating *cognitive-interpersonal cycle*" (Safran 1990a, p. 97). An early study of the therapeutic relationship in behavior therapy (Ford 1978), observing that individual differences in therapists related to clients' perceptions of the therapeutic relationship, anticipated aspects of Safran's formulations. A more recent study (Kazdin et al. 1989) is also related and brings attention to the power of enactments in treating children. These investigators randomly assigned children, referred because of severe antisocial behaviors, to one of three treatment conditions. One group participated in problem-solving skills training (PSST) (e.g., developing alternative solutions; taking the perspective of others). The bulk of this treatment "was devoted to enacting interpersonal situations through role play" (p. 525). Another group participated in problem-solving skills training with in-vivo practice (PSST-P). In addition to receiving the identical treatment provided to participants in the PSST program, these children received "in-vivo practice which consisted of therapeutically planned activities outside of the sessions" (p. 527) that involved parents and sibs. Initially the therapist provided assistance during these in-vivo enactments before or after a session. Gradually the parents assisted the child, and the therapist's role during these moments "faded" (p. 527). A third group participated in relationship therapy (RT). Here the therapist used play materials to help the child talk and express feelings. Children who participated in PSST and PSST-P programs showed significantly greater reduction in antisocial behavior than children who participated in RT programs.

Safran (1990a) noted that his concept of cognitive-interpersonal cycles is similar to Wachtel's (1977, 1987) cyclical psychodynamics, discussed earlier. While each of these concepts bears some resemblance to the notion of cycles of dialectical enactments proposed in this volume, there is an important difference. With cycles of dialectical enactments, two persons negotiate the paradox between what each construes and expects. In Safran's concept, the person's cognition construes and constructs the environment, and in Wachtel's formulation a person construes another, and on this basis, searches for experiences with others that fit this construction. Neither of these formulations emphasizes a process in which persons negotiate the difference between what each construes and expects. Other cognitive-behavioral therapists, who take the position that words spoken by the therapist and patient are not primary, have proposed that "nonspecific factors" in the relationship between patient and therapist change the way a person feels, acts, and experiences herself/himself.

The developmental-dialectical model agrees that verbal conceptualizing should be subordinated, especially in psychotherapy with children, and takes a step further in operationalizing what these "cognitive-interpersonal cycles" and "nonspecific relationship factors" are. Given the model's roots in the first years of life, and the pivotal role played by embodied meanings, the model takes the position that nonspecific factors are in fact quite specific. They consist of child and therapist engaging in ritualized, circular dialectical interactions and enactments. As child and therapist interact, a child negotiates the dialectic among what she/he says, imagines, and does, while the therapist negotiates the dialectic among what she/he says, imagines, and does. At the same time, child and therapist respond to, influence, and contour, the other's patterns of words, fantasies, and actions as they co-construct an intersubjective world unique to them and within which the child reorganizes her/his metaphors, cognitive functioning, and modes of expression. This dialectical process defines how change takes place both within a person and between persons, forming a bridge connecting intrapsychic interactions with interpersonal interactions. Unless words are rooted in ritualized interactions, the meanings they express float like detached balloons.

The model I propose, then, disagrees with treatment approaches that emphasize verbalizing (e.g., interpretations, self-talk, discourse) as vehicles for change, whether conducted within a cognitive-behavioral or psychodynamic framework. It seems to me Freud (1912) recognized that meanings, cognitions, and behaviors are revised more by interpersonal transactions than by verbal statements when he noted, "I dislike making use of analytic writings as an assistance to my patients. I require them to learn from personal experience, and I assure them that they will acquire wide and more valuable knowledge than the whole literature of psychoanalysis could teach them" (pp. 119–120). The clinical cases discussed provide illustrations of dialectical, circular interactions and enactments, and of the therapist as an active participant, rather then someone who verbalizes feelings, motives, and self instructions, whether she/he is sitting quietly at a table or crawling on all fours in a treatment room or outdoors.

CAN YOU SAY MORE ABOUT THE PRIMACY OF CHANGE AS INTEGRATION AND CONSOLIDATION?

The model proposed here, with its roots in development and dialectics, views change and growth as a process that assimilates and consolidates previous behaviors into emerging behaviors, rather than a process in which old behaviors are eliminated by new ones, a principle at the heart of the organismic-developmental viewpoint. Following this principle, the model also takes the position that unconscious meanings and cognitive and behavioral modalities that are structured during infancy and the toddler years, are extended into unconscious and conscious meanings, and into cognitive and behavioral modalities that become constructed during childhood and beyond. Therefore, as a child and adolescent interact with others and negotiate developmental issues, these earlier structures continually influence the organization of structures formed throughout childhood and adolescence. In addition, since the model distinguishes between levels of functioning that are interrelated, change processes that occur within a level are distinguished from processes of change involved as a behavioral organization spirals from one level to another. Therefore, different therapeutic techniques are required to facilitate each type of change process. When applied to treatment, the focus of the proposed development-dialectical model, then, is on setting into motion processes that promote change rather than processes that attempt to achieve a predetermined end state (see also Brems 1993).

A CLOSING COMMENT

Almost a century ago Mary Cover Jones (1924) desensitized a child of his fear of rabbits by moving a caged rabbit closer and closer to the child while the child ate. Lightmer Witmer (1908) administered cognitive tasks to a child who was a poor speller. And Sigmund Freud (1909) supervised a father in using verbal and conceptual interactions with his son, interpreting unconscious meanings associated with the boy's fear of horses. Each of these early attempts to help a suffering child could be viewed as forecasting the three approaches to child psychotherapy that have emerged as dominant. The dialectical-developmental model and its therapeutic guidelines, described in this volume, represent one probe searching for a way of integrating valuable aspects of each approach in order to treat the whole child.

Modifying a leaf from Mitchell (1988), the model views unconscious, embodied meanings/metaphors as the skeletal system, representing experiences with others in the past and what one expects from others in the present. These representations are not visible to the naked eye, but ever active in construing situations and prescribing what a person can do. Symbols constructed and shared by a child in interactions with others make up the child's skin near consciousness, providing a continuous flow of stimulation, and representing what the child wants and prohibits and what the environment wants and prohibits. Cognitive functions, and modalities of action, fantasy, and language, form the child's neural, vascular, and muscular networks, connecting and coordinating the requirements and performance of the skeletal system and skin. The more successful we are in developing therapeutic techniques that interrelate and coordinate a child's skin, with a child's skeletal, muscular, and vascular systems, the more a child will be treated holistically and set on a growth-fostering, developmental course throughout childhood and adolescence.

In his concluding remarks to the participants at the First World Congress of Infant Psychiatry held in Cascais, Portugal in 1980, Erikson (1983) shared a view that to my mind captures the holistic, developmental-dialectical approach to child and adolescent therapy I presented in this volume. "As we learned to treat . . . children (and their families), we found that [therapeutic] intervention in the widest sense really means involvement in the overall dynamic of 'growing together' . . . which alone can heal" (p. 425).

References

Altman, N. (1994). A perspective on child psychoanalysis 1994: the recognition of relational theory and technique in child treatment. *Psychoanalytic Psychology* 11:383–395.

Anthony, E. J. (1956). The significance of Jean Piaget for child psychiatry. *British Journal of Medical Psychology* 29:20–34.

Arkowitz, H. (1984). Historical perspective on the integration of psychoanalytic therapy and behavioral therapy. In *Psychoanalytic Therapy and Behavioral Therapy: Is Integration Possible?* ed. H. Arkowitz and S. B. Messer, pp. 1–30. New York: Plenum.

——— (1992). Integrative theories of therapy. In *History of Psychotherapy: A Century of Change*, ed. D. K. Freedkeim, pp. 261–303. Washington, DC: American Psychological Association.

Arkowitz, H., and Messer, S. B., eds. (1984). *Psychoanalytic Therapy and Behavioral Therapy: Is Integration Possible?* New York: Plenum.

Arnkoff, D. B. (1980). Psychotherapy from the perspective of cognitive therapy. In *Psychotherapy Process: Current Issues and Future Directions*, ed. M. J. Mahoney, pp. 339–361. New York: Plenum.

Arnkoff, D. B., and Glass, C. R. (1982). Clinical cognitive constructs: examination, evaluation, and elaboration. In *Advances in Cognitive-Behavioral Research and Therapy*, vol. 1, ed. P. C. Kendall, pp. 1–34. New York: Academic Press.

Baldwin, A. L. (1967). *Theories of Child Development*. New York: Wiley.

Baltes, P. B., and Schaie, K. W., eds. (1973). *Life-Span Developmental Psychology: Personality and Socialization*. New York: Academic Press.

Bandura, A. (1969). *Principles of Behavior Modification*. New York: Holt, Rinehart and Winston.

——— (1977). *Social Learning Theory*. Englewood Cliffs, NJ: Prentice-Hall.

Barnard, R. E., and Brazelton, T. B., eds. (1990). *Touch: The Foundation of Experience*. Madison, CT: International Universities Press.

Barratt, B. B. (1984). *Psychic Reality and Psychoanalytic Knowing*. Hillsdale, NJ: Analytic Press.

Bearison, D. J., and Zimiles, H. (1986). Developmental perspectives of thought and emotion: an introduction. In *Thought and Emotion: Developmental Perspectives*, ed. D. J. Bearison and H. Zimiles, pp. 1–10. Hillsdale, NJ: Erlbaum.

Beck, A. T. (1976). *Cognitive therapy and the emotional disorders*. New York: International Universities Press.

Bedrosian, R. C. (1981). The application of cognitive therapy techniques with adolescents. In *New Directions in Cognitive Therapy*, ed. G. Emery, S. D. Hollon, and R. C. Bedrosian, pp. 68–83. New York: Guilford.

Beebe, B., and Lachmann, F. M. (1994). Representation and internalization in infancy: three principles of salience. *Psychoanalytic Psychology* 11:127–165.

Billow, R. M. (1977). Metaphor: a review of the psychological literature. *Psychological Bulletin* 84:81–92.

Blaisdell, O. (1972). *Developmental changes in action aggression and in fantasy aggression*. Unpublished doctoral dissertation. Boston University, Boston.

Blake, R. R., and Ramsey, G. V., eds. (1951). *Perception: An Approach to Personality*. New York: Ronald.

Blatt, S. J., and Behrends, R. S. (1987). Internalization, separation-individuation, and the nature of the therapeutic action. *International Journal of Psychoanalysis* 68:279–297.

Bohart, A. C. (1993). Experiencing: the basis of psychotherapy. *Journal of Psychotherapy Integration* 3:51–67.

Brems, C. (1993). *A Comprehensive Guide to Child Psychotherapy*. Boston: Allyn & Bacon.

Breuer, J., and Freud, S. (1895). Studies on hysteria. *Standard Edition* 2:1–306. London: Hogarth Press.

Bronfenbrenner, U. (1951). Toward an integrated theory of personality. In *Perception: An Approach to Personality*, ed. R. R. Blake and G. V. Ramsey, pp. 206–257. New York: Ronald.

———— (1963). Developmental theory in transition. In *Child Psychology*, ed. H. W. Stevenson, pp. 517–542. Chicago: University of Chicago Press.

Brown, F. (1958). The psychodiagnostic test battery. In *Progress in Clinical Psychology*, ed. D. Brower and L. E. Abt, pp. 60–71. New York: Grune & Stratton.

Bruner, J. S. (1951). Personality dynamics and the process of perceiving. In *Perception: An Approach to Personality*, ed. R. R. Blake and G. V. Ramsey, pp. 121–147. New York: Ronald.

———— (1986). Thought and emotion: Can Humpty Dumpty be put back together again? In *Thought and Emotion: Developmental Perspectives*, ed. D. J. Bearison and H. Zimiles, pp. 11–20. Hillsdale, NJ: Erlbaum.

———— (1990). *Acts of Meaning*. Cambridge, MA: Harvard University Press.

———— (1992). Another look at the New Look I. *American Psychologist* 47:780–785.

Bucci, W. (1985). Dual coding system: a cognitive model for psychoanalytic research. *Journal of the American Psychoanalytic Association* 33:571–607.

Calicchia, J. A., Moncata, S. J., and Santostefano, S. (1993). Cognitive control differences in violent juvenile inpatients. *Journal of Clinical Psychology* 49: 731–740.

Campbell, S. F., ed. (1977). *Piaget Sampler: An Introduction to Jean Piaget through His Own Work*. New York: Jason Aronson.

Cangelosi, D. M. (1993). Internal and external wars: psychodynamic play therapy. In *Play Therapy in Action: A Case Book for Practitioners*, ed. T. Knottman and C. Schaefer, pp. 347–370. Northvale, NJ: Jason Aronson.

Cash, T. F., and Pruzinsky, T., eds. (1990). *Body Images: Development, Deviance and Change*. New York: Guilford.

Cicchetti, D., ed. (1984). Developmental psychopathology [special issue]. *Child Development* 55:(1).

Clark, D. M., and Fairburn, C. G., eds. (1997). *Science and Practice of Cognitive Behavior Therapy*. New York: Oxford University Press.

Clark, M. S., and Fiske, S. T., eds. (1982). Preface. *Affect and Cognition* (pp. ix–x). Hillsdale, NJ: Erlbaum.

Cohen, L. B., and Salapatek, P., eds. (1975). *Infant Perception: From Sensation to Cognition*, vols. 1–2. New York: Academic Press.

Cohen, R., and Schleser, R. (1984). Cognitive development and clinical intervention. In *Cognitive Behavior Therapy with Children*, ed. A. W. Craighead, pp. 45–68. New York: Plenum.

Colby, K. M., and Stoller, R. J. (1988). *Cognitive Science and Psychoanalysis*. Hillsdale, NJ: Analytic Press.

Conn, J. H. (1993). The play-interview. In *Play Therapy Techniques*, ed. C. E. Schaefer and D. M. Cangelosi, pp. 9–44. Northvale, NJ: Jason Aronson.

Coonerty, S. (1993). Integrative child therapy. In *Comprehensive Handbook of Psychotherapy Integration*, ed. G. Stricker and J. R. Gold, pp. 413–425. New York: Plenum.

Coppolillo, H. P. (1987). *Psychodynamic Psychotherapy of Children: An Introduction to the Art and the Techniques*. Madison, CT: International Universities Press.

Corsini, R. J., and Wedding, D., eds. (1989). *Current Psychotherapies*, 4th ed. Itasca, IL: Peacock.

Cotugno, A. J. (1987). Cognitive control functioning in hyperactive and non-hyperactive children. *Journal of Learning Disabilities* 20:563–567.

Davis, L. J. (1997). The encyclopedia of insanity: a psychiatric handbook lists a madness for everyone. *Harper's Magazine*, February, pp. 61–66.

Diagnostic and Statistical Manual of Mental Disorders (1994). 4th ed.—revised. Washington, DC: American Psychiatric Association.

DiGiuseppe, R. A. (1981). Cognitive therapy with children. In *New Directions in Cognitive Therapy*, ed. G. Emery, S. D. Hollon, and R. C. Bedrosian, pp. 50–66. New York: Guilford.

Division of Child, Youth and Family Services (1994). Multicultural issues in clinical training. *The Child, Youth and Family Services Quarterly* 17:1–27.

Dobson, K. S., and Craig, K. D., eds. (1996). *Advances in Cognitive-Behavioral Therapy*. Thousand Oaks: Sage.

Eichler, J. (1971). *A developmental study of action, fantasy, and language aggression in latency aged boys.* Unpublished doctoral dissertation, Boston University, Boston.

Emery, G., Hollon, S. D., and Bedrosian, R. C. (1981). *New Directions in Cognitive Therapy.* New York: Guilford.

Epstein, S. (1994). Integration of the cognitive and psychodynamic unconscious. *American Psychologist* 49:709–724.

Erikson, E. H. (1950). *Childhood and Society.* New York: Norton.

——— (1964). Clinical observations of play disruption in young children. In *Child Psychotherapy,* ed. M. Hayworth, pp. 246–276. New York: Basic Books.

——— (1980). *Identity and the Life Cycle.* New York: Norton.

——— (1983). Concluding remarks: infancy and the rest of life. In *Frontiers of Infant Psychiatry,* ed. J. D. Call, E. Galenson, and R. L. Tyson, pp. 425–428. New York: Basic Books.

Erlenmeyer-Kimling, L., and Miller, N. E., eds. (1986). *Life-Span Research on the Prediction of Psychopathology.* Hillsdale, NJ: Erlbaum.

Faust, J. (1993). Oh, but a heart, courage and a brain: an integrative approach to play therapy. In *Play Therapy in Action: A Case Book for Practitioners,* ed. T. Knottman and C. Schaefer, pp. 417–456. Northvale, NJ: Jason Aronson.

Feuerstein, R. (1980). *Instrumental Enrichment: An Intervention Program for Cognitive Modifiability.* Baltimore: University Park Press.

Fischer, J. (1995). Uniformity myths in eclectic and integrative psychotherapy. *Journal of Psychotherapy Integration* 5:41–56.

Fisher, S. (1990). The evolution of psychological concepts about the body. In *Body Images: Development, Deviance, and Change,* ed. T. F. Cash and T. Pruzinsky, pp. 3–20. New York: Guilford.

Fisher, S., and Cleveland, S. E. (1958). *Body Image and Personality.* New York: Van Nostrand.

Flavell, J. H. (1963). *The Developmental Psychology of Jean Piaget.* New York: Van Nostrand.

Ford, J. D. (1978). Therapeutic relationships in behavior therapy: an empirical analysis. *Journal of Consulting and Clinical Psychology* 46:1302–1314.

Ford-Clark, M. E. (1992). *A developmental assessment of the cognitive principle of leveling-sharpening in two interpersonal-emotional contexts: aggression and affliction.* Unpublished doctoral dissertation, Antioch University/New England Graduate School.

Franklin, A. J., Carter, R. T., and Grace, C. (1993). An integrative approach to psychotherapy with Black/African Americans: the relevance of race and culture. In *Comprehensive Handbook of Psychotherapy Integration,* ed. G. Stricker and J. R. Gold, pp. 465–482. New York: Plenum.

Freedkeim, D. K., ed. (1992). *History of Psychotherapy: A Century of Change.* Washington, DC: American Psychological Association.

Frenkl-Brunswick, E. (1951). Personality theory and perception. In *Perception: An*

Approach to Personality, ed. R. R. Blake and G. V. Ramsey, pp. 356–420. New York: Ronald.

Freud, A. (1946). *The Ego and Mechanisms of Defense.* New York: International Universities Press.

——— (1965). *Normality and Pathology in Childhood.* New York: International Universities Press.

Freud, S. (1900). The interpretation of dreams. *Standard Edition* 4, 5:1–626. London: Hogarth Press.

——— (1904). Freud's psycho-analytic procedure. *Standard Edition* 7:249–256. London: Hogarth Press.

——— (1905). On psychotherapy. *Standard Edition* 7:257–270. London: Hogarth Press.

——— (1909). Analysis of a phobia in a five-year-old boy. *Standard Edition* 10:5 147. London: Hogarth Press.

——— (1912). Recommendations to physicians practicing psychoanalysis. *Standard Edition* 12:111–120. London: Hogarth Press.

——— (1914). Remembering, repeating and working-through (further recommendations on the technique of psychoanalysis: II). *Standard Edition* 12:145–156. London: Hogarth Press.

——— (1915). Instincts and their vicissitudes. *Standard Edition* 14:117–140. London: Hogarth Press.

——— (1916). Introductory lectures on psychoanalysis. *Standard Edition* 15:15–239. London: Hogarth Press.

——— (1923). The ego and the id. *Standard Edition* 19:87–174. London: Hogarth Press.

——— (1930). Civilization and its discontents. *Standard Edition* 21:64–145.

——— (1932). New introductory lectures on psycho-analysis. *Standard Edition* 22:7–182.

Galton, F. (1884). Measurement of character. *The Fortnightly Review* 36:179–185.

Gardner, H. (1985). *The Mind's New Science: A History of the Cognitive Revolution.* New York: Basic Books.

Garfield, S. L. (1994). Eclecticism and integration in psychotherapy: developments and issues. *Clinical Psychology Science and Practice* 6:123–137.

Gaston, L., Goldfried, M. R., Greenberg, A. O., et al. (1995). The therapeutic alliance in psychodynamic, cognitive-behavioral, and experiential therapies. *Journal of Psychotherapy Integration* 5:1–26.

Gelfand, D. M., and Peterson, L. (1985). *Child Development and Psychopathology.* Beverly Hills, CA: Sage.

Gholson, B., and Rosenthal, T. L., eds. (1984). *Applications of Cognitive Developmental Theory.* New York: Academic Press.

Gill, M., ed. (1967). *Collected Papers of David Rapaport.* New York: Basic Books.

Gill, M. M. (1984). Psychoanalysis and psychotherapy: a revision. *International Review of Psychoanalysis* 11:161–179.

Gold, J. R. (1994). When the patient does the integrating: lessons for theory and practice. *Journal of Psychotherapy Integration* 4:133–158.

Goncalves, O. (1995). Cognitive narrative psychotherapy: the hermeneutic construction of alternative meanings. In *Cognitive and Constructive Psychotherapies: Therapy, Research, and Practice*, ed. M. J. Mahoney, pp. 139–162.

Goulet, L. R., and Baltes, P. B., eds. (1970). *Life-Span Developmental Psychology: Research and Theory*. New York: Academic Press.

Greenson, R. (1977). That impossible profession. In *Human Dimension in Psychoanalytic Practice*, ed. K. A. Frank, pp. 95–110. New York: Grune & Stratton.

Gruber, H. E., Hammond, K. R., and Jessor, R., eds. (1957). *Contemporary Approaches to Cognition*. Cambridge, MA: Harvard University Press.

Guidano, V. F., and Liotti, G. (1983). *Cognitive Processes and Emotional Disorders: A Structural Approach to Psychotherapy*. New York: Guildford.

Hammer, M., and Kaplan, A. M. (1967). *The Practice of Psychotherapy with Children*. Homewood, IL: Dorsy.

Harris, D. B. (1957). Problems in formulating a scientific concept of development. In *The Concept of Development: An Issue in the Study of Human Behavior*, ed. D. B. Harris, pp. 3–14. Minneapolis: University of Minnesota Press.

Hartmann, H. (1939). *Ego Psychology and the Problem of Adaptation*, 1st English ed. New York: International Universities Press, 1958.

Heard, H. L., and Linehan, M. M. (1994). Dialectical behavior therapy: an integrative approach to the treatment of borderline personality disorders. *Journal of Psychotherapy Integration* 4:55–82.

Hilgard, E. R. (1951). The role of learning in perception. In *Perception: An Approach to Personality*, ed. R. R. Blake and G. V. Ramsey, pp. 95–120. New York: Ronald.

Hoffman, M., ed. (1984). *Foundations of Cognitive Therapy*. New York: Plenum.

Hollin, C. R. (1990). *Cognitive-Behavioral Interventions with Young Offenders*. New York: Pergamon.

Hollon, S. D., and Kriss, M. R. (1984). Cognitive factors in clinical research and practice. *Clinical Psychology Review* 4:35–76.

Holt, R. R. (1964). The emergence of cognitive psychology. *Journal of the American Psychoanalytic Association* 12:650–655.

Horowitz, M. J., ed. (1988). *Psychodynamics and Cognition*. Chicago: University of Chicago Press.

Hughes, J. N. (1988). *Cognitive Behavior Therapy with Children in Schools*. New York: Pergamon.

Izard, C. E. (1978). On the ontogenesis of emotions and emotion-cognitive relationships in infancy. In *The Development of Affect*, ed. M. Lewis and L. A. Rosenblum, pp. 389–414. New York: Plenum.

Izard, C. E., Kagan, J., and Zajonc, R. B. (1984). Introduction. In *Emotions, Cog-*

nition and Behaviors, ed. C. E. Izard, J. Kagan, and R. B. Zajonc, pp. 1–14. Cambridge, MA: Cambridge University Press.

Jacobson, N. S. (1994). Behavior therapy and psychotherapy integration. *Journal of Psychotherapy Integration* 4:105–119.

Jellinck, E. M. (1939). Some principles of psychiatric classification. *Psychiatry* 2:161–165.

Johnson, M. (1987). *The Body in the Mind: The Bodily Basis of Meaning, Imagination and Reason*. Chicago: University of Chicago Press.

——— (1993). A culturally sensitive approach to therapy with children. In *A Comprehensive Guide to Child Psychotherapy*, ed. C. Brems, pp. 68–73. Boston: Allyn and Bacon.

Jones, M. C. (1924). A laboratory study of fear: the case of Peter. *Pedagogical Seminary* 31:308–315.

Jung, C. G. (1952). *Symbols of Transformation*. New York: Bollingen Foundation.

Kagan, J. (1978). On emotion and its development: a working paper. In *The Development of Affect*, ed. M. Lewis and L. Rosenblum, pp. 11–41. New York: Plenum.

Kaplan, B. (1959). The study of language in psychiatry: the comparative developmental approach and its application to symbolization and language in psychopathology. In *American Handbook in Psychiatry*, vol. 3, ed. S. Arieti. New York: Basic Books.

Katz, M. M., and Cole, J. O. (1965). Reflections on the major conference issue. In *The Role of Classification in Psychiatry and Psychopathology*, ed. M. M. Katz, J. O. Cole, and W. E. Barton, pp. 563–568. Chevy Chase, MD: U.S. Department of Health, Education and Welfare.

Katz, M. M., Cole, J. O., and Barton, W. E., eds. (1965). *The Role and Methodology of Classification in Psychiatry and Psychopathology*. Chevy Chase, MD: U.S. Department of Health, Education and Welfare.

Kay, P. (1972). Psychoanalytic theory of development in childhood and pre-adolescence. In *Handbook of Child Psychoanalysis*, ed. B. B. Wolman, pp. 53–142. New York: Van Nostrand Reinhold.

Kazdin, A. E. (1989). Developmental psychopathology: current research, issues and direction. *American Psychologist* 44:180–187.

Kazdin, A. E., Bass, D., Siegel, T., and Thomas, C. (1989). Cognitive-behavioral therapy and relationship therapy in the treatment of children referred for antisocial behavior. *Journal of Counseling and Clinical Psychology* 57:522–535.

Kazdin, A. E., Siegel, T. C., and Bass, D. (1990). Drawing on clinical practice to inform research on child and adolescent psychotherapy: survey of practitioners. *Professional Psychology: Research and Practice* 21:189–198.

Kelly, G. A. (1965). The role of classification in personality theory. In *The Role and Methodology of Classification in Psychiatry and Psychopathology*, ed. M. Katz, J. O. Cole, and W. E. Barton, pp. 155–162. Chevy Chase, MD: U.S. Department of Health, Education and Welfare.

Kendall, P. C., and Braswell, L. (1985). *Cognitive-Behavioral Therapy for Impulsive Children*. New York: Guilford.

Kendall, P. C., and Hollon, S. D., eds. (1979). *Cognitive-Behavioral Interventions: Theory, Research and Procedures*. New York: Academic Press.

Kendall, P. C., and Morison, P. (1984). Integrating cognitive behavioral procedures for the treatment of socially isolated children. In *Cognitive Behavior Therapy with Children*, ed. A. W. Meyers and W. E. Craighead, pp. 261–288. New York: Plenum.

Klein, G. S. (1951). The personal world through perception. In *Perception: An Approach to Personality*, ed. R. R. Blake and G. V. Ramsey, pp. 328–355. New York: Ronald.

——— (1954). Need and regulation. In *Nebraska Symposium on Motivation*, ed. M. R. Jones, pp. 224–274. Lincoln: University of Nebraska Press.

Klein, G. S., and Schlesinger, H. J. (1949). Where is the perceiver in perceptual therapy? *Journal of Personality* 18:32–47.

Knapp, P. H. (1988). Steps toward a lexicon: discussion of "unconsciously determined defensive strategies." In *Psychodynamics and Cognition*, ed. M. J. Horowitz, pp. 95–114. Chicago: University of Chicago Press.

Knell, S. M. (1995). *Cognitive-Behavioral Play Therapy*. Northvale, NJ: Jason Aronson.

Kohlenberg, R. J., and Tsai, M. (1994). Functional analytic psychotherapy: a radical behavioral approach to treatment and integration. *Journal of Psychotherapy Integration* 4:175–201.

Kottman, T., and Schaefer, C., eds. (1993). *Play Therapy in Action: A Casebook for Practitioners*. Northvale, NJ: Jason Aronson.

Kramer, S., and Akhtar, S., eds. (1992). *When the Body Speaks: Psychological Meanings in Kinetic Clues*. Northvale, NJ: Jason Aronson.

Kruger, D. W. (1990). Developmental and psychodynamic perspectives on body-image change. In *Body Images: Development, Deviance and Change*, ed. T. F. Cash and T. Pruzinsky, pp. 255–271. New York: Guilford.

Kuhn, T. S. (1962). *The Structure of Scientific Revolutions*. Chicago: University of Chicago Press.

——— (1977). *The Essential Tension*. Chicago: University of Chicago Press.

Lazarus, A. A. (1995). Different types of eclecticism and integration: let's be aware of the dangers. *Journal of Psychotherapy Integration* 5:27–40.

Lear, J. (1990). *Love and Its Place in Nature: A Philosophical Interpretation of Freudian Psychoanalysis*. New York: Farrar, Straus & Giroux.

Lewis, M. (1977). Language, cognitive development, and personality. *Journal of the American Academy of Child Psychiatry* 16:646–661.

Lichtenberg, J. D. (1983). *Psychoanalysis and Infant Research*. Hillsdale, NJ: Erlbaum.

Lindzey, G. (1952). TAT: interpretive assumptions and related empirical evidence. *Psychological Bulletin* 49:1–25.

London, P. (1964). *The Modes and Morals of Psychotherapy*. New York: Holt, Rinehart & Winston.

Magnusson, D. (1981). *Toward a Psychology of Situations*. Hillsdale, NJ: Erlbaum.

Mahl, G. F. (1987). *Explorations in Nonverbal and Vocal Behavior*. Hillsdale, NJ: Erlbaum.

Mahler, M. (1979). *Selected Papers of Margaret S. Mahler*. New York: Jason Aronson.

Mahoney, M. J., ed. (1980). *Psychotherapy Process: Current Issues and Future Directions*. New York: Plenum.

——— (1985). Psychotherapy and human change processes. In *Cognition and Psychotherapy*, ed. M. J. Mahoney and A. Freeman, pp. 3–48. New York: Plenum.

——— (1993). Diversity and the dynamics of development in psychotherapy integration. *Journal of Psychotherapy Integration* 3:1–13.

——— , ed. (1995a). *Cognitive and Constructive Psychotherapies: Theory, Research, and Practice*. New York: Springer.

——— , ed. (1995b). Theoretical developments in cognitive psychotherapies. In *Cognitive and Constructive Psychotherapies: Theory, Research, and Practice*, ed. M. J. Mahoney, pp. 3–19. New York: Springer.

Mahoney, M. J., and Freeman, A., eds. (1985). *Cognition and Psychotherapy*. New York: Plenum.

Mandler, G. (1982). The structure of value: accounting for taste. In *Affect and Cognition*, ed. M. S. Clark and S. T. Fiske, pp. 3–36. Hillsdale, NJ: Erlbaum.

Marmor, J., and Woods, S. M., eds. (1980). *The Interface between the Psychodynamic and Behavioral Therapies*. New York: Plenum Medical.

Masling, J. M., and Bornstein, R. F., eds. (1994). *Empirical Perspectives on Object Relations Theory*. Washington, DC: American Psychological Association.

Matson, J. L., and Ollendick, T. H. (1988). *Enhancing Children's Social Skills: Assessment and Training*. New York: Pergamon.

McCleary, R., and Lazarus, R. S. (1949). Autonomic discrimination without awareness. *Journal of Personality* 18:171–179.

McMullin, R. E. (1986). *Handbook of Cognitive Therapy Techniques*. New York: Norton.

Meichenbaum, D. (1977). *Cognitive-Behavior Modification: An Integrative Approach*. New York: Plenum.

——— (1995). Changing conceptions of cognitive behavior modification: retrospect and prospect. In *Cognitive and Constructive Psychotherapies: Theory, Research, and Practice*, ed. M. J. Mahoney, pp. 20–26. New York: Springer.

Mendelsohn, E., and Silverman, L. H. (1984). The activation of unconcious fantasies in behavioral treatments. In *Psychoanalytic Therapy and Behavior Therapy: Is Integration Possible?*, ed. H. Arkowitz and S. B. Messer, pp. 255–294. New York: Plenum.

Messer, S. B., and Winokur, M. (1984). Ways of knowing and visions of reality in psychoanalytic therapy and behavior therapy. In *Psychoanalytic Therapy and*

Behavioral Therapy: Is Integration Possible?, ed. H. Arkowitz and S. B. Messer, pp. 63–100. New York: Plenum.

Meyers, A. W., and Craighead, W. E. (1984). Cognitive behavior with children: a historical, conceptual and organizational overview. In *Cognitive Behavior Therapy with Children*, ed. A. W. Meyers and W. E. Craighead, pp. 1–17. New York: Plenum.

Mitchell, S. A. (1988). *Relational Concepts in Psychoanalysis: An Integration*. Cambridge, MA: Harvard University Press.

——— (1994). Recent developments in psychoanalytic theorizing. *Journal of Psychotherapy Integration* 4:93–103.

Mounoud, P. (1982). Revolutionary periods in early development. In *Regressions in Mental Development*, ed. T. G. Bever, pp. 119–132. Hillsdale, NJ: Erlbaum.

Muran, J. C., and DiGiuseppe, R. A. (1990). Towards a cognitive formulation of metaphor use in psychotherapy. *Clinical Psychological Review* 10:69–85.

Nagel, E. (1957). Determinism and development. In *The Concept of Development: An Issue in the Study of Human Behavior*, ed. D. B. Harris, pp. 15–24. Minneapolis: University of Minnesota Press.

Nannis, E. D. (1988). A cognitive-developmental view of emotional understanding and the implications for child psychotherapy. In *Cognitive Development and Child Psychotherapy*, ed. S. R. Shirk, pp. 91–115. New York: Plenum.

Neisser, V. (1976). *Cognition and Reality: Principles and Implications of Cognitive Psychology*. San Francisco: Freeman.

Norcross, J. C., and Goldfried, M. R., eds. (1992). *Handbook of Psychotherapy Integration*. New York: Basic Books.

O'Connor, K. (1993). Child, protector, confidant: structured group ecosystemic play therapy. In *Play Therapy in Action*, ed. T. Kottman and C. Schaefer, pp. 245–280. New York: Jason Aronson.

Ogden, T. H. (1979). On projective identification. *International Journal of Psychoanalysis* 60:357–373.

Ohlmann, T., and Marendez, C. (1991). Vicarious processes involved in selection/control of frames of reference and spatial aspects of field dependence-independence. In *Field Dependence-independence: Cognitive Style Across the Life Span*, ed. S. Wapner and J. Demick, pp. 105–130. Hillsdale, NJ: Erlbaum.

Orlinsky, D. E., and Howard, K. I. (1987). A genetic model of psychotherapy. *Journal of Integrative and Eclectic Psychotherapy* 6:6–27.

Ortony, A., ed. (1979). *Metaphor and Thought*. New York: Cambridge University Press.

Ottenson, J. P., and Holzman, P. S. (1976). Cognitive controls and psychopathology. *Journal of Abnormal Psychology* 85:125–139.

Overton, W. F. (1994a). The arrow of time and the cycle of time: concepts of change, cognition, and embodiment. *Psychological Inquiry* 5:215–237.

———— (1994b). Contexts of meaning: the computational and the embodied mind. In *The Nature and Ontogenesis of Meaning*, ed. W. F. Overton and D. S. Palermo, pp. 1–18. Hillsdale, NJ: Erlbaum.

———— (1997a, in press). Developmental psychology: philosophy, concepts and methodology. In *Theoretical Models of Human Development*, 5th ed. ed. R. M. Lerner.

———— (1997b, in press). Relational-developmental theory: A psychological perspective. In *Children, Cities and Psychological Theories: Developing Relationships*, ed. D. Gorlitz, H. J. Harloff, J. Valsiner, and G. Mey. New York: de Gruyter.

Overton, W. F., and Horowitz, H. A. (1991). Developmental psychopathology: integrations and differentiations. In *Rochester Symposium on Developmental Psychopathology, vol. 3: Models and Integration*, ed. D. Cicchetti and S. L. Toth, pp. 1–42. Rochester, NY: University of Rochester Press.

Pearson, G. H. (1968). *A Handbook of Child Psychoanalysis*. New York: Basic Books.

Piaget, J. (1952). *The Origins of Intelligence in Children*. New York: Norton.

———— (1954). *The Construction of Reality in the Child*. New York: Basic Books.

———— (1973). The affective unconscious and the cognitive unconscious. *Journal of the American Psychoanalytic Association* 21:249–266.

———— (1975). Foreword. In *Explorations in Child Psychiatry*, ed. E. J. Anthony, pp. vii–ix. New York: Plenum.

———— (1977). The role of action in the development of thinking. In *Knowledge and Development*, ed. W. F. Overton and J. M. Gallagher, pp. 17–42. New York: Plenum.

———— (1981). *Intelligence and Affectivity: Their Relationship during Child Development*. Palo Alto, CA: Annual Reviews.

Pruzinsky, T. (1990). Somatopsychic approaches to psychotherapy and personal growth. In *Body Images: Development, Deviance and Change*, ed. T. F. Cash and T. Pruzinsky, pp. 296–315. New York: Guilford.

Psychoanalytic Psychology (1995). Special section. Contemporary structural psychoanalysis and relational psychoanalysis. Vol. 12, No. 1.

Rapaport, D. (1960). Psychoanalysis as a developmental psychology. In *Perspectives in Psychological Theory*, ed. B. Kaplan and S. Wapner, pp. 209–255. New York: International Universities Press.

Reese, H. W., and Overton, W. F. (1970). Models of development and theories of development. In *Life Span Developmental Psychology*, ed. L. R. Goulet and P. B. Baltes, pp. 116–145. New York: Academic Press.

Reeve, J., Inck, T. A., and Safran, J. (1993). Toward an integration of cognitive, interpersonal, and experiential approaches to therapy. In *Comprehensive Handbook of Psychotherapy Integration*, ed. G. Stricker and J. R. Gold, pp. 113–124. New York: Plenum.

Reinecke, M. A., Dattilio, F. M., and Freeman, A., eds. (1996). *Cognitive Therapy with Children and Adolescents*. New York: Guilford.

Reisman, J. M. (1973). *Principles of Psychotherapy with Children*. New York: Wiley.

Rhoads, J. M. (1984). Relationships between psychodynamic and behavioral therapies. In *Psychoanalytic Therapy and Behavioral Therapy: Is Integration Possible?*, ed. H. Arkowitz and S. B. Meiser, pp. 195–211. New York: Plenum.

Rieder, C., and Cicchetti, D. (1989). Organizational perspective in cognitive control functioning and cognitive affective balance in maltreated children. *Developmental Psychology* 25:382–393.

Safran, J. D. (1990a). Towards a refinement of cognitive therapy in light of interpersonal theory: I. Theory. *Clinical Psychology Review* 10:87–105.

——— (1990b). Towards a refinement of cognitive therapy in light of interpersonal theory: II. Theory. *Clinical Psychology Review* 10:107–121.

——— (1993). The therapeutic alliance rupture as a transtheoretical phenomenon: definitional and conceptual issues. *Journal of Psychotherapy Integration* 3:33–49.

Sander, L. W. (1962). Issues in early mother-child interaction. *Journal of the American Academy of Child Psychiatry* 3:141–166.

——— (1964). Adaptive relationships in early mother–child interaction. *Journal of the American Academy of Child Psychiatry* 3:231–264.

——— (1969). Regulation and organization in the early infant-caretaker system. In *Brain and Early Behavior*, ed. R. Robinson. London: Academic Press.

——— (1975). Infant and caretaking environment: investigation and conceptualization of adaptive behavior in a system of increasing complexity. In *Explorations in Child Psychiatry*, ed. E. J. Anthony, pp. 129–166. New York: Plenum.

——— (1976). Primary prevention and some aspects of temporal organization in early infant–caretaker interaction. In *Infant Psychiatry: A New Synthesis*, ed. E. Rexford, L. Sander, and T. Shapiro, pp. 187–206. New Haven, CT: Yale University Press.

——— (1989). Investigations of the infant and its caregiving environments as a biological system. In *The Course of Life*, ed. S. I. Greenspan and G. H. Pollack, 2nd ed., pp. 359–391. Madison, WI: International Universities Press.

Santostefano, S. (1960a). An exploration of performance measures of personality. *Journal of Clinical Psychology* 6:373–377.

——— (1960b). Anxiety and hostility in stuttering. *Journal of Speech and Hearing Research* 3:337–347.

——— (1962a). Miniature situations test as a way of interviewing children. *Merrill-Palmer Quarterly of Behavior and Development* 8:261–269.

——— (1962b). Performance testing of personality. *Merrill-Palmer Quarterly of Behavior and Development* 8:83–97.

——— (1964a). A developmental study of the cognitive control leveling-sharpening. *Merrill-Palmer Quarterly of Behavior and Development* 10:343–360.

——— (1964b). Cognitive controls and exceptional states in children. *Journal of Clinical Psychology* 20:213–218.

———— (1965a). Construct validity of the miniature situations test: I. The performance of public school, orphaned and brain-damaged children. *Journal of Clinical Psychology* 21:418–421.

———— (1965b). Relating self-report and overt behavior: the concepts of levels of modes for expressing motives. *Perceptual Motor Skills* 21:940.

———— (1968a). Miniature situations and methodological problems in parent–child interaction research. *Merrill-Palmer Quarterly of Behavior and Development* 14:285–312.

———— (1968b). Situational testing in personality assessment. In *International Encyclopedia of the Social Sciences*, ed. D. L. Sills, pp. 48–55. New York: Macmillan/Free Press.

———— (1970). Assessment of motives in children. *Psychological Reports* 26:639–649.

———— (1971). Beyond nosology: diagnosis from the viewpoint of development. In *Perspectives in Child Psychopathology*, ed. E. Rie, pp. 130–177. New York: Aldine-Atheston.

———— (1976a). Shepherd Ivory Franz: the father of research for clinical practice. *McLean Hospital Journal* 1:49–55.

———— (1976b). Tell me the first word that comes to mind: the free association method and the concept of levels of expressing motives. *McLean Hospital Journal* 1:174–189.

———— (1977). Action, fantasy and language: developmental levels of ego organization in communicating drives and affects. In *Communicative Structures and Psychic Structures*, ed. N. Freedman and S. Grand, pp. 331–356. New York: Plenum.

———— (1978). *A Biodevelopmental Approach to Clinical Child Psychology, Cognitive Controls and Cognitive Control Therapy*. New York: Wiley.

———— (1980a). Clinical child psychology: the need for developmental principles. *New Directions for Child Development* 7:1–19.

———— (1980b). Cognition in personality and the treatment process: a psychoanalytic view. *Psychoanalytic Study of the Child* 35:41–66.

———— (1985a). *Cognitive Control Theory with Children and Adolescents*. New York: Pergamon.

———— (1985b). Metaphor: an integration of action, fantasy, and language in development. *Imagination, Cognition, and Personality* 4:127–146.

———— (1986). Cognitive controls, metaphors and contexts: an approach to cognition and emotion. In *Thought and Emotion*, ed. D. Bearison and H. Zimiles, pp. 175–210. Hillsdale, NJ: Erlbaum.

———— (1988a). *The Cognitive Control Battery*. Los Angeles: Western Psychological Services.

———— (1988b). Process and change in child therapy and development: the concept of metaphor. In *Organizing Early Experience: Imagination and Cognition in Childhood*, ed. D. Morrison, pp. 139–172. Amityville, NY: Baywood.

———— (1991a). Cognitive style as process coordinating outer space with inner self: lessons from the past. In *Field Dependence-Independence: Bio-psycho-social*

Factors across the Lifespan, ed. S. Wapner and J. Demick, pp. 269–286. Los Angeles: Erlbaum.

———— (1991b). Coordinating outer space with inner self: reflections on developmental psychopathology. In *Constructivist Perspectives on Developmental Psychopathology and Atypical Development*, ed. D. P. Keating and H. Rosen, pp. 11–40. Hillsdale, NJ: Erlbaum.

———— (1992a). *The Action Test of Body Image: Manual of Instructions and Scoring*. Unpublished manuscript.

———— (1992b). *Life Stressor Interview: Manual of Instructions and Scoring*. Unpublished manuscript.

———— (1992c). *The leveling-sharpening friends, shoot-out and trauma tests: manual of instructions and scoring*. Unpublished manuscript.

———— (1995a). *Integrative Psychotherapy for Children and Adolescents with ADHD*, rev. Northvale, NJ: Jason Aronson.

———— (1995b). Embodied meanings, cognition and emotion: probing how three are one. In *Rochester Symposium on Developmental Psychopathology, vol. 6: Emotion, Cognition and Representation*, ed. D. Cicchetti and S. L. Toth, pp. 59–130. Rochester, NY: University of Rochester Press.

———— (In press). Cycles in the life of one psychotherapist. In *Becoming a Psychotherapist*, ed. J. Reppen. New York: Psychoanalytic Books.

Santostefano, S., and Baker, H. (1972). Research in child psychopathology: the contributions of developmental psychology. In *Manual of Child Psychopathology*, ed. B. B. Wolmann, pp. 1113–1153. New York: McGraw-Hill.

Santostefano, S., and Berkowitz, S. (1976). Principles of infant development as a guide in the psychotherapeutic treatment of borderline and psychotic children. *McLean Hospital Journal* 1:236–261.

Santostefano, S., and Calicchia, J. (1992). Body image, relational psychoanalysis, and the construction of meaning: implications for treating aggressive children. *Development and Psychopathology* 4:655–678.

Santostefano, S., and Moncata, S. (1989). A psychoanalytic view of cognition within personality: cognitive dysfunction and educating troubled youth. *Resident Treatment for Children and Youth* 6:41–62.

Santostefano, S., and Rieder, C. (1984). Cognitive controls and aggression in children: the concept of cognitive-affective balance. *Journal of Consulting and Clinical Psychology* 52:46–56.

Santostefano, S., Rieder, C., and Berk, S. (1984). The structure of fantasized movement in suicidal children and adolescents. *Journal of Suicide and Life-Threatening Behavior* 14:3–16.

Santostefano, S., and Stayton, S. (1967). Training the pre-school retarded child in focal attention: a program for parents. *American Journal of Orthopsychiatry* 37:732–743.

Santostefano, S., and Wilson, S. (1968). Construct validity of the miniature situations test: II. The performance of institutionalized delinquents and public school adolescents. *Journal of Clinical Psychology* 24:355–358.

Schacht, T. E. (1984). The varieties of integrative experience. In *Psychoanalytic and Behavior Therapy: Is Integration Possible?*, ed. H. Arkowitz and S. B. Messer, pp. 107–132. New York: Plenum.

Schaefer, C. E., and Cangelosi, D. M., eds. (1993). *Play Therapy Techniques.* Northvale, NJ: Jason Aronson.

Schilder, P. (1935). *The Image and Appearance of the Human Body.* New York: International Universities Press.

Schneider, S. F. (1990). Psychology at a crossroad. *American Psychologist* 45:521–529.

Sechrest, L., and Smith, B. (1994). Psychotherapy is the practice of psychology. *Journal of Psychotherapy Integration* 4:1–29.

Shakow, D. (1965). The role of classification in the development of the science of psychopathology. In *The Role and Methodology of Classifications in Psychiatry and Psychopathology*, ed. M. Katz, J. O. Cole, and W. E. Burton, pp. 116–142. Chevy Chase, MD: U.S. Department of Health, Education and Welfare.

Shapiro, E. K., and Weber, E. (1981). Preface. In *Cognitive and Affective Growth: Developmental Interaction*, ed. E. K. Shapiro and E. Weber, pp. vii–viii. Hillsdale, NJ: Erlbaum.

Shirk, S. R. (1988). Causal reasoning and children's comprehension of therapeutic interpretations. In *Cognitive Development and Child Psychotherapy*, ed. S. R. Shirk, pp. 53–89. New York: Plenum.

Siegel, M. G. (1989). *Psychological Testing from Early Childhood through Adolescence: A Developmental and Psychodynamic Approach.* Madison, CT: International Universities Press.

Smith, N. R., and Franklin, M. B., eds. (1979). *Symbolic Functioning in Children.* Hillsdale, NJ: Erlbaum.

Sollod, R. N., and Wachtel, P. L. (1980). A structural and transactional approach to cognition and clinical problems. In *Psychotherapy Process: Current Issues and Future Directions*, ed. M. J. Mahoney, pp. 1–28. New York: Plenum.

Spiegel, S. (1989). *An Interpersonal Approach to Child Therapy: The Treatment of Children and Adolescents from an Interpersonal Point of View.* New York: Columbia University Press.

Stern, D. N. (1985). *The Interpersonal World of the Infant: A View from Psychoanalysis and Developmental Psychology.* New York: Basic Books.

Stoops, J. W. (1974). *The assessment of aggression in children: arguments for a multimodal approach.* Unpublished doctoral dissertation, Kent State University, Kent, OH.

Stricker, G. (1994). Psychotherapy, psychology and science. *Journal of Psychotherapy Integration* 4:21–38.

Stricker, G., and Gold, J. R., eds. (1993). *Comprehensive Handbook of Psychotherapy Integration*. New York: Plenum.

Strupp, H. (1973). On the basic ingredients of psychotherapy. *Journal of Counseling and Clinical Psychology* 41:1–8.

——— (1986). Psychotherapy: research, practice and public policy (how to avoid dead ends). *American Psychologist* 41:120–130.

Temkin, O. (1965). The history of classification in the medical sciences. In *The Role and Methodology of Classification in Psychiatry and Psychopathology*, ed. M. Katz, J. O. Cole, and W. E. Marton, pp. 11–19. Chevy Chase, MD: U.S. Department of Health, Education and Welfare.

Thompson, J. K., Penner, L. A., and Altabe, M. N. (1990). Procedures, problems and progress in the assessment of body images. In *Body Images: Development, Deviance and Change*, pp. 21–50. New York: Guilford.

Thompson, S. C. (1981). Will it hurt less if I can control it? A complex answer to a simple question. *Psychological Bulletin* 90:89–101.

Tiemersma, D. (1989). *Body Schema and Body Image*. Amsterdam/Lisse: Swets and Zeitlinger.

Tuber, S., Frank, M. A., and Santostefano, S. (1989). Children's anticipation of impending surgery. *Bulletin of the Menninger Clinic* 53:501–511.

Valenstein, A. F. (1983). Working through and resistance to change: insight and the action system. *Journal of the American Psychoanalytic Association* 31:353–373.

Verbrugge, R. R., and McCarrell, N. S. (1977). Metaphoric comprehension: studies in reminding and resembling. *Cognitive Psychology* 9:454–533.

Wachtel, P. L. (1977). *Psychoanalysis and Behavior Therapy: Toward an Integration*. New York: Basic Books.

——— (1984). On theory, practice and the nature of integration. In *Psychoanalytic and Behavior Therapy: Is Integration Possible?*, ed. H. Arkowitz and S. B. Messer, pp. 31–52. New York: Plenum.

——— (1987). *Action and Insight*. New York: Guilford.

———, ed. (1982). *Resistance: Psychodynamics and Behavioral Approaches*. New York: Plenum.

Wapner, S., and Demick, J., eds. (1991). *Field Dependence-Independence: Cognitive Style across the Life Span*. Hillsdale, NJ: Erlbaum.

Wapner, S., and Werner, H., eds. (1965). *The Body Perfect*. New York: Random House.

Watzlawick, P., Weakland, J., and Fisch, R. (1974). *Change: Principle of Problem Formation and Problem Resolution*. New York: Norton.

Weimer, W. B. (1980). Psychotherapy and the philosophy of science. In *Psychotherapy Process: Current Issues and Future Directions*, ed. J. M. Mahoney. New York: Plenum.

Weiner, M. L. (1985). *Cognitive-Experiential Therapy: An Integrative Ego Psychotherapy*. New York: Brunner/Mazel.

Weisz, J. R., Suwanlerts, S., Chaiyasit, W., and Walter, B. R. (1987). Over- and under-controlled referral problems among children and adolescents from Thailand and the United States. *Journal of Consulting and Clinical Psychology* 55:719–726.

Weisz, J. R., and Weiss, B. (1993). *Effects of psychotherapy with children and adolescents.* Newbury Park, CA: Sage.

Wells, F. L. (1911). Some properties of the free association method. *Psychological Review* 18:1–23.

——— (1912). The association experiment. *Psychological Bulletin* 9:435–438.

Werner, H. (1948). *Comparative Psychology of Mental Development.* New York: International Universities Press.

——— (1949). Introductory remarks. *Journal of Personality* 18:2–5.

——— (1964). *Comparative Psychology of Mental Development*, rev. ed. New York: International Universities Press.

Werner, H., and Kaplan, B. (1963). *Symbol Formation: An Organismic-Developmental Approach to Language and the Expression of Thought.* New York: Wiley.

Werner, H., and Wapner, S. (1949). Sensory tonic field theory of perception. *Journal of Personality* 18:88–107.

Wertlieb, D. L. (1979). *Cognitive organization, regulations of aggression and learning disorders in boys.* Unpublished doctoral dissertation, Boston University, Boston

White, S. H. (1991). The child as agent: issues of cognitive style and personal design in human development. In *Field Dependence-Independence: Cognitive Style Across the Life Span*, ed. S. Wapner and J. Demick, pp. 7–25. Hillsdale, NJ: Erlbaum.

Wilber, K. (1979). *No Boundary: Eastern and Western Approaches to Personal Growth.* Boston: Shambhala.

Winnicott, D. W. (1971). *Therapeutic Consultations in Child Psychiatry.* New York: Basic Books.

Witkin, H. A. (1949). The nature and importance of individual differences in perception. *Journal of Personality* 18:145–170.

Witzum, E., van der Hart, O., and Friedman, B. (1988). The use of metaphors in psychotherapy. *Journal of Contemporary Psychotherapy* 18:270–290.

Wohlwil, J. F. (1973). *The Study of Behavioral Development.* New York: Academic Press.

Wolf, D., and Gardner, H. (1979). Style and sequence in early symbolic play. In *Symbolic Functioning in Childhood*, ed. N. R. Smith and M. B. Franklin, pp. 117–138. Hillsdale, NJ: Erlbaum.

Wolff, P. (1960). The developmental psychologies of Jean Piaget and psychoanalysis. *Psychological Issues* 2(5), whole issue.

Wolman, B. B. (1972). Psychoanalytic theory of infantile development. In *Handbook of Child Psychoanalysis*, ed. B. B. Wolman, pp. 3–52. New York: Van Nostrand Reinhold.

————, ed. (1982). *Handbook of Developmental Psychology*. Englewood Cliffs, NJ: Prentice-Hall.

Wozniak, R. H. (1986). Notes toward a co-constructive theory of the emotion-cognition relationship. In *Thought and Emotion: Developmental Perspectives*, ed. D. J. Bearison and H. Zimiles, pp. 39–64. Hillsdale, NJ: Erlbaum.

Zajonc, R. B., and Markus, H. (1984). Affect and cognition: the hard interface. In *Emotion, Cognition, and Behavior*, ed. C. E. Izard, J. Kagan, and R. B. Zajonc, pp. 73–102. Cambridge, London: Cambridge University Press.

Zimmerman, B. J. (1983). Social learning theory: a contextualist account of cognitive functioning. In *Recent Advances in Cognitive-Developmental Theory*, ed. C. J. Brainerd, pp. 1–50. New York: Springer-Verlag.

Index